Shak
Apprei

# Shakespeare's Apprenticeship

## Identifying the Real Playwright's Earliest Works

RAMON JIMÉNEZ

McFarland & Company, Inc., Publishers

*Jefferson, North Carolina*

LIBRARY OF CONGRESS CATALOGUING-IN-PUBLICATION DATA

Names: Jimenez, Ramon L., author.
Title: Shakespeare's apprenticeship : identifying the real playwright's
    earliest works / Ramon Jimenez.
Description: Jefferson, North Carolina : McFarland & Company,
    Inc., 2018. | Includes bibliographical references and index.
Identifiers: LCCN 2018037619 | ISBN 9781476672649
    (softcover : acid free paper) ∞
Subjects: LCSH: Shakespeare, William, 1564–1616—Authorship. |
    Shakespeare, William, 1564–1616—Criticism and interpretation.
Classification: LCC PR2937 .J56 2018 | DDC 822.3/3—dc23
LC record available at https://lccn.loc.gov/2018037619

BRITISH LIBRARY CATALOGUING DATA ARE AVAILABLE

ISBN (print) 978-1-4766-7264-9
ISBN (ebook) 978-1-4766-3331-2

Front cover image of ink and quill © 2018 DNY59/iStock

Printed in the United States of America

*McFarland & Company, Inc., Publishers
    Box 611, Jefferson, North Carolina 28640
    www.mcfarlandpub.com*

This is for Jonah and his family—
Gayle, William, Bianca and Colson

# Table of Contents

# Preface

Of all the historic events and developments that took place during the lengthy reign of Queen Elizabeth I, the founding and flourishing of the English public theater are among the most prominent, and the ones that in modern times command the most attention. Her reign is the most studied period in the history of English drama, not only because of Shakespeare, but also because of the extraordinary number of plays performed. The intense appetite for entertainment, and the establishment of purpose-built theaters, led to a thriving market for popular drama.

Week after week, in more than a dozen inns and public theaters in London alone, as many as thirty-five different playing companies, a third of them "boy companies," offered comedies, tragedies and histories for a trifling price of admission. The individual companies were sponsored or maintained by wealthy aristocrats, assorted nobles, grammar schools, churches and the Queen herself, who never attended a public theater but regularly invited select companies to play for her at court. To meet the demand, a host of clever men, more than a hundred, turned out play after play, often collaborating to produce a script as quickly as possible. The result was a rapid evolution of the art of playwriting and the emergence of three or four of England's finest dramatists.

Of the several dozen remarkable plays that reached the stage at that time, many, including all of those by Shakespeare, are still being performed today. However, most of the hundreds of plays performed during Elizabeth's reign have been lost. We do not even know their names. And most of those that were published, a small fraction of the total, bore no author's name. It was my curiosity about some of those anonymous plays that caused me to read them and to try to identify the authors.

I have occasionally been asked why it mattered who wrote a four-hundred-year-old play that is now only rarely performed. It is true that for the great majority of anonymous Elizabethan plays the author's name is of interest only to scholars of the period. But to attach the name of Shakespeare to an obscure and anonymous play, not to mention five of them, is a matter of the greatest importance. More than that, these plays are not masterpieces of the sort that we find in the Shakespeare canon. In most respects, especially in their dialogue, they do not rise to the level of skill that informs even his earliest canonical plays. But they show the signs, especially in their structure and plots, of a nascent genius, and they can be seen as the earliest efforts of a novice dramatist who would then master every facet of his craft before he was thirty.

Despite the nearly-total absence of evidence connecting the putative author from Stratford with the canon, the circumstances of his life have been the subject of the most intense research—far more than for any other writer. Hardly a year passes without another biography or two that rearranges and reassesses the small number of mundane facts about him that have been uncovered. But a subject of even greater interest, and of even more study, has been the contents of the canon. Here again, no playwright's works have been so meticulously scrutinized and so endlessly interpreted.

*Shakespeare's Apprenticeship* supplies the evidence for a major addition to that canon. It is the product of several years of investigation into the background and authorship of five anonymous plays that have obvious connections to the Shakespeare canon. My research has taken me to manors and museums, castles and Public Record Offices throughout England, and to more than a dozen libraries in England and the United States. My study of these plays has been the most rewarding intellectual exercise that I have ever undertaken. That is because so few scholars have paid any attention to these plays, and very little has been written about them. In a certain sense, they constitute a new field of research, where new explanations of facts, and new facts, are open to discovery.

My companion on this journey has been my wife, Joan Leon, whose unfailing encouragement and loving support have been indispensable to its completion. I am also most grateful to those who have read all or part of my manuscript and offered helpful comments and suggestions—Katherine Chiljan, Gary Goldstein, John Hamill and William Ray.

# References, Abbreviations and Bibliographical Notes

All quotations from the orthodox canon of Shakespeare's plays and poems are from G. Blakemore Evans, et al., eds. *The Riverside Shakespeare*, 2d ed. 1997.

## Abbreviations

| | |
|---|---|
| CSP | *Calendar of State Papers* |
| ODNB | *Oxford Dictionary of National Biography* |
| OED | *Oxford English Dictionary* |
| PMLA | *Publications of the Modern Language Association* |

## A Short List of Books on the Authorship Question

*"Shakespeare" Identified in Edward de Vere, Seventeenth Earl of Oxford* by John T. Looney. 1920. 3rd ed. 1979. An independent and non-academic scholar presented the evidence and made the first argument for Edward de Vere as the author of the Shakespeare canon.

*Hidden Allusions in Shakespeare's Plays* by Eva Turner Clark. 1931. A comprehensive discussion of the evidence for the date and authorship of each play.

*The Mysterious William Shakespeare* by Charlton Ogburn, Jr. 1987. 2nd ed. 1994. A scholarly and well-documented treatment of the authorship question.

*Shakespeare, Who Was He?* by Richard F. Whalen. 1994. A short and succinct introduction to the authorship question.

*"Shakespeare" by another Name, The Life of Edward de Vere, Earl of Oxford, the Man Who Was Shakespeare* by Mark K. Anderson. 2005. A well-documented biography of the author of the Shakespeare canon.

## Editions of the Apprenticeship Plays

### THE FAMOUS VICTORIES OF HENRY THE FIFTH

Seymour M. Pitcher. *The Case for Shakespeare's Authorship of the Famous Victories.* 1961. Modern spelling, with scene and line numbers.

Joseph Quincy Adams, ed. *Chief Pre-Shakespearean Dramas.* 1924. Original spelling, in prose.

Geoffrey Bullough. *Narrative and Dramatic Sources of Shakespeare.* v. 4. 1962 Original spelling, in verse.

Maynard Mack, ed. *Henry IV, Part One.* 1963. Signet Classic. Includes text of *Famous Victories.* Modern spelling, in prose.

*Queen's Men Editions.* Complete texts in both original and modern spelling. http://qme.internetshakespeare.uvic.ca/

http://public.wsu.edu/~delahoyd/shakespeare/victories.html. A scene-by-scene synopsis.

## The True Tragedy of Richard the Third

Horace H. Furness, ed. *The Tragedy of Richard the Third.* 1909. Includes text of *True Tragedy,* absent scene divisions and line numbers.

Malone Society Reprint. *The True Tragedy of Richard the Third.* 1929. Original spelling with line numbers.

*Queen's Men Editions.* Complete text in original spelling. http://qme.internetshakespeare. uvic.ca/

## The Troublesome Reign of John, King of England

Geoffrey Bullough. *Narrative and Dramatic Sources of Shakespeare.* v. 4. 1962. Original spelling, with scene and line numbers.

J. W. Sider, ed. *The Troublesome Raigne of John, King of England.* 1979. Original spelling, with scene and line numbers.

## The Taming of a Shrew

W. C. Hazlitt. *Shakespeare's Library* (1875) 1965 ed. AMS Press v. 6. Original spelling; no line numbers.

Stephen Roy Miller, ed. *The Taming of a Shrew, The 1594 Quarto.* 1988. Modern spelling, with scene and line numbers.

## King Leir

W. C. Hazlitt. *Shakespeare's Library.* (1875) 1965 ed. AMS Press v. 6. Original spelling; no line numbers.

Joseph Satin. *Shakespeare and His Sources.* 1966. Modern spelling, with act, scene and line numbers.

Sidney Lee, ed. *The chronicle history of King Leir.* 1909. Modern spelling, with scene and line numbers. https://archive.org/stream/chroniclehistory00leesuoft/chroniclehistory00leesuoft_djvu.txt

Donald M. Michie. *A Critical Edition of The True Chronicle History of King Leir and His Three Daughters, Gonorill, Ragan and Cordella.* 1991. Modern spelling, with scene and line numbers.

Queen's Men Editions. Complete texts in both original and modern spellings. Videos of performances of several scenes. http://qme.internetshakespeare.uvic.ca/Library/Texts/Leir/

# Introduction

The purpose of *Shakespeare's Apprenticeship* is to present the evidence and make the argument that five anonymous plays performed during Queen Elizabeth's reign were written by the author of the Shakespeare canon, and were probably his first efforts at dramatic writing. He subsequently rewrote all five of them, and they were then republished under his pseudonym, each with a slightly modified title. He transformed one of them—*The Famous Victories of Henry the Fifth*—into the Prince Hal trilogy, *1* and *2 Henry IV* and *Henry V*. Although many scholars disagree, the accumulation of historical, theatrical and literary evidence for their precedence and authorship is substantial and compelling.

In each of the following numbered chapters, I describe a single anonymous play and detail the external and internal evidence connecting it to a later canonical play or plays. The external evidence is contained in printed publications of all types—play quartos, registration records, broadsides, letters, dedications and court records. The internal evidence, from the play-texts themselves, varies in type and strength, and ranges from the minutiae of word usage to imagery, dramatic devices and major and minor characters. On the other hand, each of the plays has been entirely rewritten, and although the playwright carried over many linguistic and dramatic practices, there is very little identical language. Shakespeare revised nearly all of his plays, but none as substantially as he did these five, even assigning slightly different names to his revisions.

These five plays form a unique group in the drama of the time in that each has been similarly modified and rewritten, the resulting seven plays making up a large fraction of the accepted Shakespeare canon. Several other early plays, such as *Edmund Ironside* and *Edward III* may also be classified as Shakespearean juvenilia, but are not included in this book because we have no rewritten versions.

The premise of this book is that the author of the Shakespeare canon was Edward de Vere, seventeenth Earl of Oxford, and that he deliberately concealed his name from the public throughout his life by using a pseudonym. After his death, the suppression of his name was continued, and his plays and poems were attributed to a minor actor and theater sharer with a name similar to his pseudonym—William Shakspere of Stratford-upon-Avon. In the course of time, the Stratford man became so strongly associated with the Shakespeare canon that three hundred years would elapse before the hoax was uncovered, and the true author revealed.

This premise has been explicated numerous times since Lord Oxford was revealed as the author of the canon in 1920. The lack of evidence that William Shakspere had anything to do with playwriting is striking, but I will not attempt to demonstrate it here. A short list of the best treatments of the subject is included in a Bibliographical Note. The personal and literary evidence that the Earl of Oxford is the real Shakespeare is overwhelming, and I include a summary of it in "The Author of the Canon," at the end of this Introduction. Evidence of his authorship of these plays during his teen years is included in each chapter. In accordance with my premise, I will use the names *Oxford*, *Edward de Vere* and *Shakespeare* interchangeably to indicate the author of the canon. To indicate William Shakspere of Stratford-upon-Avon, I will use *Shakspere*, the name by which he was known in his native county.

## *The Size of the Canon*

The precise size of the canon of Shakespearean drama has fluctuated little in the nearly four hundred years since the publication of thirty-six plays in the First Folio in 1623. Three plays now accepted as Shakespeare's by most modern editors, *Pericles*, *The Two Noble Kinsmen* and *Edward III*, were absent from the first two Folios, and the latter two were absent from all four (1623, 1632, 1663, 1685). Six of the seven plays added to the second edition of the Third Folio (1664), such plays as *The Puritan Widow* and *A Yorkshire Tragedy*, have never been accepted as Shakespeare's. The seventh, *Pericles*, was printed anonymously six times before its appearance in the Third Folio, but was not accepted as a Shakespeare play until late in the eighteenth century. *The Two Noble Kinsmen* was not generally acknowledged as Shakespeare's until the nineteenth century, and it now appears in most editions of the complete works, albeit as a collaboration with John Fletcher. After Eric Sams made a decisive case for it in 1996, *Edward III* was included in the 2nd edition of *The Riverside Shakespeare* in 1997 and in the New Cambridge series in 1998. Sams' equally convincing brief for the inclusion of *Edmund Ironside* (1986) has not been accepted by orthodox scholars.

It is clear, then, that the Shakespeare Folios are not reliable documents for determining Shakespeare's authorship, and there is ample precedent to question their accuracy. But the result is that there is less agreement today about the size and nature of the canon than ever before. Several plays and parts of plays have been added by some editors, and parts of plays that were once accepted as wholly Shakespeare's have been assigned to other authors under the rubric of collaboration.

In 2002, Brian Vickers assembled evidence that *The Two Noble Kinsmen* and *Henry VIII* were co-authored by John Fletcher, and that three other authors in addition to Shakespeare were responsible for *Pericles* (George Wilkins), *Titus Andronicus* (George Peele), and *Timon of Athens* (Thomas Middleton). In 2013, there was published for The Royal Shakespeare Company a collection of ten plays, most of which had been ascribed by some scholars to Shakespeare, but were not part of the currently accepted canon. The editors termed them "apocryphal" Shakespeare, but offered internal evidence, "stylometric" evidence, that at least five of them were "highly likely" to have been co-written by Shakespeare (Bate, et al., eds., *Shakespeare & Others*).

In 2016, the editors of *The New Oxford Shakespeare* added several more plays to the canon, expanding it to forty-four, and assigned eight different co-authors, including Christopher Marlowe and Thomas Nashe, to as many as seventeen of them. These claims of collaboration are highly questionable because convincing evidence is lacking. There is only one instance of external evidence—John Fletcher's name on a Quarto of *The Two Noble Kinsmen*, published in 1634, long after both playwrights were dead. The internal evidence is inconsistent and contradictory, and varies greatly, depending on which scholar is alleging it, and which analytical system is used. Furthermore, if Oxford chose to collaborate he would most likely have done so with Anthony Munday or John Lyly, two playwrights who were in his employ.

In this book I add five plays—apprenticeship plays—to the Shakespeare canon, none of which, except in a few isolated instances, has ever been assigned to him. There is no evidence that he collaborated with anyone in writing them, and I am confident in attributing them to him in their entirety. They were all performed during the author's lifetime, and two different Quartos of *The Troublesome Reign of John, King of England*, in 1611 and 1622, were clearly attributed to him on their title pages. But they have all been excluded from the Shakespeare canon by orthodox scholars, that is, those who adhere to the Stratfordian theory of authorship. They have also been largely ignored in discussions of Shakespearean apocrypha, and are absent from collections of such apocrypha.

The reason given is that they are too poorly conceived and written to deserve Shakespeare's name. Although this is a subjective judgment, there is little question that they are generally inferior to those in the accepted canon. Nevertheless, the evidence that they are products of Shakespeare's pen, admittedly a novice's pen, is considerable and consistent for each of them.

There are two general ideas underlying my attribution of these plays to Shakespeare—his juvenilia and his penchant for revising his work. I assign all five of these anonymous plays to his teen age, that is, between 1563 and 1570. As is clear from the evidence provided in the following pages, they are not only his juvenilia, but are also the original versions of seven of his accepted plays. Today's orthodox scholars reject these ascriptions almost unanimously, and mistakenly, I argue, because they do not take into account these ideas, nor do they address the logical conclusion of their position—that Shakespeare was guilty of persistent plagiarism.

## Juvenilia

As Shakespeare is the Elizabethan dramatist with the largest number of surviving plays, it is puzzling that none of his apprentice work has been securely identified. Even his earliest accepted plays reveal, at the least, a journeyman's skill at creating believable characters and compelling plots. It stands to reason that this prolific playwright must have written a bad play, or at least a play with the defects of the five described here. But only a few scholars of any period have given any consideration to the idea of a substantial corpus of Shakespearean juvenilia.

In 1982, the Norwegian scholar Kristian Smidt wrote that "We know nothing about Shakespeare's earliest attempts at playwriting, but it is intrinsically improbable that he made no attempts before he tackled *Henry VI*, or whatever play of the canon may be assumed to be the first in time. It seems likely enough, too, that some of the plays we still have were built on earlier versions which were discarded when they had served their turn. This may be particularly true of the histories" (159).

While it is true that we have no recognized juvenilia of any Elizabethan playwright, we do have texts and records of performance of five anonymous plays with Shakespearean titles that have not been convincingly attributed to any dramatist of the period. And each of them is considered by most scholars to be a partial or major source of a canonical Shakespeare play or plays. But as Eric Sams remarked in *The Real Shakespeare*, "...several of Shakespeare's Folio plays, though none of anyone else's, exist in two or more very different versions, including totally different treatments of the same theme. The simple and obvious explanation, now universally overlooked, is that the earlier publications were his first versions"; (180). We can be sure that Shakespeare did not always write like Shakespeare.

## Revision

For many decades until the mid–1980s, the prevailing view was that once Shakespeare "brought a play to a finished state, he did no more to it" (Wells, "Unstable Image" 309). For example, as recently as 1982, Harold Jenkins asserted that "There has been too much irresponsible conjecture about Shakespeare's supposed revisions of supposed earlier attempts. My conception of Shakespeare is of a supremely inventive poet who had no call to rework his previous plays when he could always move on to a new one" (5). But as long ago as 1920, the founder of the Oxfordian movement, John T. Looney, broached the idea of the courtier-poet repeatedly returning to his plays throughout his lifetime:

> Everything points to "Shakespeare" being given to storing, elaborating, and steadily perfecting his productions before issuing them ... "Love's Labour's Lost," ... was not issued in its final form until 1598, and every line of it bears marks of most careful and exacting revision. "Hamlet," too, there is evidence, underwent similar treatment.... Everything bespeaks the loving and leisurely revision of a writer free from all external pressure; and this, combined with the amazing rapidity of issue, confirms the impression of a long foreground somewhere [*"Shakespeare" Identified* 1:322].

More recently, scholars have accepted the fact that Shakespeare was a persistent and meticulous reviser of his own work, especially his history plays. In her study, *Revising Shakespeare*, Grace Ioppolo noted that "Shakespeare's revising hand, exercised over a period of several years, appears clearly and brilliantly in the English history plays..." (124). There is patent evidence of revision in all eight plays of the two tetralogies, which Ioppolo described as "substantial, painstaking ... practiced some years after composition..." (130).

Of the fifty-three quartos of Shakespeare plays issued before the First Folio, fifteen quartos of six plays bore such phrases as "newly corrected," "newly augmented," "amended" or "enlarged" on their title pages (Erne 270–3; Bartlett 20–7, 36. 123). In most cases, Shakespeare was named as the reviser, even though many of these quartos were issued after his death. The Folio texts of *Hamlet, King Lear, Troilus and Cressida* and *Othello* are now generally acknowledged to have been substantially revised by the author of the earlier versions, published or not. Since he returned to these four masterful tragedies, it is reasonable to believe that he returned to his earliest plays, especially since in three of them he had portrayed a favorite king—Henry V, Richard III and King Lear. His motivation for rewriting *The Troublesome Reign of John* and *The Taming of a Shrew*, described in Chapters III and IV, is equally clear.

## Plagiarism

The nearly-unanimous view of orthodox scholars is that Shakespeare had nothing to do with any of the five anonymous plays treated here. Some scholars acknowledge that he used them as sources for his canonical plays, but even among this group most see only a slight connection. The majority of orthodox scholars regard them as some variety of "bad quarto," "piracy," "memorial reconstruction," "imitation" or "compilation." In most cases, such judgments place the composition of the anonymous play *after* the corresponding canonical play. But the documentary evidence is clear. Four of the five were printed and performed before their canonical counterparts, and the fifth, the anonymous *King Leir*, although not printed until 1605, was recorded by Philip Henslowe as performed in 1594. Evidence for the composition, performance and publication of each of the apprenticeship plays and their canonical counterparts is included in the appropriate chapter.

In most of the seven canonical plays derived from these apprenticeship works, Shakespeare used nearly the same plot structure and plot elements, and many of the same characters. In many cases, the reappearing characters have the same names as in the earlier plays. One critic describes this practice as "the deft perfecting of numerous earlier experiments in the field, usually covering similar subject matter" (Richmond 343). But if these plays were the work of other writers, as most scholars claim, then Shakespeare would be guilty of multiple acts of blatant plagiarism, not a label to be lightly applied to the world's most renowned dramatist. Such wholesale borrowing by Shakespeare from other writers' plays would be entirely untypical. Rather, it was his custom to improve and refine a phrase or a passage from one of his own earlier works. As Kenneth Muir wrote, "Hundreds of examples could be given of similar recurrences in plays whose authenticity no one disputes; and in nearly every case the second version is more pregnant and impressive" ("A Reconsideration" 47). One of Shakespeare's contemporaries, Leonard Digges, devoted four lines in a commendatory poem to affirming that he "doth not borrow,"

> "Nor Plagiari–like from others gleane,
> Nor begges he from each witty friend a Scene,
> To peece his Acts with, all that he doth write,
> Is pure his owne, plot, language exquisite,"
> —Commendatory verses to Shakespeare's *Poems* (1640).
> Quoted in Chambers, *William Shakespeare* 2:232

There could hardly be a more forceful disagreement with the opinions of most scholars on the subject of Shakespeare's use of these plays.

The best explanation for the five anonymous plays treated here is that they were the work of Shakespeare himself, at a very early stage of his career. In the following chapters, the details of evidence and the reasoning behind my claims are arranged similarly for each play, in specific Sections. In this form, the discussion of each aspect of each play can be found easily in the appropriate chapter. As the plays are covered in the probable order of composition, *Shakespeare's Apprenticeship* can also be read as a narrative.

# THE AUTHOR OF THE CANON

The underlying premise of this book is that the author of the Shakespeare canon, and of the plays treated here, was Edward de Vere, the seventeenth Earl of Oxford (1550–1604), a recognized courtier-playwright and an important literary figure in Elizabethan England. The evidence that the name "William Shakespeare" was his pseudonym has been detailed numerous times during the past century, and is buttressed every year by additional research and analysis.

It is a well-known observation that the serious writer is revealed in his or her writing. And so it is with Shakespeare, states one leading Shakespeare scholar—Jonathan Bate. In his recent biography of the playwright, Bate wrote: "Gathering what we can from his plays and poems: that is how we will write a biography that is true to him" (*Soul of the Age* xix). This statement acknowledges a widely recognized truth—that a writer's work reflects his milieu, his experiences, his thoughts and his own personality. But another Shakespeare scholar, a University of Birmingham professor, admitted recently that "Shakespeare ... is authorial dark matter, absent from his writing and from historical record to an extraordinary degree..." (Sharpe 641). It was the remarkable gap between the known facts about William Shakspere of Stratford and the traits and characteristics of the author revealed in the Shakespeare canon that led an English schoolmaster to suppose that the real author was someone else, and to search for him in the backwaters of Elizabethan poetry.

This search led him to the discovery that "William Shakespeare" was a *nom de plume* that concealed the identity of England's greatest poet and dramatist, and that continued to hide it from readers, playgoers and scholars for hundreds of years. In 1920, John T. Looney published his unique work of investigative scholarship demonstrating that the man behind the Shakespeare name and the Shakespeare canon was Edward de Vere, seventeenth Earl of Oxford.[1] Since then, hundreds of books and articles have augmented the evidence that this unconventional nobleman and courtier not only wrote the plays and poems attributed to Shakespeare, but concealed the fact of his authorship throughout his life. It appears that after his death his descendants and those in their service deliberately substituted an alternative author and fabricated physical and literary evidence to perpetuate the hoax.

The web of evidence associating Oxford with the Shakespeare canon is robust and far-reaching, and grows stronger and more complex every year.

Although he was recognized by his contemporaries as an outstanding writer of poetry and plays, he is the only leading dramatist of the time whose name is not associated with a single play. This fact, alone, about any other person would be sufficient to stimulate intense interest and considerable research. Yet the Shakespearean academic community has not only failed to undertake this research itself, it has willfully and consistently refused to allow presentations or to publish research on the Authorship Question by anyone who disputes the Stratfordian theory. What Oxfordian research it does not ignore, it routinely dismisses, usually with scorn and sarcasm, as unworthy of serious consideration.

However, during the many decades since Looney's revelations, the continuing and comprehensive investigation of the biography of the alleged author, William Shakspere of Stratford-upon-Avon, has failed to produce any evidence of his connection to the Shakespeare canon, other than several ambiguous phrases in the prefatory material to the First Folio, published seven years after his death (Price, *Unorthodox* 190–1). The bust in Stratford's Holy Trinity Church, alleged to be that of William Shakespeare, and the cryptic epitaph beneath it, have been shown to be clumsy attempts to associate Shakspere with the author of the canon (Whalen, "Stratford Bust"). In addition, repeated examinations of the documents of the Elizabethan theater have unearthed nothing that supports the theory of the Stratford man's authorship, and have revealed that no one who knew him associated him with literature of any kind (Jiménez, "Eyewitnesses"). On the other hand, Looney's conclusions, drawn from the plays and poems themselves, about the playwright's personality, his education, his selection of plots and characters, his familiarity with foreign countries and languages, his attitudes about women, money, public order and the crown all comport with what we have learned about Edward de Vere.

## Attributes of the Playwright

Walt Whitman was one of the first to doubt the Stratford theory and to suggest that the author was an aristocrat—"one of the 'wolfish earls' so plenteous in the plays themselves, or some born descendant and knower…" (2:404). It is a truism that Shakespeare almost always wrote from an aristocratic point of view and tended to support the interests and reflect the attitudes of the aristocracy. Most of his heroes and his villains are members of royal families, the nobility or the merely wealthy, and they are most often found in their royal courts or homes, or on the battlefield. A great number of the images and metaphors that Shakespeare used come from the hobbies and diversions of Elizabethan aristocrats and wealthy people: falconry; hunting, especially with dogs; fencing and dueling; archery; horsemanship; bowls; and card games.

Shakespeare reveals not only a precise and comprehensive knowledge of all these activities, but a facile and consistent use of language, imagery, simile and metaphor based upon them (Spurgeon 26–7, 30–2, 110–11). There is little argument that the canon reflects these characteristics. The historian Hugh Trevor-Roper described Shakespeare as a "cultured, sophisticated aristocrat, fascinated alike by the comedy and tragedy of human life, but unquestioning in his social and religious conservatism" (42).

Another distinctive characteristic of the playwright is his obvious interest and competence in music. "In no author are musical allusions more frequent than in Shakespeare" (Squire 32). In the plays and poems there are hundreds of images, metaphors and passages relating to music, as well as numerous ballads, love songs, folk songs and drinking songs. The playwright demonstrates a clear technical knowledge of musical theory and practice, and includes numerous allusions to musicians, to instruments and even to the notes (Squire 32–49).

These attributes and characteristics comport precisely with those of the seventeenth Earl of Oxford—a courtier, aristocrat and important landowner who was an intimate of both Queen Elizabeth and her Principal Secretary, William Cecil, whose daughter he married at age twenty-one. Oxford was praised for his affection for and competence in music, and for his patronage of musicians and composers, notably John Farmer and William Byrd (Ward, *Seventeenth Earl* 203–4; Anderson 205). However, these are only the most obvious similarities between him and the playwright Shakespeare. The details of his education, his literary and theatrical activities, his personal experiences, his travels and the people surrounding him all supply strong evidence that he is the author of the Shakespeare canon.

## Oxford's Early Environment and Education

Among scholars of the period, there is general agreement that Shakespeare was one of the best-read and most broadly-educated playwrights of the Renaissance. In the words of Ralph Waldo Emerson, "His mind is the horizon beyond which, at present, we do not see" (254). He displays a wide-ranging familiarity with the literature of Elizabethan England and the continent, as well as with the classics of ancient Rome and Greece. Besides literature, he was also obviously interested in and familiar with a variety of scholarly subjects, such as botany, astronomy, medicine and philosophy. Scholars have identified hundreds of plays, poems, novels, histories, etc., by dozens of authors that he referred to, quoted or used as sources (Gillespie 521–8). His use of untranslated works in Latin and Greek, as well as his frequent use of words, and creation of words, derived from those languages, attest to his competence in both (W. Theobald 14–15).

The facts and circumstances surrounding Oxford's childhood and adolescence suggest an environment and an upbringing that would have been an ideal preparation for a poet and dramatist, especially one who would write about the characters and subjects that dominate the Shakespeare canon. The tradition of sponsoring playing companies by the de Vere family was in place no later than 1490, during the tenure of John, the thirteenth Earl (Lancashire 106, 407)—a tradition maintained by Oxford's father and Edward himself. John Bale, the author of one of the earliest English history plays, *King Johan,* wrote it for Oxford's grandfather in the 1530s and subsequently revised it for a performance for Queen Elizabeth during her visit to Ipswich in 1561 (Harris 71, 75). It is likely that Oxford was in attendance. As a young child he lived with, and was tutored by, Sir Thomas Smith, one of England's greatest scholars, and the owner of an extensive library (Hughes 1, 9). His father's sister Frances was the widow of Henry Howard, Earl of Surrey, a major poet who is credited with the first sonnets written in the distinctive Shakespearean form, a modification of the Petrarchan sonnet.

Oxford matriculated at Cambridge at age eight, and was later awarded masters' degrees by both Oxford and Cambridge Universities (Ward, *Seventeenth Earl* 11, 22, 27). In his collection of studies of the Elizabethan drama, Frederick A. Boas refers to "the curious fact that Shakespeare shows familiarity with certain distinctively Cambridge terms" (*Shakespeare and the Universities* 47–9).[2] In 1562, Oxford's father died, and the twelve-year-old became a royal ward. He was sent to London to live in the home of William Cecil, later Lord Burghley. A surviving schedule of Oxford's rigorous daily schooling in Cecil's household confirms that he was a student in what G. P. V. Akrigg has called "the best school for boys to be found in Elizabethan England" (25–6).

As the inheritor of one of England's oldest earldoms and a member of the Cecil household, Oxford was embedded in an environment that figured prominently in the Shakespeare canon—the royal court and the center of English culture, power and wealth. "Cecil House was England's nearest equivalent to a humanist *salon.*... As a meeting place for the learned it had no parallel in early Elizabethan England" (van Dorsten 195). Besides being the dedicatee of dozens of literary works, Cecil was also one of the premier book and manuscript collectors of the Elizabethan age, and modern scholars have described his extensive library (Jolly, "'Shakespeare' and Burghley's Library" 6). There is clear documentation that Oxford, before he was twenty, purchased a Geneva Bible, and editions of Chaucer and Plutarch, all major sources of Shakespeare's plays (Ward, *Seventeenth Earl* 33). When he was in his early teens, his uncle Arthur

Golding, who was also living in William Cecil's house (Golding 36–7), translated Ovid's *Metamorphoses*, probably Shakespeare's most important source. Thus, Oxford's early education and environment prepared him to be the writer Shakespeare was, and led him to fill his dramas with the same kings and queens, aristocrats, clergymen and courtiers he saw about him.

## Literary and Theatrical Activities

Evidence of Oxford's literary activity and his association with the Elizabethan theater extends from his teen years to the end of his life. Beginning in 1564, he was the dedicatee of more than two dozen books, half of which were works of translation and imaginative literature, produced by poets, playwrights and translators, such as Thomas Watson, Robert Greene and Arthur Golding. The interests of Shakespeare the playwright are reflected in several other books dedicated to the Earl of Oxford—on medicine, on music, and on the military.[3] The Earl was repeatedly cited as a generous patron and a keen reader of poetry and prose, foreign and English, both contemporary and classical.

Poems first appeared in print over the Earl of Oxford's initials in a widely-read Elizabethan collection, *The Paradyse of Dainty Devices*, published in 1576 and repeatedly reprinted for the rest of the century. These poems have been praised as skillful, experimental and innovative. According to the critic Stephen W. May, Oxford's youthful poems in *Paradyse* "create a dramatic break with everything known to have been written at the Elizabethan court up to that time." He describes poem 4, in which the author cries out against "this loss of my good name," as a "defiant lyric without precedent in English Renaissance verse" (*Elizabethan Courtier Poets* 53). The charged subject of this eighteen-line *cri de coeur* has been associated with an accusation made by Oxford's half-sister Katherine in 1563, when he was thirteen, that he was born of a bigamous marriage, and was therefore illegitimate (Anderson 24). Oxford's poems have been linked to Shakespeare by Joseph Sobran, who found some 250 phrases, lines and images in twenty of his poems that are repeated one or more times in the Shakespeare canon, an average of about a dozen per poem (231–70). He found hundreds of similar echoes of the canon in Oxford's letters (170–1).[4]

At the age of twenty-one, the Earl of Oxford sponsored the translation into Latin of Castiglione's *Il Cortegiano* and wrote a prefatory note in Latin to the translator Bartholomew Clerke. The following year he commissioned and wrote an introductory letter to Thomas Bedingfield's English translation of *De Consolatione* (*Cardanus's Comfort*), a work recognized by orthodox scholars as "Hamlet's book" (Hardin Craig 17–37; L. Campbell 17, 133–4). He employed well-known literary men, such as John Lyly, Anthony Munday and Abraham Fleming as his secretaries, the former two being playwrights (Anderson 482). For almost a decade he maintained an unconventional literary salon near the theater district that was a headquarters for impecunious poets and playwrights (Anderson 156–61).

In 1573, the Cambridge scholar Gabriel Harvey wrote that Oxford's introduction to *Cardanus's Comfort* was an example of "how greatly thou dost excel in letters," and praised him as the writer of "many Latin verses" and "many more English verses" (Anderson 139). There is good evidence that Oxford was entertaining the court and the Queen with dramatic productions and performances as early as the 1570s. For instance, in a March 1579 letter, Gilbert Talbot wrote to his father that "before Her Majesty this Shrovetide at night" there was "a device presented by the persons of the Earl of Oxford, the Earl of Surrey, the Lords Thomas Howard and Windsor" (Ward, *Seventeenth Earl* 163–164).

Oxford was cited by name in three different works of literary commentary as a leading poet and playwright. In *A Discourse of English Poetry* (1586) William Webbe praised the Earl of Oxford as the "most excellent" of poets at court (G. G. Smith 1:243), and the anonymous author of *The Arte of English Poesie* (1589) asserted that he would be known as the best of the courtly poets "if their doings could be found out" (G. G. Smith 2:65). This judgment is confirmed by more recent critics, such as A. B. Grosart, W. J. Courthope, and Sidney Lee, who asserted that Oxford "wrote verse of much lyric beauty" (Looney, *"Shakespeare" Identified* 1:124–5; Lee, "Vere, Edward de" 228).

De Vere's life-long association with the theater, with players and with playwrights is unquestionable. During the 1580s, and as late as 1602, he sponsored his own playing companies, and in 1583 leased one of the earliest private Elizabethan theaters, the Blackfriars, for the use of his own troupe, the Earl of Oxford's Boys (Anderson 187–8). In *Palladis Tamia* (1598), a commonplace book of similes, quotations and observations on a variety of subjects, Francis Meres included him in a list of the best comic playwrights. However, no play bearing his name has survived, nor has his name ever been associated with any play.

Over a period of more than four decades, repeated opaque suggestions were made that there was an unknown writer behind the Shakespeare name who could not be named. In the "L'envoy" to his poem "Narcissus" (1595), Thomas Edwards devoted fifteen stanzas to describing several contemporary poets, identifying each of them by a name from one of their poems. In the three stanzas describing the author of "Adon" (referring to *Venus and Adonis*), he used such phrases as "in purple robes destain'd," "one whose power floweth far," "the only object and the star," and "he differs much from men / Tilting under Frieries." These and other phrases have been shown to point in general to a leading nobleman, and in particular to the Earl of Oxford (Stritmatter, "Tilting" 1, 18–20).

In his pamphlet *The Scourge of Folly* (1610), the poet John Davies of Hereford addressed "Shake-speare" [*sic*] as "our English Terence" (2:26), a comparison very likely referring to the tradition that the comedies of the former slave and Roman playwright Terence were actually written by the aristocrats Scipio Africanus and Gaius Laelius. The assertion was first made in 50 BCE by Cicero in a letter to his friend Atticus (271), and again in the next century by the rhetorician Quintilian (4:57). In *The Schoolmaster* (1570), Roger Ascham repeated the assertion (143–4), as did Montaigne, whose essays were translated by John Florio in 1603 (199). Similar suggestions about a concealed poet were made in 1598 by John Marston in *Scourge of Villanie* (Ogburn Jr. 401–2) and in 1612 by Henry Peacham in *Minerva Britanna* (Stritmatter, "Minerva").

These examples do not exhaust the abundant evidence that Oxford was a significant literary figure throughout his lifetime, and that he was several times referred to as the concealed author behind the Shakespeare pseudonym.

## Legal Training, Medical Knowledge and Experience in the Military

Shakespeare's familiarity with the law and his frequent use of legal language has long been a subject of intense interest. The most recent analysis of the legal terms, concepts and procedures occurring in the Shakespeare canon conclusively demonstrates that he had an extensive and accurate knowledge of the law (M. Alexander 110–11). He used more than two hundred legal terms and legal concepts in numerous ways—as case references, as similes and metaphors, images, examples and even puns—with an aptness and accuracy that can no longer be questioned. In February 1567, the sixteen-year-old Oxford was admitted to Gray's Inn, one of the Elizabethan law colleges. He was a member of the House of Lords for more than thirty years. He was a juror in two of the most important treason trials of the period, and was involved in legal matters and court suits throughout his life.

The author of the canon was equally familiar with the latest medical theories and practices, as well as the anatomy and processes of the human body. Scholars have identified hundreds of medical references in his plays and poems, most of them major references in which he used an image or a metaphor. He was especially prolific in his use of imagery to describe mental and physical illness, injury and disease—far more so than his fellow dramatists (F. Davis 56, n.1). He was aware of the major medical controversy between the adherents of Galen and those of Paracelsus, and referred to both authorities in *All's Well That Ends Well* (II.iii.12). Moreover it appears that his medical references were not random, irrelevant or inappropriate, but reflected the most advanced opinions at the time.

Shakespeare's intimate knowledge of military affairs was noticed in the mid–nineteenth century, and has more recently been fully documented. According to the compiler of a dictionary of his military language, Shakespeare possessed "an extraordinarily detailed knowledge of warfare, both ancient and modern" (Edelman, *Military Language* 1). Nearly all the history plays, as well as *Othello, Antony and Cleopatra* and *Troilus and Cressida*, are set in a place and time of armed conflict, and numerous obscure military analogies and references can be found throughout the canon. Several of Shakespeare's most enduring characters are soldiers or ex-soldiers, including the *faux* soldier Sir John Falstaff. One of Oxford's most fervent wishes as a young man was to serve his Queen in the military against her enemies. After missing a chance because of illness, he rode with an English army in the Scottish campaign in 1570 before he was twenty, and later faced the Spanish in the Netherlands as Commander of the Horse in 1585 (Anderson 41–3, 204–206).

Shakespeare's knowledge of the sea and ships is just as striking and comprehensive. According to naval officer A. F. Falconer, there is a "surprisingly extensive and exact use of the technical terms belonging to sailing, anchor work, sounding, ship construction, navigation, gunnery and swimming" in the Shakespeare canon. He adds that "Shakespeare does not invent sea terms and never misuses them" (vii). Again, Oxford had ample opportunity to become familiar with ships and the sea. The trip from the de Vere home in Essex to London was routinely made by ship from the seaside town of Wivenhoe at the mouth of the Colne River, where the de Veres had an estate for over a century. Oxford made at least two Channel crossings during his twenties, and traveled extensively by water in and around Italy during his visit in 1575–6. There is also evidence that he was aboard ship in the preliminary maneuvers against the Spanish Armada in the summer of 1588 (Anderson 223–25).

Thus, four distinctive characteristics that the author of the Shakespeare canon displayed—an authoritative knowledge of the law, medicine, the military, and ships and the sea, are readily explained by the record of Oxford's activities. No other candidate for the authorship, including Shakspere of Stratford, had these kinds of personal experiences.

## France and Italy Prominent in the Canon

The concordance between Shakespeare's detailed knowledge of the language, culture, and geography of Italy and France, and the travels of Edward de Vere in those countries is one of the strongest indicators that they were the same person. It is well-known that Elizabethan imaginative literature, especially its drama, was heavily indebted to Italian sources and models, and made use of such devices from Italian drama as the chorus, the dumb show and the play within the play (Grillo 65). To no other writer did this apply more than to Shakespeare. Almost a third of the plays in the canon take place in Italy, including ancient Italy, and more than a dozen are wholly or partially derived from Italian plays or novels.

Scholars have repeatedly documented Shakespeare's unexplained familiarity with the geography, social life and local details of many places in Italy, especially northern Italy.[5] "When we consider that in the north of Italy he reveals a ... profound knowledge of Milan, Bergamo, Verona, Mantua, Padua and Venice, the very limitation of the poet's notion of geography proves that he derived his information from an actual journey through Italy and not from books" (Grillo 146). Italian scholar Noemi Magri identified the locales and documented the accuracy of numerous details in *Two Gentlemen of Verona* ("No Errors in Shakespeare") and *The Merchant of Venice* ("Places in Shakespeare").

Nor is Shakespeare's knowledge of Italy limited to details of geography and local custom. It is clear that he directly observed and was profoundly affected by Italian painting and sculpture, and used several specific works—murals, sculptures and paintings—as the bases for incidents, characters and imagery in his plays and poems. For instance, the language and imagery in *The Winter's Tale, Love's Labor's Lost, Venus and Adonis* and *Lucrece* have been traced to the sculpture and murals of Giulio Romano in Mantua's Ducal Palace and Palazzo Te, and elsewhere in the same city (Hamill, "Ghosts" 86–92). (Further evidence of Shakespeare's knowledge of Italian customs is detailed in Chapter IV.)

After waiting several years for permission from the Queen to leave England, Oxford was allowed to travel to Paris in February 1575 and then to Italy via Strasbourg. After leasing quarters in Venice, he toured Italy for more than a year, visiting nearly all the locations in Shakespeare's Italian plays, including Milan, Padua, Verona, Florence, Mantua and Palermo (Anderson 74–107). Significantly, the Italian cities and city-states that Oxford did not visit, such as Naples and Ravenna, etc., are not mentioned in the Shakespeare canon. Shakespeare's Italy, it turns out, is the Italy that Oxford visited.

## *Why the Anonymity?*

One of the central questions about the case for Oxford that has not been definitively answered is why he concealed his authorship of the plays and used a pseudonym. Of the several possible reasons for this, the most obvious is the so-called "stigma of print," the idea that the creative work of self-respecting aristocrats, including most courtiers, was merely a pastime, a leisure activity. Allowing it to appear in print over their own names suggested a crass seeking of publicity or even monetary compensation.[6] The stigma applied especially to playwriting. Even late into Elizabeth's reign, "the condemnation of public plays and the people concerned with them was fairly general" (Bentley 43).

Another reason for anonymity was simple custom. Most of the plays performed during Elizabeth's reign were never published, and most of those printed appeared without an author's name (B. Maxwell 5–6). Many plays now attributed to Lyly, Peele, Greene, Kyd, Marlowe, Heywood, Drayton, Shakespeare, and dozens of others were first printed anonymously. As Alfred Hart wrote about Elizabethan printed plays, "It is correct to state that anonymity was the rule rather than the exception" (*Stolne* 6). There is no evidence that the author of the Shakespeare canon had any interest or role in the publication of his plays. Nor is there any record that he objected or intervened when corrupt or allegedly "pirated" editions were published (Price, *Unorthodox* 129–30, 170). But it is possible that he had a hand in the publication of his two narrative poems, *Venus and Adonis* (1593) and *Lucrece* (1594), both of which appear to have been carefully edited.

A third reason for anonymity, one that appears to apply directly to the Earl of Oxford, has to do with his position as hereditary Lord Great Chamberlain of England, and his close association with Queen Elizabeth. Many prominent figures in the court and in the highest levels of government were the targets of satire in the Shakespeare plays, some of it extremely disparaging. Knowledge that the author was a genuine insider who had a personal acquaintance with the subjects of his satire would make them easier to identify and would lend credence to his mocking portraits. In this case, it might have been William Cecil, or even the Queen, who required that Oxford remain anonymous.

Finally, Oxford might have imposed anonymity upon himself, or had it imposed by higher authorities, because of some aspect of his personal behavior. Late in 1580, he confessed to the Queen that he and several others had been reconciled to the Catholic Church. This led to the arrest of two of his acquaintances, Henry Howard and Charles Arundel, who then unleashed a lengthy screed against him that accused him of everything from treason to pederasty (Anderson 165–9). In March of the next year, Anne Vavasour, a nineteen-year-old lady-in-waiting to the Queen, gave birth to Oxford's son, the pregnancy being actually her second by him. The three of them were sent to the Tower, where Oxford remained until released by the Queen in June, but he was banned from the court for another two years (Anderson 172–3). At the time, Oxford had been living apart from his wife for five years because of his suspicion that she had betrayed him with another man. Although he reunited with her in 1582, these scrapes and scandals, and certain other indignities, might have led him to consider himself in disrepute and disgrace, which, along with regret and awareness of imminent death, are the themes of a dozen or more of his sonnets.

It appears that Oxford assented to the publication of *Venus and Adonis* and *Lucrece*, and wrote the very personal dedications to Henry Wriothesley, third Earl of Southampton, who is widely believed to be the Fair Youth of the Sonnets. It might have been that he was anxious that his relationship with him, whatever it was, not be known to the public, and for this reason caused the dedications to be signed with the pseudonym "William Shakespeare." The name recalls the Greek goddess Athena, who was said to have sprung from the brow of Zeus, brandishing a spear. She was the protector of Athens, the birthplace of classical drama, and was widely perceived as both a patron goddess of poets and fearless warrior in battle.[7] As such, she was most likely the inspiration behind a common English name that concealed a nobleman and a dramatist who had martial aspirations.

How, when and why the pseudonym came to be associated with the man from Stratford with the same name is unknown. What is clear is that it continued to be used after Oxford's death in 1604. The perpetrators appear to have been his surviving relatives, who might have had the same motivation as he did. Their roles in the production of the First Folio are described below.

## Oxford's Personal Life and Circumstances Reflected in the Plays

Every work in the Shakespeare canon contains allusions to circumstances, events and people in Oxford's life. Portraits of him, his family and his contemporaries have been identified in most of them by both orthodox and Oxfordian scholars. These allusions and portraits are "too numerous, consistent, complex and intimate to be mere coincidences" (Malim, "Will"). Of all the plays, *Hamlet* contains the most autobiographical material, including characters that appear to represent Oxford's father-in-law William Cecil (Polonius), his wife Anne Cecil (Ophelia), Cecil's son Robert (Laertes) and Oxford himself, whose circumstances, interests and experiences are clearly depicted in the portrait of

Prince Hamlet (Sobran 189–95). Oxford can also be identified as Bertram in *All's Well That Ends Well* (Ogburn Jr. 489–91) and Timon in *Timon of Athens* (Anderson 323–4). His street quarrel with the Knyvet family is echoed in *Romeo and Juliet* (Anderson 180–1).

*Twelfth Night* is perhaps the play that connects Oxford with the Shakespeare canon more strongly than any other, for two reasons. In the first place, the plot and the characters depict an episode in which Oxford had a strong interest—the courtship of Queen Elizabeth (Olivia) by the French Duc d'Alençon (Duke Orsino) in 1579. Also identifiable in the cast are Oxford's sister Mary (Maria), his friend Peregrine Bertie (Sir Toby Belch), the poet Sir Philip Sidney (Sir Andrew Aguecheek), Sir Christopher Hatton (Malvolio), and Oxford himself, whom the dramatist portrayed in Feste, the professed fool in Olivia's court (Clark 220–232).[8] Secondly, in 1732 the antiquarian Francis Peck described a manuscript that he proposed to publish as "a pleasant conceit of Vere, earl of Oxford, discontented at the rising of a mean gentleman in the English court, circa 1580," a statement that particularly applies to *Twelfth Night*. Although this manuscript was never published and has probably been lost, it was identified by Peck as belonging to the library of Abraham Fleming (c. 1552–1607), a London translator, poet, historian and clergyman who was a secretary to the Earl of Oxford, c. 1580 (Anderson 486, "p. 154").

Oxford's anger and despair at Anne's supposed infidelity, which he later came to doubt, is a recurring theme in at least four plays—*Measure for Measure*, *Othello*, *Cymbeline* and *The Winter's Tale*, in all of which a husband is deceived by slanders against his innocent wife. The hot-tempered and blunt-speaking Welshman Fluellen in *Henry V* has been identified by both Oxfordian and orthodox scholars as Sir Roger Williams, a follower of the Earl of Oxford (Barrell, "Shakespeare's 'Fluellen'" 59–62). A prank ambush of two of Lord Burghley's servants by three of Oxford's men at Gad's Hill near Rochester in 1573 is re-enacted in *1 Henry IV* (II.ii) by Falstaff and three of Prince Hal's servants (Ogburn Jr. 529). *The Merchant of Venice, King Lear, Twelfth Night, The Taming of the Shrew, The Tempest* and other plays contain names, incidents and situations that can be found in the biography of Edward de Vere (Anderson xxvii).

Shakespeare's *Sonnets* are an especially rich source of associations with Oxford. They are filled with autobiographical details and references that are directly linked to what is known about his life—the author's intention that his identity remain unknown (My name be buried where my body is," Sonnet 72); his lameness, his shame and his "outcast state" (89, 129, 29); and his preoccupation with the ravages of time and old age, and his own imminent death (16, 62, 73). Several sonnets suggest that the writer is a nobleman (91, 125), and Sonnet 76 contains an unmistakable reference to "E. Vere"—"That every word doth almost tell my name." Most scholars and editors agree that the *Sonnets* are in some way autobiographical, but beyond that opinions vary widely as to their actual meaning.

Some scholars have found evidence of homosexual love of the Fair Youth by the *Sonnets'* author, and evidence of the same in several of the plays (Sobran 98–100, 198–201; Hamill, "Sexuality" 49–53). Others detect a father-son relationship between them (Ogburn Jr. 342–6; Whittemore, "Chronicles"). There are several significant connections between Oxford and Henry Wriothesley, the presumed subject of the Fair Youth sonnets, but the role of the young man, whether patron, son, lover or merely dear friend, is still a much-debated question. Regardless of these uncertainties, however, the basic facts about the *Sonnets* supply further evidence that they were written by Edward de Vere.

## Dating of the Plays and Oxford's Death in 1604

Orthodox scholars typically dismiss the Oxfordian argument with the claim that several of Shakespeare's plays, as many as a dozen, were written after 1604, the year of Oxford's death. But no post–1604 allusion or source has been shown to be essential to any Shakespeare play. In no play is there a reference to any natural phenomenon, scientific discovery or topical event that occurred after 1604, nor is there a reference to anything published after 1604 (Whalen, "Dozen" 75–6).

Despite intense research and analysis, scholars have been unable to establish an unambiguous date of composition for any Shakespeare play. Registration, publication and performance dates have been obtained from various documents, but they can only indicate a *terminus ante quem*, a date before which the play must have been written. It is clear that several canonical plays were written many years before they were mentioned anywhere (Sobran 161). Eighteen plays that appeared in the First Folio in 1623 had never been printed before, and for three of them, *Coriolanus*, *Timon of Athens* and *All's Well That Ends Well*, there is no surviving record of any kind before that date.

There is evidence, however, that the playwright ceased writing in 1604. Critics have noted Shakespeare's frequent references to contemporary astronomical events and scientific discoveries, such as the supernova of 1572 that is remarked upon by Bernardo in *Hamlet* (I.i.36–8); William Gilbert's theory of geomagnetism, which he published in 1600, that is referred to twice in *Troilus and Cressida* (III.ii.179 and IV.ii.104–5); and the lines in *1 Henry VI* that allude to the uncertainty of the orbit of Mars (I.ii.1–2).[9] But similar events and discoveries that occurred after 1604 are absent from the canon. The discovery of

Jupiter's moons (by Galileo in 1610), the explanation of sunspots (also by Galileo, in 1612), and the invention of the working telescope (1608), for instance, go unmentioned in plays supposedly written after 1604.

Another indication that the author wrote nothing after 1604 is the fact that of forty-three major sources of Shakespeare's plays, all but one, the so-called Strachey Letter (discussed below), were published before Edward de Vere died, in 1604 (Sobran 156–7). In fact, a few orthodox scholars have even concluded that Shakespeare stopped writing in 1604.[10]

The most persistent argument for a post–1604 Shakespeare play is that for *The Tempest*, which was mentioned for the first time in a record of its performance at court in 1611. Its earliest appearance in print was in the First Folio. For many decades, orthodox critics have routinely claimed that the travel narratives of Sylvester Jourdain (1610) and William Strachey were the sources for the storm and shipwreck material in *The Tempest*. But recent research has demonstrated convincingly that the Strachey Letter (which was not actually published until 1625) could not have been written and taken to London in time to be used as a source for the play. The precise details and language of the storm and shipwreck scenes in *The Tempest* appear to have their sources in the colloquy *Naufragium* (*Shipwreck*) by Erasmus, published in 1518, and a collection of travel narratives by Peter Martyr, *The Decades of the Newe Worlde or West India*, that was translated from the Latin by Richard Eden (Stritmatter and Kositsky, "Voyagers"). Significantly, Eden was a friend and former student of Sir Thomas Smith, with whom Oxford was living in 1555, the year that *Decades* was published (S. Hughes 9).

## Oxford's Descendants and The First Folio

The evidence that the author of the canon was actually the Earl of Oxford continued to accumulate after his death in 1604. The mysterious dedication to *Shake-speare's Sonnets*, published in 1609, with its enigmatic phrase—"our ever-living poet," suggested that the author was dead (Price, *Unorthodox* 145–6). An even more pointed message appeared in the cryptic epistle titled "A never writer, to an ever reader. News" that was added to the second version of the first Quarto of *Troilus and Cressida*, published in the same year. The phrase is easily read as "an E. Vere writer to an E. Vere reader." Moreover, the epistle refers to the "scape" of the manuscript from certain "grand possessors," suggesting that, Oxford being dead, someone other than the author was in control of his plays.[11]

The collection of Shakespeare's plays published in 1623, the First Folio, gives every appearance of being the fruit of twenty years of association among Ben Jonson, the three de Vere daughters, Elizabeth, Bridget and Susan, and the Herbert brothers, William, third Earl of Pembroke and Philip, Earl of Montgomery. Both Oxford's son, Henry de Vere (b. 1593), and Henry's friend and close ally Henry Wriothesley, third Earl of Southampton and dedicatee of *Venus and Adonis* and *Lucrece* (b. 1573), were also associated with the Herbert brothers.

In 1590, her grandfather William Cecil proposed a marriage between Oxford's oldest daughter, Elizabeth Vere, and Henry Wriothesley, who had entered Cecil's household as a nine-year-old ward in 1582 (Akrigg 20–22). Wriothesley is generally regarded as the addressee of the first seventeen of Shakespeare's sonnets—the "procreation" sonnets. Whether or not this belief is correct, they failed to convince him, and he avoided the marriage. The parents of William Herbert, and Edward de Vere himself, favored the marriage of William to de Vere's second daughter Bridget, but in 1598 she married someone else (Anderson 313–14). In 1604, the younger Herbert, Philip, married Oxford's youngest daughter Susan. During the next few years, Susan and her sister Elizabeth, as well as other ladies of the court, performed in several of Jonson's masques, and Susan was the subject of one of the epigrams that appeared in his *Works*, published in 1616 (Ogburn Jr. 221–2). The association of Jonson and William Herbert began about 1605, and a decade later Jonson dedicated to him the *Epigrams* section of his Folio (Riggs 179, 226). In 1615, after a determined campaign for the position, Herbert obtained the office of Lord Chamberlain of the Household, and gained control of the Revels Office, as well as the playbooks of the King's Men, who had performed many of the Shakespeare plays.

The names of two former King's Men actors, John Heminges and Henry Condell, appear under the dedication of the First Folio to the two Herbert Earls, who may have financed its publication. Although Heminges and Condell claim to have collected the plays, it is far more likely that this was done by the Folio's publishers. And there is strong evidence that it was Ben Jonson who not only edited the plays but also wrote both the dedication and the subsequent epistle that also bore the two actors' names (Price, *Unorthodox* 170–4).

The orchestration and financing of the First Folio by the Herbert brothers, and editorial work by Ben Jonson, who had a long-standing association with them and with Oxford's daughter Susan, are additional strong indications that Oxford was the author of the plays. Furthermore, an extensive analysis of the prefatory material in the First Folio concludes that it is "littered with hints that the poet was a man of rank..." (Price, *Unorthodox* 176). The deliberate concealment of the actual author and the alleged allusions to Shakspere of Stratford in the First Folio accord with the efforts made by Oxford during his lifetime to remain anonymous and, after 1593, to allow his work to be credited to a man whose name happened to be similar to his pseudonym.

It is only in, and not until, the First Folio of 1623 that the few ambiguous phrases appear that purport to connect the Shakespeare plays with the William Shakspere of Stratford, who died in 1616. There is substantial evidence that the only other connection—the putative monument to the author in Stratford's Holy Trinity Church—was originally a bust of John Shakspere that was altered to represent his son (Kennedy). It is upon this scanty evidence that the entire case rests for the Stratford businessman's authorship of the world's most illustrious dramatic canon.

## The Future of Oxford

Cases of mistaken or concealed identity of authors and the people they write about are relatively common in literature. But it is rare that a literary deception has had an impact as important and as widespread as the Shakespeare hoax. Ralph W. Emerson was one of the earliest to recognize its importance when he asserted, in 1854, that the Stratfordian narrative was improbable, and that the identity of the writer posed "the first of all literary problems" (Deese 114). The accumulation of evidence for Oxford, here much condensed and summarized, is the most comprehensive and detailed solution to the "problem." It is hard to believe that it will not eventually result in the acceptance of Edward de Vere as the genuine Shakespeare.

When this occurs, all the biographies of the Stratford man, and at least one of Oxford, will become comical literary curiosities. Every Stratfordian analysis of every play and poem will have to be rewritten, and dozens of speculations about sources, meanings, characters and allusions will prove to be incorrect. The canon will be expanded, and most of Shakespeare's plays and poems will be re-dated at least fifteen years earlier. More than that, the history of Elizabethan drama and poetry will be drastically revised by the revelation that Sidney, Lyly, Watson, Daniel, Greene, Kyd, Lodge and Marlowe, all younger and less talented than de Vere, did not influence, and were not precursors of, Shakespeare, but the reverse. The re-dating of the canon will change antecedents into derivations and lenders into borrowers. The map of Elizabethan creative literature will be turned upside-down or, more properly, right-side-up, and this extraordinary man will finally be accorded his rightful place in the history of drama, of poetry and of the language itself.

# I

# The Famous Victories
# of Henry the Fifth
# and the Prince Hal Plays

## The Plays and Their Sources

In the first scene of the anonymous *The Famous Victories of Henry the Fifth*, in which appear the heir to the English throne and five comic characters, we may have the earliest surviving dramatic passages from the hand of the author of the Shakespeare canon—Edward de Vere, seventeenth Earl of Oxford. It is the first of ten such comic scenes in one of the earliest plays about English history, thus forecasting the eventual appearance of more than a hundred comedians of various sorts and a dozen plays about English kings. The evidence in the following pages will demonstrate that Lord Oxford wrote *Famous Victories* at a very early age, probably in his teens; that he expanded it into the three Prince Hal plays two decades later; that in *Henry V*, he responded extensively, with humor, sarcasm and ridicule, to criticism of the three earlier plays by a fellow courtier-poet and that he did all this by the spring of 1584, before the age of thirty-four.

The following four plays were published in the order listed between February 1598 and August 1600:

*The Famous Victories of Henry the fifth: Containing the Honourable Battell of Agin-court.* 1598

*The History of Henrie the fourth; With the battell at Shrewsburie, betweene the King and Lord Henry Percy, surnamed Henrie Hotspur of the North. With the humorous conceits of Sir Iohn Falstalffe.* 1598

> *The Second part of Henrie the fourth, continuing to his death and corona-*
> *tion of Henrie the fift. With the humours of sir Iohn Falstaffe, and swaggering*
> *Pistoll.* 1600
>
> *The Cronicle History of Henry the fift, With his battell fought at Agin*
> *Court in France. Togither with Auncient Pistoll.* 1600

Despite their titles, the central figure in each was Henry, Prince of Wales, also known as Prince Hal, who succeeded to England's throne as Henry V in 1413, and died only nine years later. As one of the country's most heroic kings, he had been the subject of numerous biographies, ballads and histories by the late sixteenth century, but so far as we know, these four plays, in which six different publishers and printers participated, were the first printed dramatic works about him. Three of the four were initially anonymous; the third—*The Second part of Henrie the fourth*—bore the words "Written by William Shakespeare" on the title page. The second (1599) through the sixth (1622) Quartos of the first *Henry IV* play bore the words "Newly corrected by W. Shake-spear," but *The Cronicle History of Henry the fift* remained anonymous in three Quartos until its publication in the First Folio in 1623.[1] The authorship of the earliest, *The Famous Victories of Henry the Fifth*, has never been established.

## THE FAMOUS VICTORIES OF HENRY THE FIFTH

Thomas Creed registered this anonymous play in May 1594 (Arber, ed. *Transcript* 2:648) and published it in 1598, "As it was played by the Queen's Majesty's Players." Only two copies of this edition are extant. The play has such similarities in terms of historical background, plot, characters and language with Shakespeare's 1 and 2 *Henry IV* and *Henry V* that it might reasonably be investigated as his first effort to dramatize the life of England's fourth and fifth Henrys. In 1928, B. M. Ward asserted that it was written by Edward de Vere, and that it was Shakespeare's principal source ("Famous Victories").

The Quarto of 1598 comprises about 1550 lines of black letter prose printed as verse that later editors have divided into twenty scenes that alternate roughly between historical exposition and comic relief. Among the more than forty speaking characters are a dozen comics, including Sir John Oldcastle, also known as "Jockey," who cluster around the young Prince Hal. Another prominent character is Richard de Vere, eleventh Earl of Oxford, a close advisor to both Kings. The play is set in the second decade of the fifteenth century, ending with the invasion and defeat of France by Henry V in 1415.

*Famous Victories* opens as Prince Hal, Oldcastle and two others have just ambushed and robbed the King's receivers of a thousand pounds at Gad's Hill

FAMOVS VIC=
tories of Henry the
fifth:

Containing the Honou-
rable Battell of Agin-court:

*As it was plaide by the Queenes Maiesties
Players.*

LONDON
Printed by Thomas Creede, 1598.

Title page of the anonymous Quarto 1 of *The Famous Victories of Henry the Fifth*, 1598, very likely Shakespeare's first play. The play's 1550 lines, all in prose, were printed in black letter. A second Quarto was issued in 1617 (© Huntington Art Collections, San Marino, California).

in Kent, and have fled to the outskirts of London. The four retire to celebrate at an "old tavern in Eastcheap." After "a bloody fray" the Sheriff arrives and takes them all before the Lord Chief Justice. When the Justice finds one of the robbers guilty, and says he must be executed, Prince Hal objects and demands that "my man" be released. When the Justice refuses, Hal "gives him a box on the ear," and the Justice commits him to the Fleet (4.104–5).[2] After another comic scene, Prince Hal is free and meets with his father and repents of all his bad behavior, calling himself "an unworthy son for so good a father!" (6.17).

Two scenes later, the King is on his deathbed in the Jerusalem Chamber of Westminster Abbey when Prince Hal enters, finds him asleep and, thinking he is dead, takes the crown. When the King awakens and finds the crown missing, he sends the Earl of Oxford to investigate. When Oxford returns with the Prince and the crown, the King rebukes his son, who tries to explain his behavior. The King forgives him, hands over the crown, and dies. Sir John Oldcastle and his companions greet the new King Henry V with great familiarity, but he urges them to change their way of life as he has his, and then orders them to keep a distance of ten miles from him. The remaining scenes of the play focus on Henry's negotiations with, and invasion of, France, interspersed with three comic episodes of military life. Henry V defeats the French at Agincourt and, as he demands the French throne, courts Katherine, the French King's daughter. In the final scene, Henry is designated heir to the throne of France, and his coming marriage to Katherine is announced.

*Famous Victories* has a poor reputation among literary scholars. It has been described as "crude," "primitive," "almost imbecilic," a "decrepit pot-boiler" and as "a medley of nonsense and ribaldry" (quoted in Pitcher 5). One of the most succinct judgments was made by J. A. Symonds, who called it "a piece of uncouth, but honest old English upholstery" (378). Its stylistic shortcomings are readily apparent. One critic calls it "heavily formulaic" with "poor verbal quality and abrupt and jerky action" (Maguire 250–1). Repeated questions are used to establish identity, place and situation. The play is replete with empty oaths, redundant declarations and observations that refer to action already in progress (L. Nichols 160–1). Confusing stage directions and speech prefixes, and abrupt dialogue suggest a novice playwright.

Nevertheless, *Famous Victories* must have been a popular play. It was reissued in 1617 by Bernard Alsop, after performances by a second playing company—the King's Men (Chambers, *Elizabethan Stage* 4:17). Its prose has been described as "forceful and straightforward, close to the language of the common folk, and easy and conversational in tone…" (Clemen 194–5). "For all its acknowledgement of the horror of war there is nothing in *Henry V* that catches the stench of a battlefield so acutely as the scene in *Famous Victories* in which one of the clowns steals shoes from dead French soldiers" (Leggatt 16). There are only three speeches that exceed twenty lines, and the plot moves at a rapid tempo. The comic subplot is well-integrated with the main plot in the first half, but then disintegrates into unrelated episodes. The characters do not develop, except that Prince Hal suddenly ceases his bad behavior and abandons his riotous comrades once he becomes king, just as he does in *2 Henry IV.* And it was the author of *Famous Victories* who first used the dramatic device of alternating comic scenes with those containing characters from English history, an innovation that Shakespeare repeated in the Prince Hal trilogy (Ribner 74).

There are roughly four opinions about the relationship between *Famous Victories* and the Shakespearean trilogy:

1. *Famous Victories* is a garbled or abridged version of an earlier play or plays about Prince Hal that was also a source of Shakespeare's trilogy.
2. *Famous Victories* was itself derived from Shakespeare's trilogy—either by a memorial reconstruction, or by deliberate abridgement or "dumbing down" for the public theater, or for a provincial production.
3. *Famous Victories* was by another playwright, and was a source for Shakespeare's Prince Hal trilogy.
4. Shakespeare wrote *Famous Victories* himself at an early age, and later expanded it into his trilogy. It is this position that is supported in the pages below.

The circumstances of the play's printing are little help in determining who wrote it. Although Thomas Creede printed *Famous Victories* in 1598 without an author's name, and in the same year put the name "Shake-speare" on Quarto 2 of *Richard III,* his reliability for correctly assigning authorship is poor (Bartlett 127, 20). In the decade after 1594, he printed several Shakespeare quartos without the author's name, including *Romeo and Juliet,* and in 1605 he attached Shakespeare's name to *The London Prodigal* (Bartlett 65, 23). By 1598, half-a-dozen Shakespeare plays had been printed anonymously, including *The History of Henrie the fourth,* and it was not until that same year that any play appeared with Shakespeare's name on it.[3]

Most orthodox scholars contend that *Famous Victories* was by another playwright, and was a source for Shakespeare's Prince Hal trilogy, but there is no agreement about who that playwright was. Scholars also differ widely about how much Shakespeare used *Famous Victories.* Some say his use was minor, and that his principal source was Rafael Holinshed's *Chronicles,* published in 1577 and reissued in an expanded version in 1587 (Chambers, *William Shakespeare* 1:383, 395; Norwich 139). Others, such as Geoffrey Bullough, say his debt was substantial (*Narrative* 4:167–68), and John Dover Wilson wrote that "a very intimate connection of some kind exists between Shakespeare's plays and this old text" ("Origins" 3). In the most recent Arden edition of *Henry IV, Part 2* (2016), James C. Bulman calls *Famous Victories* "enormously influential on Shakespeare's *Henry IV* plays," and devotes half-a-dozen pages to detailing the incidents and language that he took from it (14–15, 128–33).

In 1954, an obscure American scholar, Ephraim Everitt, attributed *Famous Victories* to Shakespeare, but supplied only general evidence (171–2). Seven years later, Seymour M. Pitcher published a full-scale study of the play, attributing it to Shakespeare, and describing in detail its similarity to the Prince Hal plays. His findings are a major source for this chapter.

## 1 HENRY IV

*The History of Henrie the fourth*, was registered by Andrew Wise in February 1598, probably before the publication of *Famous Victories*, and subsequently printed by P(eter) S(hort), in both cases minus an author's name.[4] It was reprinted five times by five different printers before appearing in the First Folio, each reprint bearing the phrase "Newly corrected" by "W. Shake-speare" or "William Shake-speare" on the title page (Bartlett 26–27). Editors agree that the Quartos were set up from each other successively, and that the Folio was set up from Q5, printed in 1613 (Weil & Weil 219; Kastan 111).

According to E. K. Chambers, "conjectural alterations" and the "usual misprints" are the only justification for the "Newly corrected" phrase on the title pages (*William Shakespeare* 1:379). Speech prefixes are fairly uniform. Most of the oaths and profanity in the Quartos, and a few of the biblical references, have been excised from the Folio. Act and scene divisions are absent from all the Quartos, but in the Folio, the play is divided into eighteen scenes in five acts. Modern editors have added a scene in Act V by dividing scene ii in two. A character list first appeared in Nicholas Rowe's edition of 1709.

Part 1 treats the years 1402 and 1403, in which Henry "Hotspur" Percy refuses to turn over to Henry IV the rebel Sir Edmund Mortimer, whom he has captured. At the same time, Henry's son Prince Hal plots, with his companions Ned Poins and Sir John Falstaff, a robbery of a group of travelers at Gad's Hill, near Rochester. After absenting themselves from the actual robbery, which is carried out by Falstaff and three others, Prince Hal and Poins disguise themselves and ambush the robbers, who flee without their booty. The whole episode is then recounted among all the participants during a riotous evening at the tavern in Eastcheap, which ends when the sheriff arrives and arrests them all, including Prince Hal. King Henry later rebukes Prince Hal for his behavior, but forgives him and gives him a command in the campaign against Hotspur. When the King's army engages the rebels near Shrewsbury, Prince Hal saves his father's life and then slays Hotspur as the rebels are defeated. Prince Hal and his father then depart to fight another rebel army in Wales.

Of the 3176 lines in the play, about 47 percent are in prose, 50 percent in blank verse, and the remainder in rhyme (Chambers, *William Shakespeare* 2:398). There are thirty-three speaking parts and half-a-dozen additional non-speaking characters. Gary Taylor concludes that the play was first performed in 1596 ("James" 352).

## 2 Henry IV

The play was registered in August 1600 by Andrew Wise, and was printed for Wise in the same year by V(alentine) S(immes). The Stationers' Register entry contained the phrase "Wrytten by master Shakespere." On the title page were the words "As it hath sundrie times been publickly acted by the right honourable, the Lord Chamberlain his servants. Written by William Shakespeare" (Chambers, *William Shakespeare* 1:377–78). The play appeared next in the First Folio, the text of which includes an additional 168 lines, and omits about forty. Profanity, indelicacy and an anti-patriotic passage in the Quarto were removed. As one Arden editor remarked, the relationship between the Folio and the Quarto is "a first-class puzzle" (Humphreys, ed. *King Henry IV, Part II*, lxxiv). Most editors and critics agree with him that the Folio was set up from a transcript prepared "from a Q and a MS concurrently" rather than from "an elaborately annotated Q" (lxxxii). These distinctions make little difference in determining the actual date of composition.

The play treats events in the remainder of Henry IV's reign until his death in 1413, but not in chronological order. At the opening, a rebel army remains at large in Northumberland. Three of the four scenes in Act II are given over to comic episodes in which Mistress Quickly unsuccessfully attempts to have Falstaff arrested, and Prince Hal and Poins play an elaborate trick on Falstaff by disguising themselves as servers. The death of Owen Glendower and withdrawals from the conflict by several noblemen deplete the rebels' ranks, and they agree to a peace settlement with Henry's son Prince John. But once they have disbanded their army, the rebel noblemen are executed and their troops pursued and slaughtered. At Westminster Abbey, King Henry is ill and asleep when Prince Hal enters and, believing him dead, takes the crown from his pillow. In the next scene, his father rebukes him and, after Prince Hal tries to explain his behavior, forgives him, and then dies, just as in *Famous Victories*.

After two more comic scenes, the new King Henry V, in a conversation with the Lord Chief Justice, recalls the latter's commitment of him to prison, but praises his conduct and asks him to stay in his post. When Falstaff greets the King familiarly, Henry reproaches him at length, and orders him and the other "misleaders" "not to come near our person by ten mile" (V.v.63–4). The play ends as the Lord Chief Justice orders Falstaff and all his companions taken to the Fleet.

## HENRY V

The first mention of *Henry V* in the Stationers' Register occurred on August 4, 1600, when it was listed as "to be staied," along with three other plays.[5] As mentioned above, about the same time, or even earlier, a Quarto printed by Thomas Creede, the printer of *Famous Victories* two years earlier, was published by Thomas Millington and John Busby. The title page indicated that the play had been performed "sundry times" by the Chamberlain's Men. According to Andrew Gurr, "The quarto of *Henry V* was not entered for printing in the Stationers' Register in 1600, because Thomas Creede had already entered his copy for *The Famous Victories* back in 1594" (*First Quarto* 6). This treatment of the two plays suggests that they were considered to be the same, or at least written by the same author.

Creede printed a second Quarto of *Henry V* for Thomas Pavier in 1602 after "copyright was established by a transfer" to Pavier in August 1600 (Chambers, *William Shakespeare* 1:130). William Jaggard printed a third Quarto in 1619, also for Pavier, but with a false date of 1608.[6] None of these three Quartos bore an author's name. The Quarto versions are nearly identical with each other, but are only about half as long as the Folio text. They eliminate or transpose several entire scenes; they cut or shorten all the longer speeches, especially those of Henry, and they cut the Prologue, Epilogue and all speeches by the Chorus that introduce each act. Eleven small speaking parts are eliminated, creating a smaller and simpler playing text that could be performed in just two hours. It has been observed that "...the quarto text of *Henry V* ... is in many ways closer to *The Famous Victories* than the version of the play we are familiar with from the Folio" (Clare 112). In the last 350 years, no company has acted the Quarto version (Gurr, *First Quarto* 4).

Although a few scholars contend that the Quarto was the playwright's first version, a consensus has emerged that the text printed in the First Folio was the author's original composition, and that the Quarto text was extracted from his copy, and then printed in 1600 (Gurr, ed. *First Quarto* 9). How, why and by whom the Quarto version was derived from the original are also in dispute. The usual theories abound—playhouse piracy, memorial reconstruction, abridgement for playing on tour, etc. But regardless of the method, it appears that a shorter version of the original text was performed, and then printed.

The ten different Quartos of these four plays present a messy and uneven publication history that includes six different owners and seven different printers. Three additional Quartos of *1 Henry IV* were printed after the First Folio by three other printers for three other owners (Bartlett 25–9; 127–8). This suggests that no author was involved in the process of copying, editing and publication, and that the manuscripts were acquired, perhaps illegitimately, then registered, printed and sold in a random manner. The Folio versions of the three canonical plays are roughly the same length, within three hundred lines of each other, but the three Quartos of *Henry V* are only half as long as the others. This supports the view that the Folio *Henry V* was the author's original version. However, some scholars now think that the opposite is the case—that the quarto version of the play preceded that of the Folio. For a discussion of these opinions, see "Contrary Evidence," below.

Francis Meres listed "*Henry the 4*" among Shakespeare's tragedies in *Palladis Tamia*, registered in September 1598. According to the argument made in this chapter, by that date all four Prince Hal plays had been performed; but the last two had yet to be printed.

## SOURCES OF THE PLAYS

### Famous Victories

The idea that *Famous Victories* was a garbled version of an earlier play or plays about Prince Hal has been advanced by Andrew Cairncross, John Dover Wilson, Gary Taylor and others. "A piracy of the loose type" is the phrase used by Cairncross (*Hamlet* 144, 148). Taylor considered *Famous Victories* a "memorially reconstructed" play that "debases" an earlier play on the same subject (ed. *Henry V*, 4, n. 3; 28). In the opinion of John Dover Wilson, *Famous Victories* was a memorial reconstruction of a "highly-abridged and much degraded version" of two other plays about Henry IV and V "written in the eighties" and owned by the Queen's Men. He surmised that the company, in dire straits during the plague years of 1592–4, sold the plays, and that they were subsequently "reported from memory" and published as *Famous Victories* (ed. *Henry V* 116–7).

Needless to say, there is no trace of the unknown play or plays preceding *Famous Victories*, nor of their unknown author and, as Gary Taylor admitted, "...this is all speculation" (ed. *Henry V* 4, n. 3). E. M. W. Tillyard made the unusual, if not unique, suggestion that *Famous Victories* "may well be an abridgement—a kind of dramatic Lamb's Tale—of Shakespeare's early plays on Henry IV and Henry V" (174). These "early plays" of Shakespeare fall into the same category as those imagined by Taylor and Wilson, that is, no trace of them can be found.

In his study of the play, Seymour Pitcher cited Sir Thomas Elyot's *The Book of the Governor* (1531) and three chronicles—those of Edward Hall

(1548), Rafael Holinshed (1577), and John Stow's *Chronicles of England* (1580) as sources of *Famous Victories*.

B. M. Ward examined the details and language in the play that also appeared in the first edition of Holinshed's *Chronicles* and found that all but one had previously appeared in Edward Hall's *Chronicle*, first published in 1548.[7] The single exception that Ward identified is an eight-line speech by the Duke of Burgundy in the last scene that is "practically a verbatim transcript (somewhat condensed) of a paragraph in Holinshed." However, as Ward pointed out, "Holinshed's authority (quoted by him in the margin) was the Latin history of the reign of King Henry V written by Titus Livius about 1440" ("Famous" 280). Ward was referring to *Vita Henrici Quinti*, written by Tito Livio, dei Frulovisi, an Italian historian who had traveled in England in the 1430s.[8] Although this work remained in manuscript until 1716, it was used by both Stow in the 1560s and Holinshed in the 1570s, but apparently not by Hall. Thus, the manuscript containing this incident, and several other incidents in *Famous Victories*, was in circulation in the mid-sixteenth century and available to the playwright. Ward also identified "five instances of phrases in the play" that appeared in Hall's *Chronicle*, but not in Holinshed's ("Famous" 279). According to Andrew Gurr, [*Famous Victories*] "certainly uses Hall and not Holinshed" (ed. *Henry V* 235).

It appears that the playwright took the incident of the gift of tennis balls from the Dolphin in scene 9 from the manuscript of *Historia Regum Anglie*, a chronicle compiled in the 1420s by John Strecche, canon of Kenilworth.[9] The mention of a carpet in the gift has its origin in the phrase "soft cushions to lie on" in Strecche's account, which appears in no other.[10] Pitcher attributes certain details and language in the play (226, n. 8) to John Stow's *A Summarie of English Chronicles* (1565). Most of them can also be found in Hall or Elyot. Others are from one of Stow's many sources, such as Titus Livius or *Gregory's Chronicle*.[11]

The play's title echoes the title of Hall's third chapter—"The Victorious Acts of King Henry the Fifth." It was perhaps also echoed by Queen Elizabeth at Tilbury, just before the arrival of the Spanish Armada in July 1588, when she predicted that "We shall shortly have a famous victory" (Cheney 410–11).

### 1 and 2 Henry IV

The two plays have a striking relationship to the first half of *Famous Victories*. The structure of Part 1 is clearly based on scenes 1 through 6, and that of Part 2 on scenes 7 through 9, up to line 58 in Pitcher's edition (Weis 23–4). As David Scott Kastan remarks about Part 1, Shakespeare "found the focus of the play in the anonymous *The Famous Victories of Henry the Fifth*" (342).

For both plays, Bullough cites as "sources" and "probable sources" Holinshed's *Chronicles* (1587) and Samuel Daniel's *Civil Wars* (1595). For Part 1, he adds Stow's *Chronicles of England* (1580); for Part 2 he adds Hall's *Chronicle* (1548) and *Famous Victories*.[12] Most critics and editors agree, and some add such other sources as *The Mirror for Magistrates*, a collection of linked verse biographies of tragic figures in English history by various authors that was first published in 1555.[13] But virtually all the historical background and incidents in both Parts that are not in *Famous Victories* are contained in Edward Hall's *Chronicle* (1548), or in other chronicles published before it.

John Dover Wilson and others have cited language in several of Thomas Nashe's works published after 1589 that is identical or nearly so to words and phrases in the two *Henry IV* plays.[14] These editors suggest that either Nashe had a hand in the composition of the plays or that Shakespeare borrowed language from Nashe. Wilson wrote that the matter was "an unsolved, perhaps insoluble, puzzle" ("Origins" 12) and that he had "no explanation to offer" (ed. *Henry IV, Part 1*, 191). But a satisfactory explanation emerges when one considers the evidence below for the Earl of Oxford's authorship of these plays, and for composition dates in the early 1580s. Any similarities of language between them and Nashe's works can only be the result of borrowings by Nashe after seeing the plays or manuscripts of the plays.

### Henry V

The sources for *Henry V* are roughly the same as for its two predecessors. Bullough cites Holinshed's *Chronicles* (1587) and the *Annals* of Tacitus, specifically the "Description of Germanie" in an English translation by Richard Grenewey published in 1598 (*Narrative* 4:361–4). The pronouncements of the Archbishop of Canterbury about the Salic Law in scene 9 of *Famous Victories* are taken up and expanded in I.ii of *Henry V*, followed in both plays by the presentation of the tennis balls by the French Ambassador. The balance of scene 9 and the remaining ten scenes of *Famous Victories* supply the skeleton for the twenty-three scenes in *Henry V*. According to one scholar, the three Prince Hal plays are "heavily indebted" to *Famous Victories*, serving as a "theatrical pre-text" for them (Clare 102–3). Numerous details of plot, language, characterization and dramatic devices in *Famous Victories* are scattered throughout the trilogy. These are described below in "The Prince Hal Plays and Edward de Vere." As with both Henry IV plays, all the historical background and incidents in *Henry V* that are not in *Famous Victories* can be found in Edward Hall's *Chronicle* (1548), or in other chronicles published before it.

One example is the lines spoken by the Archbishop of Canterbury, Henry Chichele, in the opening scene of the play, in which he argues against the Lollard's Bill of 1410, which called for the appropriation of Church lands and wealth by the crown (I.i.1–19). Editors of *Henry V* routinely cite and quote

Holinshed as the source for this passage (Taylor, ed. *Henry V* 94, 306; Craik, ed. *King Henry V* 122; Gurr, ed. *King Henry V* 80). But the incident was recorded in the *Chronicles of London* (Kingsford, ed. 65–7), and appeared in print in both Robert Fabyan's *The New Chronicles of England and France*, first published in 1516, and three more times before 1560 (578), and in Hall's *Chronicle* (49–50).

The dramatic devices of intermingling historical and comical scenes, and the appearance of both a clown and a king in the same scene that first appeared in *Famous Victories* are repeated in *Henry V*. And in this play, Shakespeare added a third device that appeared originally in *Famous Victories*—the depiction of "strangers," or foreigners, who speak broken English. This is treated in "The Prince Hal Plays and Edward de Vere" below.

## *Relationships Between* Famous Victories *and the Prince Hal Plays*

The connections between *Famous Victories* and the Prince Hal plays are legion, and range from structure and plot to characters, and from language and style to dramatic devices.

### STRUCTURE AND PLOT

The structure and plot of *Famous Victories* align almost exactly with those of Shakespeare's Prince Hal trilogy, except that each episode in the anonymous play has been rewritten and expanded and many new ones added. The fifty-seven scenes in the Prince Hal plays are a natural expansion of the twenty scenes in *Famous Victories*. The first scene of *Famous Victories* matches the second scene of *1 Henry IV,* and the last scene of *Famous Victories*, in which Henry V woos the French Princess Katherine, matches the last scene in *Henry V*, in which he does the same thing. Thus the anonymous play might be seen as a rudimentary skeleton within the full body of the trilogy.

The following plot elements occur in both *Famous Victories* and in the Prince Hal trilogy:

- the robbery of the King's receivers at Gad's Hill in Kent (*Famous Victories*, sc. 1; *1 Henry IV* II.ii).
- the meeting of the robbers in an Eastcheap tavern (*Famous Victories*, sc. 2; *1 Henry IV* II.iv).
- Prince Hal's "box on the ear" of the Chief Justice (*Famous Victories*, sc. 4; referred to in *2 Henry IV*, I.ii.52–3 and I.ii.187–8).

- the Chief Justice's commitment of Prince Hal to prison (*Famous Victories*, sc. 4; referred to in *2 Henry IV* I.ii.52–3 and V.ii.67–79).[15]
- the Prince's visit to his sick father (*Famous Victories*, sc. 6; *1 Henry IV* III.ii).
- the reconciliation of the newly-crowned King Henry V with the Chief Justice (*Famous Victories*, sc. 9; *2 Henry IV* V.ii.101–39).
- Prince Hal's former comic companions expecting favors from the new King (*Famous Victories*, Scs. 5 and 9; *2 Henry IV* V.iii.120–35).
- the new King's rejection of his former companions (*Famous Victories*, sc. 9; *2 Henry IV* V.v.46–70).
- the rigorous defense of Henry's right to the crown of France by the Archbishop of Canterbury (*Famous Victories*, sc. 9; *Henry V* I.ii.33–95.).
- the gift of tennis balls from the Dolphin (*Famous Victories*, sc. 9; *Henry V* I.ii.259).
- the episode of forced military recruitment (*Famous Victories*, sc. 10; *2 Henry IV* III.ii).
- the overconfidence of the French about the war with England (*Famous Victories*, scs. 11 and 13; *Henry V* II.iv.14–28).
- the refusal of the French king to allow his son, the Dolphin, to fight at Agincourt (*Famous Victories*, sc. 11; *Henry V* III.v.64).
- Derick's encounter with a French soldier (*Famous Victories*, sc. 17; Pistol's in *Henry V* IV.iv.).
- the comics' conversation on the battlefield about returning to England (*Famous Victories*, sc. 19; *Henry V* V.i).
- the courting of the French Princess Katherine by the victorious Henry V (*Famous Victories*, scs. 18 and 20; *Henry V* V.ii.99–277).

Not only are all these plot elements common to *Famous Victories* and the Prince Hal plays, they all occur roughly in the same order.[16] One additional similarity between *Famous Victories* and *Henry V* is the complete absence of the historical Henry V's second campaign in France from 1417 to 1420. As one scholar put it, "Shakespeare's trilogy emulates the stagecraft" and follows "exactly the contour" of *Famous Victories*" (Clare 113).

Besides the plot elements listed above, there are several dozen specific details of action and characterization that appear in both *Famous Victories* and in Shakespeare's trilogy. For example: the character "Gads Hill" ("Gadshill" in *1 Henry* IV) involved in the robbery; Gad's Hill as the place of the robbery; the Chief Justice's defense of his sending the Prince to prison; the meetings between Henry V and the French herald; the defiant Henry V telling the French herald that his only ransom will be his worthless dead body; Henry V's assurance that the French Ambassador may speak his mind; Henry V's naming of the battle after the nearby castle; Henry V's requirement of an oath of fealty from the Duke of Burgundy.[17] The French Captain's claim that the English soldier is lost without "his warm bed and stale drink" (*Famous Victories*, sc. 13) is echoed at III.vii in *Henry V*, where the Duke of Orleans and the Constable of France assure each other that the English cannot fight without beef.

The key interaction between Henry IV and his son is structured in the same way in the *Henry IV* plays as it is in *Famous Victories*. In both versions, Prince Hal reassures his father that he has reformed himself and abandoned his previous misbehavior. But then, in scene 8 of *Famous Victories*, and in IV.v of *2 Henry IV*, he takes the crown from his sleeping father's pillow and leaves the chamber. When the King awakens, he is alarmed that the crown is gone and sends Oxford in *Famous Victories*, Warwick in *2 Henry IV*, to find it. In both plays, Prince Hal is found with the crown and brought back to his father's chamber, where he delivers a long speech of apology and repentance, and is immediately forgiven by the King. Again, not only are all forty-two specific details common to both, they occur in the same order. Moreover, most of these details cannot be found in the chronicles of the period; they are additions by the playwright himself.

In addition to the above similarities, there are several incidents and passages of dialogue attributed to historical characters in Shakespeare's Prince Hal trilogy for which there is little or no evidence in the more than twenty historical chronicles available in the middle years of Elizabeth's reign. However, many of them appear in *Famous Victories*—the most notable being the scene in which Henry woos the French princess Katherine in the last act of *Henry V*.

In 1961, Seymour Pitcher advanced the claim that in writing his Henry trilogy Shakespeare used *Famous Victories* "ingeniously" and "instinctively." "He knew it by heart, by total assimilation"—because he wrote it himself (6). The most important structural similarity among the four plays is the alternation of comic scenes with those based on historical events. *Famous Victories* was the first history play to include an important comic subplot, and to pursue that plot throughout the play in alternating scenes. There are nine scenes in *Famous Victories* devoted entirely to the comic subplot (1, 2, 4, 7, 10, 13, 16, 17, 19), eight scenes based on historical events (3, 8, 11, 12, 14, 15, 18, 20), and three scenes in which there is some combination of the two (5, 6, 9).

In contrast, there is no comic subplot in any of the six canonical history plays that Shakespeare wrote between *Famous Victories* and the Prince Hal trilogy, and just a handful of humorous lines.[18] But the comic subplot reappears in each of the plays in the trilogy, nineteen of the fifty-seven scenes in the three plays being fully occupied by comics, and eight others containing some comic material, an arrangement very much like that in *Famous Victories*. This is further support for the claim that the playwright took *Famous Victories* as his source and template for the Prince Hal trilogy.[19]

## CHARACTERS

Nearly all the characters in *Famous Victories* reappear in one or more of the Prince Hal plays, including seven of the eight English officials and aristocrats, and five of the six French nobility, including King Charles VI, his son the "Dolphin" and Princess Katherine. Most of the comic characters are carried over, and several are exactly duplicated. For the most part, the characters who reappear in the Prince Hal plays say and do the same things that they say and do in *Famous Victories*. Prince Hal is the main character in all four plays. His interaction in *Famous Victories* with his comic companions, with his generals, with the French royalty and nobility, and with Princess Katherine are in large part duplicated, but greatly enhanced and enlarged, in the Folio trilogy.

The interactions between Prince Hal and his father in *1 Henry IV* (III.ii) and in *2 Henry IV* (IV.v) are the same as in scenes 6 and 8 of *Famous Victories*, except that Shakespeare rewrote them as extended conversations. But most of the details remain—the music that soothes the King, the King dozing as the Prince takes the crown, the repentance of the Prince as he weeps and returns it, and his promise to safeguard it when he is king. In the words of one editor, "The death-bed scene, above all, shows a kinship [with *Famous Victories* ] of conception and even of phrasing, though not of quality."[20]

Henry V's cousin, Edward, Duke of York, appears briefly in scenes 9 and 12 of *Famous Victories*. In scene 12 he requests and is granted command of the vanguard at Agincourt, and three scenes later is reported as a casualty of the battle. In his only two lines in *Henry V* (IV.iii.129–30), he makes the same request, and is reported killed in IV.viii.104. Henry V's uncle, Thomas Beaufort, whom he created Duke of Exeter after Agincourt, speaks only four lines in *Famous Victories*, but his role is greatly expanded in *Henry V.*

Richard de Vere, eleventh Earl of Oxford, is one of the main characters in *Famous Victories*, and speaks eighteen times in seven scenes, more than any other historical character except the Lord Chief Justice and the two Henrys. He is the first historical character to speak, except for Prince Hal, and he speaks only to Henry IV or to Prince Hal, who is crowned King between the eighth and ninth scenes. More than that, in *Famous Victories* de Vere has been elevated to the place of principal counselor to both Henrys, even though the chronicles report that York, Exeter and the Earl of Westmoreland acted in that capacity.

In fact, the eleventh Earl of Oxford is mentioned only twice in Hall's *Chronicle*, the principal source of the play, and only once by Holinshed. Neither writer assigns to him any of the actions he takes or words he speaks in the play, except to say that he was present when Henry landed in France and was with him at Agincourt (Ward, *Oxford* 282–3; Corbin and Sedge 146). Oxford is the only English aristocrat in *Famous Victories* who is entirely absent from all the Prince Hal plays. (See "*Famous Victories* and Edward de Vere," below).

Aside from the Archbishop of Bourges, who is replaced by an unnamed secular Ambassador, all the members of the French nobility in *Famous Victories* reappear in *Henry V*, where they play the same roles, albeit much enlarged and enhanced. The most prominent comic characters in *Famous Victories* who reappear in the Prince Hal plays are Ned (Edward Poins in 1 and 2 *Henry IV*), Mistress Cobbler (Mistress Quickly in 1 and 2 *Henry IV* and *Henry V*), and the Sir John Oldcastle and Derick characters, who are combined and transformed into Sir John Falstaff.

## Sir John Falstaff

Of the ten comics in *Famous Victories*, Shakespeare combined two—Sir John Oldcastle and Derick—to create Sir John Falstaff, his most memorable comic figure. Derick appears in six scenes and speaks more than 170 lines in *Famous Victories*, but he and Oldcastle never appear in the same scene, suggesting to some scholars that they were played by the same person (Fiehler 25; Bevington, ed. *Henry IV, Part 1* 32). Between them, they appear in nine of the play's twenty scenes, and display the same characteristics, say many of the same things, and interact with other characters in the same way, as Falstaff in the two *Henry IV* plays. The Oldcastle/Derick character bears the same relationship to Prince Hal in *Famous Victories* that Falstaff bears to him in Shakespeare's plays.[21] In the words of one scholar, "A superficial examination of the two plays [*Famous Victories* and 1 *Henry IV*] will show that in each we have a swaggering soldier, in service against his will, aggressive when his enemies are unarmed, and running away when they are armed; in each he is a coward, braggart, glutton, thief, rogue, clown and parasite; in each he has the same monumental unblushing effrontery and loves a jest even at his own expense" (Monaghan 358). Furthermore, in *Famous Victories* Sir John Oldcastle is a companion of Prince Hal, and tends to lead him into mischief, the same role played by Falstaff in the *Henry IV* plays.[22] As Robert Weimann suggests, if Kemp acted the part of Falstaff, "he must have done so in much the same way as Tarlton had played Dericke in the Chief Justice scene in *Famous Victories*" (191).

As described above, the Oldcastle of *Famous Victories* and Falstaff in II.ii of 1 *Henry IV* both participate in a robbery on Gad's Hill, although the outcome of the episode is slightly different in the latter play. In a conversation with Old-castle in scene 5 of *Famous Victories*, Prince Hal notes the prevalence "nowa-days" of prisons, hanging and whippings, and adds "But I tell you, sirs, when I am King we shall have no such things" (14–15). In *1 Henry IV*, Falstaff asks of Prince Hal, "Shall there be gallows standing in England when thou art king?" Hal's reply suggests that hangings will be rare (I.ii.56–65). Both Oldcastle in *Famous Victories* (scene 5) and Falstaff in *1 Henry IV* (I.ii) expect that they will prosper when Prince Hal becomes king. Both welcome King Henry's death, but both are among the group that is rejected by the new King Henry.

In scene 7 of *Famous Victories*, Derick complains bitterly about the meal prepared for him by Mistress Cobbler, and calls her a knave and a whore. They clash again in scene 10 and physically assault each other. In Act III of *1 Henry IV*, Falstaff and Mistress Quickly argue at length about money he owes her for food and wine. He calls her "Dame Partlet," a traditional name for a scolding woman, questions her honesty, and suggests that she is a prostitute (III. iii).[23]

Derick's boasts and tricks on the battlefield of Agincourt in scene 19 of *Famous Victories* are nearly identical with those of Falstaff after he and his companions are robbed by Poins and Prince Hal in *1 Henry IV*. Derick brags to John Cobbler that he was "four or five times slain" and that he was called "the bloody soldier amongst them all" because "Every day when I went into the field I would take a straw and thrust it into my nose and make my nose bleed...." He adds that when he was confronted by an actual French soldier, he "skipped quite over a hedge; and he saw me no more that day." In Act II of *1 Henry IV*, Prince Hal and his companions exchange accounts in the Eastcheap tavern about the two robberies that have just taken place. Falstaff claims that after he and the others robbed the King's receivers he was set upon by eleven men, and that he drove off seven of them. Prince Hal replies that only he and Poins assaulted Falstaff and his three companions, and that Falstaff fled without a fight. He accuses Falstaff of hacking his sword to make it look like he used it to defend himself, and Peto later confirms it. Bardolph reports that Falstaff told them to "tickle our noses with spear-grass, to make them bleed" (II. iv).

Some scholars have attempted to associate Falstaff with one or the other of two historical figures who were prominent in early fifteenth century England. The historical Sir John Oldcastle was a friend of Henry V, but turned against him and against the Catholic establishment of England and embraced Lollardy, a religious and political movement that advocated a major reform of Western Christianity. In 1408, he married Joan de la Pole, fourth Baroness Cobham, and in consequence, bore the nominal title of Lord Cobham. In 1414, he led a Lollard rebellion that was easily put down and, after being excommunicated, impris-oned and then escaping, he was eventually recaptured, tried, and convicted of treason and heresy. He suffered an especially gruesome execution in 1417, being hanged in chains and burnt (Corbin and Sedge 2–6). By the mid–sixteenth century, he was among the pantheon of Protestant martyrs, and was depicted as such in an adulatory biography by John Bale in 1544 (*Select Works* 1–59) and in John Foxe's *Acts and Monuments* in 1563 (3:321–401).

The record is clear that in his revision and expansion of *Famous Victories*, Shakespeare retained the name Oldcastle in *1 Henry IV* (Taylor, "James" 341). But it is claimed that he was pressured to change it by a person "descended from his title," ostensibly William Brooke, tenth Lord Cobham, who was a favorite of Elizabeth and, for a short time in 1596–7, her Lord Chamberlain (Lock). The connection between Oldcastle and William Brooke was extremely tenuous, however, the former being the stepfather of the great-great-great-grandmother of the latter (Gibson 102). Some assert that the pressure came from prominent Elizabethan Protestants, who were outraged at Shakespeare's portrayal of one of their revered heroes (Corbin and Sedge 9–12, Pendleton 66). The latter claim is more likely, since the appearance of Oldcastle on the stage in two popular plays—*Famous Victories* and *1 Henry IV*—stimulated at least two responses in defense of him—*Sir John Oldcastle* (1600), written by Michael Drayton and others, and a poem by John Weever, *The Mirror of Martyrs* (1601).[24]

The other historical character who has been linked to Falstaff was Sir John Fastolf (1380–1459), a soldier and landowner who accompanied Henry V during his wars in France, fought at Agincourt, and was made a Knight of the Garter in 1426. In mid-career he was accused of cowardice after losing a battle against the French, but was eventually exonerated. A Sir John Fastolfe appears briefly in *1 Henry VI*, where he is depicted as a coward (III.ii.105–8), but there is otherwise no description of him.[25] Neither of these men resembles the fat comic and *faux* soldier in Shakespeare's plays.

In light of the evidence presented in "The Date of *Famous Victories*" below, it is hard to imagine a teen-age Oxford deliberately satirizing a fifteenth century Protestant martyr. It may be that the slightly humorous name "Oldcastle" appealed to him as a name for his slightly humorous knight/comic. He appears in only one scene and speaks only eight lines in *Famous Victories*. (Under the name "Jockey," colloquial for "John," he speaks only another twenty-three lines) This thinly-drawn portrait of the double-named Oldcastle/Jockey character can hardly be called a serious satire, or even a recognizable portrait, of Sir John Oldcastle. It smacks of confusion or carelessness on the part of the author, rather than purpose.

The subsequent choice of "Falstaff" as an alternative name, and the enlargement of the role, admit of two explanations. It may be that Oxford came across the name "Fastolf" and found that by rearranging the letters he would have a perfect name for a failing or retreating soldier, a soldier whose staff or banner is falling. And in *1 Henry IV*, he took the opportunity to flesh out, as it were, a portrait of a *miles gloriosus*, a boastful, cowardly, sometime soldier—a stock comic character who appeared first in Greek drama, and then in the Latin comedies of Plautus and Terence. Both Plautus's *Miles Gloriosus* and Terence's *Eunuchus* contained *miles gloriosus* (swaggering soldier) characters, and both were performed on Elizabethan stages, *Eunuchus* at Queens' College, Cambridge in 1564 (G. Smith 58) and *Miles Gloriosus* before Queen Elizabeth in January 1565 by the Children of Westminster (Chambers, *Elizabethan Stage* 3:20).

On the basis of these facts, it is clear that Falstaff is not a historical figure, but a character derived from a composite of Sir John Oldcastle and Derick in *Famous Victories* (Satin 215, n. 2; Bullough, *Narrative* 4:171).

### Edward Poins

The Edward Poins of the two *Henry IV* plays is identical with the Ned of *Famous Victories*. In all three plays, Prince Hal repeatedly calls him "Ned," and in two of them they carry out a robbery at Gad's Hill. In *Famous Victories*, they are joined by Tom and Sir John Oldcastle in a robbery of the King's receivers. In *1 Henry IV*, after Oldcastle and the others have robbed the receivers, Poins and the Prince rob them. In all three plays, Poins speaks familiarly to Prince Hal and is his closest companion.

In scene 9 of *Famous Victories*, Poins suggests to the new King Henry V that he does not grieve over his father's death. Henry then tells him to "mend thy manners" and that he must "change" in the same way as *he* has. In a long conversation between them in *2 Henry IV*, Poins calls the new King a hypocrite for pretending to grieve over his father's illness. Henry responds coolly, and suggests that it is the "vile company" of Falstaff and Poins that has caused him to appear unmoved by his father's illness (II. ii. 28–55).

Although a Poins family was prominent in the early fifteenth century, no member of it was a close associate of Prince Hal either before or after he became Henry V. The Poins of the Shakespeare plays is a replica of the Poins of *Famous Victories*, and neither is a historical character.

### Mistress Quickly

The literary ancestor of the Mistress Quickly in the two *Henry IV* plays is Mistress Cobbler, the wife of John Cobbler in *Famous Victories*. Both women are members of the group of comics associated with Prince Hal before and after he becomes Henry V. In scene 7 of *Famous Victories*, Mistress Cobbler engages in the dispute described above over a meal with the Oldcastle/Derick character. Mistress Quickly has a similar dispute with Falstaff about the bill for his food and wine in *1 Henry IV* (III.iii.65–82). In all three plays, the Oldcastle/Derick/Falstaff character insults and slanders the woman who has served him food. In scene 10 of *Famous Victories*, after Oldcastle/Derick and Mistress Cobbler have assaulted each other, he threatens to "clap the law on your back," and suggests to the recruiting Captain that he "press her for a soldier." In *2 Henry IV*, Mistress Quickly attempts to have Falstaff arrested for debt, and they exchange mutual threats (II.i).[26]

It is clear that Shakespeare has, in the two *Henry IV* plays, simply re-used and renamed the female foil to the Oldcastle/Derick character in *Famous Victories*. He has broadened her role considerably and made her a more believable character, but retained her behavior, her language and her relationship with the fat knight.

### Ralph Mouldy and Francis Feeble

James C. Bulman called attention to two characters in *Famous Victories* who might have inspired a scene and contributed to the behavior of two comics in Shakespeare's revision. In scene 10 of *Famous Victories*, "…a captain conscripts two clowns for the wars in France, one of whom, John Cobbler, like Mouldy in *2 Henry IV*, begs to be allowed to stay at home to do his husbandry, while the other, Derick, like Feeble in the same play, is willing to do his patriotic duty" (133).

## LANGUAGE AND STYLE

Individual words and phrases, images, ideas and dramatic devices in *Famous Victories* reappear throughout Shakespeare's three Prince Hal plays. In most cases, they are associated with the same character or situation as in the earlier play. Nor are they limited to one type of character. They appear in the conversations among the comics; in Henry IV's comments about his illness and his seizing of the crown; in Henry V's response to the Dauphin's gift of tennis balls; in his remarks on the battlefield in France; in his triumphal scene in the French court; and in the scenes in which he courts Katherine, the daughter of Charles VI.

### Examples in *Famous Victories* and in *1 Henry IV*

*Jockey*                              but the best is

                we are ahorseback and they be a foot    *Famous Victories* 1.28–9

*Fal.*         A' horseback, ye cuckoo, but afoot
              he will not budge a foot.                    *1 Henry IV* II.iv.353–4

* * *

*Jockey.*                                        For the
              town of Deptford is risen with hue and cry after your man,
                                                *Famous Victories* 1.18–19.

*Sher.*                                      A hue and cry
              Hath follow'd certain men unto this house.
                                                *1 Henry IV* II.iv.507–8

* * *

*Derick.*                                  Nay, I am quickly
              pacified.                              *Famous Victories* 2.55–6

*Fal.*         Thou seest I am pacified still         *1 Henry IV* III.iii.172

* * *

*Ned.*        Shall I be Lord Chief Justice? By Gog's wounds,
              I'll be the bravest Chief Justice that ever was in Eng-
              land!                                *Famous Victories* 5.22–4

*Fal.*         Shall I? Oh, rare! By the Lord, I'll be a brave judge
                                                *1 Henry IV* I.ii.171

Falstaff is described with similar phrases by Henry IV in *Famous Victories* and by Prince Hal in *1 Henry IV*:

*King*                                      and follow this
              vilde and reprobate company, which abuseth youth so mani
              festly                              *Famous Victories* 6.3–5

*Prince*      That villanous abominable misleader of
              youth …                            *1 Henry IV* II.iv.462–3

* * *

Henry IV uses language to describe Worcester that is similar to language used by the King of France to describe Henry V in *Famous Victories*:

| King of France. | You are very peremptory, my good brother of England. | *Famous Victories* 18.23–4 |
|---|---|---|
| King. | O, sir, your presence is too bold and peremptory, | |
| | | *1 Henry IV* I.iii.17 |

Henry IV's allusion to his impending death in *Famous Victories* is echoed by Prince Hal in *1 Henry IV*:

| King | I see it boots me not to take any physic, for all the physicians in the world cannot cure me; no, not one; | *Famous Victories* 8.1–3 |
|---|---|---|
| Prince. | Which would have been as speedy in your end As all the poisonous potions in the world | *1 Henry IV* V.iv.55–6 |

Derick's unusual figure of speech in *Famous Victories* is repeated by Prince Hal in *1 Henry IV*:

| Derick. | If it be thy fortune to be hanged, be hanged in thy own language, whatsoever thou dost! | *Famous Victories* 19.39–40 |
|---|---|---|
| Prince | To conclude, I am so good a proficient in one quarter of an hour, that I can drink with any tinker in his own language during my life. | *1 Henry IV* II.iv.17–20 |

## Examples in *Famous Victories* and in *2 Henry IV*

As Derick is being pressed into military service by a Captain, he exclaims, "Marry, I have brought two shirts with me…"          *Famous Victories* 10.29

As Falstaff departs to join the King's forces against the rebels, he remarks, "I take but two shirts out with me…"          *2 Henry IV* I.ii.209

\* \* \*

Prince Hal's remark about his father in *Famous Victories* is echoed by his brother in *2 Henry IV*:

| | |
|---|---|
| *Prince.* | To the Court; for I hear say my father lies very |
| | Sick                                    *Famous Victories* 5.38–9 |
| *P. John.* | I hear the King my father is sore sick.    *2 Henry IV* IV.iii.77 |

* * *

Henry IV recalls his seizure of the crown in similar language in *Famous Victories* and in *2 Henry IV*:

| | |
|---|---|
| *King.* | For |
| | God knows, my son, how hardly I came by it, and how |
| | hardly I have maintained it.    *Famous Victories* 8.63–5 |
| *King.* | God knows, my son, |
| | By what by-paths and indirect crook'd ways |
| | I met this crown,                      *2 Henry IV* IV.v.183–5 |
| *King* | How I came by the crown, O God forgive;    *2 Henry IV* IV.v.218 |

⁂

The newly-crowned Henry V rejects his former companions with the same language in *1 Henry IV* as he does in *Famous Victories*:

| | |
|---|---|
| *King.* | And |
| | therefore, not upon a pain of death to approach my presence |
| | by ten miles space.                    *Famous Victories* 9.53–5 |
| *K. Hen.* | Till then I banish thee on pain of death, |
| | As I have done the rest of my misleaders, |
| | Not to come near our person by ten mile    *2 Henry IV* V.v.63–4 |

⁂

In *Famous Victories* and in *2 Henry IV*, the Lord Chief Justice uses the same words to criticize Prince Hal and defend himself as representing the King:

| | |
|---|---|
| *Judge.* | therefore, in striking |
| | me in this place, you greatly abuse me; and not me only but |
| | also your father, whose lively person here in this place I do |
| | represent                              *Famous Victories* 4.95–8 |
| *Ch. Just.* | I then did use the person of your father, |
| | … |

Your Highness pleasèd to forget my place,

The majesty and power of law and justice,

The image of the King whom I presented,

And stroock me in my very seat of judgment;

*2 Henry IV* V.ii.73–80

## Examples in *Famous Victories* and in *Henry V*

The lengthy exchange between Henry V and the French Ambassador in *Famous Victories* yields several phrases and ideas that are carried over into the same exchange in *Henry V*:

*Archbishop.*   My lord, hearing of your wildness before

your father's death, sent you this, my good lord, meaning

that you are more fitter for a tennis court than a field, and

more fitter for a carpet than the camp  *Famous Victories* 9.130–3

*1 Amb.*   … the prince our master

Says that you savour too much of your youth,

And bids you be advised: there's nought in France

That can be with a nimble galliard won;    *Henry V* I.ii.249–52

\* \* \*

*King [of*   My Lord Prince Dolphin is very pleasant with me!
*England].*   But tell him, that instead of balls of leather we will toss him

balls of brass and iron—          *Famous Victories* 9.134–6

*K. Hen.*   We are glad the Dolphin is so pleasant

with us,                  *Henry V* I.ii.258–9

…

And tell the pleasant prince this mock of his

Hath turn'd his balls to gun-stones,        *Henry V* I.ii.281–2

*King*   My Lord of York, deliver him our
*[Henry].*   safe conduct under our broad seal emanuel.

*Famous Victories* 9.47–8

*K. Hen.*   Convey them with safe conduct.        *Henry V* I.ii.297

\* \* \*

In *Henry V* the King urges his troops into battle at Agincourt with language that echoes his words in *Famous Victories*, before the siege of Harfleur:

| | |
|---|---|
| *King* | Why, then, with one voice, and like true |
| *[Henry].* | English hearts, with me throw up your caps, and for Eng |
| | land, Cry, "St. George!" And God and St. George help |
| | us!                            *Famous Victories* 14.57–60 |
| *K. Hen.* | Follow your spirit; and upon this charge |
| | Cry, "God for Harry, England, and St. George!" |
| | *Henry V* III.i.33–4 |

In the context of the battle of Agincourt, King Charles of France in *Famous Victories* and an English soldier in *Henry V* use a similar antithetical phrase:

| | |
|---|---|
| *King of* | Ay, for by this hot beginning we shall |
| *France.* | scarce bring it to a calm ending.    *Famous Victories* 18.31–2 |
| *Will.* | We see yonder the beginning of the day, but |
| | I think we shall never see the end of it.    *Henry V* IV.i.89–90 |

Certain words between Derick and the Frenchman in their encounter on the battlefield of Agincourt in *Famous Victories* are carried over into the encounter in the same place between Pistol and the French soldier in *Henry V*:

| | |
|---|---|
| *Frenchman.* | Come quickly, you peasant! |
| *Derick.* | I will, sir. What shall I give you? |
| *Frenchman.* | Marry, thou shalt give me one, two, tre, four |
| | hundred crowns. |
| *Derick.* | Nay, sir, I will give you more; I will give as |
| | many crowns as will lie on your sword. |
| | *Famous Victories* 17.4–9 |
| *Pist.* | Peasant, unless you give me crowns, brave crowns; |
| | Or mangled shalt thou be by this my sword. |
| | *Henry V* IV.iv.38–9 |

In the aftermath of Agincourt, the French herald makes the same request of King Henry in both plays:

Herald.          He hath sent me to desire your Majesty to give

                 him leave to go into the field to view his poor countrymen,

                 that they may all be honourably buried.

                                                    *Famous Victories* 15.25–7

Mont.                        O, give us leave, great King,

                 To view the field in safety, and dispose

                 Of their dead bodies!                    *Henry V* IV.vii.81–3

In the same exchange, Henry V asks the identical question and receives the identical reply in both plays:

King.                        But, Herald, what castle is this

                 so near adjoining our camp?

Herald.          If it please your Majesty, 'tis called the Castle

                 of Agincourt.                    *Famous Victories* 15.35–8

K. Hen.          What is this castle call'd that stands hard by?

Mont.            They call it Agincourt                    *Henry V* IV.vii.88–91

Several scholars have pointed out that the fictional fifty-line passage in *Famous Victories,* in which Henry V woos the French Princess Katherine, bears a close resemblance to the longer passage in V.ii of *Henry V,* in which he does the same thing (Monaghan 356; Gurr, ed. *Henry V* 208). The scenes differ mainly in that Katherine speaks fluent English in *Famous Victories,* but in *Henry V* she speaks broken English with a heavy French accent. The conversation is greatly expanded in *Henry V,* but Henry asks many of the same questions and receives many of the same answers in both plays. After addressing her as "fair Lady Katherine of France" in *Famous Victories,* and "Fair Katherine, and most fair" in *Henry V,* Henry immediately shifts to "Kate" in both plays.

In scene 18 of *Famous Victories* Henry asks, "But tell me, canst thou love the King of England?" and Katherine answers, "How shall I love him that dealt so hardly with my father?" (69–72). In *Henry V,* he asks "And what sayest thou then to my love? Speak, my fair, and fairly, I pray thee," and she answers, "Is it possible dat I sould love de enemie of France?" (V.ii.166–70). When Henry repeats his question, she replies in the same way in both plays:

| | |
|---|---|
| *Katherine.* | If I were of my own direction I could give |
| | you answer; but seeing I stand in my father's direction, I |
| | must first know his will.      *Famous Victories* 18.76–8 |
| *Kath.* | Dat is as it shall please de *roi mon père*      *Henry V* V.ii.247 |

In both plays Henry deprecates his courting ability, devoting just three lines to it in *Famous Victories*:

| | |
|---|---|
| *King of* | I cannot do as these |
| *England.* | countries do that spend half their time in wooing. Tush, |
| | wench, I am none such.      *Famous Victories* 18.61–3 |

In rewriting the scene in *Henry V*, Shakespeare devotes twice the lines to the same idea, which is absent from the chronicles:

| | |
|---|---|
| *K. Hen.* | And while thou liv'st, |
| | dear Kate, take a fellow of plain and uncoin'd con- |
| | stancy; for he perforce must do thee right, because he |
| | hath not the gift to woo in other places; for these |
| | fellows of infinite tongue, that can rhyme themselves |
| | into ladies' favors, they do always reason themselves |
| | out again.      *Henry V* V.ii.152–8 |

    The preceding examples from *Famous Victories* and the three Prince Hal plays illustrate how words, phrases, images and ideas from the earlier play were carried over into the rewritten plays.[27] Another carry-over is the extended use of prose. In his previous six history plays, Shakespeare wrote primarily in verse, prose accounting for no more than 17 percent of the lines in *2 Henry VI*, and less or none in the other five. But in the three Prince Hal plays, prose accounts for 47, 53 and 40 percent, respectively, of each play's total lines (Campbell and Quinn 932). One scholar suggests that this significant movement to prose was Shakespeare's response to "developments in London's theatrical world" having to do with audience preferences and the move of the Lord Chamberlain's Men to the Curtain theater in 1597 (Bruster 121–3). But Shakespeare wrote his Prince Hal trilogy long before 1597, and it is much more likely that when he revised his old *Famous Victories* play, he was prompted by the all-prose manuscript to set nearly half of each of the three revised plays in prose.

## DRAMATIC DEVICES

The exchange of identities by which Derick and John Cobbler parody the confrontation between Prince Hal and the Chief Justice in scene 4 of *Famous Victories* is another Shakespearean marker—a reversal of roles that results in an artificial episode, or play, within the play. Shakespeare re-uses this particular device in II.iv of *1 Henry IV* (381–429) where, at the same point in the story, he inserts two mock interviews between Prince Hal and his father so that the former can "practice an answer" to King Henry's expected interrogation. In the first, Falstaff takes the role of King Henry as he reproves his son for his bad behavior; in the second, Prince Hal plays the King, and Falstaff, in the role of the Prince, defends his companion. The parody and the mock interviews are the playwright's inventions; they do not appear in the historical record.

Another device of the playwright's invention is the garbled syntax and mispronunciation of English by foreigners, an unusual phenomenon at the time *Famous Victories* was written. Scene 13 consists entirely of a comical conversation among three French soldiers, a drummer, and a Captain. Although the Captain speaks perfect English, the others misuse *me* for *I*, *sh* for *ch* and *t* for *th*. Shakespeare re-uses this device several times in *Henry V*, first in a similar exchange among four soldiers in Henry's army about the tactics of siege warfare that becomes a celebration of the comic mispronunciation of English (III.ii). Two scenes later (III.iv), Katherine and Agnes engage in a dialogue in which Katherine's misunderstanding and mispronunciation of English culminate in a bilingual sexual pun. Again, in V.ii, she attempts a conversation in English with Henry in which her mispronunciation of English reaches its comic zenith.

## Famous Victories *and the Shakespeare Canon*

Numerous elements of plot, characterization and language in *Famous Victories* reappear not only in the Prince Hal trilogy, but throughout the Shakespeare canon.

The stubborn porter who briefly bars Prince Hal and his friends from King Henry's court in scene 5, for instance, is the literary ancestor of two other porters in the canon who are slow to admit visitors. The most notable, in *Macbeth*, soliloquizes at length about his role before opening the gate (II.iii). In *The Comedy of Errors*, Dromio of Syracuse, in his capacity as porter, refuses to allow his brother and Antipholus of Ephesus entry to the latter's house (III.i).

In his repentance speech in scene 20 of *Famous Victories*, Prince Hal offers his dagger to his father as a token of remorse, and invites him to stab him. Three characters in the canon make the same invitation to convince others of their sincerity, Cassius offering his to dagger Brutus in *Julius Caesar* (IV.iii.100), Imogen her sword to Pisanio in *Cymbeline* (III.iv.69) and Richard III his sword to Lady Anne in *Richard III* (I.ii.175).

Prince Hal's condescending banter with the coy Princess Katherine, whom he calls Kate, is repeated by several Shakespearean characters, notably Hotspur, Petruchio, and Dumaine in *Love's Labor's Lost*—all to a woman they call Kate.

In scene 2 of *Famous Victories*, in which three neighbors keep the watch on St. John's Eve, we get the first hints of a comic scene among watchmen that appears in the anonymous *King Leir* and again in *Much Ado About Nothing*. (See "*King Leir* and the Shakespeare Canon" in Chapter V.)

In *3 Henry VI*, Prince Edward defies the three York brothers with the same language that Henry V uses to defy the French before Agincourt in *Famous Victories*.

King.          … wrongful usurpers of my right:

*Famous Victories* 12.27–8

Prince.      And thou usurp'st my father's right and mine

*3 Henry VI* V.v.37

Prince Hal's descriptions of those who would be punished when he is king are echoed by Hamlet:

Prince.      Thou shalt hang none but pick-purses, and

horse-stealers, and such base-minded villains

*Famous Victories* 5.28–9

Ros.          My lord, you once did love me.

Ham.        And do still, by these pickers and stealers.    *Hamlet* III.i.335–6

At a low point in English fortunes, Henry V, just before Agincourt, and Reignier (the Duke of Anjou), after the English defeat at Orleans in *1 Henry VI*, use the same words to describe the celebrations of the French:

| | |
|---|---|
| *King.* | Well, my lords, our battles are ordained, and the |
| | French making of bonfires, and at their banquets. |

Famous Victories 14.35–6

| | |
|---|---|
| *Reig.* | Why ring not out the bells aloud throughout the town? |
| | Dolphin, command the citizens make bonfires, |
| | And feast and banquet in the open streets, |
| | To celebrate the joy that God hath given us. |

1 Henry VI I.vi.11–14

Derick's association of a knave and a drab are repeated in two later Shakespeare plays:

| | |
|---|---|
| *Derick.* | And she is a very |
| | knave, and thou a drab if thou take her part. |

Famous Victories 7.14–15

| | | |
|---|---|---|
| *Glou.* | Follow the knave; and take this drab away. | 2 *Henry VI* II.i.153 |
| *Pom.* | If your worship will take order for the drabs and | |
| | the knaves, you need not to fear the bawds. | |

Measure for Measure II.i.234–5

In contemplating his usurpation by Bolingbroke, Richard II uses the same words that Henry V uses in *Famous Victories* when he is told that he cannot have the crown of France.

| | | |
|---|---|---|
| *King of* | What! not King of France? Then | |
|  *England.* | nothing. | *Famous Victories* 20.6–7 |
| *K. Rich.* | | and by and by |
| | Think that I am unking'd by Bullingbrook, | |
| | And straight am nothing: | *Richard II* V.v.36–8 |

In *3 Henry VI*, the Duke of Gloucester (later Richard III) associates the words *blood* and *drunk* with a lance, just as Henry V associates them with a sword in *Famous Victories*:

| | | |
|---|---|---|
| *King.* | Come, my Lords come! By this time our swords | |
| | are almost drunk with French blood. | *Famous Victories* 15.1–2 |

| | |
|---|---|
| *Glou.* | Thy brother's blood the thirsty earth hath drunk, |
| | Broach'd with the steely point of Clifford's lance; |

*3 Henry VI* II.iii.15–16

In two subsequent history plays, Shakespeare re-uses Henry IV's phrase *ruin and decay* in *Famous Victories* to refer to the potential fate of England:

| | |
|---|---|
| *King.* | I had |
| | thought once-whiles I had lived to have seen this noble realm |
| | of England flourish by thee, my son; but now I see it goes |
| | to ruin and decay.            *Famous Victories* 5.82–5 |
| *K. Rich.* | Cry woe, destruction, ruin and decay: |

*Richard II* III.ii.102

| | |
|---|---|
| *K. Rich.* | Death, desolation, ruin and decay: |

*Richard III* IV.iv.409

In *Famous Victories*, Henry V uses a phrase that Shakespeare re-uses repeatedly in the three *Henry VI* plays:

| | |
|---|---|
| *King.* | Ay, truly, my Lord; and for revengement I have |
| | chosen you to be my protector over my realm |

*Famous Victories* 9.167–8

| | |
|---|---|
| *Win.* | Gloucester, what e'er we like, thou art Protector |
| | And lookest to command the Prince and realm. |

*1 Henry VI* I.i.37–8

| | | |
|---|---|---|
| *Glou.* | There's none protector of the realm but I. | *1 Henry VI* I.iii.12 |
| *Win.* | I do, thou most usurping proditor, | |
| | And not Protector, of the King or realm | *1 Henry VI* I.iii.31–2 |
| *Win.* | Because he is Protector of the realm, | *1 Henry VI* I.iii.66 |
| *Glou.* | Madam, I am Protector of the realm; | *2 Henry VI* I.iii.123 |
| *Q. Mar.* | The Duke is made Protector of the realm; | |

*3 Henry VI* I.i.240

Henry V's use of *king* and *kingly* to modify the same word in *Famous Victories* reappears in three of Shakespeare's history plays:

*King.*          No, Herald; 'tis a kingly resolution, and the resolu-

                 tion of a king.                          *Famous Victories* 14.50–1

*K. Rich.*       A king, woe's slave, shall kingly woe obey.

                                                          *Richard II* III.ii.210

*Glou.*          More like a king, more kingly in my thoughts;

                                                          *2 Henry VI* V.i.29

Buck.            Then I salute you with this kingly title:

                 Long live Richard, England's royal king!

                                                          *Richard III* III.vii.239–40[28]

Henry IV's association of the word *drowsy* with death in *Famous Victories* reappears in two subsequent plays:

*King.*          Well, my lords, I know not whether it be for sleep,

                 Or drawing near of drowsy summer of death,

                                                          *Famous Victories* 8.75–6

*K. Hen.*        The organs, though defunct and dead before,

                 Break up their drowsy grave and newly move

                                                          *Henry V* IV.i.21–2

*Obe.*           Through the house give gathering light,

                 By the dead and drowsy fire,

                                                          *A Midsummer Night's Dream* V.i.391–2

Derick's opposition of the words *jest* and *earnest* in *Famous Victories* is found again in four different canonical plays:

*Derick.*        Hear you, sir, is it your man's quality to rob folks

                 in jest? In faith, he shall be hanged in earnest.

                                                          *Famous Victories* 4.60–1

*Launce.*        Marry, after they clos'd in earnest, they

                 parted very fairly in jest.     *Two Gentlemen of Verona* II.v.12–13

*S. Dro.*        Hold, sir, for God's sake! Now your

                 jest is earnest                          *The Comedy of Errors* II.ii.24

| | |
|---|---|
| *Buck.* | That high, All-Seer, that I dallied with, |
| | Hath turn'd my feigned prayer on my head, |
| | And given in earnest what I begg'd in jest. |

*Richard III* V.i.20–3

| | |
|---|---|
| *Celia.* | But, turning these |
| | jests out of service, let us talk in good earnest. |

*As You Like It* I.iii.25–6

℘

Mistress Page uses the same phrases about Doctor Caius and Anne Page in *The Merry Wives of Windsor* that Henry V uses about himself and Katherine in *Famous Victories*:

| | |
|---|---|
| *King of* | Ay, but I love her, and must crave her— |
| *England.* | Nay, I love her, and will have her!     *Famous Victories* 18.47–8 |
| *Mrs. Page.* | He, none but he, shall have her, |
| | Though twenty thousand worthier come to crave her. |

*The Merry Wives of Windsor* IV.iv.89–90

℘

The idea of a king as a god occupying a "seat" or a throne, first expressed in *Famous Victories*, reappears in two subsequent plays:

| | |
|---|---|
| *Jockey.* | Oh, how it did me good, to see the King when he |
| | was crowned! Methought his seat was like the figure of |
| | heaven, and his person was like unto a god. |

*Famous Victories* 9.24–5

| | |
|---|---|
| *Ver.* | I saw young Harry with his beaver on, |
| | His cushes on his thighs, gallantly arm'd, |
| | Rise from the ground like feathered Mercury, |
| | And vaulted with such ease into his seat, |
| | As if an angel [dropp'd] down from the clouds |
| | To turn and wind a fiery Pegasus,     *1 Henry IV* IV.i.104–109 |
| *Nest.* | With due observance of [thy] godlike seat, |
| | Great Agamemnon,     *Troilus and Cressida* I.iii.31–2 |

℘

The use of the verb *take* in connection with a blow on the ear, first used in *Famous Victories*, reappears twice in a different context in *Henry V*, and again in *Measure for Measure*:

Derick.        Why, then, take you that [*boxing his ear* ] till
               more come! Zounds, shall I not have him?

                                                            *Famous Victories* 4.134–5

K. Hen.                                                     If ever thou
               come to me and say, after to-morrow, "This is my
               glove," by this hand, I will take thee a box on the
               ear.                                         *Henry V* IV.i.213–16

Will.          And't please your Majesty, a rascal that
               swagger'd with me last night; who if alive and ever
               dare to challenge this glove, I have sworn to take him
               a box a' th' ear;                            *Henry V* IV.vii.125–8

Escal.         If he took you a box o' th' ear, you might
               have your action of slander too.

                                                            *Measure for Measure* II.i.180–1

A distinctive phrase used by Prince Hal in *Famous Victories* reappears in a similar context in *Coriolanus*:

Prince.                        But we stand prat-
               ing here too long; I must needs speak with my father.

                                                            *Famous Victories* 5.57–8

1. Cit.        The other side a' th' city is risen; why stay we prating
               here? To th' Capitol!                       *Coriolanus* I.i.47–8

The mock interview between Prince Hal and his father in II.iv of *1 Henry IV*, and Lear's mock trial of Goneril and Regan in *King Lear* (III.vi.20–85) both echo the exchange in *Famous Victories* between the Lord Chief Justice and Prince Hal at the time the thief, Cuthbert Cutter, is brought to trial. After receiving a box on the ear from the Prince, the Lord Chief Justice commits him to the Fleet (4.116–50). Later in the scene, Derick and John Cobbler re-enact the exchange. In *Famous Victories*, Shakespeare devotes about thirty-five lines to the mock interview, which begins:

*Derick.*          Faith, John, I'll tell thee what; thou shalt be my

Lord Chief Justice, and thou shall sit in the chair; and I'll be

the young prince, and hit thee a box on the ear;

*Famous Victories* 4.116–118

Shakespeare dropped this particular scene from *1 Henry IV* when he rewrote *Famous Victories*. But in its place, at the same point in the story, he inserted a mock interview between Prince Hal and his father to "practice an answer" to King Henry's expected interrogation. In II.iv of *1 Henry IV*, Falstaff takes the role of King Henry as he reproves his son for his bad behavior, and at the same time remarks upon the "cheerful look" and "noble carriage" of a certain corpulent companion of his:

*Prince.*          Do thou stand for my father and examine

me upon the particulars of my life.

*Fal.*               Shall I? Content. This chair shall be my state,

this dagger my scepter, and this cushion my crown.

*Prince.*          Thy state is taken for a join'd-stool, thy

golden sceptre for a leaden dagger and thy precious

rich crown for a pitiful bald crown.          *1 Henry IV* II.iv.376–82

They eventually exchange places and continue the drollery until they are interrupted by the sheriff (383–481).

In III.vi of *King Lear*, Lear, Edgar and the Fool prepare to stage a mock trial of Goneril and Regan:

*Lear.*             It shall be done, I will arraign them straight.

[*To Edgar.*]   Come sit thou here, most learned [justicer];

[*To the Fool.*] Thou, sapient sir, sit here ...          *King Lear* III.vi.20–22

A moment later, Kent addresses Lear:

*Kent.*             How do you, sir? Stand you not so amaz'd.

Will you lie down and rest upon the cushions?

*King Lear* III.vi.33–4

A few lines later, the Fool picks up a stool and addresses it:

*Fool.*             Come hither, mistress. Is your name

Goneril?

| | |
|---|---|
| *Lear.* | She cannot deny it. |
| *Fool.* | Cry you mercy, I took you for a join-stool. |

*King Lear* III.vi.49–52

The connection among the plays is evidenced by strikingly similar language in all three scenes. Half-a-dozen words—*justice/justicer, sit, chair, took/taken, cushion, stand, joined stool*—appear in two or more of them. It seems that the same idea of a mock trial or interview, and the particular language to describe it, planted in his first play, stayed with Shakespeare and reappeared in one of his last plays. Although none of the preceding examples of the author's re-use of images and language is persuasive in itself, their cumulative effect strongly suggests the same mind at work. There are numerous other examples in Pitcher at 94–103 and 120–62.

## Famous Victories *and Other Apprenticeship Plays*

As noted above, in *Famous Victories* Prince Hal invites his father to stab him as a sign of his sincerity. Shakespeare re-used the idea three more times in subsequent plays. But before writing any canonical play, he re-used it in the second scene of *The True Tragedy of Richard the Third*, as Edward IV, on his deathbed, attempts to reconcile two of his nobles, Lord Hastings and Thomas Grey, Marquess of Dorset. After repeated prompting by the King and Queen Elizabeth, Hastings agrees to a reconciliation. As proof of his sincerity, he makes the same offer that Prince Hal made:

| | |
|---|---|
| *Hastings.* | And would rather that my body shall be prey to mine enemy. |
| | Rather than I will offend my Lord at the hour |
| | And instance of his death.        *True Tragedy* 2.140–2 |

Grey makes the same pledge:

| | |
|---|---|
| *Marc. (Grey)* | My gracious Lord, I am content, |
| | And humbly crave your gracious pardon on my knee, |
| | For my foul offence, |
| | And see, my Lord, my breast opened to mine adversary, |

*True Tragedy* 2.147–50[29]

In a conversation with Oldcastle in scene 5 of *Famous Victories*, Prince Hal remarks that when he becomes king "we shall have no such things" as prisons, hanging and whippings. He repeats the sentiment in *1 Henry IV* (I.ii.56–65). But even before that, Christopher Sly expresses the same thought in *The Taming of a Shrew*:

| | |
|---|---|
| *Sly.* | I say we'll have no sending to prison! |
| *Lord.* | My lord, this is but the play, they're but in jest. |
| *Sly.* | I tell thee Sim, we'll have no sending to prison, |
| | That's flat! |

*The Taming of a Shrew*   Sly Interlude 3.45–8[30]

## Famous Victories *and Edward de Vere*

The notorious prank robbery at Gad's Hill is the first comic incident in both *Famous Victories* and the canonical *1 Henry IV*. The difference is that in the former play Prince Hal has just participated in the robbery, but in the canonical play he only robs the robbers, and then promises to pay back the money. The incident is ultimately based on a passage in *The First English Life of King Henry the Fifth*, an anonymous biography written in 1513. According to the account in this manuscript, Prince Hal and his "younge Lords and gentlemen would await in disguised aray for his own receiuers, and distres them of theire money," which he later restored to them (Kingsford, ed. *First English Life* 17). The playwright of *Famous Victories* crystallized this vague reference into a single robbery at a particular place—Gad's Hill in Kent—and on a particular date— "the 20th day of May last past, in the fourteenth year of the reign of our sovereign lord King Henry the Fourth" (4.21–4), that is, in 1413. As B. M. Ward first pointed out, the date is spurious, Henry IV having died in March of 1413.

But if the date is spurious, the incident itself has a striking counterpart in the life of Edward de Vere. Among the letters surviving in the Elizabethan State Papers is one dated May 1573 from two servants of Lord Burghley, William Faunt and John Wotton—complaining to him that they have been ambushed between Rochester and Gravesend and shot at by three men in the employ of the Earl of Oxford.[31] They further claim that the Earl was the "procurer of that wiche is done" (Ward, *Famous* 285–6). The connection between this incident and the similar episode in *Famous Victories* (and in *1 Henry IV*) is not clear, but Ward suggested that the play was written by Oxford "fairly soon after May 1573, and that the author definitely had in mind the Faunt and Wotton episode when he constructed the first few scenes of his plot" (*Famous* 286–7). But in view of the evidence supplied below in "The Date of *Famous Victories*," this is too late a date for the play. It is more likely that Oxford took the idea for the robbery from the anonymous *First English Life*, a manuscript that was also used by de Vere's contemporaries, John Stow and Rafael Holinshed (Kingsford, *Early Biographies* 73–4. 81). In the mid-sixteenth century, Gad's Hill was still well-known as a propitious location for a robbery—as attested by a now-lost ballad titled "The Robery at Gaddes Hill" that was registered in London in 1558 (Arber, ed. *Transcript* 1:96).

Further evidence supporting Oxford's authorship of *Famous Victories* is the portrayal of the obscure Richard de Vere, eleventh Earl of Oxford, who died in 1417 at the age of thirty-two. Both Hall and Holinshed report his participation in Henry V's campaign of 1415 in France and his role in the "middleward" of the English army at Agincourt, but nothing more (Ward, *Famous Victories* 282–3). As noted earlier, however, he is one of the main characters in the play. In the ninth scene, Richard de Vere urges the new King Henry V to ignore the advice of the Archbishop of Canterbury to attack Scotland first, but to invade France first instead. This was in fact the advice that Henry took, but in the chronicle sources it comes from the Duke of Exeter (Pitcher 211–12). On the eve of the Battle of Agincourt, Oxford asks the King for command of the vanguard, but it has already been promised to the Duke of York. On the morning of the battle, Oxford brings information to the King about the number of French facing him, and a few moments later volunteers to take charge of the archers whom the King has ordered to plant sharpened stakes in the ground to break the French cavalry charge. (The English were badly outnumbered, and military historians agree that this tactic was the key to their victory.) To this request, Henry V replies, "With all my heart, my good Lord of Oxford. And go and provide quickly" (14.32–3). It appears that the author of the play was a good friend of the House of de Vere. There is no surviving documentation for these actions of the eleventh Earl, but it is conceivable that de Vere relied on family records or traditions about him. Or he might have simply made them all up. (The same motivation might have led him to only briefly mention the infamous Robert de Vere, ninth Earl of Oxford, in *The Tragedy of Richard II, Part One*, also known as *Thomas of Woodstock*, a Shakespeare play that has not yet been added to the canon. See D. L. Wright at 14–15 and M. Egan at 1:575). This evidence connects Edward de Vere more closely to *The Famous Victories of Henry the Fifth* than to any other dramatic work.

Four other de Veres, two of them earls, are mentioned in the Shakespeare canon. In the first four Quartos of *Richard II*, Aubrey, the tenth Earl, is erroneously mentioned as executed (V.vi) but isn't in the cast (Stokes 336). In one of only a dozen short speeches in *3 Henry VI*, John, the thirteenth Earl, a loyal supporter of Henry, alludes to the executions of his father, the twelfth Earl, and his older brother, Aubrey (III.iii.101–105). In *Richard III*, King Edward IV credits the thirteenth Earl with striking him down at the battle of Tewkesbury (II.i.113–114), but the historical thirteenth Earl was not present at Tewkesbury. He was with the Earl of Richmond in the same play, however, at Tamworth in 1485, where he speaks two lines (V.ii.17–18) and at Bosworth (V.iii.27–8), where, as the chroniclers report, he was put in command of the vanguard of Richmond's troops (Ross 85–6). (His substantial role in *The True Tragedy of Richard the Third*, Oxford's first version of *Richard III*, is described in Chapter II.)

After his first two plays, Oxford minimized his portrayal of his de Vere ancestors. For instance, in neither *The Troublesome Reign of John* nor *King John* does he mention the second Earl of Oxford, Aubrey de Vere, or the third, Robert de Vere, the former having supported King John during the barons' revolt in 1215, and the latter joining those who successfully curbed his powers (Ogburn Jr. 419).[32] It is logical that in his earliest plays—composed when he was barely a teenager—Oxford would want to glorify his ancestors. But he might have been warned, even at this early date, that it was not suitable for an earl to be known as a writer of plays, and that too many heroic Earls of Oxford in his history plays might give him away. It could be that he donned his veil of anonymity at this time. As we know, his name was never associated with any play. It is true that his initials appeared as the author of several poems in *The Paradyse of Dainty Devices*, published in 1576. But this collection was assembled by Richard Edwards no later than 1566, the year of his death. In any event, it was commonplace for the nobility to acknowledge their authorship of occasional poetry, especially songs of the type included in this collection.

## The Annotations in a Copy of Edward Hall's Chronicle

In 1940, two antiquarian book dealers in Kent, Alan Keen and Roger Lubbock, discovered a 1550 edition of Hall's *Chronicle* in a country library they had just purchased. In the margins of Hall's narratives of the reigns of Richard II, Henry IV, Henry V and Henry VI, they found over 400 annotations in the secretary hand of a young Elizabethan man, as well as various crosses, marginal lines, underlinings, and two simple drawings. In the Henry IV section of the book, the name "Edward" had been written in an Italic hand, and elsewhere in the book the same name pricked out with a pin.[33] As Keen and Lubbock also report, another person, "Rychard Newport," has written his name twice in the margins "in a hand completely different from that of the annotator," and "put his initials with the date '6 *Apll. ao* 1565'" in another margin (5). They identified him as Sir Richard Newport, Lord of Ercall and Sheriff of Shropshire, who died in 1570.

Seymour Pitcher listed twenty-three annotations in the Henry V portion of the Hall volume that reappear in similar form in *Famous Victories*, all of which strongly suggest, some with special force, that the annotator is the author of the play, and many of which also appear in the Folio *Henry V* (233–50, especially 250). Keen and Lubbock also found many instances "where a detail or expression is selected from Halle (*sic*) by A. [the annotator] and also used, verbatim or in the same general sense, by Shakespeare" (21). Considering these facts, all three investigators, Keen, Lubbock and Pitcher, concluded that there is a strong likelihood that the annotator was the author of the Shakespeare canon.[34]

If it is correct that the annotator is the author of the Shakespeare canon, the most likely scenario is that Oxford made the annotations in a copy of Hall's *Chronicle* in Sir Thomas Smith's library while he was living with him, or that he made them in a copy of Hall in William Cecil's library after moving into his household in 1562. In either case, the annotated copy would then have passed by some way to Sir Richard Newport, who wrote his name in it in 1565. An inventory of Smith's library made in August 1566 included a copy of Hall's *Chronicle* (Strype 276), so the annotated copy cannot have been his, unless he owned a second copy. A 1687 sale catalogue of some of the books and manuscripts in Cecil's library does not list the book at all (Jolly 6–9). But considering Cecil's book-collecting habits, it hardly seems likely that he didn't own a copy of Hall's *Chronicle*. Thus, it is possible that in the first year or two of his residence with Cecil the young de Vere annotated the copy of Hall's *Chronicle* discovered in 1940, but confirming evidence is lacking. Although we have no example of Oxford's secretary hand, there is good evidence that many educated Elizabethans wrote in both secretary and Italic styles (Hamilton 9–37).

## *The Date of* Famous Victories

That *Famous Victories* was at least ten years old when it was published in 1598 is attested by clear documentary evidence that the comic actor, Richard Tarlton, who died in September 1588, played the role of the Derick the clown.[35] His fellow actor, William Knell, who played Prince Hal in the same Queen's Men production, at the Bull in Bishopsgate, died in June 1587 (A. and V. Palmer 140), making it certain that the play was written no later than the same year. From this scanty record, most scholars contend that *Famous Victories* was written in the mid-1580s (McMillin and Maclean 89–90; Griffin 59, n. 50). However, considering the playwright's personal history and the other plays, anonymous or not, for which he is responsible, Oxford is far more likely to have written *Famous Victories* much earlier—during his teen years. It is the shortest, only 1550 lines, entirely in prose, and poorest of his plays, and is certainly his earliest surviving one.

A probable reference to the final scene in the play appeared in Thomas Nashe's pamphlet *Pierce Penilesse* in 1592:

> … what a glorious thing it is to have Henry V represented on the stage, leading the French king prisoner, and forcing him and the Dolphin to swear fealty! [Nashe, *Works* 1:213].

As Eric Sams noted, "This was obviously *FV*, even though those sworn to fealty are in fact the Dolphin and the Duke of Burgundy, not the French king. Further, Nashe mentions it in the general context of plays by Shakespeare."[36] He might have been right. Two pages later, Nashe praises "Tarlton, Ned Allen, Knell, Bentlie." The association of Nashe's remarks with Tarlton, Knell and the Queen's Men's production of *Famous Victories* at the Bull is much stronger than with Edward Alleyn and any production of *Henry V*.

There is further evidence that supports such an early date for *Famous Victories*. It is clear that the author of the Shakespeare canon must have had some kind of extended legal training (M. Alexander 110–11). Legal terminology and legal concepts are profuse throughout the canon. A survey of legal terms and phrases appearing in Shakespeare's plays reveals that they are most abundant in his history plays, appearing an average of forty-two times in each (Sokol 320–29). But in *Famous Victories* they are absent, except for a few common words, such as *judge, justice* and *heir*—words that might be used by any layman without legal training. This suggests that Oxford wrote *Famous Victories* as a teen-ager, even before he began his legal studies in 1567 at Gray's Inn. This is borne out by the plain prose, flat characters and clumsy action of the play— all reflecting the first efforts of a novice playwright.

Of the five apprenticeship plays discussed in this book, only *King Leir* can be dated after Oxford's 1567 admittance to Gray's Inn. The other four are essentially devoid of serious legal issues and legal terms, whereas *King Leir* and the entire orthodox canon are replete with them. Therefore, it is reasonable to assign the composition of *Famous Victories* to the year just following Oxford's tragic loss of his father, and his sudden removal to London in September 1562. This misfortune was much greater than the loss of his father. When he was sent to London, he was also deprived of the remainder of his family—his sisters, his mother and his aunts and uncles, except Arthur Golding. He was also suddenly separated from his friends, his home and his familiar surroundings. He was abruptly relocated to the largest city in the country and to an unfamiliar household, surrounded and supervised by people he didn't know.

It is well-known that a trauma or great misfortune often stimulates creative activity, and a fair speculation is that Oxford turned to writing a play to assuage his shock and grief on the death of his father. The idea has been expressed succinctly by two well-known writers:

> "No one has ever written, painted, sculpted, modeled, built, or invented except literally to get out of hell." Antonin Artaud 1947.
>
> "The artist is extremely lucky who is presented with the worst possible ordeal which will not actually kill him." John Berryman 1976.[37]

In his new home, Oxford came into contact with the court and with the diversions of the capital, including public playhouses and, very likely, taverns and street life. Assuming that this was the occasion when he began to write plays, the subject matter of his first effort bears a close relationship to his circumstances at the time. As noted above in the first Section, *Famous Victories* tells the story of a young nobleman, a prince, who, with a band of good fellows, conducts a prank robbery of the King's couriers. After the robbery, the ensuing riotous celebration, and the arrest of the Prince, the King rebukes him, and complains that he "hath gotten a son which with grief will end his father's days!" (3.45–46). Prince Hal quickly repents of all his bad behavior, calling himself "an unworthy son for so good a father!" (6.17).

There follows the deathbed scene, the taking of the crown, and the Prince's explanation of his behavior:

*Prince.*        … finding you at that time past all recovery, and dead, to my thinking—God is my witness—and what should I do, but with weeping tears lament the death of you, my father? And after that, seeing the crown, I took it…. But, seeing you live, I most humbly render it into your Majesty's hands.

*Famous Victories* 8.46–52

His father again forgives him, and then dies. In the room at this moment, with the King and Prince Hal, is one of Oxford's ancestors, the eleventh Earl. The chronicles report this scene, but do not mention the presence of the Earl of Oxford (Ward, *Famous* 282–284).

To recapitulate the first eight scenes of *Famous Victories*, there is a recollection of some mischief with good friends, some bad behavior and an apology for it, a reconciliation with a father, a renunciation of the crown, and a father's death. The young man unaccountably and suddenly reforms himself, and rejects his disreputable companions. The remainder of the play is devoted to incidents of the young man's personal success. Prince Hal becomes King of England and invades England's traditional enemy, France. Against great odds, he defeats the French army, and is named heir to the throne of France. He then marries Katherine, the French King's daughter. It seems that in this play Oxford is recalling his life before he was sent to London, agonizing over his behavior and his father's death, and then fantasizing about his future. Several of the earliest Oxfordian scholars made this same observation. In 1928, B. M. Ward asserted that "In it [*Famous Victories*] he portrayed himself" ("*Famous*" 291). In 1931, E. T. Clark made the same claim (9–10) and, in 1952, Dorothy and Charlton Ogburn wrote that in *Famous Victories* "he himself was thinly disguised as the truant Prince who begs forgiveness of the King, his father..." (77). They also took Shakespeare's description of Henry V—"This star of England" for the title of their book about Oxford (Epil. 7).

However, all three contended that Oxford wrote the play to make amends for the sudden trip to the continent that he took in 1574 without the required permission from the Queen. The evidence detailed above places the composition of *Famous Victories* at least ten years earlier.

There is further support for the claim that Oxford was sufficiently competent to write *Famous Victories* at thirteen or fourteen. Tutored privately from the age of four, Oxford matriculated at Cambridge University at the age of eight (Ward, *Seventeenth Earl* 11). We have no information about his performance at Cambridge, or how long he remained there, but the mere fact that he was enrolled suggests an extremely precocious child. In a 1563 letter to Cecil, Oxford's tutor, the antiquary Laurence Nowell, wrote, "I clearly see that my work for the Earl of Oxford cannot much longer be required" (Ward, *Seventeenth Earl* 20). In a dedication to him in 1564, Arthur Golding praised him for his "desire ... to read, peruse, and communicate with others as well the histories of ancient times, and things done long ago ... and that not without a certain pregnancy of wit and ripeness of understanding" (Chiljan, *Dedications* 6–7). Since Oxford was not a teacher and, so far as we know, wrote no histories or chronicles, it is quite possible that Golding was referring to dramatic works that Oxford wrote on historical subjects. Some scholars suggest that Oxford wrote the long poem *The Tragicall History of Romeus and Juliet* in 1562[38] and/or the play mentioned in the poem (Ogburn Jr. 449–450), and that he, not Arthur Golding, was the translator of Ovid's *Metamorphoses*, printed in 1565 and 1567 (Whittemore "Oxford's Metamorphoses").

We also know that Oxford was writing competent poetry before the age of sixteen, poetry that is still anthologized today (Anderson 121–123). Such precocity is unusual, but not unheard of. There are many examples of extraordinary educational achievement by children and significant literary works written by teenagers. For instance, Jeremy Bentham wrote in Latin and Greek at age four; Thomas Macaulay composed a twenty-four-page world history at age six (Radford 5). Madame de Staël wrote a play, *The Inconveniences of Parisian Life*, at age twelve. Both Victor Hugo and Alfred Tennyson wrote five-act plays at age fourteen. Tennyson's play—*The Devil and the Lady*—an imitation of an Elizabethan comedy, is the same length as *Famous Victories*. When it was finally published in 1930, *The Times* reviewer called it "astonishingly mature." So, it is entirely believable that Oxford could have written *Famous Victories* in his early teen years.[39]

Further evidence supporting an early date is the fact that the commonly accepted sources of the play—*Holinshed's Chronicles*, in either edition, 1577 or 1587, and John Stow's *Chronicles of England* (1580)—are entirely unnecessary as sources for the historical events depicted. Aside from the single exception described above in "Sources of the Plays," all the historical incidents in *Famous Victories*, and even their particular details, can be found in Edward Hall's *Chronicle*, published in 1548, or in earlier chronicles (Ward, "Famous" 280–81, 287). And in many cases the language used is closer to Hall than to Holinshed.

Thus, the weight of evidence supports the claim that *Famous Victories* is not an adaptation, a memorial reconstruction or a playhouse piracy. Rather, it is an early and original work by the author of the Shakespeare canon—Edward de Vere, seventeenth Earl of Oxford.

## Dates of the Prince Hal Plays

As noted in the previous Section, there is clear documentation that *Famous Victories* was seen by London audiences in 1588. The passage quoted from Nashe's 1592 pamphlet *Pierce Penilesse* was the first mention in print of a play in which Henry V appeared, and the evidence is strong that he was referring to *Famous Victories*.

There are several other references in the theatrical records to a play about Henry V during the decade before 1599. In 1592, between February and June, Philip Henslowe recorded in his Diary four performances by Lord Strange's Men of *"harey of cornwell,"* a title not appearing elsewhere in Elizabethan documents, except in a letter from Edward Alleyn to his wife in July or August of the same year. Alleyn was with Lord Strange's Men in Bristol, and mentioned that they were preparing to perform *"Hary of Cornwall."* In 1946, Charles Wisner Barrell suggested that these were performances of *Henry V*, and that Henslowe's title for the play was based on the conversation in IV.i in which Pistol questions the disguised Henry V:

| *Pist.* | | What is thy name? |
|---|---|---|
| *K. Hen.* | Harry Le Roy. | |
| *Pist.* | Le Roy? a Cornish name. Art thou of Cornish crew? | |
| *K. Hen.* | No, I am a Welshman. | *Henry V* IV.1.48–51[40] |

In Barrell's words, "In misidentifying the incomparable "Harry of Monmouth" as a Cornishman through his ignorance of the simple French term for *king*, the presumptuous [*sic*] Pistol would make even the most humble patrons of the Rose howl with glee. Moreover, in that day the natives of the Land's End were considered a race apart—and not entirely civilized. As Ned Alleyne, [*sic*] who was nearly seven feet tall with a voice to match his bulk, would play the King in this comic interlude on Henslowe's stage, its effect would amply justify his father-in-law's coinage of the nickname "Harry of Cornwall" for the whole play" ("Shakespeare's *Henry V*" 53). Barrell continued: "No other popular Elizabethan play is known ... which bears this title or contains a leading character that could ... be recognized as a 'Harry of Cornwall,'" except *Henry V* (53–4). But the title is conspicuously absent from discussions of Elizabethan drama.[41]

In late 1595, Philip Henslowe recorded the following information in his Diary about a performance in his Rose theater: "28 of november 1595 ne— Rd at harey the v ... iij$^{li}$ vj$^s$." He repeated the entry at least a dozen times in various forms during the next eight months (33–7; Craik 10). E. K. Chambers described these entries as referring to "the new play of 'harey the V,'" and noted the presence of "Harry the Fifth's doublet and gown" in the Admiral's Men's inventory for March 1598 (*Elizabethan Stage* 4:17). Edmund Malone, however, thought that they referred to *Famous Victories*, and recorded his opinion on the fly-leaf of the Bodleian Library copy of the play (P. A. Daniel v–vi).

Both Geoffrey Bullough and John Dover Wilson contend that Henslowe's "harey the v" was not *Famous Victories*; nor do they think it was Shakespeare's *Henry V*, but neither they, nor Chambers, offer any explanation for what was clearly a popular play (Wilson, "Origins" 2, Bullough, *Narrative* 4:167, n. 2). There appears to be no explanation for Philip Henslowe's multiple references to a play about Henry V except that it was Shakespeare's play in either its Quarto or Folio form. But orthodox scholars uniformly ignore them, and insist that the first unmistakable reference to the canonical *Henry V* appeared in the Stationers' Register on August 4, 1600. (See the "*Henry V*" Section, above.)

More than that, they have maintained for more than a hundred years that the composition date of *Henry V* can be precisely fixed in the spring of 1599, after Queen Elizabeth had dispatched the Earl of Essex to put down an Irish rebellion. A statement by Gary Taylor is typical: "the allusion to the Irish expedition in 5.0.29–34 is the only explicit, extra-dramatic, incontestable reference to a contemporary event in the entire canon" (ed., *Henry V* 7). This dating is based upon a passage spoken by the Chorus prior to Act V, in which he describes the journey of Henry V from Agincourt, where he has just defeated the French, to Calais, to the English coast, and finally to London. The Chorus compares the crowds that poured out to meet him in London to those who swarmed after Julius Caesar when he returned victorious from Spain to Rome in 45 BCE:

> But now behold,
> In the quick forge and working-house of thought,
> How London doth pour out her citizens!
> The Mayor and all his brethren in best sort,
> Like to the senators of th'antique Rome
> With the plebeians swarming at their heels,
> Go forth and fetch their conqu'ring Caesar in;
> [*Henry V* V Cho. 22–28].

The Chorus then introduces another comparison, one that might be similar, but that has not yet taken place:

> As, by a lower but as loving likelihood,
> Were now the general of our gracious Empress,
> As in good time he may, from Ireland coming,
> Bringing rebellion broachèd on his sword,
> How many would the peaceful city quit
> To welcome him!
> [*Henry V* V Cho. 29–34].

As T. W. Craik noted in the latest Arden edition of the play, "Nearly everyone agrees that in these lines 'the General' is Robert Devereux, Earl of Essex," whom Queen Elizabeth had sent to Ireland in March 1599 to put down a major rebellion (1–2). Another scholar wrote, "The likening of Essex to Henry V by Shakespeare himself in the chorus of the Folio version is indisputable" (Albright 729). Even Eric Sams agreed that the passage refers to Essex, and added that he was "the only living person to whom Shakespeare ever alluded anywhere in his work" (*Real Shakespeare* 112). He overlooked the woman in the same line—Queen Elizabeth.

But on the face of it, the claim makes no sense, since the passages quoted, and the entire Chorus character, are absent from all three Quarto texts, including the two issued just after Essex's mission to Ireland. Moreover, a reinvestigation of the meaning and background of the passage confirms that it does not refer to Essex at all, and was not written in 1599, but at least fifteen years earlier, when *Henry V* was first seen by an Elizabethan audience. There are at least five reasons to support this conclusion.

## Evidence Against Essex as "the General"

It is true that early in 1599 Elizabeth was facing the most serious Irish rebellion of her reign. It had been building for seven years under the leadership of the perennial rebel, Hugh O'Neill, second Earl of Tyrone, who had routed an English army at the Battle of Yellow Ford in August of 1598, a battle that cost Elizabeth more than 800 troops (Guy 363).

It is true that early the next year, after much dithering, and in response to his own lobbying, Elizabeth placed the Earl of Essex in charge of a large army and dispatched him to Ireland to put an end to the rebellion. In his usual flamboyant style, Essex rode out of London late in March of 1599 with great fanfare and a huge retinue.

But Essex not only did not bring back rebellion on his sword, he failed of his mission entirely. After landing at Dublin in mid–April, he embarked on a stumbling and lackluster campaign in the southern counties, and returned to Dublin early in July with a sick and depleted army. A frustrated Elizabeth ordered him to march to the north and attack Tyrone, but when Essex set out a month later, he had trouble finding Tyrone, and when he did, he was reluctant to attack because Tyrone's army was twice the size of his.

Finally, in early September, Tyrone proposed a truce and Essex agreed to it—an act that Elizabeth angrily repudiated.[42] Essex hurried back to England, sneaked into London with a small party, and then burst unannounced into Elizabeth's chamber at Nonsuch Palace to explain himself. She apparently received him amicably, but it was the last time he was to see her. A few months later he was subjected to the judgment of a special council. In June 1600, he was stripped of most of his offices and placed under house arrest for his actions in Ireland, including bargaining with a traitor (Guy 447).

Obviously, this was not the episode the playwright had in mind when he suggested that the "general of our gracious Empress" may soon be coming from Ireland "Bringing rebellion broachèd on his sword." No one could have known what would happen in Ireland but, because of this embarrassing outcome, the period during which this passage would have to have been written lasted only about three months—from late March, when Essex departed for Ireland, to late June, when word began to reach London that his campaign was failing. It strains credulity that a reference of this kind to a general who had set out with such fanfare, and then almost immediately come to grief—then scurried back to England and been arrested for his conduct, not to mention his attempted coup d'état the next year, followed by his execution—could have remained in the text, and allowed into print by the editors of the First Folio.

The second reason why it is most improbable that the passage was written in 1599 and refers to Essex is the printing history of *Henry V*. The first Quarto appeared in August of 1600, just about sixteen months after the alleged composition date. As already mentioned, the entire Chorus role and half the remaining dialogue in the Folio version were absent from the Quarto, making it, in effect, a two-hour version of a three-hour play. According to Andrew Gurr, the Quarto gives every appearance of a play that has been deliberately cut for performance by its owners, and its immediate printing is a mark of its authority as an official version (Gurr, ed. *First Quarto* ix, 1). Thus, the orthodox claim requires the unlikely scenario of Shakespeare writing a three-hour play that is immediately cut nearly in half for performance in two hours, and the cut version then printed. Surely, the correct history of the composition, the staging and the printing of Shakespeare's *Henry V* cannot be found in this sixteen-month period.

What is much more likely is that the longer Folio version was written, and probably performed, at some earlier date, perhaps at court or for a private audience. When that version proved to be too long for popular consumption—and to have too many characters for the ordinary playing company—it was cut by nearly half for performance in the late 1590s, and then printed. The earlier and longer version survived in the author's cupboard, and then in the custody of the "grand possessors" (Ogburn Jr. 205). As with half of Shakespeare's manuscripts, it only reached print in the First Folio, where it was attributed to him for the first time.

The third reason why the passage does not refer to Essex in 1599 has to do with Queen Elizabeth's own feelings about the Earl. For all her attraction to him, the Queen's fifteen-year relationship with Essex was as stormy as her own temperament, and as erratic as his, and she was always suspicious of his potential claim to the throne. An example of this is what happened to the historian John Hayward, who published a prose history of Henry IV early in 1599, to which he attached a fawning dedication in Latin to the Earl of Essex. The Queen took the words of the dedication to suggest that if Henry IV had had as strong a hereditary claim to the throne as Robert Devereux had now, he would have been more readily accepted as King after the death of Richard II. This, she said, was treason, and called for Hayward to be "racked."[43] Her counselor, Francis Bacon, talked her out of it; but an order was issued that the dedication be cut from the book. John Hayward was subjected to surveillance, put on trial twice, and in 1600 thrown in the Tower. Even though his history was a best-seller, or perhaps because it was, he was still there when Elizabeth died three years later. Thus, the political climate in the spring of 1599 was such that a playwright took his life in his hands if he so much as mentioned the Earl of Essex in the same breath as Henry IV or Henry V.[44]

The fourth reason why it is improbable that the passage, or any of the Chorus part, was written in 1599 is that its principal message was totally inappropriate to a Shakespearean history play at that time. Beginning with his very first line, and again before each act, and finally in the Epilogue, the Chorus continually apologizes for the limitations of his stage, his players and his theater. By the orthodox reckoning, this was the ninth or tenth Shakespearean history play to reach the stage—a vast panorama of the English past, filled with marches, voyages, desperate battles, and scenes in foreign countries—all reduced to the same modest stage, the same limited company and the same compressed time period. As John Dover Wilson wrote, "...why should the dramatist suddenly in 1599 begin apologizing for the incapacity of himself and his theatre to cope with a historical theme and battle-scenes, when such things had been one of their chief stocks-in-trade for the past half-dozen years?" (ed. *Henry V* xiv). Why indeed? Wilson's only answer to his question is the unpersuasive claim that in *Henry V* Shakespeare had "no ordinary theme." A better answer will become apparent when the circumstances of the play's composition are considered below.

But the most convincing reason why it is unlikely that this passage was written in 1599 about the Earl of Essex has to do with its author. Anyone who is convinced that Edward de Vere wrote what we call Shakespeare's *Henry V* may confidently rule out Robert Devereux as the subject of this passage. The long-standing enmity between Essex and the Cecils is a matter of record, and even if Oxford were not always happy with the Cecils, it is clear that by the mid–1590s he wanted nothing to do with Essex. In his October 1595 letter to Robert Cecil, Oxford rejected a suggestion that he approach the Earl of Essex for a favor, saying that it was "a thing I cannot do in honour, sith I have already received diverse injuries and wrongs from him, which bar me from all such base courses" (Chiljan, *Letters* 53). Oxford might have been referring to the rumors circulating as early as May 1595 that his newly-married daughter, Elizabeth, Countess of Derby, was having an affair with Essex.[45] Or there might have been other reasons. But, in any case, this makes it most improbable that less than four years later Oxford would refer to the "loving likelihood" that Robert Devereux "the general of our gracious Empress" may in good time be coming from Ireland "Bringing rebellion broachèd on his sword."

## SIR THOMAS BUTLER AS "THE GENERAL OF OUR GRACIOUS EMPRESS"

But if it were not Essex in 1599, who was it, and when was it? The answer to that will lead us to the composition date of *Henry V*, and of the *Henry IV* plays.

Although orthodox scholars are unanimous in their dating of *Henry V* to 1599, non–Stratfordians have not agreed on a particular date. In 1931, Eva Turner Clark suggested that *Henry V* was written in 1586, and that if "Holland" were substituted for "Ireland," then "the general" would refer to Robert Dudley, Earl of Leicester, whom the Queen had dispatched to the Low Countries with an army late in 1585 to counter incursions by the Spanish (772–5). The history of antipathy between Oxford and Leicester rules out this possibility. But the history of Irish rebellions during Elizabeth's reign produces a much more likely scenario.

Before the protracted revolt of the 1590s, there were two serious uprisings in Ireland—known as the First and Second Desmond Rebellions. The first took place in the 1560s, and the second developed in the late 1570s under the brothers Gerald, James and John Fitzgerald, the leaders of the House of Desmond, an ancient Irish earldom in the southern province of Munster. The Second Desmond Rebellion, also called the Munster Rebellion, was a major conflict that threatened the Crown's authority and possessions in Ireland, and required a substantial mobilization of England's military apparatus. It attracted foreign intervention in the summer of 1579, and again a year later, when small armies of continental troops, described as primarily "Italian swordsmen," landed on the southwestern Irish coast, having been dispatched by Pope Gregory XIII in support of the rebellion against Elizabeth (Lennon 222–24).

In November 1579, after several years of protracted fighting and unsuccessful attempts at negotiation, the English administrators of colonial Ireland finally lost patience with the leader of the rebellion, the forty-six-year-old Gerald Fitzgerald, fourteenth Earl of Desmond, and declared him a traitor (Bagwell 3:30–1). In her attempts to settle her Irish wars with as little expense as possible, Queen Elizabeth routinely offered pardons to even the most persistent rebels if they would lay down their arms and pledge their loyalty. But the Earl of Desmond had deceived and betrayed her too often. Twice she had sent him to the Tower, and twice she had pardoned him. Finally conceding that he was an unreclaimable rebel, she declared him ineligible for a pardon, and offered "head money," a thousand pounds for his head.

Over the next few years, several different English commanders led armies into Munster with varying degrees of success, gradually killing or capturing hundreds of the Desmond rebels. In the summer of 1580, Sir James Fitzgerald was captured, hanged, and drawn and quartered (Bagwell 3:55). By May 1581, the English army in Ireland numbered more than 6,400 men, and in early January 1582 the youngest brother, Sir John of Desmond, was ambushed and killed. His turquoise and gold ring was sent to Elizabeth, and his head to the Governor of Ireland, Lord Grey of Wilton, as "a New Year's gift." Grey displayed it on a pole on a wall of Dublin castle (Bagwell 3:94).

In the summer of 1582, Lady Eleanor, the Countess of Desmond, traveled to Dublin and surrendered to Grey, but the Queen ordered that she be sent back to her husband, "unless she could induce him to surrender unconditionally" (Bagwell 3:96). Nevertheless, the rebellion dragged on, and in December 1582, on the advice of Sir Walter Raleigh, Elizabeth appointed Thomas Butler, tenth Earl of Ormond, Governor of Munster, and her commanding general in Ireland (Bagwell 3:102).

Known as "Black Tom" because of his dark hair and complexion, Thomas Butler was the scion of one of the oldest and most prominent families in Ireland, and a major figure in Anglo-Irish relations throughout Elizabeth's reign. The Butlers had been in Ireland since the end of the twelfth century, when Henry II made grants of land to Theobald Fitzwalter, and gave him the hereditary title of "Le Botiler," the king's chief butler in Ireland—from which the family then took its name (Grehan 20). Thomas Butler was a distant cousin of Elizabeth Tudor on the Boleyn side (the eighth Earl of Ormond, Thomas Boleyn, was Anne Boleyn's father), and they had both been raised at the court of Henry VIII, Butler, born in 1531, being six years older.

Young Tom was also a boyhood companion of Edward VI, and at age sixteen was knighted by Edward on his accession to the throne in 1547. As a staunch supporter of the English colonial presence in Ireland, Butler carried out a variety of diplomatic and military missions there for Queen Elizabeth during the 1560s and 1570s. According to Sidney Lee, she was so fond of him during the 1560s that "the attentions she paid him ... gave rise to no little scandal, and induced him to linger at court for the next five years."[46] Elizabeth is said to have called him her "black husband."[47] He was active in court politics, being favored by Cecil and aligned with the Sussex faction against the Earl of Leicester, whom he despised. In this context, he would have become acquainted with the young Edward de Vere, who came to London in 1562. Both of them were among the dozen diplomats and courtiers receiving Master of Arts degrees at Oxford University in September 1566, and they were admitted to Gray's Inn within weeks of each other the following year (Anderson 32; D. Edwards, "Butler, Thomas").

## "REBELLION BROACHÈD ON HIS SWORD"

When Thomas Butler arrived in Ireland in January 1583 to deal with the Desmond Rebellion, the situation in Munster had deteriorated badly. With two thousand men and two hundred horse, the Earl of Desmond was stronger than ever—threatening loyalist towns and ravaging the countryside (Falls 149). But a vigorous campaign by Butler during the spring and summer forced most of the individual rebel leaders to surrender, and reduced the rebellion to a small band of men loyal to Desmond.

By November, Desmond had retreated into the neighborhood of Tralee in County Kerry, in the southwest corner of the country. Desperate for food and horses, twenty of his men raided the farm of the O'Moriarty family and stole some horses, household goods and forty cows. The next evening, two of the O'Moriarty brothers organized a posse of two dozen men and picked up the trail of the rebels. The subsequent incident is described in a deposition taken a few days later (Rowan 97–100).

After following the trail by moonlight into the woods of Glenageenty, some six miles inland from Tralee, the pursuers spotted smoke coming from a cabin at the bottom of a glen. They waited until dawn and then crept down and burst into the cabin. All the men but one rushed away, and one of the pursuers struck him with his sword, wounding him severely. "I am the Earl of Desmond," he cried. "Save my life." "Thou hast killed thyself long ago," replied Owen O'Moriarty. "And now thou shalt be prisoner to the Queen's Majesty and the Earl of Ormond, Lord General of Munster" (Sheehan 107). They dragged him outside, but had to carry him because he was unable to walk. Afraid of being attacked by Desmond's men who were nearby, they beheaded the Earl, left his body and made their escape.

Desmond's head was taken to Thomas Cheston, Constable of Castlemaine, "who brought it on his sword point to Thomas Butler in Cork" (Sheehan 108). In his letter of November 15th to Lord Burghley recounting the death, Butler wrote "So now is this traytor come to the ende I have longe looked for, apointed by God to dye by the sword to ende his rebellion…." The summary of Ormond's letter contains the brief sentence: "Sends Desmond's head by the bearer."[48] According to tradition, Queen Elizabeth "would not believe the news of the earl's death until she saw his head, and when it was brought to her, she stared at it for hours" (Sheehan 108). In mid–December 1583, she had it mounted on a pole and placed on London Bridge.[49] As we know, the heads of criminals on London Bridge were nothing unusual, but this rebel's head was sent from Ireland to London by a general who had been dispatched there to put down a rebellion.

What more striking image could Oxford have used for this grisly incident than "Rebellion broachèd on his sword"?[50] And what more gracious compliment could Oxford have paid to a fellow earl, whom he had known since boyhood, than to allude to his service to Queen Elizabeth in connection with Henry V's conquest of France? Oxford and Ormond were not only long-time friends, they were distantly related by marriage, and had remained in contact during the 1570s. A letter from Ormond to Burghley in May 1575 refers to

Oxford's trip abroad and to "tokens and letters" that his wife Ann had received from him.[51]

Thus, all the elements in the famous passage are identified and associated with actual events and people: "the general of our gracious Empress" being Thomas Butler, tenth Earl of Ormond, a favorite of the Queen, who appointed him Lord General of her forces in Ireland; "As in good time he may, from Ireland coming," referring to his mission in Ireland, and suggesting that he may yet come to London in triumph, as did Henry V; "Bringing rebellion broachèd on his sword," signifying Ormond's dispatch to London of the head of the Queen's most persistent rebel. When Ormond had not returned by the end of January, the Queen wrote him in her own hand on the 31st, congratulating him on his success and urging that he come to England to receive her thanks. Because of opposition by his enemies at court, his return to London was delayed until the middle of May 1584.[52]

Besides Oxford, another writer, Thomas Churchyard, celebrated the success of Ormond in Ireland on this occasion. In 1584, Churchyard published *A Scourge for Rebels*, a twenty-four page pamphlet describing Ormond's appointment as Governor of Munster, and praising his successful capture and killing of the Earl of Desmond. Churchyard's relationship with Oxford is detailed in "The Thomas Churchyard Connection" in Chapter II.

This scenario places the composition date of the Act V Chorus of *Henry V* in the six-month period between mid–November 1583 and mid–May 1584, just a few months after Oxford had regained the favor of the Queen and returned to court. Since the Act V Chorus occurs with only 15 percent of the play remaining, it is likely that by November *Henry V* was nearly completed, and that the reference to Butler's return could be easily inserted before the final act. A patriotic play about an English king's victory in France would have pleased the Queen—and a reference to a lengthy rebellion in Ireland having been emphatically crushed by one of her favorite generals would have been doubly satisfying.

## AN EVENING AT THE COCKPIT

Certain other lines in the Prologue and Chorus supply clues about the audience and the venue for a performance of *Henry V* during the six-month period described above. In articles published twenty-four years apart, W. D. Smith in 1954 and G. P. Jones in 1978 suggested that particular phrases in the Chorus imply a court or private performance, rather than one in a public playhouse. Jones wrote that "the Chorus of *Henry V* is fundamentally incompatible with the public theatre and is fully comprehensible only in terms of performance under more specialised conditions" (95). He pointed out that the language alluding to "the spatial inadequacies of the theatre" and "the discrepancy between the size of the real events and the size of their theatrical representation" suggests that the manuscript for the Folio text was prepared for a performance "under more cramped conditions," such as at court or at a private residence.

Other phrases used by the Chorus speaker suggest the same thing. Such facetious solicitations as "Piece out our imperfections with your thoughts" (Pro. 23), "Play with your fancies" (III. Cho. 7), "eche [eke] out our performance with your mind" (III. Cho. 35), and "Heave him away upon your winged thoughts" (V. Cho. 8) all indicate that the audience is "confidential and personal," rather than "collective and public." (These phrases, and others of the same sort, are discussed at length in "The Prince Hal Plays and Edward de Vere," below.) As Jones remarked, such requests "might have met with ribald counter-suggestions in a public forum." Jones also cited such language as "But pardon, gentles all" (Pro. 8) and "the scene / Is now transported, gentles, to Southampton" (II. Cho. 34–5) as evidence that the Chorus is addressing an aristocratic or, at least, a private audience (96–8). The complimentary, even affectionate, reference to Queen Elizabeth—"our gracious Empress"—strongly suggests that she attended the performance.[53]

Smith went even further: "…I suspect that the choruses, replete with fawning utterances so foreign to Shakespeare, were especially designed for a performance before a sophisticated audience which may have included the Queen herself in the small theatre in Whitehall, the Cock-Pit alluded to in the opening prologue as incapable of holding 'the vasty fields of France'" (51).

If it were a royal or an aristocratic audience, it would not be an unusual venue for a Shakespeare play. In his 2004 article, "Shakespeare's Audience," Richard Whalen presented substantial evidence that Shakespeare wrote primarily for "royalty, the nobility, educated aristocrats, their retainers and court officialdom" (9). The admittedly scanty records that survive list more performances at court or aristocratic homes than in public theaters. These facts comport with the view that the Folio text of *Henry V* was derived from a manuscript prepared for use at a court or private performance. Considering the author's relationship to such an audience, they also suggest that the Chorus's remarks were personal, and that he might have been the individual delivering them. In the opening lines of the Epilogue, he appears to be referring to himself:

> Thus far, with rough and all-unable pen,
> Our bending author hath pursued the story,
> In little room confining mighty men,
> Mangling by starts the full course of their glory.
> [*Henry V* Epil. 1–4].

It is easy to imagine the Earl of Oxford, perhaps clad in the hooded, black cloak typical of the role, speaking the lines of the Chorus, carefully introducing each act to his Queen and fellow courtiers.[54]

Other phrases in the Prologue to *Henry V*—"this unworthy scaffold," "Can this cockpit hold / The vasty fields of France," "Or may we cram / Within this wooden O," "the girdle of these walls"—have been cited by editors as indications that the author was anticipating a performance by the Lord Chamberlain's Men at either the Curtain or the newly-constructed Globe in 1599 (Craik 3–4; Gurr, ed. *Henry V* 4–6; Wilson, ed. *Henry V* xiv). But these lines, and another in the Epilogue—"In little room confining mighty men"—suggest a much smaller space than either the Globe or the Curtain. The Globe was an open-air amphitheater with a yard about one hundred feet in diameter, and a capacity of over 3000 spectators (Gurr, *Stage* 128; G. Egan, 1). Nor does the Curtain seem a likely venue for the theater described by the Chorus. Although theater historians have long maintained that the Curtain was an amphitheater of about seventy-two feet in diameter (Bowsher 95, 66–7), excavations of the site in the spring of 2016 revealed the foundation of a rectangular building of approximately one hundred by seventy-two feet that could hold about 1000 spectators. This discovery also eliminates the Curtain as a venue for the performance of the Folio text of *Henry V*, regardless of the date.

Reacting to this development, Heather Knight, a senior archeologist at the London Museum of Archaeology, suggested that the play might still have premiered at the Curtain in 1599, but without the prologue. "There's a school of thought now that says prologues were actually a later addition," she said.[55] This school of thought would, of course, invalidate the claim that "the general of our gracious Empress" refers to the Earl of Essex in the spring of 1599. Any reference after July or August 1599 to the triumphal return of Essex from Ireland would have met with disbelief or laughter, or both. What seems more likely is that the performance, perhaps the first of *Henry V*, took place at Elizabeth's Whitehall Palace, her principal residence during the 1580s, and one of only two containing a "cockpit."

The history of the complex of buildings known as Whitehall confirms that such a performance could have taken place. In the 1530s, Henry VIII undertook a major expansion of York Place, Cardinal Wolsey's former residence, later called "Whitehall." According to John Stow, there were "divers fayre Tennis courtes, bowling allies, and a Cocke-pit, al built by King Henry eight" on the west side of the roadway that bisected the Palace grounds (Stow, *Survey* 2:102; quoted in Chambers, *Elizabethan Stage* 1:216, n.2). Henry VIII's Cockpit was a square two-story building, within which a quasi-circular space was constructed with tiered seating, allowing spectators to witness cock-

*Whitehall from St. James Park.* Painted by Hendrick Danckerts c. 1674–1675. The Cockpit is the square building to the right with the turreted roof, just behind the statue. Although it was built in the 1530s by Henry VIII as a venue for cock-fighting, there is evidence that it was sometimes used as a venue for plays (© Crown copyright UK Government Art Collection, London).

fighting.[56] On occasion it was modified to accommodate the performance of plays and masques. With temporary alterations, such as "added curtains for a tiring-house and scaffold planking for a stage" the space could be easily "turned to use as a simple, intimate theatre protected from wind and weather" (Wickham 47).

The Revels Accounts clearly record that in the early years of his reign, James I witnessed plays performed in the Cockpit at Whitehall (Streitberger 5, 7, 25, 30, 31, 36; Wickham 78–81). Although there is no surviving record, some modern stage historians agree with Edmund Malone that Queen Elizabeth also witnessed plays performed in Henry VIII's Cockpit (Malone 3:166; Ordish 258–9; Gurr, *Stage* 121; Kernan 18, 53). One prominent dissenter, Joseph Quincy Adams, citing the absence of such a record during Elizabeth's reign, concluded that "It was during the reign of King James that the Cockpit began to be used for dramatic representations" (34). But *Henry V* was performed at court in 1605 (Chambers, *William Shakespeare* 2:331), and it is hard to believe that a drama so popular that it played before the King nearly six years after its alleged composition had not been played at court during Elizabeth's reign.

It was not until about 1630 that Inigo Jones transformed the interior of the Whitehall Cockpit for Charles I to create a permanent theater. It would serve as such until 1698, when it and nearly all of the surrounding Palace were destroyed by fire.[57] The word "Cockpit" evolved to denote a complex of buildings on the same site that were used for various purposes, including residences of the nobility and, in later times, government offices (*OED*, cockpit. 1.c.(b)). "Its site is now occupied by the Prime Minister's London residence, No. 10 Downing Street" (Wickham 45).

Surviving records of entertainments at court, fragmentary as they are, support these conclusions about the audience and the venue for a performance of *Henry V* in late 1583 or early 1584. One of the thirteen appendices in E. K. Chambers' *The Elizabethan Stage* is "A Court Calendar," in which he summarized all the information he could obtain about the monarch's location between 1558 and 1616, and about "the plays, masks and quasi-dramatic entertainments at court" (4:75). The Court Calendar appendix indicates that the Queen arrived at Whitehall on December 20, 1583, and remained there, except for visits to Heneage House and Tower Hill, until April 20, 1584 (4:100).[58] The Calendar also records that the newly-formed Queen's Men played at court on December 26 and 29, 1583 and on March 3, 1584; that the Children of the Chapel performed at court on January 6 and February 2, 1584; and that the Earl of Oxford's Men performed on January 1 and March 3, 1584.

In another appendix, "Court Payments," Chambers listed the information

Detail of the Cockpit in the Danckerts painting. The interior of the Cockpit was transformed into a permanent theater by Inigo Jones about 1630. But the entire Whitehall palace was destroyed by fire in 1698. According to theater historians, the site is now the residence of the Prime Minister, No. 10 Downing Street (© Crown copyright UK Government Art Collection, London).

available about "the expenditures on plays or masks at court" (4:131). This appendix lists a payment of £20 made at Westminster to the Queen's Men on May 9, 1584, for the performances in the previous December and March. The plays listed for this payment were "vj histories, one Comedie" (4:159). The Court Payments appendix also lists payments to the Children of the Chapel and to the Earl of Oxford's Men for their performances during the same period, but does not indicate what plays were performed.[59]

Thus, it appears that the Queen's Men performed one or more history plays before the Queen at Whitehall on three occasions during the winter of 1583–4, and that two other companies, both controlled by the Earl of Oxford, performed there on several occasions during the same period.[60] As Jones noted, the words of the Chorus referring to a confined circular space and to a "cockpit" suggest that *Henry V* was performed at the Cockpit, rather than at the Great Chamber or the large Banqueting Hall, which were rectangular rooms also used for theatrical performances (96–7). The words of the Chorus also suggest that the audience was an aristocratic one, very likely a royal one, with the Queen present. This internal evidence comports with the external evidence detailed above that places the composition of the Chorus at some time during the six-month period ending in May 1584, when Sir Thomas Butler actually returned to London.

Ever since Edmund Malone suggested it late in the eighteenth century, the notion that Shakespeare was associated with the Queen's Men has intrigued scholars. Four of the apprenticeship plays treated in this book, including *Famous Victories*, were part of the Queen's Men's repertory in the 1590s (McMillin and Maclean 161). As the following chapters will demonstrate, they had all been written and performed, but by other companies, before the performance of *Henry V* described above. It is reasonable to conclude that the manuscript of *Henry V*, as well as those of the other apprenticeship plays, including *Famous Victories*, came to the Queen's Men from the author by the same conduit.

A secure date for the composition of *Henry V* in 1583 serves as a benchmark for an accurate dating of the first half of the Shakespeare canon. It is likely that the composition dates of the two *Henry IV* plays fall during the years just prior to that of *Henry V*. A remark by Prince Hal after Falstaff invites Doll Tearsheet to kiss him, and she obliges, is a clue to the date of *2 Henry IV*. "Saturn and Venus this year in conjunction! / What says th'almanac to that?" (II.iv.263–4). The Prince is referring to a prediction made by the astrologer Richard Harvey in the early months of 1583 that at the end of April of that year a conjunction of Saturn and Jupiter would cause a series of sudden and violent disasters that would result in the final dissolution of the world. "The total failure of the predictions brought a storm of ridicule, both in Cambridge and in London. Richard

Tarlton mocked Harvey on the stage, and William Elderton composed derisive ballads" (Capp, "Harvey, Richard"). The Prince's remark, which suggested the ageing Falstaff as Saturn and Doll Tearsheet as Venus, would have been especially topical during 1583. In fact, according to a historian of the period, "After ... the 1580's, formal defenses and attacks on astrology are wanting in England until the early years of the seventeenth century" (D. C. Allen 125).

## The Prince Hal Plays and Edward de Vere

Further evidence of the date and authorship of the four Prince Hal plays is found in the literary and personal relationships of Edward de Vere and Sir Philip Sidney. The most important evidence consists of passages in *Henry V* and in Sidney's *An Apology for Poetry* that appear to be related to each other. These passages suggest that Elizabeth's two most brilliant courtier-poets engaged in a startling and historic exchange of criticism and insults in these works that has not previously been recognized or understood.

The two men probably met as teenagers at Cecil House in the 1560s, where Oxford was a royal ward, and Sidney, four years younger, a frequent visitor (Duncan-Jones, *Courtier* 47–8). Sidney was present at Oxford University during the Queen's visit in the late summer of 1566, when Master of Arts degrees were awarded to the Earl of Oxford and the Earl of Ormond, among others. Oxford and Sidney were both admitted to Gray's Inn early in 1567, but Sidney left for Christ Church, Oxford a year later. In August 1569, an engagement was arranged between the fifteen-year-old Sidney and William Cecil's twelve-year-old daughter Anne. This engagement came to naught, and Anne married Oxford two years later (Anderson 38).

When Sidney returned from a diplomatic mission on the Continent in 1577, he became embroiled in a political spat between his father, Sir Henry Sidney, then Elizabeth's deputy in Ireland, and Sir Thomas Butler, tenth Earl of Ormond, one of her favorites at court. In September, a personal encounter was reported in which Philip snubbed the Earl, and there was rumor of a challenge. Butler apparently brushed off the matter, declaring that he wouldn't contend with a man who was "bound by Nature to defend his Father's Causes; and who is otherwise furnished with so many Vertues" (Collins 1:227). Philip then composed a lengthy defense of his father that, among other things, expressed his contempt, though obliquely, for Butler (Duncan-Jones, *Courtier* 136–7). This particular quarrel was only one facet of the long-standing competition for the Queen's favor and benefactions between the Leicester/Sidney faction and the Cecil/Sussex/Oxford faction.

Another facet of this quarrel was the prospect of a marriage between Queen Elizabeth and François-Hercule, Duke of Alençon, the youngest son of the late French King Henry II and Catherine de Medici. The Leicester/Sidney faction strongly opposed the marriage; the Cecil/Sussex/Oxford faction supported it. The controversy reached a climax of sorts in August 1579, when Alençon made his first visit to England, and he and Elizabeth spent nearly a fortnight in "a delicious whirl of amorous dalliance" (Somerset 310). Allegedly at the urging of his father, Sidney then sent a lengthy letter to the Queen outlining in detail the numerous drawbacks, and particular objections that he had, to her contemplated marriage (Sidney, *Misc. Prose* 46–57).

At about the same time, Oxford and Sidney engaged in their notorious quarrel on the tennis court, during which Oxford called Sidney a "puppy." Sidney replied intemperately, abruptly left the scene, and later sent a challenge to Oxford. In a subsequent interview with the Queen, Sidney vigorously defended his actions, but she reportedly forbade any duel, and lectured him on "the difference in degree between earls and gentlemen" and "the respect inferiors owed to their superiors."[61]

It was in the context of this background that Philip Sidney undertook his *An Apology for Poetry*, a discourse on the nature and purpose of poetry that remains a seminal work of Elizabethan criticism. Although it was not published until 1595, Sidney's biographers uniformly assign it to the years 1579–82.[62] Near the end of *An Apology*, Sidney digresses from his main subject and inserts a fourteen-hundred-word commentary that is highly critical of the current English drama. In it are what appear to be at least three references to *Famous Victories* and to Oxford's *Henry IV* plays, and it is in Oxford's next play, *Henry V*, that we find his reaction to Sidney's comments about his dramatic technique in the previous three.

In the middle of his digression, Sidney criticizes his country's playwrights because:

> all their plays be neither right tragedies, nor right comedies, mingling kings and clowns not because the matter so carrieth it, but thrust in clowns by head and shoulders, to play a part in majestical matters, with neither decency nor discretion, so as neither the admiration and commiseration, nor the right sportfulness, is by their mongrel tragi-comedy obtained [Sidney, *Critical Edition* 244].

At the time Sidney wrote, the English stage had seen less than half-a-dozen plays now extant that included in their casts a clown, that is, a comic character, and a king. Two of these were Thomas Preston's *Cambyses* and Richard Edwards' *Damon and Pythias*. However, in neither of these did a clown and a king appear in the same scene.

But in *Famous Victories*, dating from the 1560s, five comic figures, including Sir John Oldcastle, one of the progenitors of Falstaff, appear with Prince Hal, the future King Henry V, in the very first scene. There are five comics surrounding Prince Hal in scene 4, when he gives the Chief Justice a box on the ear; and in scene 5 Prince Hal cuts up with Ned, Tom and Oldcastle until King Henry enters. In scene 9, the new King Henry V chastises Ned, Tom and Oldcastle, and orders them to keep ten miles from him on pain of death, just as he does in 2 *Henry IV*. Five of the next eleven scenes contain only clowns. A play ostensibly about England's renowned warrior-king, *Famous Victories* is so riddled with clowns that it might be called a comedy punctuated by historical relief. In his two *Henry IV* plays, Oxford brought the technique of mingling clowns and kings to its finest moment, with his unique character, Sir John Falstaff, sharing the stage, the action, the language and the affection of the audience with two kings of England. This was noticed by Neil Rhodes, who wrote, "It is as though Shakespeare had looked at Sidney's injunction not to mingle kings and clowns and then tossed it straight in the bin" (117).

Thus, when Philip Sidney objected, in the early 1580s, to the playwrights' "mingling" of kings and clowns, it is highly probable that he had in mind the man who first brought English kings and clowns together on the stage—Edward de Vere.

In another passage in the same digression, Sidney protested that "our comedians think there is no delight without laughter," and explained that "Delight hath a joy in it, either permanent or present. Laughter hath only a scornful tickling." Furthermore, English playwrights "stir laughter in sinful things, which are rather execrable than ridiculous: or in miserable, which are rather to be pitied than scorned. For what is it to make folks gape at a wretched beggar or a beggarly clown; or against law of hospitality, to jest at strangers because they speak not English so well as we do?" (*Critical Edition* 245).

Among the surviving plays that were staged before Sidney wrote *An Apology for Poetry*, only two include "strangers," or foreigners, who speak broken English.[63] The anonymous *Interlude of Wealth and Health* was staged nearly thirty years before Sidney wrote (Lancashire 26), and *The Rare Triumphs of Love and Fortune*, also anonymous, was staged at the end of 1582, possibly after he wrote.[64] Sidney might have been referring to these two, or to others that have been lost, but another play he might have seen was *Famous Victories*, in which scene 13 consists entirely of a comical conversation among three French soldiers, a drummer, and a Captain. Although the Captain speaks perfect English, the others misuse "me" for "I," "sh" for "ch," and "t" for "th" (see "Dramatic Devices" in "Relationships between *Famous Victories* and the Prince Hal Plays," above).

## *Oxford's Retort*

Sidney's *An Apology for Poetry* was not published until 1595, nine years after his death, but it is well-known that manuscripts of his works circulated among the literati years before they appeared in print (Woudhuysen, *Sir Philip Sidney* 207, 232–5, 354–5; Sidney, *Selected Prose* 100, 162). Thus, there is a strong likelihood that Oxford had access to a copy within a year or two of its composition in the early 1580s. The evidence for this is found in *Henry V*, composed within the next few years, in which he reacts to Sidney's complaints by expanding and elaborating several of the offending dramatic devices, and then mocking and retorting sarcastically to another.

I suggest that in response to Sidney's criticism of the use of strangers and their broken English in *Famous Victories*, Oxford turned it up a notch in *Henry V*. Here, he not only retained the French soldier scene, but added scenes between Princess Katherine and her maid in III.iv, and between Katherine and Henry V in V.ii, in which he exploited the French King's daughter's ignorance of English for comic purposes. The former scene then drifts into sexual innuendo of a kind that embarrasses even modern Shakespearean scholars (Norwich 212). Although Shakespeare's plays are full of sexual puns and bawdy repartee, this was perhaps an extra dose intended to twit the priggish Sidney, who was well-known as an advocate of propriety and decorum in poetry.

Furthermore, in *Henry V* Oxford introduced three additional characters, each of whom contributes his own regional dialect and stereotypical behavior. In scene ii of Act III, sometimes called the "international scene," Fluellen, a Welshman, Macmorris, an Irishman, and Jamy, a Scotchman, join the Englishman Gower in a conversation about the tactics of siege warfare that becomes a celebration of the comic mispronunciation of English. If Sidney found foreigners speaking broken English unfunny on the stage, he must have hated *Henry V*.[65] Sometime later, in *The Merry Wives of Windsor*, a play closely related to the Prince Hal trilogy, the blustering Frenchman Dr. Caius mispronounces his English just as the Frenchmen do in *Famous Victories*—another indication that the anonymous play was written by the author of the Shakespeare canon.

There is even stronger evidence of this historic exchange between these two giants of Elizabethan literature. In the same section on drama in *An Apology for Poetry*, Sidney complains that English playwrights abuse the Aristotelian principle of unity of place, and make outrageous demands upon their audiences' imagination:

> Now ye shall have three ladies walk to gather flowers, and then we must believe the stage to be a garden. By and by we hear news of shipwreck in the same place, and then we are to blame if we accept it not for a rock. Upon the back of that comes out a hideous monster

with fire and smoke, and then the miserable beholders are bound to take it for a cave. While in the meantime two armies fly in, represented with four swords and bucklers, and then what hard heart will not receive it for a pitched field? [Sidney, *Critical Edition* 243].

At the time Sidney wrote, few pitched battles, as distinguished from two-man duels, had been presented on the English stage (Edelman, *Brawl ridiculous* 13, 52), and it is highly probable that any he had seen would have been in Oxford's history plays. There is at least one battle scene in each of the *Henry VI* plays, one in *Richard II*, and several in *Edward III*—all written and staged, according to orthodox scholars, before *Henry V*. Sidney's complaint about "two armies" flying in, "represented with four swords and bucklers," might well have been directed at *Famous Victories* because that is what takes place at the opening of scene 15, where the stage direction "The Battle" signals a depiction of the Battle of Agincourt. The evidence for this conclusion is the lengthy satirical response to Sidney's complaints that Oxford made in the next play he wrote, culminating in an extraordinary retort by the playwright when he again presented the Battle of Agincourt on stage.

In *Henry V*, where the second half of *Famous Victories* is more fully dramatized, Oxford made use of a Chorus to respond to Sidney's criticism. As noted above, the Choruses preceding each of the five acts in *Henry V* are monologues by a speaker who sets the scene, explains the action, and urges the audience to suspend disbelief and imagine the physical place suggested by the dialogue. The first Chorus, or Prologue, is devoted entirely to answering Sidney's complaint that the audience must imagine too much:

> O for a Muse of fire, that would ascend
>
> The brightest heaven on invention,
>
> A kingdom for a stage, princes to act,
>
> And monarchs to behold the swelling scene!
>
> ...
>
>          Can this cockpit hold
>
> The vasty fields of France? Or may we cram
>
> Within this wooden O the very casques
>
> That did affright the air at Agincourt?
>
> ...
>
> Suppose within the girdle of these walls
>
> Are now confin'd two mighty monarchies,
>
> Whose high upreared and abutting fronts

> The perilous narrow ocean parts asunder;
> Piece out our imperfections with your thoughts;
> Into a thousand parts divide one man,
> And make imaginary puissance;
> Think, when we talk of horses, that you see them
> Printing their proud hoofs I' th' receiving earth.

The speaker ends this lengthy tongue-in-cheek appeal with a final request:

> Admit me Chorus to this history;
> Who, prologue-like, your humble patience pray
> Gently to hear, kindly to judge, our play.     *Henry V* Prologue

Less than 400 lines later, at the beginning of Act II, the Chorus is again asking the audience to bear with him:

> The King is set from London; and the scene
> Is now transported, gentles, to Southampton.
> There is the playhouse now, there must you sit;
> And thence to France shall we convey you safe,
> And bring you back, charming the narrow seas
> To give you gentle pass; or, if we may
> We'll not offend one stomach with our play.
> > *Henry V* II, Chorus 29–42

Before Act III, a similar exhortation by the Chorus ends with the line:

> Still be kind,
> And eche [eke] out our performance with your mind.
> > *Henry V* III, Chorus 24–5

The Choruses before Acts IV and V, each about fifty lines long, are similar adjurations to suspend disbelief, and it is in the Chorus before Act IV that we find what must be a personal retort to Sidney by Oxford about his method of portraying battles in the playhouse.[66] The speaker sets the scene by describing the tension and fear in the French and English camps on the night before Agincourt. But in the last six lines he speaks about the battle itself:

And so our scene must to the battle fly,

Where—O for pity!—we shall much disgrace

With four or five most vile and ragged foils,

(Right ill-disposed in brawl ridiculous)

The name of Agincourt. Yet sit and see,

Minding true things by what their mockeries be.

*Henry V* IV, Chorus 48–53

"O for pity!," Oxford writes, that "we shall much disgrace" the name of Agincourt by portraying it with just four or five fellows armed only with light and blunted weapons used in fencing. This is clearly a reference to Sidney's "two armies … represented with four swords and bucklers," and many editors have pointed to the similarity of the two phrases. But most of them merely quote the passage in Sidney's *Apology* or direct the reader to it. In the latest Arden edition, T. W. Craik comments that "Shakespeare echoes Sidney's criticism of stage conventions" (256). But with the exclamation "O for pity!" Oxford is not "echoing" Sidney, he is deriding him. The phrase is facetious, even sarcastic. In fact, the entire device of apologetic Choruses before each act in *Henry V* is best read as a witty rebuff of Sidney's complaint that English dramatists strain their audiences' imagination with the exotic settings of their plays.[67]

Samuel Johnson was the first critic to remark on the incongruity of the Chorus's apologies: "…nor can it be easily discovered," he wrote, "why the intelligence given by the Chorus is more necessary in this play than in many others where it is omitted" (Woudhuysen, *Johnson* 211). Today, we are entitled to ask why, other than facetiously, would the playwright in the six Chorus speeches in *Henry V* refer to the limitations of his stage, and ask the forbearance of his audience *more than thirty times*? As noted above, such a welter of apologies would have been totally inappropriate in his ninth or tenth history play. My answer is that he did so to rebuke the fatuous Sidney whom, a few years before, on the tennis court, he had called a "puppy."

Although many critics have noticed the connection between Sidney's complaints and the *Henry V* Choruses, one scholar has taken the next step and suggested a motivation. In a 1987 article, Sharon Tyler wrote: "It is tantalizing but pure speculation to see Shakespeare deliberately taking up the artistic gauntlet flung by Sidney" (76). More than tantalizing, it is irresistible. Oxford takes Sidney's contemptuous phrase "four swords and bucklers," turns it into two lines of verse, and tosses it back at him: With four or five most vile and ragged foils, Right ill-disposed in brawl ridiculous) *Henry V* IV, Chorus 50–1.

But then, instead of attempting any serious depiction of a battle, as he did in the *Henry VI* plays, Oxford inserts, as the battle starts in IV.iv, only two words in the stage directions—"Alarum" and "Excursions." He then trots out Pistol and his Frenchman, and the Boy, who engage in another comic dialogue in French and English that takes its humor from Pistol's bluster and fractured French. We may have, in the Choruses of *Henry V*, Shakespeare's first response to a bad review. If these Choruses are actually the retort to Sidney that they appear to be, they supply further evidence that the same man wrote *Famous Victories* and the Prince Hal trilogy.

## OXFORD AND SIDNEY

There is further evidence that Sidney was criticizing Oxford in *An Apology for Poetry.* Following his complaints about dramatists, he takes aim at "prose-printers":

> Now for similitudes, in certain printed discourses, I think all herbarists, all stories of beasts, fowls, and fishes are rifled up, that they come in multitudes to wait upon any of our conceits; which certainly is as absurd a surfeit to the ears as possible … a most tedious prattling [Sidney, *Critical Edition* 247].

Sidney scholars have identified this passage as a criticism of *Euphues, the Anatomy of Wit* (1578) and *Euphues and his England* (1580), both by Oxford's protégé John Lyly, who dedicated the latter to him (Sidney, *Apology*, Shepherd, ed. 230; Duncan-Jones, *Courtier* 237). In her biography of Sidney, Duncan-Jones suggests a similar purpose in another passage, where Sidney complains about "derivative and unconvincing love poets"—a likely reference to Thomas Watson and his collection of one hundred poems about love, *Hekatompathia,* which Watson dedicated to Oxford in the spring of 1582.[68]

There is still another instance in *Henry V* where it is clear that Oxford intended to ridicule Philip Sidney. It appears that he went out of his way to make fun of Sidney's fondness for horses. Sidney was given a pony at age eleven (M. Wilson 36), and seems to have developed a particular affinity for horses and horsemanship. He performed several times with great skill at the tilt, and is said to have travelled almost exclusively on horseback during his three-year tour of Europe in the early 1570s (Duncan-Jones, *Courtier* 63–4). His first name even derives from the Greek Φίλιππος "lover of horses." Throughout his works, there are admiring references to horses and horsemanship, a notable one being the famous opening paragraph of *An Apology for Poetry*, where he recounts the opinions of John Pietro Pugliano, his riding instructor during his visit to the Imperial Court in Vienna in 1574:

He said soldiers were the noblest estate of mankind, and horsemen the Noblest of soldiers. He said they were the masters of war, and ornaments of peace, speedy goers, and strong abiders, triumphers both in camps and courts. Nay, to so unbelieved a point he proceeded, as that no earthly thing bred such wonder to a Prince, as to be a good horseman—skill of government was but a *pedanteria* [pedantry] in comparison. Then would he add certain praises, by telling us what a peerless beast the horse was, the only serviceable courtier without flattery, the beast of most beauty, faithfulness, courage, and such more, that if I had not been a piece of a logician before I came to him, I think he would have persuaded me to have wished myself a horse [Sidney, *Critical Edition* 212].

If there is a hint of humor in this passage, it would be rare in Sidney's writings. Nevertheless, it is clear that Pugliano's sentiments were not far from Sidney's. A more personal declaration may be his sonnet on his horse and his love in *Astrophil and Stella*:

### Sonnet 49

I on my horse, and love on me doth try
Our horsemanships, while by strange work I prove
A horseman to my horse, a horse to love;
And now man's wrongs in me, poor beast, descry.
The reins wherewith my rider doth me tie
Are humbled thoughts, which bit of reverence move,
Curbed in with fear, but with gilt boss above
Of hope, which makes it seem fair to the eye.
The wand is will; thou, fancy, saddle art,
Girt fast by memory; and while I spur
My horse, he spurs with sharp desire my heart:
He sits me fast, however I do stir:
And now hath made me to his hand so right,
That in the manage myself takes delight.

                                         Sidney, *Critical Edition* 172[69]

This was, perhaps, too easy a target for Oxford. Near the end of Act III of *Henry V*, as the English and French armies prepare for the battle at Agincourt, he ridicules Sidney by putting his sentiments into the mouth of the eighteen-year-old Louis de Valois, the Dauphin of France, referring to him as the "Dolphin." Oxford devotes nearly all of scene vii, more than one hundred lines, to a conversation among three French aristocrats that appears to have no purpose other than to illustrate at great length the Dolphin's infatuation with his horse. In response to a remark by the Duke of Orleans about horses and armor, the Dolphin replies, "I will not change my / horse with any that treads but on four pasterns" (III.vii.11–12). The conversation continues in this vein:

| | |
|---|---|
| *Dol.* | When I bestride him, I soar, I am a hawk: he trots the air; the earth sings when he touches it; the basest horn of his hoof is more musical than the pipe of Hermes. |
| *Orl.* | He's of the color of the nutmeg. |
| *Dol.* | And of the heat of the ginger. It is a beast for Perseus. He is pure air and fire; and the dull elements of earth and water never appear in him, but only in patient stillness while his rider mounts him. He is indeed a horse; and all other jades you may call beasts. |
| *Con.* | Indeed, my lord, it is a most absolute and excellent horse. |
| *Dol.* | It is the prince of palfreys: his neigh is like the bidding of a monarch, and his countenance enforces homage. |
| *Orl.* | No more, cousin. |
| *Dol.* | Nay, the man hath no wit that cannot, from the rising of the lark to the lodging of the lamb, vary deserved praise on my palfrey. It is a theme as fluent as the sea; turn the sands into eloquent tongues, and my horse is argument for them all. 'Tis a subject for a sovereign to reason on, and for a sovereign's sovereign to ride on; and for the world, familiar to us and unknown, to lay apart their particular functions and wonder at him. I once writ a sonnet in his praise and began thus: "Wonder of nature"— |
| *Orl.* | I have heard a sonnet begin so to one's mistress. |
| *Dol.* | Then did they imitate that which I compos'd to my courser, for my horse is my mistress. |
| *Orl.* | Your mistress bears well. |
| *Dol.* | Me well; which is the prescript praise and perfection of a good and particular mistress. |

| | |
|---|---|
| *Con.* | Nay, for methought yesterday your mistress |
| | shrewdly shook your back. |
| *Dol.* | So perhaps did yours. |
| *Con.* | Mine was not bridled. |
| *Dol.* | O then belike she was old and gentle, and you |
| | rode like a kern of Ireland, your French hose off, and |
| | in your straight strossers. |
| *Con.* | You have good judgment in horsemanship. |
| *Dol.* | Be warn'd by me then: they that ride so, and |
| | ride not warily, fall into foul bogs. I had rather have |
| | my horse to my mistress. |
| *Con.* | I had as live have my mistress a jade. |
| *Dol.* | I tell thee, Constable, my mistress wears his |
| | own hair. |
| *Con.* | I could make as true a boast as that, if I had a |
| | sow to my mistress.          *Henry V* III.vii.15–63 |

This strange conversation is entirely superfluous to the plot, and even to the background, of the play. The entire scene is absent from the Quartos, and Andrew Gurr even omitted it from his edition of the first Quarto of *Henry V* on the grounds that the Quarto text was Shakespeare's revision for the stage (ed., *The First Quarto* ix).[70]

Besides the several obvious sexual puns and metaphors in the passage, which seem to have escaped notice by recent editors,[71] the Dolphin's description of his horse as a "palfrey" is another horse-related mockery of Sidney. The palfrey is a lightweight, nimble horse, more suited to be a lady's mount than to ride into combat. Oxford is suggesting that the Dolphin, i.e., Sidney, is effeminate, and unprepared to take the field in battle.[72]

The satire was all the sharper in that during the siege of Harfleur the historical Henry V challenged the Dolphin Louis to a "single combat" to decide who would inherit the crown of France. Louis, who was known to be fat and sluggish, declined the challenge, and was not even present at Agincourt, being kept from the battlefield by his father, the King (Seward, *Henry V* 69). He died before the end of the year. It should be noted that neither the Prologue nor the Choruses remain in the texts of the three Quartos, and that the Dolphin's role is substantially reduced. Half of his lines in the Folio are given to the Duke of Bourbon, and others are simply deleted. It is clear that by the end of the 1590s the satire of Sidney was no longer relevant or, perhaps, even understandable.

This additional connection between *Henry V* and Sidney's *Astrophil and Stella* further supports a date for the play in the early 1580s. Oxford's response to Sidney must have been written before Sidney's death in 1586 from wounds sustained in a cavalry charge on the battlefield. He was given a hero's funeral of a type usually reserved for great noblemen. He was an extremely popular supporter and patron of literature, and the recipient of dozens of literary dedications. On his death, almost every English poet composed verses in his praise. (Oxford did not.) It is unlikely that after this hero's death Oxford would have openly mocked his poetry, his person and his opinions about the English drama.

A dating of *Henry V* to the early 1580s is also consistent with the claim that Oxford's gratuitous reference in the Act V Chorus to "the general of our gracious Empress" was a reference to the impending triumphal return from Ireland of Sir Thomas Butler, Oxford's long-time friend, and for several years the antagonist of Sidney and his faction.

Oxford would continue to satirize Sidney in subsequent plays. As long ago as 1922, John T. Looney identified the real-life counterparts of several characters in *The Merry Wives of Windsor*, a play that follows *Henry V* and includes several of its characters. The elaborate plot to humiliate Falstaff is supplemented by what is clearly a dramatization of Philip Sidney's courtship of Anne Cecil, and its failure—Oxford marrying her instead.[73] The trio of Abraham Slender, Anne Page and Master Fenton are easily identified as Philip Sidney, Anne Cecil and the Earl of Oxford. Sidney's uncle, Robert Dudley, Earl of Leicester, is caricatured in Slender's wealthy uncle, Robert Shallow; and Anne's parents, the Cecils, in Mr. and Mrs. Page.[74] The engagement of Anne and Slender is negotiated by Shallow and Mr. Page, just as Anne's and Sidney's engagement was negotiated by Dudley, Sidney's wealthy uncle, and Anne's father, William Cecil.

Throughout the latter part of the first scene of *Merry Wives*, Oxford presents Slender as eager to do his uncle's bidding, but seemingly lacking the motivation to marry Anne. He claims that he has been bruised "with playing at sword and dagger with a master of fence," and repeatedly utters malapropisms and non-sequiturs. In a single line, "I keep but three men and a boy yet, till my mother be dead," he pronounces the name given him by Oxford in *Love's Labor's Lost*—Boyet, and refers to his poor financial condition until he inherits wealth on his mother's death, as was the case with Sidney (I.i.274–5). In the third act, Oxford ridicules Sidney's declarations to Penelope Rich in *Astrophil and Stella* by putting his language, "Have I caught thee, my heavenly jewel?," in the mouth of Falstaff as he courts Mistress Ford.[75] As Looney puts it, the "body of precise details" in the play—the specific financial arrangements, the attributes and relationships of the characters, and even several Christian names—all reflect the actual circumstances of the proposed marriage ("*Shakespeare" Identified* 2:169–76).

Looney also identified another satirization of Sidney in *Love's Labor's Lost*, where he is portrayed as the messenger/courtier Boyet, who is a borrower of wit from other poets:

> Ber.        This fellow picks up wit as pigeons pease.
>
>            And utters it again when God doth please.
>
>                                *Love's Labor's Lost* V.ii.315–16[76]

This couplet refers to a perception by some that Sidney often made free use of other writers' phrases, ideas and images—as he admits in the first Sonnet in *Astrophil and Stella*:

> . . .
> I sought fit words to paint the blackest face of woe;
> Studying inventions fine her wits to entertain,
> Oft turning others' leaves to see if thence would flow
> Some fresh and fruitful showers upon my sunburnt brain.
> But words came halting forth, wanting invention's stay;
> . . .
> Thus, great with child to speak, and helpless in my throes,
> Biting my truant pen, beating myself for spite,
> "Fool," said my muse to me, "look in thy heart and write."
>                     Sidney, *Critical Edition* (153)

As one of Sidney's earliest biographers wrote, "Sidney did much more than look into his heart before writing. Even those who see tragic meaning in his sonnets must admit that; there was frequent turning of 'others' leaves', and much studying of 'inventions fine,' in his efforts to paint for Stella's entertainment 'the blackest face of woe'" (Bourne 273). In the words of Sidney Lee, "Petrarch, Ronsard and Desportes inspired the majority of Sidney's efforts, and addresses to abstractions like sleep, the moon, his muse, grief, or lust are almost verbatim translations from the French" (*A Life* 706). It appears that this criticism surfaced while Sidney was still writing, and he responded in Sonnet 74:

> And this I swear by blackest brook of hell,
> I am no pick-purse of another's wit.
>             Sidney, *Critical Edition* 184

Although he might have been replying to someone else, it is hard to believe that these lines are not a direct response to the couplet in *Love's Labor's Lost*.

There are multiple allusions to Boyet as Sidney, and to Berowne as Oxford, throughout Act V. The most obvious are the references to the New Year's gifts that Sidney and Oxford made to the Queen. Half-way through the act, the Princess mentions the jewel that Berowne has given her (V.ii.456–7) and, a few lines later, Berowne dresses down Boyet for his part in the plot, ending with the line—"Die when you will, a smock shall be your shroud" (V.ii.479). Oxford's gift to the Queen in 1580 was "a fayre juell of golde" (J. B. Nichols 1:289). Sidney's gift, in 1578, was "a smock of camerick, the sleves and collor wrought with blac worke (J. B. Nichols 2:77).[77]

The gaunt and doltish Andrew Aguecheek in *Twelfth Night* is another Sidney caricature, his surname reflecting the pockmarks and "mines" left by measles and smallpox on his face while still a child (Moffett 71). More than that, his Christian name suggests the apostle St. Andrew, whose feast day—November 30th—coincides with Sidney's birthday. He is drawn as a ridiculous figure who is both confused and boastful, and who imagines himself a ladies' man, but is unattractive and socially inept.[78] The portrait of Sidney is rounded out as Aguecheek challenges Viola/Cesario to a duel, but becomes terrified when he learns that his opponent is a noted fencer. "Pox on't. I'll not meddle with him," he declares, and offers his horse in exchange for the matter to be forgotten (III.iv.142–310).

Oxford returned to the subject in *Cymbeline*, where the oafish Cloten (rhymes with *rotten*)[79] and the worthy Posthumus, a ward of the king, can be identified as Sidney and Oxford—in competition for the affection of Imogen as Anne Cecil. In a conversation with two Lords in I.ii, Cloten brags about an aborted sword fight that he started with Posthumus in the previous scene. But the two Lords whisper aside to each other about the forbearance of Posthumus and the cowardice of Cloten as he thrust ineffectually at Posthumus, and avoided any actual swordplay. The Lords continue their asides to each other, suggesting that Imogen made the better choice by marrying Posthumus instead of Cloten, just as Anne Cecil married Oxford, instead of Sidney. Finally, one Lord simply utters the word "Puppies," a clear allusion to Oxford's scornful rebuff of Sidney on the tennis court in 1579. In a departure from the plot similar to that in *Henry V*, Oxford devotes the entire scene to equating Cloten with Sidney, and ridiculing them both.[80]

A. Bronson Feldman detected a caricature of Sidney in Michael Cassio, the young officer who is Iago's rival in *Othello*: "…both men were soldiers who had learned the trade from books"; both were quick-tempered and rash; both were associated with the woman Oxford/Othello loved, Sidney a wooer of Anne Cecil, Cassio accused of wooing Desdemona; and both suffered a serious wound in the leg, Sidney subsequently dying. Feldman also notes Iago's two references to Cassio as a dog, reminiscent of Oxford's "canine insult" of Sidney on the tennis court (166–7).

Thus, in as many as six plays Oxford responded sharply to Sidney's criticism and repeatedly ridiculed his person and his poetry. These multiple insults to Sidney in several Shakespeare plays, reflecting the actual quarrel and persistent hostility between Sidney and Oxford, further support the identification of Oxford as the author of the canon.

The last issue to be considered is Oxford's access to the essential sources of the Prince Hal plays. It is well known that as a child Oxford lived with, and was tutored by, Sir Thomas Smith, one of England's greatest scholars, and the owner of an extensive library (S. Hughes 1, 9). The most important sources for *Famous Victories*—Hall's *Chronicle*, Robert Fabyan's *The New Chronicles of England and France*, and the *Vita Henrici Quinti* of Tito Livio, were available to Oxford in Smith's library (Jolly and O'Brien 19–20). In 1562, at age twelve, de Vere was sent to live in the home of William Cecil in London, and it is likely that he remained there, except for brief absences, until his marriage in 1571. As noted in the Introduction, Cecil was one of the premier book and manuscript collectors of the Elizabethan age. A catalog of his holdings at his death lists 1700 books and about 250 manuscripts (Jolly 6). It is likely that some of these sources were also available in Cecil's library, as well as such others in print as Sir Thomas Elyot's *The Book of the Governor* (1531), John Stow's *A Summarie of English Chronicles* (1565), and the 1559 edition of *The Mirror for Magistrates*.

## Contrary Evidence

Aside from those mentioned above, only a few scholars have attempted to assign *Famous Victories* to a particular author. In 1891, F. G. Fleay attributed it to Richard Tarlton (*Biographical Chronicle* 2:258–9), but adduced no evidence other than the fact that Tarlton appeared in the play as Derick the clown. In 1920, H. D. Sykes attributed the play to Samuel Rowley on the basis of similarities that he found among *Famous Victories*, Rowley's *When You See Me You Know Me* (1604), and the 1602 additions to Marlowe's *Doctor Faustus* (*Authorship* 4–8). Rowley and William Bird were the two playwrights to whom Philip Henslowe paid £4, in 1602, for the additions to Marlowe's play. Sykes was on firmer ground when he concluded that *Famous Victories* and the prose scenes in *The Taming of a Shrew* had a common author. But both plays date to the 1560s, and Rowley appears to have been born about 1570. Alice-Lyle Scoufos, in *Shakespeare's Typological Satire*, suggested that the author of *Famous Victories* was Henry Evans, a Welshman who intermittently managed several boys' playing companies between 1583 and 1608—including the one patronized by the

Earl of Oxford (179). But there is nothing to connect Evans with the play, and no evidence that he ever wrote anything. A suggestion was made by Philip Brockbank in 1971 that the author was Robert Greene, but he presented no evidence (150). Oxfordian scholars uniformly assign the authorship of *Famous Victories* to the Earl of Oxford.

In support of the orthodox dating of *Henry V*, Gary Taylor cites "the play-wright's preoccupation with Irish affairs" and his "allusion to the Irish expedition" as additional evidence for the composition of the play in the spring of 1599, when Essex was sent to Ireland. He refers to early 1599 as "a period of great nationalist enthusiasm for an expansionist military adventure" (ed. *Henry V* 7). But these conditions were also present in the early 1580s, when Ireland and England's role in Ireland were very much on the minds of Elizabeth and the English public, as well. The campaign against the Desmond rebels, the widespread suffering of the Irish people, and the controversial massacre of six hundred foreign troops at Smerwick in County Kerry in November 1580 caused much comment by English observers. Serious Irish rebellions commenced as early as 1565, and "Irish expeditions" followed shortly after, and continued to the end of Elizabeth's reign.

Another example that Taylor cites of the playwright's preoccupation with Irish affairs in *Henry V* is the exclamation "calen o custure me" that Pistol utters in response to the French soldier's question in IV.iv. The phrase is an English corruption of a popular Irish song, *cailin óg a stór* ("maiden, my treasure"), as Taylor himself reports (ed. *Henry V* 234). The song was registered in March 1582 (Arber, ed. *Transcript* 2:407) and was issued on a broadside between that date and 1584, when it was included in the ballad collection *A Handful of Pleasant Delights* (Rollins viii). Frequent references to it suggest that it was popular at that time; so it was clearly more topical in the early 1580s than in 1599.[81]

Two other candidates for "the general" have been proposed—Sir John Norris and Sir Charles Blount, eighth Lord Mountjoy. In 1595, the Queen put Sir John Norris in command of a small army and dispatched him to Ireland against the rebel Earl of Tyrone, Hugh O'Neill. But over the next two years, Norris' campaign floundered, and in May 1597 he was superseded by another commander (Trim). Norris died a few months later and O'Neill was still at large in 1599 when Essex was sent against him. There was nothing in Norris' campaign that would have suggested to the playwright that he would return to London "Bringing rebellion broachèd on his sword."

The theory that Baron Mountjoy (1563–1606), was "the general," and that the four lines in the Act V Chorus referred to his return from Ireland, was advanced by W. D. Smith in 1954. Such a scenario would require the Choruses to have been written after February 1600, when Elizabeth sent Mountjoy to

Ireland in pursuit of O'Neill. Smith's theory was largely ignored for fifty years, except for a paper by R. A. Law ("Choruses"), before it was revived by several prominent scholars—Richard Dutton, Stephen Orgel, Andrew Gurr and Lukas Erne. Dutton proposed that the four lines referred to Mountjoy's victory at the battle of Kinsale in County Cork in December 1601, and that this was the reason "for a rewriting of the play, most plausibly in 1602" ("Methinks" 197). Orgel argued, similarly, for a rewritten *Henry V* in 1602 (11). Gurr suggested that "…the Folio text, with its famous Choruses and speeches … was unlikely to have been heard at the Globe any time before 1623…," thus robbing the passage in the Act V Chorus of any alleged topicality with respect to either Essex or Mountjoy ("First Quarto" ix). Along the same line, Erne conjectured that "the Chorus was not performed in front of audiences but only printed for the benefit of readers…" (248).

It is true that Mountjoy succeeded Essex, and traveled to Ireland in February 1600 to take command of the English army pursuing O'Neill. But it was nearly two years before the two met in a significant battle, at Kinsale in County Cork, in December 1601. The result of the battle was a clear victory for the English, but O'Neill merely retreated, albeit with a much-reduced army, and the rebellion persisted. During the ensuing year, Mountjoy lobbied Elizabeth and Robert Cecil for permission to negotiate with O'Neill, which was granted in February 1603. It was not until the end of the following month, after Elizabeth's death, that O'Neill finally submitted, and the settlement allowed him generous concessions, retention of his earldom, most of his property, and a royal pardon (Guy 367; W. Palmer 137). Again, there was nothing about Mountjoy's campaign or its outcome that would give rise to Oxford's trenchant image.

Several editors have asserted that the "beard of the general's cut" remark by Gower at III.vi.77 of *Henry V* (scene 9 in the Quarto) refers to the square-cut beard that the Earl of Essex affected after the Cadiz expedition of 1596 (Craik 237). But a glance at the contemporary painting of Sir Thomas Butler attributed to Steven van der Meulen, plainly illustrates Gower's remark—he is wearing a square-cut beard.[82]

Those Oxfordian scholars who assign a date to *Famous Victories* associate it with the 1573 Gad's Hill robbery described in "*Famous Victories* and Edward de Vere," above, and date its composition to that year or the next (Ward, *Famous* 285; Clark 682; Ogburn Jr. 773). But, as detailed in "The Date of *Famous Victories*" and elsewhere in this book, the evidence is much stronger that Oxford wrote *Famous Victories* in the early 1560s, and the four other apprenticeship plays before 1570.

Oxfordian scholars date *Henry V* in a range between 1578 (Hess 3:260) and 1592 (Moore 195), but don't supply much evidence for their dates. Moore accepts the reference to Essex in 1599 and suggests that it, and the entire Chorus apparatus, are additions made by the playwright to the original text that he composed years earlier. He points out that the half-a-dozen lines following the reference to Essex "contain textual corruption" (183–4). But the anomaly of the absence of all the Chorus's speeches from the 1600, 1602 and 1619 quartos, and their reappearance in the Folio, remains unexplained. The scenario outlined above in "Dates of the Prince Hal Plays," is a much better explanation for these facts.

## Conclusion

The Earl of Oxford's obvious precocity, and the attestations of his youthful literary talent, combined with the circumstances of his early teen years, support his authorship of a short and simple play in prose, such as *Famous Victories*. The absence of legal terms and legal issues in the play suggests that he wrote it before he undertook his legal education in 1567.[83] The clear similarities of character, plot and language between *Famous Victories* and the Prince Hal trilogy indicate that the latter plays were a wholesale expansion and refinement of the former. The identification of Sir Thomas Butler as "the general of our gracious Empress," Oxford's retort to Sidney's criticisms in *An Apology for Poetry*, and his subsequent ridicule of him in several plays supply the evidence for the conclusion that he wrote *Henry V* in the early 1580s.

The fixing of the composition date of *Henry V* in 1583 establishes an important benchmark in the chronology of Shakespeare's history plays. The last six lines of the precise fourteen-line Shakespearean sonnet that is the Epilogue to *Henry V* tell us that the *Henry VI* trilogy was already a staple of the stage:

> Henry the Sixt, in infant bands crown'd King
> Of France and England, did this king succeed;
> Whose state so many had the managing,
> That they lost France, and made his England bleed;
> Which oft our stage has shown; and for their sake,
> In your fair minds let this acceptance take.
> [*Henry V* Epilogue 9–14]

As there are no other extant Elizabethan plays about Henry VI, virtually all modern scholars agree that Shakespeare completed the *Henry VI-Richard III* tetralogy before his Prince Hal series, and most of them think that the *Henry VI* trilogy, to the extent that he wrote it, was his first attempt to dramatize English history. This rough sequence accords with the evidence presented above, but only in terms of sequence. With the exception of *Henry VIII*, Shakespeare's history plays must be dated before 1584, and *Famous Victories* earlier still. The traditional dating of c. 1588–1599 can no longer be sustained.

But aside from Seymour Pitcher, and the free-thinking critic Eric Sams, no orthodox Shakespearean scholars accept *Famous Victories* as a Shakespeare play. In *The English History Play in the Age of Shakespeare*, Irving Ribner wrote that "the suggestion ... that the play represents an early work by William Shakespeare need scarcely be taken seriously" (68). Samuel Schoenbaum called it "a preposterous thesis" (167). But neither scholar offered any rebuttal to the evidence for Shakespeare's authorship, nor any evidence for another author.

# II

## The True Tragedy of Richard
## the Third and Richard III

The anonymous history play, *The True Tragedy of Richard the Third*, printed in 1594, has occasionally been cited as a source for Shakespeare's *Richard III*, printed in 1597, also anonymously. *True Tragedy* was not reprinted until 1821, and was not commented on at length until 1900, when G. B. Churchill found sufficient parallels between the two plays to assert that Shakespeare made substantial use of incidents and language in the anonymous play when composing *Richard III* (524). Fifty years later, John Dover Wilson agreed, and pointed out additional links between the plays ("Shakespeare's *Richard III*" 299–306). In 1960, Geoffrey Bullough concurred with Churchill and Wilson (3:222, 238), and printed most of *True Tragedy* at the end of his discussion of *Richard III* in his *Narrative and Dramatic Sources of Shakespeare*.

On the other hand, most commentators, including E. K. Chambers, see only scattered minor borrowings by Shakespeare from *True Tragedy*. Several early critics ascribed the play variously to Lodge, Peele, Kyd, and the author of *Locrine* (Chambers, *Elizabethan Stage* 4:44). Aside from occasional comments about its insignificance, *True Tragedy* has been largely ignored by scholars for the past fifty years. With the exception of a hint from Eric Sams in 1995 (*Real Shakespeare* 59), no one has ever claimed the play for Shakespeare, nor has it been included in discussions or collections of Shakespearean apocrypha.[1]

However, a review of the published evidence, and a further analysis of the two plays, lead to the conclusion that *True Tragedy* was not only a major source for Shakespeare's *Richard III*, but it was Shakespeare himself who wrote it—one of his earliest attempts at playwriting. There are also significant links between this anonymous play and Edward de Vere, seventeenth Earl of Oxford, that add to the evidence that he was the actual author of the Shakespeare canon.

In addition, the evidence suggests that this play was performed for an aristocratic audience, possibly including Queen Elizabeth herself, in the early 1560s, when de Vere was between thirteen and fifteen years old.[2]

## *The Anonymous* True Tragedy of Richard the Third

The title page of the anonymous Quarto printed in 1594 by Thomas Creede reads: "*The True Tragedie of Richard the Third: Wherein is showne the death of Edward the fourth, with the smothering of the two yoong Princes in the Tower: With a lamentable ende of Shore's wife, an example for all wicked women. And lastly the conjunction and joyning of the two noble Houses, Lancaster and Yorke. As it was playd by the Queenes Majesties Players*" (Greg, ed. *True Tragedy* xiii). Three copies of this edition survive. An entry credited to Thomas Creede in the Stationers' Register in June of the same year contained roughly the same language, except that it begins "An enterlude entituled, The Tragedie of Richard the Third" (Greg, ed. *True Tragedy* v). *True Tragedy* next appeared in print in 1821, when it was included in Edmund Malone's *Variorum* (v. 19). It was subsequently published by the Shakespeare Society in 1844 (Barron Field, ed.) and in W. C. Hazlitt's *Shakespeare's Library* in 1875 (pt. 2, vol. 1). In the Malone Society reprint of 1929, the only subsequent edition, W. W. Greg wrote: "Nothing whatever is known of the history of the piece beyond the statement on the title-page that it 'was playd by the Queenes Majesties Players'" (v). There is no record of its performance, nor is it mentioned in any document from the period.

The Quarto text of 2500 lines reproduced in the Malone Society edition gives every appearance of being set from a manuscript prepared by someone listening to the play being performed or dictated, the latter being more likely. Although the spelling is erratic throughout, there are numerous misspellings based on apparent mishearings. There are also long stretches of misaligned text, that is, verse printed as prose and vice versa. A large portion of another Queen's Men play registered by Creede in 1594, *The Famous Victories of Henry the Fifth*, was printed as verse (in 1598), even though the entire play was written in prose. The misaligned text in these Quartos is not easily explained, and might have been due to errors or deliberate changes by one or more transcribers and/or one or more compositors.

*Opposite:* **Title page of the anonymous *The True Tragedy of Richard the Third*. 1594. It was registered in the same year, but there is no record of its performance, nor is it mentioned in any other document from the period. The canonical *Richard III* was printed in 1597, also anonymously. *True Tragedy* was not reprinted until 1821 (by permission of the Folger Shakespeare Library).**

# THE
# True Tragedie of Ri=
### chard the third:

Wherein is fhowne the death of Edward the
fourth, with the fmothering of the two
yoong Princes in the Tower:

*With a lamentable ende of Shores wife, as example
for all wicked women.*

And laftly, the coniunction and ioyning of the two noble
Houfes, *Lancafter* and *Yorke*.

As it was playd by the Queenes Maiefties
Players.

### LONDON

Printed by Thomas Creede, and are to be fold by
William Barley, at his fhop in Newgate Market, neare
Chrift Church doore.   1594.

## The Canonical Richard III

The canonical *The Tragedie of King Richard the Third* was published in six Quartos between 1597, when it was registered by Andrew Wise, and 1622, just a year before it appeared in the First Folio. Each Quarto bore, with minor variations, the subtitle, *Containing his treacherous plots against his brother Clarence: the pitiful murther of his innocent nephews; his tyrannical usurpation: with the whole course of his detested life, and most deserved death.* The title page of Q1 lists no author, but each of the remaining five, beginning with Q2 in 1598, bears the words "by William Shakespeare" or "by William Shake-speare." The title pages of Quartos 3 (1602) through 6 (1622) include the words "Newly augmented by" just before Shakespeare's name. But, according to E. K. Chambers, "There are no augmentations," except for "occasional corrections" and "a progressive accumulation of errors" (*William Shakespeare* 1:296–300). Approximately thirty-seven copies of these six Quartos are extant (Bartlett 19–21).

In the Folio, the title is listed under "Histories" as "*The Life and Death of Richard the Third*" and the running title is the same. But the Head-title reads "*The Tragedy of Richard the Third: with the Landing of the Earle Richmond, and the Battell at Bosworth Field*" (Jowett 118–19). The Folio and Quarto texts differ from each other sufficiently to lead Chambers to declare them "distinct texts" (*William Shakespeare* 1:297). The usual disagreement prevails as to which precedes the other and, if the Folio were the original, whether the Q1 text were memorially reconstructed or a deliberate revision by the author, or someone else. Nor is there agreement about the best copy text, the latest Arden (Siemon 2009) and New Cambridge Shakespeare (Lull 1999) editors using the Folio as the copy text, and the Oxford editor (Jowett 2000) using the Quarto. A separate edition of Q1 appeared in 1996, edited by Peter Davison. The textual history of the play is comprehensively treated in Appendix 1 of Siemon's edition.

## Sources of the Plays

The original source for *True Tragedy* was Sir Thomas More's *The History of King Richard the Third*, a short biography first published in 1543 by Richard Grafton as a continuation of John Hardyng's rhymed *Chronicle of John Hardyng*. The apparent immediate source was Edward Hall's *Chronicle*, published by Grafton in 1548.[3] Language and details about Shore's Wife in *True Tragedy* were based on the poem about her by Thomas Churchyard that was added to *The Mirror for Magistrates* in 1563, in the third edition (Churchill 409–13; also, see "The Thomas Churchyard Connection," below).

The principal sources for the canonical *Richard III* were also More's *History* and Hall's *Chronicle*. For the period covered by the play, the *Chronicles* of Hall and Holinshed are nearly identical with each other and with the More biography. Some editors have found details in the play that they claim are unique to Holinshed's *Chronicles*, in either edition, but most of these are either popular superstitions or historical incidents that cannot be tied to a particular source. Moreover, all the Tudor chroniclers copied extensively from previous writers; Holinshed himself cited more than 190 sources, most of which were available to the author of *Richard III*. Another probable source was the history of George, Duke of Clarence in the 1559 edition of *The Mirror for Magistrates*.[4]

Robert J. Lordi (142–4), Geoffrey Bullough (*Narrative* 3:235–7) and others cite incidents and ideas in Thomas Legge's Latin play *Richardus Tertius* (c. 1579) that they think had an influence on *Richard III*. But considering the substantial evidence that Oxford composed the *Henry VI-Richard III* tetralogy before traveling to Italy in 1575, detailed below in "The Date of *Richard III*," any influence would have been in the opposite direction.[5]

As to the influence of *True Tragedy* on the canonical *Richard III*, scholarly opinion is sharply divided. It ranges from the multiple instances of borrowing in every act cited by Churchill and Bullough to E. K. Chambers' extraordinary statement that "There is very little trace of any use by Shakespeare of this play for his *Richard III*" (*Elizabethan Stage* 4:44). But the evidence in the following Section demonstrates that in writing *Richard III* Shakespeare made substantial use of *True Tragedy* in every part of the play and in every element of its composition.

# Relationships Between True Tragedy and Richard III

## STRUCTURE AND PLOT

As John Dover Wilson observed, "*Richard III* and *T. T.*, for all their differences, are strikingly similar in general structure" ("Shakespeare's *Richard III*" 300). The first act of *Richard III* corresponds roughly to the first scene in *True Tragedy*, in which the ghost of George, Duke of Clarence, appears briefly to the characters Truth and Poetry, and calls, in Latin, for a quick and bloody revenge. Truth then recounts to Poetry the events of the 1460s—the seizing of the throne from Henry VI by Richard, Duke of York; Richard's subsequent death at Wakefield; the accession of George's brother Edward IV; and the murder (in 1471) of Henry VI by Richard, Duke of Gloucester. When Poetry asks the identity of the ghost, Truth replies that it is Clarence, and that he was also a victim of Richard, by drowning in a butt of wine, a death that occurred in 1478. Truth then describes Richard:

*Truth.*        A man ill shaped, crooked backed, lame armed, withall,

Valiantly minded, but tyrannous in authoritie.

*True Tragedy* 57–8[6]

Finally, Truth suggests to the audience that they imagine that Edward IV, after reigning twenty-two years, has summoned his nobles to the court to hear his death-bed wishes, an event recorded in the chronicles as taking place in April 1483. Here the action of *True Tragedy* begins, with the departure of Truth and Poetry and the entrance of King Edward, Lord Hastings, Queen Elizabeth and her son Thomas Grey, Marquess of Dorset. The concluding sentence of the stage directions reads "To them, Richard."

In the first act of *Richard III*, there is a similar compression of historical events, from the funeral of Henry VI in 1471 to the murder of Edward's brother George, Duke of Clarence in 1478. In his opening soliloquy, Richard describes himself in language similar to that used in *True Tragedy*—"not shap'd for sportive tricks," etc. Act II opens at the same time and in the same place that *True Tragedy* begins—in 1483, with King Edward on his death-bed attempting to reconcile his nobles. The cast of characters is nearly the same, and Richard enters, with Ratcliffe, after forty-four lines. The remainder of both plays is based on events in the sixteen-month period ending with the Battle of Bosworth and the crowning of Henry VII in August 1485.

Shakespeare's *Richard III* departs from *True Tragedy* in only two significant ways. One is in the depiction of women and Richard's interaction with them. Queen Elizabeth, the widow of King Edward, and her daughter, also named Elizabeth, are present in both plays. *True Tragedy* includes two other women, Jane Shore and her maid Hursly—Jane being the unfortunate former mistress of Edward IV. Nowhere in *True Tragedy* does Richard speak to any of them.

In the canonical *Richard III*, Shakespeare deleted Shore and Hursly, but added three other women. One is the widowed Duchess of York, mother of the infamous Plantagenet brothers, Richard, Edward and George. Another is the widow of Henry VI, Margaret of Anjou, who died in 1482, but was such a brilliant character in the three *Henry VI* plays that Shakespeare brought her back for a fourth appearance in *Richard III*. The third was another widow, Lady Anne Neville, whom Richard successfully courted, and who became his queen briefly before she mysteriously died. And Richard speaks to all of them, at length, with great irony and wit.

Shakespeare has also spiced up the action by adding two courtships, both by Richard—one of Anne Neville, and the other directed to Edward's widow

Elizabeth for the hand of her daughter, also Elizabeth. These additions illustrate his maturity and increasing dramatic skill—and bring humor, irony, depth and balance to the rather grim story told in *True Tragedy*. They also reflect the older writer's experience with women, ranging from the evil to the innocent, something more likely to lie in the future of a teen-aged boy.

The other major difference between the two plays is the treatment of the murders of Edward IV's two young sons, and of his brother George. In *True Tragedy*, it is the murder of the two princes in the Tower that is dramatized; the murder of George, Duke of Clarence, is only reported. In *Richard III*, it is the murder of Clarence that is dramatized, and the murder of the princes that is only reported. With respect to time and circumstance, the murder of the princes in *True Tragedy* adheres more closely to the sources. It occurred in 1483, after Richard was crowned King, and there is still disagreement about his guilt. The murder of Clarence in *Richard III* occurred five years before the action of the play, and it is likely that Richard was not responsible for it.

## LANGUAGE, INCIDENT AND DETAIL

In his introduction to the Malone Society reprint of *True Tragedy*, W. W. Greg described the play as "a strangely amateurish composition," and continued:

> The text certainly seems to be in a rather chaotic state. Some parts are written in straightforward if stilted prose, others in tolerable blank verse: the end shows an irregular mixture of quatrains and couplets. In places, however, the prose tends to fall into verse cadence and even contains cases of rime, while at times the verse becomes irregular. There are passages especially near the beginning, which might equally be regarded as prose cut up into lengths or verse in the last stages of decay: there are also distinct fragments of fourteener couplets. It is hard to imagine that the play should have been composed in this manner.
>
> [ed. *True Tragedy* vi–vii].

In addition, the text lacks any scene or act divisions, and contains many misplaced or confusing stage directions. As Churchill remarked, "As it stands, the play is wretchedly corrupt and abominably printed" (404). It is true that many of the textual anomalies can be laid to a degraded manuscript or to a careless compositor, as well as mishearings attending on an "oral stage" in the composition to printing process. The play is full of bombast, declarative dialogue and vigorous metaphoric language. There is no question that it is the work of an inexperienced playwright, and that it is one of the earliest examples of the use of a revenge motif in a history play. See "Further Dating Evidence," below, for additional details of the play's style.

The canonical *Richard III* has many of the same characteristics. E. K. Chambers described the style of *Richard III* as follows:

… a highly-mannered, rhetorical style, extravagant in utterance, with many appeals and exclamations. There is much violent and vituperative speech: the word *blood* runs like a *leit-motif* through the play. Epithets, and sometimes nouns, are piled up, in pairs, with or without a conjunction; … A "clinching" line at the end of a speech is also common.

[*William Shakespeare* 1:302].

Chambers' remarks apply equally well to *True Tragedy*. For instance, the words *blood* and *bloody* appear more than two dozen times in the text. In his revision, Shakespeare cut the bombast down a notch and treated the blood theme more expertly. The verse and dramaturgy are markedly superior, as well.

But there are dozens of instances of language, incident and detail in *True Tragedy* that Shakespeare carried over into *Richard III*. They fall into two categories—those that are clearly derived from one or more of the sources, and those that are unsupported by the sources, and are peculiar to the two plays. In their aggregate they are unmistakable, and supply convincing evidence of Shakespeare's familiarity with *True Tragedy*, and frequent borrowing from it.

In the second category are the following examples of language, incident and detail in both plays that are not found in the sources:

1. The King's death-bed scene, and his attempt to reconcile his nobles, are described in the chronicles and recur in both plays, although the group of participants is not identical. But in both plays Richard is present, whereas none of the chronicle accounts place him there; and he was actually in Yorkshire at the time (Seward, *Wars* 260).

2. In *True Tragedy*, the playwright uses an unusual dramatic device to show Richard cleverly claiming for himself the blessing Buckingham intends for King Edward:

*Buckingham.* Sound trumpet in this parley, God save the King.

*Richard.*                                             Richard.  *True Tragedy* 785–6

In the long scene after the funeral of Henry VI in Act I of *Richard III*, Shakespeare employs the identical device to show Richard deflecting Queen Margaret's curse on him back on herself:

*Q. Mar.*      … Thou loathed issue of thy father's loins,
                   Thou rag of honour, thou detested—

*K. Rich.*                      Margaret!          *Richard III* I.iii.232–4

3. In *True Tragedy*, it is the murder of the two princes that is dramatized; in *Richard III* it is the murder of Clarence. However, the instructions to the hired murderers, by James Tyrell in *True Tragedy*, and by Richard

in *Richard III*, are similar, as are the responses, and have no basis in any chronicle:

| | |
|---|---|
| *Terrell.* | Come hither, sirs. To make a long discourse were but a folly. You seem to be resolute in this cause that Myles Forest hath delivered to you. Therefore, you must cast away pity, and not so much as think upon favour, for the more stern that you are, the more shall you please the King. |
| *Will.* | Zounds, sir! Ne'er talk to us of favour. Tis not the first that Jack and I have gone about.     *True Tragedy* 1223–29 |

| | |
|---|---|
| *K. Rich.* | … When you have done, repair to Crosby Place.<br>But, sirs, be sudden in the execution,<br>Withal obdurate, do not hear him plead,<br>For Clarence is well-spoken, and perhaps<br>May move your hearts to pity if you mark him. |
| *1. Mur.* | Tut, tut, my lord, we will not stand to prate.<br>Talkers are no good doers. Be assured,<br>We go to use our hands, and not our tongues.<br>     *Richard III* I.iii.345–52 |

4. The murderers' discussion of how they will do the deed, the depiction of the actual murder, and their conversation about disposing of the bodies are similar in the two plays (1295–1316 in *True Tragedy*; I.iv.99–152, 258–73 in *Richard III*). In each case, one of the murderers is reluctant to proceed, but after the other remonstrates with him, he readily turns to the task. Another similarity is how the murders are reported. In *True Tragedy*, Tyrell asks, "How now Myles Forest, is this deed dispatcht?" Forest answers, "I sir, a bloodie deed we have performed" (1319–20). In *Richard III*, the second Murderer says "A bloody deed and desperately dispatch'd" (I.iv.261). None of these details appear in the sources (Boswell-Stone 348).

5. There is similar language and detail in the lamentation scenes in both plays. In *True Tragedy*, Queen Elizabeth mourns the loss of her husband Edward IV (789–811). In *Richard III*, she does the same, and the Duchess of York, using similar language, mourns the loss of her husband and sons, Clarence and Edward (II.ii.1–100). In both plays, the children of

the mourning women are called "images" of their fathers. In both plays, children ask the women whom they are mourning. In *True Tragedy*, Elizabeth is comforted by her three children, her daughter saying, "Good mother expect the living, and forget the dead" (792). In *Richard III*, the Duchess is comforted by Clarence's children, and Elizabeth by Earl Rivers, who says "Drown desperate sorrow in dead Edward's grave, / And plant your joys in living Edward's throne" (II.ii.99–100). These scenes and this language have no sources in the chronicles (Lull 104).

6. As Churchill pointed out, young Prince Edward displays an unusual maturity for a thirteen-year-old in both plays, "for which the chronicle offers no hint" (505–6). His remarks about what he will accomplish as King in *True Tragedy* (530–3) are similar to those in *Richard III* (III.i.76–94).

7. The repeated references to Thomas, Lord Grey, as the uncle of Prince Edward are identical errors in both plays. He was actually the Queen's oldest son by her first husband, Sir John Grey, and therefore Edward's half-brother. None of the sources contains this error.

8. The discussion of the size of the train to accompany Prince Edward to London for his coronation in *True Tragedy* (492–503) is echoed in *Richard III* (II.ii.117ff). Although this discussion is mentioned by both More and Hall, the dialogue in both plays includes several identical words—*train, malice, green,* and *break*—that do not occur in the sources. These "verbal links" were strong enough to convince both John Dover Wilson ("Shakespeare's *Richard III*" 301) and W. W. Greg (*Editorial Problem* 80–1) that Shakespeare was influenced by the language in the same scene in *True Tragedy*. Churchill remarked that "The agreement between these two passages and especially the agreement between the two speeches of Rivers, is far closer than the agreement of either scene with the chronicle" (505).

9. In both plays, the plan to separate Prince Edward from his kinsmen on their trip to London originates with Buckingham (*True Tragedy* 409–13; *Richard III* II.ii.146–50). However, in the only mention of this detail in the chronicles (More, copied by Hall), it is Hastings, Buckingham and Richard who are responsible for the scheme.

10. The scene in which the Queen is informed of her relatives' imprisonment is dramatized similarly in both plays. The stage direction, "Enter a messenger," is identical. In *True Tragedy*, the dialogue proceeds:

| | |
|---|---|
| *York.* | What art thou that with thy ghastly looks presseth in- |
| | to sanctuary, to affright our mother Queene. |
| *Messen.* | A sweet Princes, doth my countenance bewray me? |
| | My newes is doubtfull and heavie.          *True Tragedy* 813–16 |

In *Richard III*:

| | |
|---|---|
| *Arch.* | Here comes a messenger. What news? |
| *Mess.* | Such news, my lord, as grieves me to report. |
| | *Richard III* II.iv.38–9 |

11.  The responses to young Prince Edward's reaction to the arrest of Lord Rivers and Lord Grey are similar in the two plays. In *Richard III* (III.i.1–16) Prince Edward expresses sadness and frustration that his uncles are not in London to welcome him. In *True Tragedy* (747–76), his complaint is more extensive and pointed. In both plays, he protests that Lord Grey, in particular, is innocent of wrongdoing. In *True Tragedy*, Richard responds by suggesting that what has taken place is "too subtil for babes," and that the Prince is a child and being used as such. In *Richard III*, Richard responds similarly to the effect that the Prince is too young and inexperienced to understand the duplicity of dangerous men. In the only chronicle that mentions any response to the Prince's remarks, Hall merely notes that Buckingham, not Richard, tells the Prince that his uncles have concealed their actions from him (Churchill 506).

12.  At the same place in the action in both plays, after the execution of Rivers, Grey and Vaughan, and just prior to the condemnation of Hastings, Richard makes a similar observation about his rising late, and then adds a distinctive remark. In *True Tragedy* he says:

| | |
|---|---|
| *Richard.* | Go to no more ado Catesby, they say I have bin a long |
| | sleeper to day, but ile be awake anon to some of their costs. |
| | *True Tragedy* 925–6 |

In *Richard III*, he says:

| | |
|---|---|
| *Glou.* | My noble lords and cousins all, good morrow: |
| | I have been long a sleeper; but I trust |
| | My absence doth neglect no great design, |
| | Which by my presence might have been concluded. |
| | *Richard III* III.iv.22–5 |

More and Hall use the identical language to describe this scene: "These lords so sitting together communing of this matter, the protector came in among them, first about nine of the clock, saluting them courteously, and excusing himself that he had been from them so long, saying merely that he had been a sleeper [More writes "a slepe"] that day." In both plays, the dramatist took two separated and unrelated words, "long" and "sleeper," and combined them into a distinctive phrase. In both, he then added a remark by Richard that neither occurs, nor is implied in any of the chronicles. In *True Tragedy* it is a veiled threat; in *Richard III* it is facetious, if not sarcastic.

13.  In both plays, the author uses an identical dramatic device to reveal that Richard is being called "King" even before Prince Edward's planned coronation. In *True Tragedy*, Prince Edward (whom the playwright has identified as King since the death of his father) asks Myles Forest who was given the keys to the Tower:

| | |
|---|---|
| Forest. | My Lord, it was one that was appointed by the King |
| | to be an ayde to sir Thomas Brokenbury. |
| King. | Did the King, why Myles Forest, am not I King? |
| Forest. | I would have said, my Lord, your unckle the Protector. |

*True Tragedy* 1271–74

In *Richard III*, Shakespeare uses the same slip of the tongue for the same purpose, except that the exchange is between Brakenbury, the Keeper of the Tower, and Queen Elizabeth. Brakenbury refuses to allow her to visit her two sons, saying:

| | |
|---|---|
| Brak. | I may not suffer you to visit them, |
| | The King hath strictly charg'd the contrary. |
| Q. Eliz. | The King? who's that? |
| Brak. | I mean the Lord Protector.          *Richard III* IV.i.16–19 |

14.  In scene iv of *True Tragedy*, Richard muses upon the prospect of wearing the crown:

| | |
|---|---|
| Richard. | Why so, now fortune make me a King, Fortune give |
| | me a kingdome, let the world report the Duke of Gloster was a |
| | King, therefore Fortune make me King, if I be but King for a |
| | yeare, nay but halfe a yeare, nay a moneth, a weeke, three dayse, |
| | one day, or halfe a day, nay an houre, swoundes half an houre, nay |

sweete Fortune, clap but the Crowne on my head, that the vassals may but once say, God save King *Richard's* life, it is inough.

*True Tragedy* 443–49

As he ascends the throne in the canonical play, Richard says:

K. Rich.                              Thus high, by thy advice

And thy assistance, is King Richard seated;

But shall we wear these glories for a day?

Or shall they last, and we rejoice in them?

*Richard III* IV.ii.3–6

Although Shakespeare eschews the bombast, he includes a similar reflection on the transitory nature of the kingship. It need hardly be noted that there are no such musings in any of the sources.

15.  Identical distinctive phrases are used several times in both plays. In *True Tragedy* two different characters use the phrase "in good time" in connection with the entrance of another person (700, 1581). In *Richard III*, Shakespeare uses the same phrase four times in the same context, in three of them followed by the words "here comes the" (II.i.45, III.i.24, III.i.95), and in the fourth by the words "here the Lieutenant comes" (IV.i.12). Churchill adds the information that the phrase "in good time" does not occur in the plays of Peele or Greene, and only once, in a different context, in the entire Marlowe canon (524). The playwright of *True Tragedy* uses "no doubt" and "undoubtedly" ten times. Shakespeare uses the same words fifteen times in *Richard III*, but only eleven times in the balance of the canon (Churchill 523).

16.  In *True Tragedy*, Richard says to Sir Francis Lovell, "...keep silence, villaine, least I by poste do send thy soule to hell" (1928–9). In *Richard III*, referring to his sickly brother Edward IV, and his other brother George, he says "He cannot live, I hope, and must not die / Till George be pack'd with post-horse up to Heaven." (I.i.145–6) This unusual, and now obsolete, use of the verb "to post," meaning "to transport a person swiftly," was not elsewhere recorded in English before it appeared in *Cymbeline* (II.iv.27) in the First Folio (*OED* post, v.2 II.7).

17.  In his death-bed scene in *True Tragedy*, King Edward IV uses the word "Redeemer" (187). In *Richard III*, he uses the same word twice in the

same scene (II.i.4 and 124), but it is used nowhere else in the entire canon.

## SIMILARITIES IN THE FINAL SCENES OF BOTH PLAYS

It is in the last act of *Richard III*, and in the corresponding last four scenes of *True Tragedy*, that the major concurrences between the two plays occur. The first appearance of Henry Tudor, second Earl of Richmond, is strikingly similar in both plays. He enters at scene xv in *True Tragedy* and at V.ii in *Richard III*—in the former accompanied by Sir James Blount, Peter Landois, and the Earl of Oxford, and in the latter by Blount, Oxford, Sir Walter Herbert and unnamed others. In both cases, he has been marching nearly two weeks since his landing in Wales, and is within a day or two of engaging Richard's army at Bosworth. His opening words to his company in each play sound the same themes and use many of the same words:

*Richmond.*     Welcome deare *friends* and *loving* country-men,

Welcome I say to Englands blissfull *Ile*,

Whose forwardnesse I cannot but commend,

That thus do aide us in our enterprise,

My right it is, and sole inheritance,

And Richard but *usurps* in my authoritie,

For in his *tyrannie* he slaughtered those

That would not succour him in his attempts,

Whose guiltlesse *blood* craves daily at *Gods* hands,

Revenge for outrage done to their harmlesse lives;

Then *courage* countrymen, and never be dismayd,

Our quarels good, and *God* will helpe the right,

For we may know by dangers we have past,

That *God* no doubt will give us victorie.

*True Tragedy* 1640–53 (emphasis added)

*Richm.*     Fellows in arms, and my most *loving friends*

Bruis'd underneath the yoke of *tyranny*,

Thus far into the bowels of the land,

Have we march'd on without impediment;

And here receive we from our father Stanley

Lines of fair comfort and *encouragement.*

The wretched, *bloody*, and *usurping* boar,

That spoil'd your summer fields and fruitful vines,

Swills your warm *blood* like wash and makes his trough

In your embowell'd bosoms—this foul swine

Is now even in the centry of this *isle,*

Near to the town of Leicester, as we learn.

From Tamworth thither is but one day's march.

In *Gods* name cheerly on, *courageous friends,*

To reap the harvest of perpetual peace

By this one *bloody* trial of sharp war.

*Richard III* V.ii.1–16 (emphasis added)

Although these words appear in the chronicle accounts of Richmond's oration to his troops, the identical time and location of the speech, the same number and nearly identical characters present, and the similar language all suggest that Shakespeare used the scene in *True Tragedy* as the model for the scene in *Richard III.* Furthermore, in both plays this opening speech of Richmond's is immediately followed by supportive remarks by the Earl of Oxford and then by Sir James Blount. Although it is known that Oxford and Blount accompanied Richmond, neither is mentioned by any chronicler in the account of the invasion, except for Richmond's assignment of Oxford, on the morning of the battle of Bosworth, to command the archers. In fact, all the chronicles name half-a-dozen other men as prominent in Richmond's campaign. Thus, the presence of these particular men with Richmond at his entrance, and their responses to his speech are peculiar to the two plays.

The well-known scene in Act V of *Richard III,* in which Richard is visited by the ghosts of those he has murdered, is another example of Shakespeare's extension and elaboration of a device first used in *True Tragedy.* It is true that ghosts appeared in other Elizabethan plays, notably in *Locrine, The Spanish Tragedy, The Misfortunes of Arthur* and *James IV,* all of which, according to the orthodox chronology, pre-dated *Richard III.*[7] But in this case, the particular ghost of Clarence that appeared in *True Tragedy* also appears (among others) in Shakespeare's play. Although Richard's disturbing dreams are mentioned in the chronicles, no ghosts appear in any of them. The chronicles refer to "horrible images" of "evil sprites" (Churchill 151) and "terrible devils" (Hall, quoted in Bullough, *Narrative* 3:291) that frighten Richard—but no ghosts. Furthermore, Clarence's ghost does not merely frighten Richard in *True*

*Tragedy,* he clamors for revenge (4–5, 53–5), and in *Richard III* demands that Richard "despair and die" (V.iii.136). In Shakespeare's revision, the same imprecation is repeated by each of the nine other ghosts. As Churchill wrote, "It is not likely that the two [playwrights] hit upon the idea independently" (514).

In his soliloquy in each play, Richard expresses the same fears that the "ghosts" or "souls" of those he has murdered will exact revenge or vengeance upon him. In *True Tragedy*:

| | |
|---|---|
| *Richard.* | Meethinks their ghoasts comes gaping for revenge, |
| | Whom I have slaine in reaching for a Crowne, |
| | Clarence complaines, and crieth for revenge. |
| | My nephues bloods, Revenge, revenge, doth crie. |
| | The headlesse Peeres comes preasing for revenge. |
| | And every one cries, let the tyrant die.          *True Tragedy* 1880–5 |

In *Richard III,* after all ten ghosts have spoken to him, Richard says:

| | |
|---|---|
| *K. Rich.* | Methought the souls of all that I had murther'd |
| | Came to my tent, and every one did threat |
| | Tomorrow's vengeance on the head of Richard. |
| | *Richard III* V.iii.204–6 |

Just a few lines later, when Richard describes his "fearful dream" to Ratcliffe, he uses familiar Shakespearean imagery:

| | |
|---|---|
| *K. Rich.* | By the apostle Paul, shadows to-night |
| | Have stroock more terror to the soul of Richard |
| | Than can the substance of ten thousand soldiers |
| | Armed in proof and led by shallow Richmond. |
| | *Richard III* V.iii.216–19 |

This is clearly an echo of his line "Tush, a shadow without a substance" in *True Tragedy* (468)—where he uses the same imagery in a similar context of threatening troops.

Richard's final speech on the field of Bosworth is the most obvious example of Shakespeare's use of ideas from *True Tragedy.* In this case, he improved greatly on Richard's opening line, in which he calls for a horse—turning it into one of the most memorable in the entire canon. Richard's last words in *True Tragedy,* here converted into verse from the prose of the Quarto, remind us of the Shakespeare we know, and this passage, except for the jarring first line, is probably the finest in the play:

| | |
|---|---|
| *King.* | A horse, a horse, a fresh horse. |
| *Page* | A flie my Lord, and save your life. |
| *King.* | Flie villaine, look I as tho I would fly, no first shall |
| | this dull and sencelesse ball of earth receive my bodie cold and |
| | void of sence, you watry heavens rowle on my gloomy day, and |
| | darksome cloudes close up my cheerfull sownde, downe is thy |
| | sunne Richard, never to shine againe, the birdes, whose feathers |
| | should adorne my head, hover aloft & dares not come in sight, |
| | yet faint not man, for this day, if Fortune will, shall make thee |
| | King possest with quiet Crown, if Fates deny, this ground must |
| | be my grave, yet golden thoughts that reachéd for a Crowne, |
| | danted before by Fortunes cruell spight, are come as comforts |
| | to my drooping heart, and bids me keepe my crowne and die |
| | a King. These are my last, what more I have to say ile make re- |
| | port among the damned soules.      *True Tragedy* 1985–99 |

The passage in *Richard III*:

| | |
|---|---|
| *K. Rich.* | A horse, a horse! my kingdom for a horse! |
| *Cate.* | Withdraw, my Lord. I'll help you to a horse. |
| *K. Rich.* | Slave, I have set my life upon a cast, |
| | And I will stand the hazard of the die. |
| | I think there be six Richmonds in the field; |
| | Five have I slain today instead of him. |
| | A horse, a horse! my kingdom for a horse.  *Richard III* V.iv.7–13 |

In both plays, it is the same cry for a horse, the same admonition to flee, the same curt rebuff, and the same declaration by Richard that he will accept the outcome of the gamble he has made. There are no such details and no such dialogue in the sources. The import and the language of the scene in *Richard III* are obviously drawn from the anonymous play. In Shakespeare's revision, Richard indulges in no further rhetoric, perhaps because he has already, two scenes earlier, announced to his company that if he is the loser his next destination will be hell:

| K. Rich. | March on, join bravely, let us to it pell-mell; |
| | If not to heaven, then hand in hand to hell. |
| | *Richard III* V.iii.312–13 |

This echoes his last words in *True Tragedy*:

| King. | These are my last, what more I have to say Ile make re- |
| | port among the damned souls.          *True Tragedy* 1998–9 |

Finally, even in the manner of Richard's death, Shakespeare has carried over the dramatic detail that he introduced in *True Tragedy*. In both plays, the Earl of Richmond personally slays Richard, a detail contrary to all the sources, which uniformly report that Richard died in the general fighting. As John Jowett, the play's editor, remarked, "The single combat, found also in *True Tragedy*, is a fiction" (354).

At the conclusion of his summary of more than thirty similarities between the two plays, only some of which have been listed here, Churchill wrote: "I have endeavored to include every case in which a careful examination discovered a resemblance that cannot be accounted for by the common chronicle source of the two plays" (524). Thus, the argument is reasonable that Shakespeare borrowed liberally from *True Tragedy* in terms of structure, incident, style and vocabulary. While he might have seen a manuscript, or even a performance, of *True Tragedy* before its printing in 1594, the strongest inference from such borrowing is that he was its author.

Despite his extraordinary interest in *True Tragedy* and his comprehensive effort to elucidate it, Churchill devoted only three sentences to the identity of its author. The first sums up his attitude: "The question is of so dark a nature that the most careful investigation yields no satisfactory result" (528). One may think that a question "of so dark a nature" would attract the attention and scrutiny of numerous scholars. But even though Churchill detailed these extensive borrowings by Shakespeare more than a century ago, Shakespearean scholars have ignored or dismissed them as non-existent or trivial ever since. John Dover Wilson even suggested that the obvious similarities between the two plays meant that each was based on the same lost play on the same subject by a third author ("Shakespeare's *Richard IIII*" 306). But it is unnecessary to imagine an *Ur-Richard III* to account for two existing plays about Richard III with such remarkable similarities. To imagine a nonexistent play, and two unknown dramatists, does violence to common sense. The evidence for Shakespeare's authorship of both plays is a better solution.

# True Tragedy *and Other Canonical Plays*

The earlier and anonymous *True Tragedy* shares numerous stylistic and lexical characteristics with canonical Shakespeare plays, especially the early ones. Perhaps the most well-known and well-established feature of Shakespeare's writing is his verbal inventiveness. He is credited in the *Oxford English Dictionary* with the introduction to the language of slightly over 2000 new words or new usages (Schäfer 83), an average of about fifty per play. The author of *True Tragedy* displayed the same type of creativity. As many as eighty words and usages found in the play are described by the *OED* as first used by Shakespeare (forty), or other writers in 1594, or later. For example, the following dozen words, in their particular meanings in *True Tragedy*, are not recorded elsewhere by the *OED* until the seventeenth century: *bloodsucker, brambles, enchased, fruitful, huffer, jostle, regard, ringleader, second sight, twil, uncouth* and *wounded*. At least seven usages in the play have not yet been defined by the *OED*.

John Dover Wilson identified as "very common in Shakespeare" the use of the word "even" for emphasis at the beginning of a line (ed. *Titus* xxi), such as "Even for his sake am I pitiless" in *Titus Andronicus* (II.i.162). He cited six other examples from the play, as well as three from other plays. *True Tragedy* contains several similar formulations, such as "Farewell, even the woorst guest that ever came to my / house" (580–1) and "even from this daunger is / George Standley come" (2142–3).

David Lake, in his study of Thomas Middleton and Shakespeare, wrote: "Through all his work, Shakespeare prefers *them* to 'em and *hath* to *has*; he makes very little use of *I'm* (only five authentic instances outside *Timon*) or of *'Has* for *he has* (14 authentic instances outside *Timon*)" (281). These same preferences are obvious in *True Tragedy*: *them* occurs sixty-three times, 'em never; *hath* eighty-two times, *has* three (and *hast* nine). Neither *I'm* nor *'Has* for *he has* occurs at all.

In *The authorship of Shakespeare's plays*, Jonathan Hope counted the incidence of all forms of the words *thou, thy, thine* and *thee* in the plays of Shakespeare, and compiled an index that reflected their use in each play. For the nine history plays (excepting the late *Henry VIII*), the average index is fourteen (61–3). A similar calculation for *True Tragedy* reveals an index of fifteen.

In its use of words with the "venge" root, *True Tragedy* conforms with the other early Shakespeare plays in which revenge is an important motif. In *Titus Andronicus*, there are forty-three such words; in *3 Henry VI*, twenty-three; in *Richard III*, twenty; and in *True Tragedy*, twenty-nine. The phrase "Lord Protector over the realm" in the first scene of *True Tragedy* occurs again six times in the three *Henry VI* plays.

As mentioned above, in scene iv of *True Tragedy* Richard says, "Tush a shadow without a substance, and a fear with-out a cause" (468–9). The following examples attest to the dramatist's liking for the formulation: "he takes false shadows for true substances" (*Titus Andronicus* III.ii.80); "Each substance of a grief hath twenty shadows" (*Richard II* II.ii.14); "the very substance of the ambitious is merely the shadow of a dream" (*Hamlet* II.ii.257–9); "For since the substance of your perfect self is else devoted, I am but a shadow" (*Two Gentlemen of Verona* IV.ii.123–4).

The phrase "ruine and decaie" in scene iii of *True Tragedy* (268) is a favorite phrase of Shakespeare's. As noted in Chapter I, the phrase is used in *Famous Victories*, and again in *Richard II* (III.ii.102) and *Richard III* (IV.iv.409).

Jane Shore's question about a name in *True Tragedy*, "O Fortune, wherefore wert thou called Fortune?" (195) is echoed in a similar context by Juliet: "O Romeo, Romeo, wherefore art thou Romeo?" (*Romeo and Juliet* II.ii.33).

In *True Tragedy*, the word "latest" is used twice to mean "last" in the context of dying: "Outrageous Richard breathed his latest breath" (32) and "sweete death, my latest friend" (1976). This usage is echoed in both 3 *Henry VI*: "breath'd his latest gasp" (II.i.108), and in 2 *Henry IV*: "And hear, I think, the very latest counsel / That I shall ever breathe" (IV.v.182–3).

In 1985, Naseeb Shaheen pointed out that a distinctive phrase in *True Tragedy* was repeated three times in two later Shakespeare plays (32–3). In scene xii, Denton, one of the princes' murderers says, "I had rather than fortie pounds I had / neer taen it in hand" (1296–7), meaning that he wished that he had never undertaken the murder even more than he wished he had forty pounds. The identical formulation in a different context occurs twice in *Twelfth Night*, once referring to the same forty pounds (V.i.177–8) and once to forty shillings (II.iii.20–1). In *The Merry Wives of Windsor*, Slender says, "I had rather than forty shillings I had my Book of Songs and Sonnets here" (I.i.198–9), a reference to Richard Tottel's collection of poems, *Tottel's Miscellany*, published in 1557.

In his analysis of *Edward III* as a Shakespeare play, Kenneth Muir considered the many examples in it of language that is paralleled in canonical Shakespeare plays. He wrote, "Of course, even if these parallels are valid, Shakespeare might conceivably be echoing and improving on a play by another dramatist, in which perhaps he had himself acted. But if this were so, it would be unique in his career...." He also referred to "Shakespeare's usual custom ... to refine on a passage he had written earlier" ("A Reconsideration" 47).

This evidence demonstrates that Shakespeare was intimately familiar with *True Tragedy*, and incorporated numerous words and phrases, stylistic elements and dramatic details—and even errors of fact—into his *Richard III*. It is also apparent that many of the words and phrases, stylistic elements, and lexical characteristics that occur in *True Tragedy* reappear throughout the Shakespeare canon, especially in the earlier plays. The conclusion can hardly be avoided that he was the author of *True Tragedy*.

## *The Two* Richard III *Plays and Edward de Vere*

Even a cursory perusal of Edward de Vere's letters and poems reveals many of the linguistic markers found in *True Tragedy*—alliteration, subject-verb disagreements, unusual words, new words, archaic words, etc. One particular example echoes the phrase "a shadow without a substance" mentioned above. In a 1581 letter, Oxford wrote, "But the world is so cunning as of a shadow they can make a substance, and of a likelihood a truth" (Chiljan, *Letters* 32). Another example from *True Tragedy* is Jane Shore's remark about her husband's reaction to her relationship with Edward IV: "yea, my owne husband knew / of my breach of disloyaltie, and yet suffered me, by reason hee / knew it bootlesse to kicke against the pricke" (1023–5). Writing from Siena in 1576, Oxford resorted to Italian to express his frustration: "…and for every step of mine a block is found to be laid in my way, I see it is but vain, *calcitrare contra li busi*…" (Chiljan, *Letters* 23), literally "to kick against blows."

Certain external evidence supports the association of *True Tragedy* with Shakespeare and with Edward de Vere. Between 1594 and 1612, its printer and publisher, Thomas Creede, printed *Richard III* four times, as well as four other Shakespeare plays, three of which bore no author's name. (He also printed two non–Shakespearean plays—*Locrine* (1595) and *The London Prodigal* (1605) with Shakespeare's name or initials on them.)[8] During the 1590s, he printed or registered nine plays that were clearly or probably the property of the Queen's Men, the playing company named on the title page of *True Tragedy* (Pinciss 323). The Queen's Men company is well-known for its alleged association with Shakespeare and his plays.

### THE THIRTEENTH EARL

The most convincing evidence of Oxford's authorship of *True Tragedy* is found in the portrayal of the historical John de Vere, thirteenth Earl of Oxford, as the future Henry VII's principal supporter in the play. It is well known that the thirteenth Earl was one of the leading Lancastrian noblemen who fought on the side of Henry VI against the Yorkists. After years of opposition, he was finally captured, attainted and then imprisoned at Hammes Castle near Calais for more than ten years until he escaped in late 1484, assisted by his jailer,

Sir James Blount (Seward, *Wars* 216, 297). Oxford and Blount joined Henry Tudor, Earl of Richmond, in France, and accompanied him on his invasion of England in August 1485. Oxford commanded the forward troop of archers at Bosworth, and was later rewarded handsomely by the victorious Henry VII.

Several of the chronicles describe the thirteenth Earl as a leading supporter and close friend of Henry Tudor. But they do not mention him in connection with Henry's invasion until the actual Battle of Bosworth, when Henry gave him his command. However, in each of the three scenes in which Henry Tudor appears, the author of *True Tragedy* has placed the Earl of Oxford at his right hand, and made him the leading spokesman for his supporters. In the play, Richard III himself speaks of Oxford, something that is not recorded in the chronicles. Here is his reaction when he is told that Oxford and Blount have escaped their prison in France and joined the Earl of Richmond:

*King.*          Messenger staie, hath Blunt betraid, doth Oxford re-

bel and aide the Earle Richmond, may this be true, what is our

prison so weake, our friends so fickle, our Ports so ill lookt too,

that they may passe and repasse the seas at their pleasures, then

everie one conspires, spoyles our Conflex, conqueres our Ca-

stles, and Armes themselves with their own weapons, unresi-

sted? O villaines, rebels, fugetives, theeves, how are we betrayd,

when our own swoords shall beate us, and our own subiects

seekes the subvertion of the state, the fall of their Prince, and

sack of their country, of his, nay, neither must nor shall, for I will

Army with my friends, and cut off my enemies, & beard them

to their face that dares me, and but one, I one, one beyond the

seas that troubles me: wel, his power is weak, & we are strong,

therfore I will meet him with such melodie, that the singing of a

bullet shall send him merily to his longest home. Come folow me

                                                          *True Tragedy* 1624–38

It is after this speech at the end of scene xiv that the future Henry VII strides onto the stage for his first appearance in *True Tragedy*. It is the Earl of Oxford and Sir James Blount who accompany him, just as they do in *Richard III*. But thereafter, the two plays diverge, Oxford's significant role in *True Tragedy* being reduced to only two lines in *Richard III* (V.ii.17–18). After Henry's opening speech in *True Tragedy*, it is the Earl of Oxford who responds first with assurances that he will fight for his "cousin Richmond" until he is crowned King. After Henry promises to root out corruption and tyranny if he is successful, it is the Earl of Oxford who replies again that he will not be frightened or deterred by the vicious acts of Richard. And in the last scene of the play, after Richard has been slain, it is the Earl of Oxford who vows "perpetuall love" to Henry and showers him with compliments, while making references to Cicero, Caesar, Hector and Troy. Finally, after Thomas Stanley presents the crown of England to his stepson, Henry, it is the Earl of Oxford who shouts, "Henry the seventh, by the grace of God, King of Eng- / land, France, and Lord of *Ireland*; God save the King" (2094–5), a proclamation repeated by the rest of the cast.

In another instance, the playwright of *True Tragedy* emphasizes the closeness of the two men by giving to Oxford the role of gently chiding Richmond for his unexplained disappearance two nights before the Battle of Bosworth. The chronicles report that Richmond became separated from his army in the darkness, and found himself alone and unable to locate any of his soldiers. He spent the night incognito in a small village, and by good luck found his army early the next morning. He explained his mysterious absence to his greatly-relieved officers with a story about visiting some "prevy frendes and secret alies" (Bullough, *Narrative* 3:290). No other person is mentioned in connection with this incident. But in scene xvi of *True Tragedy*, when only Oxford and Richmond are on stage, Oxford remarks:

*Oxford.*    Good my Lord have a care of your self, I like not these
        night walkes and scouting abroad in the evenings so disguised,
        for you must not now that you are in the usurpers dominions,
        and you are the onely marke he aimes at, and your last nights
        absence bred such amazement in our souldiers, that they like
        men wanting the power to follow Armes, were on a sodaine
        more liker to flie then to fight ...        *True Tragedy* 1810–16

Richmond responds by repeating his affection for Oxford and asking him to excuse his behavior. There is no historical basis for Oxford's role in this dialogue; it has been arbitrarily assigned to him by the playwright.

In all, the thirteenth Earl of Oxford speaks forty lines in *True Tragedy*, a larger role than any Earl of Oxford has in any Elizabethan play. He is repeatedly referred to in such laudatory terms as "good Oxford," "the valiant Earl of Oxford," "this brave Earl." When Henry assigns the Earl his position at the Battle of Bosworth, he addresses him as "my Lord of Oxford, you as our second self." After the battle, the victorious Henry, after thanking "his Deitie," says, "woorthy Oxford for thy / service showne in hote encountring of the enemy, Earle Rich- / mond bindes himselfe in lasting bondes of faithfull love & per- / fect unitie" (2039–42). Except for the reference to him on the night before the Battle of Bosworth, none of this is reported in the chronicles. It has all been inserted by the anonymous author.

A reasonable explanation for this anomaly is that the author of *True Tragedy* was one of the thirteenth Earl's successors to the Oxford Earldom— one who was known as both a poet and a playwright. Edward de Vere's keen interest in history, both ancient and recent, was noted by others when he was no older than fourteen.[9] The most obvious historical sources for the play— the chronicles of Polydore Vergil, Edward Hall and John Hardyng, as well as several others—appear on a list of volumes in Sir Thomas Smith's library made in 1566, only a few years after de Vere's residence in his household (Strype 276–7). If de Vere were the author, he would have been in an ideal position to make use of family records or an oral tradition to dramatize the role of the thirteenth Earl in the series of events that put the first Tudor on the throne of England. A story of such importance, only eighty to ninety years in the past, might still be remembered and repeated by people in his household at Hedingham Castle, or in his circle of acquaintances, who had known the participants.[10] Besides the fact that the thirteenth Earl himself lived until 1513, well within the lifetime of someone alive in 1560, there is further reason to believe that those living in and around Hedingham Castle would have had a particular interest in the doings of Richard III.

In 1471, after the disastrous Battle of Barnet, in which Edward IV defeated the forces of Henry VI, John de Vere, the twenty-eight-year-old thirteenth Earl of Oxford, fled to Scotland and then to France. His mother, Elizabeth, the widow of the executed twelfth Earl, was confined by Edward IV to Bromley Prior at Stratford-le-bowe, outside London. Edward then granted all of John de Vere's property, including Hedingham Castle, to his own brother Richard Plantagenet, later Richard III. The following year, Richard's henchmen kidnapped the dowager Countess Elizabeth and bullied her into signing over to him all the real property she held in her own name, including the manor at Wivenhoe (Seward, *Wars* 216–17). After Henry Tudor's capture of the throne in 1485, the property of the thirteenth Earl was restored to him by Act of Parliament, but it took another ten years and another Act before he obtained return of his mother's property. The dramatic story of the loss of all the de Vere holdings to Richard Plantagenet, and the heroic acts that led to their restoration, would have been routinely told in the de Vere household throughout the sixteenth century.

In the canonical *Richard III*, the thirteenth Earl of Oxford is a member of the cast, but speaks only two lines (V.ii.17–18), which are attributed to him only in the Folio version.[11] We can only guess that de Vere reduced his ancestor's role so drastically in his revision for the same reason that he chose to conceal himself behind a pseudonym for the rest of his life. But as a young man, especially one so recently bereft of his father, he might have had an understandable urge to draw attention to the deeds of one of his most heroic ancestors.

## THE STANLEY FAMILY EPISODE

Further evidence of Oxford's authorship of both plays is the depiction of the role of the wealthy and prominent Stanley family in the last year of Richard's reign. Both playwrights depart in similar ways from the relevant chronicle accounts, and emphasize the Stanleys' contribution to the defeat of Richard III.

In late spring of 1483, Richard Plantagenet completed his seizure of the throne and was crowned early in July. After an aborted invasion of England later in the year, Henry Tudor retreated to Brittany, and to France the next year, where he began gathering support for another invasion. Late in 1484, the thirteenth Earl and James Blount made their escape from Hammes Castle and joined Henry's nascent Tudor court at Montargis in the Loire Valley (Seward, *Wars* 297). Ironically, Richard's seizure of the crown, and the subsequent alienation of many Yorkists who had supported his brother Edward, led to Oxford's escape. According to a Burgundian chronicler, Jean Molinet, it was Thomas, Lord Stanley, who persuaded Blount to transfer his allegiance to Henry Tudor and to flee Hammes Castle with Oxford.[12] Oxford's reputation, military experience and lengthy opposition to the Yorkists made him a welcome addition to Henry's cause.

In the meantime, Thomas Stanley remained at the English court, where Richard had appointed him High Constable of England late in 1483. Despite this, Richard was suspicious of Stanley because, a dozen years earlier, he had married Margaret Beaufort, the widow of the Henry Tudor's father, and was thus Henry's stepfather. This affinity would have given Stanley ample reason to support him and to facilitate Oxford's escape. The chronicles report that in the summer of 1485, when Stanley asked Richard if he might travel to his property to visit his family (but actually to prepare to support Richmond's invasion), Richard refused to allow him to go unless he left his son George in court as a hostage.

In both plays, this scene is dramatized similarly, beginning with Richard's greeting of Stanley with the phrase "What news?" In both plays, Stanley answers ambiguously. In *True Tragedy*, Richard persists with questions about Richmond's plans and his strength—to which Stanley replies that he knows nothing. Richard becomes sarcastic:

King.        Oh, good wordes Lord Standley, but give

             me leave to gleane out of your golden field of eloquence, how

             brave you pleade ignorance, as though you knew not of your

             sonnes departure into *Brittaine* out of England.

                                                  *True Tragedy* 1515–18

To Stanley's ambiguous answer in *Richard III*, King Richard replies sarcastically:

K. Rich.     Hoyday, a riddle! Neither good nor bad

             What need'st thou run so many miles about,

             When thou mayst tell thy tale the nearest way?

             Once more, what news?          *Richard III* IV.iv.459–62

In both plays, Stanley acknowledges that Richmond is invading England to claim the throne, but protests that he is prepared to fight on Richard's side. Richard replies that Stanley intends to fight for Richmond, and that he does not trust him. He expands on his suspicions about Stanley and says that he will not let him go. But then, in both plays, after Richard has decided against Stanley's leaving, he changes his mind and agrees to let him go, on the condition that he leave his son George as a hostage. Neither Richard's surly rejection of Stanley's assurances, nor his change of mind are supported in the chronicles.

Both Thomas Stanley and his brother William were present in the vicinity of Bosworth in the days before the battle, each with his own cadre of troops. The sources agree that Thomas Stanley wanted to aid his stepson, the Earl of Richmond, against Richard, but was unable to do so openly for fear of the execution of his son George. They report that Stanley and Richmond met in secret before the battle, but say nothing about what they agreed to. Churchill listed several details that were added to the dramatization of this meeting in both plays (514). In one instance, Stanley hurries his answer to Richmond's greeting, saying "to come briefly to the purpose" in *True Tragedy* (1828) and "In brief" in *Richard III* (V.iii.87). In both plays, Stanley describes his son George similarly—as "tender George" in *Richard III* (V.iii.95), and as "being yoong and a grissell" (a young or delicate person) in *True Tragedy* (1848). In fact, George Stanley was a married man of about twenty-five at the time, and had taken his seat in the House of Lords as Lord Strange three years earlier (Tait 28). In both plays, Stanley uses the phrase "I cannot" to say that for fear of his son's life he is unable to openly assist Richmond. In both plays, he says that he will deceive Richard into thinking that he is fighting on his side. In both plays, Thomas Stanley travels to Richmond's camp, the meeting takes place at night, and Stanley warns Richmond to be prepared for battle the next day. The chronicles report that Richmond travelled to Stanley's camp, and that the meeting took place during the day, but are silent about the other details.

With respect to the fate of George Stanley, both plays reflect the outcome reported in the sources. On hearing that Thomas Stanley refused to join him, Richard ordered George beheaded. But his followers urged a delay on the grounds that attention was needed to the battle at hand. George survived and was eventually reunited with his father.

Finally, in the treatment of the Battle of Bosworth itself, both playwrights depart from the chronicle accounts in the same way: "In the chronicles Richard is shown winning even the hand-to-hand struggle with Richmond, until Stanley's forces turn the tide. On stage Richard is shown losing the battle before he meets Richmond" (Gurr, "Richard III" 44–5), just as in *True Tragedy*. In *Richard III*, Shakespeare has Stanley plucking the crown "from the dead temples of this bloody wretch" (V.v.5) before placing it on his stepson's head, a detail absent from the chronicles and from *True Tragedy*. Lastly, as Andrew Gurr adds, Shakespeare omits the role of Thomas's brother, Sir William Stanley, who intervenes, according to the chronicles, with "three thousand tall men" to win the battle for Richmond at the last minute ("Richard III" 44). The same omission occurs in *True Tragedy*. In fact, Sir William Stanley's name does not appear at all in either play, except in a list of "men of name" in IV.v of *Richard III*.

Thus, both playwrights have modified and embellished the chronicle accounts of the role of the Stanley family in the overthrow of Richard III. Several scholars have noted this, and have also pointed to Shakespeare's favorable treatment of the Stanleys in all three parts of *Henry VI* (Gurr, *Playing Companies* 262; Lefranc 156–74). In his *Lost Years*, E. A. J. Honigmann suggests that in *Richard III* Shakespeare was honoring Ferdinando Stanley, Lord Strange, the fifth Earl of Derby, a noted lover of poetry and drama and, from the late 1570s, the patron of Strange's Men. He was also blood-related to Queen Elizabeth on both sides of his family. Honigmann speculates that since "in all probability" Shakespeare was a member of Strange's Men in 1591, the alleged composition date of *Richard III*, this was a deliberate attempt to curry favor with him (*Lost Years* 63–4). But Oxford wrote *True Tragedy* and the *Henry VI–Richard III* tetralogy some years before Ferdinando Stanley took over Strange's Men, so it is more likely that he was honoring Henry Stanley, fourth Earl of Derby, who lived until 1593. It appears that Oxford conflated the actions of the two Stanley brothers, especially the parts they played during the Battle of Bosworth, so as to focus credit on Thomas, whom Henry VII created Earl of Derby just weeks later, and who was the direct ancestor of the current Earl.[13]

Even as he elevated their importance and exaggerated their merit in four different plays, Oxford had good reason to be grateful to the Stanleys, and so did Queen Elizabeth. Except for the intervention of Thomas Stanley in 1484, the thirteenth Earl might have remained confined in Hammes Castle and Henry Tudor's invasion might have faltered. Similarly, except for Sir William Stanley's last-minute support of Henry Tudor at Bosworth, it is likely that Richard would have prevailed. This is further evidence that the seventeenth Earl of Oxford was the author of the Shakespeare canon. Absent these actions by the Stanleys, the thirteenth Earl might have died in prison or fallen at Bosworth. If either Stanley had not acted as he did, it is likely that the Oxford Earldom would have been extinguished, and there would have been no Tudor dynasty.

## Dates of the Two Richard III Plays

### THE DATE OF TRUE TRAGEDY

E. A. J. Honigmann ("Shakespeare's 'Lost Source Plays'" 304–5) and Anthony Hammond (83) date True Tragedy later than Richard III, but nearly all other modern editors and scholars agree that although Richard III might have been written as early as 1591, True Tragedy was the earlier composition.[14] Besides the ample evidence for an early date, the versification, plotting, and wealth of imagery and characterization in Richard III are so superior that it is impossible to imagine a dramatist, after reading it, producing a manuscript on the same subject and with the same title, without including a great deal more of Shakespeare's language and imagery.

The evidence for a date consists of several topical references in the play, as well as certain stylistic elements and dramatic devices. The most significant topical references occur in the last scene, which ends with a wooden description of the deeds of Henry VII, followed by those of Henry VIII, Edward VI and Mary Tudor. The final words in the play are a twenty-five-line encomium to Queen Elizabeth that appears to have been written for direct delivery to her from the stage. It begins with general words of praise about her "wise life" and "civil government," which are followed by the lines:

> And she hath put proud Antichrist to flight,
>
> And bene the meanes that civill wars did cease.

True Tragedy 2204–5

It was commonplace for the Protestants of Elizabethan England to refer to Catholic nations and their rulers, among all other things Catholic, as the Antichrist. E. K. Chambers suggested that the line about the Antichrist "may pass for … a mention" of England's victory over the Spanish Armada in 1588.[15] However, the playwright had, in a previous passage, already mentioned the leading Catholic monarch in Europe, and the instigator of the Armada, King Philip II of Spain, and had described him merely as the husband of Queen Mary. Any reference in the immediate years after 1588 to Elizabeth's most stunning military victory would have merited more than a single line in a list of her achievements. It is more likely that these two lines refer to Elizabeth's invasion of Scotland, and the expulsion of the French forces there, in the second year of her reign.

In late 1559, Scottish Protestants began a rebellion against their French Queen Regent, Mary of Guise, mother of the sixteen-year-old Queen, Mary Stuart, then living in France with her husband King Francis II (Guy 264–5). Mary of Guise was the sister of the powerful Guise brothers, who had sent her to Scotland in her daughter's stead to govern the country while they schooled the young Mary in the elements of statecraft. As a foreign Catholic ruler in a largely Protestant country, Mary maintained a substantial cadre of French troops in and around Edinburgh Castle to protect herself. When the Scots, after several months of fighting, failed to dislodge her troops from their stronghold at Leith, the port of entry for Edinburgh, they asked for Queen Elizabeth's help.

Elizabeth hesitated at first, but then, in December 1559, sent fourteen ships into the Firth of Forth to prevent French ships from reinforcing their troops at Leith. The following March, she dispatched an army of nearly 5,000 troops across the border, under Lord William Grey, who began a prolonged siege of Leith. After an initial setback, the English prevailed, and within three months William Cecil was in Scotland negotiating the Treaty of Edinburgh, a pact that ended the civil war and expelled French troops from Scotland permanently (Guy 266; Neale 87–99). Thus, Elizabeth was aptly described as the monarch who was "the means that civil wars did cease" and who "put proud Antichrist to flight."

Another passage in the encomium reads:

> Twere vaine to tell the care this Queene hath had,
>
> In helping those that were opprest by warre,
>
> And how her Majestie hath still bene glad,
>
> When she hath heard of peace proclaim'd from far.
>
> *Ieneva*, *France*, and *Flanders*, hath set downe,
>
> The good she hath done, since she came to the Crowne.

> *True Tragedy* 2214–19

These lines appear to refer to events in the first year of the so-called "French Wars of Religion" between the French Protestant Huguenots and the Catholic government—the Royalists—that began in March 1562 and continued intermittently until 1580. For both religious and political reasons, Elizabeth supported the French Protestants against the Royalists. In the fall of 1562, she signed the secret Hampton Court Treaty with the Huguenot leader Louis de Bourbon, Prince of Condé. In it she agreed to send him 6,000 troops and loan him £30,000, in return for which the English would occupy the French ports of Le Havre and Dieppe. Within a few months, however, the Huguenots suffered several military defeats and de Bourbon was captured by Francis, Duke of Guise, leader of the Royalist forces. In February 1563, Francis himself was assassinated, and the next month the two sides agreed to a truce—the Peace of Amboise (Guy 267). The final two lines above refer to Elizabeth's policy of support for Protestants abroad, which earned her the gratitude of the Huguenots in France, the Protestants in Flanders, and the Protestant city of Geneva.

Another passage contains several traceable references:

> The Turke admires to heare her government,
>
> And babies in *Iury* [Jewry], sound her princely name.
>
> All Christian Princes to that Prince hath sent,
>
> After her rule was rumord foorth by fame.
>
> The Turke hath sworne never to lift his hand,
>
> To wrong the Princesse of this blessed land.
>
> *True Tragedy* 2208–13

Lines 1, 3 and 4 in this passage apparently refer to the greetings and congratulations sent to Elizabeth by foreign leaders at the time of her accession—"After her rule was rumord foorth by fame." The State Papers of the first six months of her reign contain records of such greetings from Henry II of France, the Holy Roman Emperor Ferdinand I, the King and Queen of Portugal, the Queen of Denmark, the King of Sweden, and many lesser notables.[16] Line 2 in this passage refers to the identification of Elizabeth at the time of her coronation as the "English Deborah"—the counterpart of the Biblical Deborah, the charismatic woman who was celebrated in the Book of Judges as the protector and preserver of the Israelites (Guy 250–1). Her accession was equated with the Israelites' victory over the idolatrous Canaanites, directed by the divinely-inspired Deborah, as recounted in Chapters four and five of the Book of Judges (Meyers 66–7).

At the time of Mary Tudor's death in 1558, the morale of the English and the fortunes of their country were at a low ebb after five years of religious turbulence and ineffective rule by the Catholic Queen Mary. The coronation of the new Queen in January 1559 was the occasion for much celebration and rejoicing by the London populace. Along the route of her coronation parade, the Queen was taken past five "pageants" or tableaux, each of which offered an encouraging, instructive or complimentary message. The final pageant depicted a robed and enthroned Queen, shaded by a palm tree and accompanied by a sign reading "Deborah the judge and restorer of Israel. Judges 4" (Arber, ed. *English* 4:386–7). This was a clear identification of Elizabeth with the Biblical Deborah, and of the English nation as the beleaguered Israelites of the Old Testament.[17] Jews were banished from England in 1290, and were nearly invisible during the sixteenth century, with only a few notable exceptions. There was no event during Elizabeth's reign that would have evoked celebration among the actual Jewish residents of England. The line clearly points to a similarity between events in England in 1558 and the story of the Biblical heroine who rallied her followers against unbelievers, and helped them unite in their practice of the true religion.

The final couplet in this passage reads:

> The Turke hath sworn never to lift his hand,
> To wrong the Princesse of this blessed land.
>
> *True Tragedy* 2212–13

This is the most difficult reference in the encomium to trace. During the Reformation, it was common for both Protestants and Catholics to refer to each other as "Turks," that is, non-believers in the true faith. Both John Wycliffe and the Pope were called "Turks" by their opponents. In the literature of the period, the term was a standard synonym for a cruel, barbarous and uncivilized person. In *1 Henry IV*, Falstaff referred to Pope Gregory VII as "Turk Gregory,"[18] In general, however, the term referred to the government of the Ottoman Empire at Constantinople, and more particularly to the head of that government—the Sultan. It is evident that this is the intended reference in the couplet.

The most notable Sultan of the sixteenth century was Suleiman I, who was called "the Magnificent" in the West, but who was also the foreign ruler most feared by "Christian Princes." In the forty years following Suleiman's accession in 1520, his Ottoman army—larger than any in the West and seemingly unstoppable—advanced deep into southeastern Europe on four different occasions, and swept aside Christian armies in the name of Islam. The major power defending Europe against the Ottoman Turks was the Holy Roman Empire, which was also carrying on an intermittent war with France. This led to an alliance of sorts between the Sultan and the King of France, an alliance that was viewed with alarm by the English (Green 151, 384–5).

In the couplet just quoted, the playwright may be referring to one of the following:

1. He may be simply repeating the sentiment previously expressed in the line "The Turk admires to hear her government," in which Sultan Suleiman seems to have sought to reassure the new Queen that he had no military designs on her country.

2. In February 1559, Suleiman and the Holy Roman Emperor, Ferdinand I, signed a three-year truce in which the latter agreed not to aid Spain against France, and to pay certain sums annually to Suleiman, in return for which the former agreed to halt his aggression against the Empire. This was reported in March in a letter to Queen Elizabeth from Christopher Mundt, her agent in Germany (*CSP, Foreign* 1:191), and in June, in a letter to William Cecil from Nicholas Throgmorton, the Queen's ambassador in France (*CSP, Foreign* 1:303). Such an agreement might have been interpreted in London as amounting to a non-aggression promise to Queen Elizabeth.

3. In 1562, Suleiman and the Emperor came to a similar agreement—the Peace of Prague—in which Suleiman agreed to forgo further attacks for another eight years.[19] In this treaty, Suleiman also promised safe passage to, and courteous treatment of, "all Christians" throughout his territory (Knolles 790). Cecil was also notified of this agreement (in June 1562), and might also have interpreted it as a non-aggression promise (*CSP, Foreign* 5:109, 134).

4. In February 1563, Queen Elizabeth's Ambassador in France, Sir Thomas Smith, wrote to the Privy Council (from Blois) about a planned meeting between him, a French diplomat, the Emperor's Ambassador and "the Turk's Ambassador" (*CSP, Foreign* 6:140). This was at a time when Huguenot and Royalist forces were fighting in various parts of France. Since the Turks were allied with the Royalists, and England was aiding the Huguenots, the Turkish Ambassador might have used the occasion of the meeting to assure Smith that the Sultan had no intention of attacking his country. There is no report in the relevant State Papers about the outcome of the meeting, but it might have been reported in another piece of correspondence that is lost or remains undiscovered. Admittedly, hard evidence is lacking for this specific diplomatic communication from Sultan Suleiman to Queen Elizabeth, and the possibilities cited are speculative. But they are consistent with the accompanying historical evidence, and consistent with the dates derived from the other references in the encomium.

The final four lines of the encomium hint at the death of Queen Elizabeth:

> For which, if ere her life be tane away,
>
> God grant her soule may live in heaven for aye.
>
> For if her Graces dayes be brought to end,
>
> Your hope is gone, on whom did peace depend.
>
> *True Tragedy* 2220–3

These lines may refer to the Queen's near-fatal illness with smallpox in October 1562. For two weeks she lay near death, and at one time gave instructions from her bed to Cecil and the other Privy Councilors about what should be done if she died (Read 265–6). Without question, this episode would have had a profound impact upon William Cecil and his household in the Strand, which Edward de Vere had joined only the previous month.

Although most commentators place the composition of *True Tragedy* in the late 1580s or early 1590s, only one has made a serious attempt to date the play from internal evidence. In 1921, Lewis F. Mott analyzed the references in the encomium and concluded that *True Tragedy* was written in late 1589 and first performed at court that December by the Queen's Men, the acting company named on the play's title page (71). He asserted that the congratulatory messages sent to Queen Elizabeth, and the reference to her defeat of the Antichrist, all had to do with England's victory over the Spanish Armada in 1588 (66). He claimed that the playwright "unquestionably had before him" a copy of Richard Hakluyt's *Principal Navigations,* which was published in November 1589, and contained the texts of numerous letters that passed between Queen Elizabeth and the Turkish Sultans. Most of these pertained to assurances of favorable treatment and grants of safe passage by each monarch for the travelers and traders of the other.

However, as stated above, the promise of the Turk referred to in the couplet is not about trading privileges or diplomatic immunity; it is a pledge not to aggress against Elizabeth. In fact, permission to trade throughout Turkish territory was granted by Suleiman I to the Englishman, Anthony Jenkinson, as early as 1553 (Hakluyt 3:36–8).

In 1579 William Harborne, the first government-sanctioned English trader in Turkey, arranged an exchange of letters between Queen Elizabeth and Sultan Murad III that resulted in an extensive "charter of privileges" for all English merchants in Turkey (Hakluyt 3:51–6). The Queen licensed the Levant Company in 1581, and the next year made Harborne her deputy and agent at the Sultan's court (Hakluyt 3:64–72, 85–7). The Company continued to enjoy this privileged status throughout Elizabeth's reign with only occasional interruptions. Therefore, even if it were a trade agreement that was referred to in the play, there was no particular event or occasion in the late 1580s that would merit such a reference in a catalogue of her accomplishments.

Mott also attempted to draw a connection between the line "And been the means that civil wars did cease" and events in England in 1589 by claiming that "The conflict between the peace party and the war party at Elizabeth's court is well known" (69). But to call this political conflict "civil wars" is to do violence to the phrase. He is on firmer ground with his claim that "The good she hath done" with respect to France referred to the contingent of 4000 men Elizabeth sent to aid Henry of Navarre when he became King of France in August 1589 (70–1). Although there exists a letter of thanks from Henry, Mott acknowledged that this alliance deteriorated into a quarrel between the two monarchs by February 1590. He also admitted that there are only "vague indications" of "the good she hath done" for Geneva and Flanders in this period. Finally, Mott acknowledged that "Diligent search has failed to connect the 'babes in Jewry' with any specific act of Elizabeth" (69). As shown above, the identification of Elizabeth as a modern-day Deborah at the time of her coronation fully explains the line. A reasonable conclusion, therefore, is that the evidence connecting the encomium's references to events and circumstances in the early 1560s is stronger and more consistent than Mott's claimed connections to events and circumstances in late 1589.

The final word to be said about the encomium to Elizabeth at the end of *True Tragedy* is that it bears a conspicuous resemblance to a comparable one at the end of another play with circumstantial connections to Edward de Vere. The play is *King Johan*, by the Protestant convert and dramatist John Bale (1495–1563), who wrote more than a dozen plays for John de Vere, fifteenth Earl of Oxford, in the early 1530s (Harris 75). Among the more than fourteen plays that Bale wrote for de Vere's playing company was the earliest version of *King Johan* (1534), which has been identified as "our first history play" (Ribner 39), and the first play in which a King of England appeared on stage (Harris 64).

Scholars agree that Bale revised *King Johan* several times over his lifetime, the last between September 1560 and his death three years later (Pafford xix). The twenty-two lines of praise for Queen Elizabeth that he added at the end of the play at that time have become associated with her visit to Ipswich in August 1561 because the single surviving copy was found "among some old papers, probably once belonging to the Corporation of Ipswich" (Harris 71, 104). These lines, apparently written for a performance before the Queen herself, may have been the model for the twenty-six similar lines at the end of *True Tragedy* that have the same tone and subject matter, and include many of the same words. In both are asseverations of the Queen's wisdom, her role as a lamp or light for other rulers, her mission of peace in England in the service of God, her conquest of the Antichrist, as well as the same admonition to pray for her long life. It is not difficult to imagine that *King Johan* was performed by the sixteenth Earl's own company during the Queen's five-day visit to Heding-ham Castle, only twenty-five miles from Ipswich, or at Ipswich itself, in August 1561 (Ward, *Seventeenth Earl* 12). And it is hard to imagine that the eleven-year-old de Vere was not present to meet the Queen and see the play.

## THE THOMAS CHURCHYARD CONNECTION

Another clue to the date of *True Tragedy* can be found in scene xi, in which Edward IV's former mistress, Jane Shore, bemoans her fate and her treatment at the hands of Richard III. After a long conversation with her, Lodowick, a servant of Lord Hastings, remarks:

*Lodowick.*    therefore for feare I should be seene talke with her, I will
shun her company and get me to my chamber, and there set
downe in heroicall verse, the shameful end of a Kings Concu-
bin, which is no doubt as wonderfull as the defoliation of a
kingdome.                                         *True Tragedy* 1076–79

This is an obvious reference to the narrative poem by Thomas Churchyard (1520?–1604) that was first published in 1563 in the third edition of *The Mirror for Magistrates*—"Howe Shores Wife, Edwarde the Fowerthes Concubine, Was by King Richarde Despoyled of All Her Goodes, and Forced to Do Open Penance." No other poem was published in England about the life of Jane Shore before 1593 (Harner 496–7), and "Shore's Wife" is the obvious source of the language and detail used to portray her in the play.

Churchyard's career as a writer and soldier of fortune spanned more than sixty years, and included service in several foreign countries, as well as scrapes with the authorities, quarrels with fellow writers and publication of about forty-five books and pamphlets in poetry and prose (Lyne). In his 1593 collection of prose and verse, *Churchyard's Challenge*, he reprinted "Shore's Wife," and asserted that he had written it around 1550 (B. Brown 43). As a boy, Church-yard was a page in the household of the poet Henry Howard, the Earl of Surrey, Edward de Vere's uncle by marriage. Beginning in the 1560s, Churchyard and Edward de Vere had repeated literary and personal connections over several decades. There is evidence that de Vere, or perhaps William Cecil, employed him in 1567, a relationship that might have begun some years earlier (Ward, *Seventeenth Earl* 29). In 1573, Churchyard wrote a commendatory verse for Thomas Bedingfield's translation of Cardano's *De Consolatione* (*Cardanus's*

*Comforte*), a work dedicated to Oxford, who contributed a prefatory letter and poem. In two of his pamphlets published in 1580, Churchyard promised future dedications to Oxford (May 9). Finally, in 1591, Churchyard, apparently again in Oxford's service, leased rooms in London from Julia Penn on Oxford's behalf (Ward, *Seventeenth Earl* 301).

The association of the author of "Shore's Wife" and the author of *True Tragedy* has another dimension—Churchyard was in the army that invaded Scotland under Lord Grey and besieged the French garrison at Leith in 1560. In fact, he wrote a poem about the siege of Leith, and included it in his 1575 collection of prose and verse, *Churchyard's Chips* (Lyne). Churchyard had also been a participant in another military campaign mentioned in the last scene of *True Tragedy*. This was Henry VIII's siege and capture of Boulogne in 1544 (A. Taylor 18). Boulogne is one of five French cities mentioned in the sixteen lines devoted to Henry VIII, just before the encomium to Queen Elizabeth begins.[20]

This association of the author of the play with the author of a source of the play, who fought in at least two military campaigns adverted to in the play, suggests that *True Tragedy* might have been written about the time they met. It is entirely possible that when the young Oxford moved into the household of William Cecil after his father's death in 1562, he came into contact with the colorful Thomas Churchyard, then a soldier-poet in his early forties. Churchyard, who had written about the mistress of Edward IV (and had certainly spoken to people who had known her), might have intrigued the young man who would later write plays about English kings. It is possible that Churchyard's stories (and his poem) about the campaign in Scotland—Elizabeth's routing of the Antichrist—might have led Oxford to include the couplet about it in the concluding passage of *True Tragedy*. At about the same time, the mid-1560s, both Oxford and Churchyard contributed songs to a compilation by Richard Edwards that was later published as *The Paradyse of Dainty Devices* (1576).[21]

Thus, all the topical references in *True Tragedy*, especially those in this final passage, can be associated with events and circumstances during the first five years of Elizabeth's reign. After several opening complimentary lines, the playwright refers to her role as the English Deborah, an identification of her made repeatedly at the time of her coronation. The next sixteen lines refer, in a nearly-accurate sequence, to diplomatic events and foreign policy decisions taken by the Queen before the summer of 1563. Finally, there is a hint at the near-fatal illness she suffered in 1562, and mention of the tragic consequences of such an event. Most of these references would have become irrelevant and stale (or incorrect) within a few years.

Lewis Mott concluded his analysis by remarking on "the amount of political information possessed by the author," and added that "The person who penned that final speech was either especially familiar with foreign affairs, or he had been exceedingly well coached" (71). This observation accords perfectly with the argument that the author was the young Edward de Vere. In the household of William Cecil, Principal Secretary to the Queen, he would very likely have been aware of political and diplomatic matters that were discussed where ministers, ambassadors and other government officials were regularly entertained. It is unlikely that any other playwright would have been privy to such information.

## FURTHER DATING EVIDENCE

Other characteristics suggesting an early date for *True Tragedy* include archaic words, meanings and spellings, and older verse forms. One of its earliest readers, John Collier, wrote in 1855:

> The style in which it is composed merits observation; it is partly in prose, partly in heavy blank-verse, (such as was penned before Marlowe had introduced his improvements, and Shakespeare had adapted and advanced them), partly in ten syllable rhyming couplets, and stanzas, and partly in the longer fourteen-syllable metre, which seems to have been popular even before prose was employed upon our stage. In every point of view it may be asserted, that few more curious dramatic relics exist in our language. It is perhaps the most ancient printed specimen of composition for a public theatre, which the subject was derived from English history [lxvi].

Fifty years later, J. A. Symonds also summed up its characteristics: "In form it contains remnants of old rhyming structure, decayed verses of fourteen feet, and clumsy prose, pieced and patched with blank verse of very lumbering rhythm" (209).

Another feature attesting to its early date is the crude treatment of the revenge motif that was prominent in the tragedies of the Roman playwright Seneca. This revenge theme is handled even less expertly than in *The Spanish Tragedy*, a play that is dated to the mid–1580s (Bevington, *Spanish* 2). It appears that the author of *True Tragedy* was not only the first to incorporate this Senecan revenge motif into an English history play, but may have been the only playwright to do so. According to G. B. Churchill, "The True Tragedy and Shakespeare's Richard III remained the only chronicle-history plays from actual English history that employed any of the motives of the [Senecan] revenge plays" (402).

Other features of *True Tragedy* suggest a beginning playwright, as well. The two long scenes depicting Jane Shore, besides being composed in vapid and clanking prose, are irrelevant to the story, and contribute only peripherally to the theme of the mutability of fortune. Throughout the play are numerous instances of dialogue explaining or announcing the coming and going of characters—such lines as "Why, here's the Lord—," and "So I take my leave," etc. The title character Richard enters at the beginning of scene ii, but when it ends more than one hundred lines later, he has not uttered a word. Other characters enter or leave scenes at the wrong moment. In sum, the evidence for a composition date for *True Tragedy* in the early 1560s is dramaturgic and linguistic, as well as topical. Thus, the three extant copies of *True Tragedy*, dated 1594, are among the earliest printed Shakespeare plays that survive.

## THE DATE OF *RICHARD III*

Orthodox editors and critics date the composition of *Richard III* to the early 1590s, and associate it with the *Henry VI* trilogy (Spencer xvi; Jowett 3; Lull 5; J. D. Wilson, ed. *Richard III* 9; Siemon 45–6). There is no question that the play belongs in Shakespeare's first tetralogy, but the orthodox dating for that sequence can only be called wildly mistaken in view of the evidence adduced in Chapter I and in the remainder of this book. There is no credible evidence for assigning *Richard III*, or the *Henry VI* trilogy, to the early 1590s.

## Contrary Evidence

As noted earlier, the authorship of *True Tragedy* has received very little attention, except for the near-unanimity among orthodox scholars that Shakespeare had nothing to do with it. Nor is there any support among modern scholars for the dating evidence outlined above. But the evidence is substantial that *True Tragedy* was one of Shakespeare's earliest plays, and his first attempt to dramatize the story of Richard III.

Attributions of *Richard III* to playwrights other than Shakespeare, such as Marlowe, Peele, Drayton, Kyd and Heywood, have been made by several scholars. These are mentioned by E. K. Chambers in his discussion of the play (*William Shakespeare* 1:301–2), but they are cursory efforts, made without much evidence, and have little support among modern critics and editors.

## Conclusion

Despite its many inept passages, and crude and clumsy structure, *True Tragedy* is full of the artful phrasing, arresting dialogue and clever turns of speech that are the marks of a superior poet in the making. Dramatic devices, such as the slip of the tongue that reveals Richard's intentions, and the dialogue between the two murderers, are worthy of a skilled playwright, and were reused by Shakespeare and others. The role of Richard, though one-dimensional, is the most powerful portrait of a dominating protagonist in any early history play. Although his soliloquies lack any wit or humor, they are the clear antecedents of the powerful speeches he delivers in *Richard III*. The play could not be mounted today, but a solo performance of most of Richard's 570 lines, one quarter of the play, would amaze and delight a modern audience.

Nevertheless, on the basis of the felicity of language and dramaturgical skill displayed, *True Tragedy* must be judged the second-worst play that can be ascribed to Shakespeare. It is a much better play than his first—*The Famous Victories of Henry the Fifth*, but not as polished as *The Troublesome Reign of John*, very likely his next. Furthermore, sexual puns and suggestive language are totally absent from the play, implying a very young author. The only reference to a sexual relationship is in the secondary story of Jane Shore, which is presented primarily as a cautionary tale about the inconstancy of friend and fortune. And finally, there are only one or two legal terms in *True Tragedy*, a distinction it shares with *Famous Victories*, *Troublesome Reign* and *The Taming of a Shrew*. The absence of legal issues and legal terms in these four plays is strong evidence that they were written before Oxford was well into his legal studies at Gray's Inn in February 1567 (Ward, *Seventeenth Earl* 27). In his revision, which he undertook less than ten years later, he would expand the text to more than 3600 lines, the second longest in the canon, and produce one of the most popular plays in all of English drama.

# III

## *The Troublesome Reign of John, King of England* and *King John*

The anonymous history play *The Troublesome Reign of John, King of England* occupies an ambiguous place in the limbo of extant Elizabethan plays whose authorship has not been determined. It has been ascribed to as many as eight different playwrights, including William Shakespeare. Nearly all the critical attention it has attracted has been as a source (and sometimes as an imitation) of Shakespeare's *King John*.

Beginning with the earliest commentators, both the play's authorship and its relationship to Shakespeare's *King John* have been in dispute. For several hundred years, most writers on the subject agreed that *Troublesome Reign*, published in 1591, was the earlier play, that it was written by someone other than Shakespeare, and that Shakespeare used it as his sole or primary source for *King John*. Several recent studies have come to different conclusions about the play's date, authorship and relationship to *King John*. However, despite these findings, the prevailing opinion has not changed.

The following re-examination of the entire matter has produced substantial evidence that *Troublesome Reign* was the earlier play, that the author of the canon wrote it himself at an early age, and that he rewrote it in his middle years as the *King John* that was published in the Folio of 1623. These conclusions are based on three categories of evidence—the striking similarity of *Troublesome Reign* and the Folio *King John*, the plethora of parallels of all types between *Troublesome Reign* and Shakespeare's acknowledged plays, and the substantial absence of such parallels from the works of other playwrights of the period. It appears that Lord Oxford wrote *Troublesome Reign* before any of his acknowledged history plays and, of all his plays, it was the first to be printed. Moreover, this evidence of early publication supports the conclusion that with few exceptions the phrases, images and ideas in the play that are also found in the plays of Marlowe and Peele, as well as in later Shakespeare plays, originated in *Troublesome Reign.*

## EARLY ASCRIPTIONS TO SHAKESPEARE

The 1591 publication of *Troublesome Reign* was in two parts, without an accompanying entry in the Stationers' Register. The title page of each part named the publisher as Sampson Clarke, and contained the sentence "As it was (sundry times) publickly acted by the Queenes Majesties Players, in the honourable Citie of London." On the basis of the ornament on the title page of Part 1, W. W. Greg identified the printer as Thomas Orwin (*Bibliography* 1:178).

A second Quarto of *Troublesome Reign*, containing both parts, was printed by Valentine Simmes for John Helme in 1611. On the title page is the same reference to the "Queenes Majesties Players," even though this company had been supplanted by the King's Men after Elizabeth's death in 1603. Also on the title page is the phrase "Written by W. Sh." A third Quarto, containing both parts, was printed by Augustine Matthews for Thomas Dewe in 1622. On that title page, the play was described as "(sundry times) lately acted" and "Written by W. Shakespeare." Scholars customarily dismiss the ascriptions to Shakespeare on the second and third Quartos as fraudulent attempts to trade on the cachet of the Shakespeare name. But the evidence does not support this conjecture. The printers of these Quartos, Simmes and Matthews, were each in business more than thirty years, and there is no record of accusations against them of piracy or false attributions. On three of the six editions of four different Shakespeare plays printed by Simmes, Shakespeare's name did not appear. And, after printing the third Quarto of *Troublesome Reign* in 1622, Augustine Matthews printed nothing by Shakespeare except the second edition of *Othello* in 1630, on which the author's name appeared. None of the three publishers— Clarke, Helme and Dewe—had any known connection with any Shakespeare play.

A more reasonable explanation for the placement of Shakespeare's name on the Q3 title page is that the edition was one of the "competing quartos," such as Q1 of *Othello*, issued in anticipation of the First Folio, the publication of which had already been announced (Sider xv; Chambers, *William Shakespeare* 1:139). This may suggest that Dewe or Matthews, or both, thought that *Troublesome Reign* were going to appear in Shakespeare's collected works. (Confusion between *Troublesome Reign* and *King John* is addressed in the "King John" Section, below.)

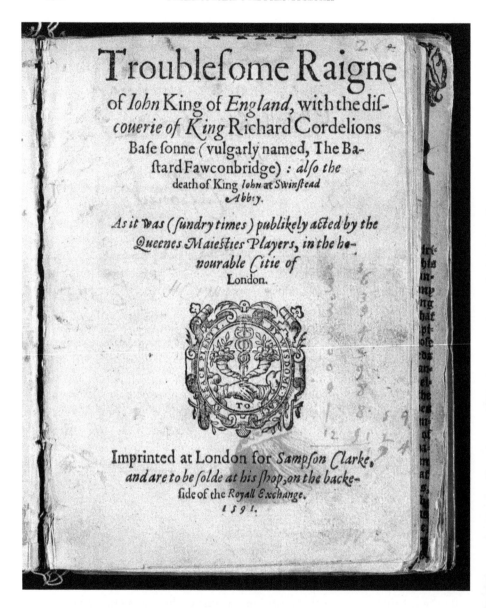

Title page of Part 1 of Quarto 1 of *The Troublesome Reign of John, King of England*. 1591. Part 2 appeared in a separate Quarto at the same time. Both Parts were printed in black letter. *Troublesome Reign* antedated Shakespeare's earliest published play, *Titus Andronicus* (1594), and by two years his first printed work—*Venus and Adonis* (1593) (courtesy Master and Fellows of Trinity College, Cambridge).

As for the alleged misuse of the Shakespeare name, Edward White, Sr., a bookseller in business since 1577, had three editions of *Titus Andronicus* printed in 1594, 1600 and 1611 to sell in his shop in St. Paul's Churchyard. Neither Shakespeare's name nor his initials appeared on any of them, even though by 1598 the play was known to be by him. The first three Quartos of *Romeo and Juliet*, published in 1597, 1599 and 1609, appeared anonymously, even though Shakespeare was identified as its author in 1598.[1] The 1598 identification of *Titus Andronicus* and *Romeo and Juliet* as Shakespeare plays was made by Francis Meres in *Palladis Tamia*. Thus, at the time of the appearance of the second Quarto of *Troublesome Reign* (1611), publishers of known Shakespeare plays were still issuing them anonymously. It is noteworthy that the other three Shakespearean "tragedies" listed by Meres were all first published anonymously.[2]

George Steevens included *Troublesome Reign* in volume 2 of his edition of *Twenty of the Plays of Shakespeare* in 1760. In his foreword, Steevens wrote that "the Author seems to have been so dissatisfied with this Play as to have written it almost entirely anew, reserving only a few of the Lines and the conduct of several Scenes" (2:Fol. N8). He is reported to have later changed his mind about Shakespeare's authorship. In 1779 Edward Capell claimed the entire play for Shakespeare, and the German critic J. Ludwig Tieck (1811) agreed with this attribution (Furness, ed. *King John* 448). However, nearly all other nineteenth century critics disparaged *Troublesome Reign* and assigned nothing in it to Shakespeare. Nor has it been included in collections of Shakespearean apocrypha.[3]

*Troublesome Reign* belongs to the category of early history plays based mainly on chronicles about English kings written or translated in the Tudor period. These plays include Peele's *Edward I* (1593), Marlowe's *Edward II* (1593), Shakespeare's *Edward III* (1595) and the *Henry VI* plays, generally assigned to 1591–93, and several other anonymous plays of the early 1590s. In dramatizing the events of John's seventeen-year reign, the author offered a full range of stagecraft typical of the early Elizabethan theater. In the words of John Munro, one of the play's editors, "he gives us three battles, disputes of monarchs, a coronation, prophecies and marvels, a betrothal, humour in a friary, plots, rebellions, proclamations, the sufferings of the innocent, a death-scene, some bombast and satire, and much patriotic feeling" (Furnivall and Munro xxii). On the religious spectrum, the play is strongly Protestant and anti-papal. In one scene, three friars and a nun are sent to the gallows for hiding their money; in another, the monk who has just poisoned King John is murdered on stage.

The style of *Troublesome Reign* is largely end-stopped blank verse, with

# THE

## First and second Part of

the troublesome Raigne of
*John* King of England.

*With the difcouerie of King* Richard Cor-
delions Bafe fonne (vulgarly named, The Baftard
Fawconbridge:) Alfo, the death of King *Iohn*
at Swinftead Abbey.

*As they were (fundry times) lately acted by
the Queenes Maiefties Players.*

Written by W. Sh.

Imprinted at London by *Valentine Simmes* for *Iohn Helme,*
and are to be fold at his fhop in Saint Dunftons
Churchyard in Fleetcftreet.
1 6 1 1.

Title page of Quarto 2 of *Troublesome Reign*—a reprint in 1611 in one volume of the two
Parts of Q1. It was printed in Roman type, with some Italic for speech heads, etc. The
attribution to "W. Sh" is routinely dismissed by scholars as an attempt to mislead buyers
into thinking it was a Shakespeare play. The canonical *King John* did not appear in print
until it was published in the First Folio in 1623 (© Huntington Art Collections, San
Marino, California).

occasional passages of rhymed iambic couplets, as well as irregular lines of wooden prose. The poetry is uneven, but the language is vigorous, declamatory and metaphorical. The author frequently employs simple rhetorical devices, such as stichomythia, antithesis, word play and heavy alliteration. The play contains more than a dozen phrases and sentences in Latin, several of them quotations from Ovid and Horace.

Although *Troublesome Reign* has been routinely reviled for its clumsy rhetoric and bombastic style, the plot structure, and especially the characterization, attracted notice because of their position in the development of the Elizabethan history play. Felix Schelling commented, "…in the personages of *Troublesome Reign*, especially in the King and Faulconbridge … we have the earliest vital representation of an historical personage upon the English stage" (Quoted in Furness, ed. *King John*, 467).

## TWENTIETH CENTURY ASSESSMENTS OF *TROUBLESOME REIGN*

In 1911, the critic and poet W. E. Courthope asserted that Shakespeare was the author of *Troublesome Reign*, and compared his rewriting of it as *King John* to his rewriting of *The First Part of the Contention* and *The True Tragedy of Richard, Duke of York* as the final two parts of the *Henry VI* trilogy. He observed that in all three instances Shakespeare employed "almost precisely the same process of reconstruction" and "kept all the characters and the entire framework of the action":

> But while he imitated the leading dramatists of the day, the writer of *The Troublesome Reign of King John* gave evidence of striking genius. In the energy and dignity of the State debates, the life of the incidents, the variety and contrast of the characters, and the power of conceiving the onward movement of a great historical action, there is a quality of dramatic workman-ship exhibited in the play quite above the genius of Peele, Greene, or even Marlowe. It is noteworthy also that the representation of mental conflict is a marked feature in *The Troublesome Reign.*              [*A History of English Poetry* 4:463–6]

Even though he cited passages in it that he considered to be imitations of their style, Courthope's overall assessment was that the play was "knit together in a manner far superior to any historic play of Marlowe, Greene, or Peele," and that it contained "more of the elements of greatness than any historic play which had yet been produced on the English stage" (4:466). John Dover Wilson commented that the author of *Troublesome Reign* might have been "an insipid versifier and an uninspired journeyman playwright, but he knew how to distil the most excellent dramatic material from the chronicles in which he was soaked" (ed. *King John* xxxix).

In his influential 1944 study of Shakespeare's history plays, E. M. W. Tillyard wrote that he did not think that *Troublesome Reign* could be considered "an authentic, consistent, and self-supporting composition," and that its "masterly construction is quite at odds with the heterogeneous execution." He suggested that *Troublesome Reign* might be a bad quarto of an even older play about King John, one also by Shakespeare (247–8).

Many other modern critics have remarked on the playwright's success in drawing together unrelated incidents throughout John's reign into a reasonably coherent story about a self-doubting ruler whose ineptness led ultimately to his banal murder. "Considerable skill as a plotter is shown by the playwright who wrote T.R." is the comment by John Elson in his 1948 study of the play's sources. He added that "Another feat of the dramatist's creative power is his depiction of the Bastard's magnetic personality" (185). While noting the mediocre verse of *Troublesome Reign*, J. L. Simmons called it "in many ways remarkable; of the known contemporary dramatists, only Shakespeare and Marlowe show the structural powers for handling such sprawling events from the chronicles" (54). Irving Ribner wrote that "There is certainly no extant play earlier than *Tamburlaine* which handles history as skillfully and maturely

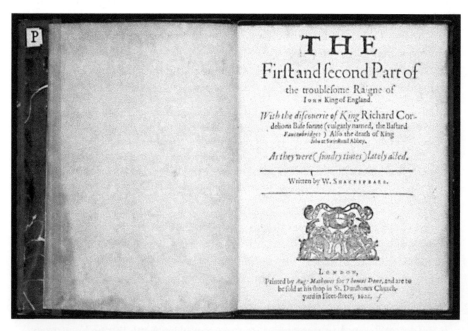

**Title page of Quarto 3 of *Troublesome Reign*. 1622. The attribution to "W. Shakespeare" may have been intended to anticipate the publication of *King John* in the First Folio the following year (© Huntington Art Collections, San Marino, California).**

as it is handled in *The Troublesome Reign*" and described it as "a heroic play which draws its hero from actual history and treats him with serious historical purpose" (77).

Despite his successful marshalling of multiple characters and events, the author of *Troublesome Reign* left us abundant evidence that he was a beginning dramatist. One early critic observed, "We may pronounce them [the two parts of *Troublesome Reign*] as his first undisputed excursions into the regions of drama; and, as such, they are but a feeble performance, sprinkl'd with some quotations from classics, and, in the comedy part, with some monkish Latin."[4] The nineteenth century critic J. A. Symonds described *Troublesome Reign* as "a dull specimen of solid play-carpentry in the earliest and crudest age of blank-verse composition."[5] Other critics have noted the play's rhetorical outbursts and heavy-handed argument. Geoffrey Bullough cited "lengthy Senecan threats," "turgid soliloquizing," and "long didactic passages" (*Narrative* 4:11, 12, 21, respectively). Other commenters mentioned pedestrian meter, bombast and brag patriotism, purple patches, and artificial sentiment (Furnivall and Munro xl). Honigmann noted the play's "extraordinary mish-mash of styles" and the fact that "the verse collapses six separate times into prose in the first scene alone" (*Impact* 133). In her analysis of forty-one "suspect texts" connected with Shakespeare, Laurie Maguire listed numerous instances in *Troublesome Reign* of missing, inconsistent, or incorrect stage directions and speech prefixes (314–16).

But even Honigmann, who decried the author as a shameless imitator of Shakespeare, praised *Troublesome Reign* as "a beautifully plotted play in its analysis of complex political manoeuveres and its dramatic control..." ("Self-Repetition" 178). Yet he and most modern scholars find *Troublesome Reign*, whether they think it preceded or followed *King John*, to be too poorly executed and too awkwardly written to be even an early Shakespeare play. Those who have an author in mind propose Marlowe, Drayton, Kyd, Thomas Lodge, William Rowley, Robert Greene, Anthony Munday or George Peele. In a recent analysis of *King John* and its sources, Michael Egan proposed that *Troublesome Reign* was a collaboration between Peele and Shakespeare, and that Shakespeare later revised it, discarding his partner's undistinguished verse and several crude scenes of monastic lechery and murder. This claim will be considered below in "A Mistaken Ascription to George Peele." Ascriptions of the entirety of *Troublesome Reign* to Shakespeare have been made by Ephraim Everitt and Eric Sams, whose findings are incorporated into this analysis.[6] But "unknown" is the only word the majority of critics can find for this scholarly and patriotic dramatist, whose poetry tended to polemic and bombast.

# King John

In *Palladis Tamia* (1598), Francis Meres included a "King John" in his list
of six of Shakespeare's "tragedies." Although there is no additional evidence,
scholars have generally assumed this to be a reference to the *King John* that was
published for the first time in the Folio in 1623. If it were a reference to the
canonical *King John*, it would be the only one of any kind before its printing.
Of the thirty-six plays in the First Folio, eighteen had already been published
in quarto editions. But the Folio publishers registered only sixteen of the
remaining eighteen in the lengthy Stationers' Register entry, omitting *The Taming of the Shrew* and *King John*. This led E. K. Chambers to remark that *King
John* was "regarded as commercially identical with its predecessor [Troublesome Reign]" (*William Shakespeare* 1:365). Aside from the title pages of *Troublesome Reign* and a mention of *King John* in a list of plays performed at Court
in 1669, there is no record of a performance of either play until 1737 (Nicoll,
*History* 315). In fact, it is quite likely that the play to which Meres referred in
1598 was *Troublesome Reign*. The play was clearly a popular one—being performed by two different playing companies, and belonging to the small group
of Elizabethan plays outside the traditional Shakespeare canon that were
printed three times, the last nearly thirty years after the first. Moreover, several
scholars have observed that the Folio text of *King John* has numerous deficiencies as a prompt book, such as confusing act and scene headings, and inconsistent stage directions and speech prefixes. Since *Troublesome Reign* was
reprinted as Shakespeare's play in 1611 and again in 1622, there is a possibility
that at the time of its printing the Folio text of *King John* had not actually been
performed.

## *Order of the Plays*

Until the twentieth century, it was generally agreed that the composition
of *Troublesome Reign* preceded that of *King John*, just as the external evidence
indicated. But in the 1930s, A. S. Cairncross, Peter Alexander and others
asserted that Shakespeare's *King John* preceded *Troublesome Reign*, and that the
similarities between the two plays were the result of the anonymous author's
borrowing from *King John*.[7] Cairncross called *Troublesome Reign* a "loose
piracy" of *King John* on the grounds that it "contains a number of lines so exactly
similar to lines in *King John*, and not derived in that form from any other known
source, that one of the plays must have been indebted to the other." He concluded that the author of *Troublesome Reign* was the debtor because of his

"indiscriminate borrowings not only from other plays of Shakespeare, but also from Peele's *Arraignment of Paris*, and from various other plays" (*Hamlet* 137).

In his 1936 Cambridge edition of *King John*, John Dover Wilson disagreed at length, describing the anonymous dramatist as the man who laid the ground for Shakespeare:

> Indeed, his play possesses all the ingredients of historical drama except dramatic life. Nor did these ingredients consist of ill-assorted lumps of information got together by laborious pedantry. The stuff had been pre-digested for Shakespeare, fused in the crucible of an imagination of no mean order, though not of a high dramatic order [ed. *King John* xxxix].

Besides the numerous parallels of thought and phrase between the plays, Wilson cited half-a-dozen instances of language, behavior and detail in *King John* that are unclear or contradictory except by reference to *Troublesome Reign*. He also pointed out that if the author of *Troublesome Reign* were the borrower he would have to have obtained a prompt copy or some kind of transcript of *King John* in 1591, or earlier, since it did not appear in print until 1623. Other critics have cited several inappropriate, or even inexplicable, stage directions in the Folio *King John* that are identical or nearly so to those at the same places in *Troublesome Reign* (Beaurline 206). Since these stage directions are perfectly appropriate in *Troublesome Reign*, this strongly suggests that Shakespeare worked from a copy of *Troublesome Reign*, routinely transferred the stage directions into his own play, and then failed to correct them after he had altered the scene.

Echoing Wilson's objections to the precedence of *King John*, A. P. Rossiter cited three details in the play—the murder of John by a monk and several remarks by the Bastard Falconbridge—that do not "make sense" except as references to incidents "*in the other play!*" (183; Rossiter's emphasis). Furthermore, no editor or critic, except those who argue its precedence to *Troublesome Reign*, assigns *King John* a date as early as 1591, virtually at the dawn of the Shakespeare canon—a re-dating that would require a major revision of the dates of the early plays. As regards the idea that *Troublesome Reign* was based upon Shakespeare's *King John*, Wilson asked:

> Why the author, having apparently ample material at his disposal, should have completely stripped the play of all its poetry and taken the trouble to dress it up in fustian verse of his own; should have reconstructed the whole in the light of an independent reading of the chronicles, so that he produced a text which followed them far more closely than Shakespeare himself had done; and should have gone out of his way not only to infuse the play with a strong anti–Catholic bias but also to substitute a harassed, if erring, martyr-king for Shakespeare's sinister John; and all this in order to prepare copy for a publisher, who could not have given him more than a few shillings for his pains! [ed. *King John* xxxii].

In his Arden edition of 1954, and in several later publications, E. A. J. Honigmann reiterated the theory of the precedence of *King John* and suggested that *Troublesome Reign* was a "bad quarto"—a hasty and thoughtless reproduction of *King John* (liv–lviii, 174–5). Despite the external evidence of its priority, and its obvious inferiority to Shakespeare's play, he maintained that both plays were written in the 1590–91 period, and that *King John* was written first. A good portion of his argument was devoted to demonstrating that Shakespeare did not use *Troublesome Reign* as a source, but depended directly on Holinshed's *Chronicles*, as well as Foxe's *Acts and Monuments*, and histories by Matthew Paris and Ralph Coggeshall (xi–xxv). But showing that Shakespeare could have obtained all the historical details he used in *King John* from sources other than *Troublesome Reign* does not go far toward showing that *King John* was the earlier play.

To support his charge of piracy, Honigmann suggested that the Queen's Men, losing ground to other companies after the death of their star comedian Richard Tarleton in 1588, resorted to copying and rewriting Shakespeare plays, such as *The Taming of the Shrew* and *Richard III*, in the early 1590s, and did the same with *King John* (ed. *King John* lv–lvi). But all three of these piracy allegations suffer from the same handicap—no text of the three Shakespeare plays existed, so far as we know, in the early 1590s. Even though it is conceivable that this was done, the piracy theory, especially as it relates to these plays, is very far from proven, and is a decidedly minority view.

In support of an early date for *King John*, Honigmann also noted more than a dozen historical details in the play that he considered to have parallels with events and circumstances in Elizabeth's reign prior to 1591 (ed. *King John* xxix). Many of these are questionable, but what is more important, they all appear in *Troublesome Reign*. Thus, they are useless to show the priority of *King John*. Two reviewers of Honigmann's Arden edition, T. A. Parrott and Alice Walker, disagreed with him about the precedence of *King John*. Parrott wrote that "there are few better examples of his skill [Shakespeare's] as an adaptor than the transformation of the crude Faulconbridge matter of T. R. into the amusing and entertaining passages in *King John*" (299). Parrott also observed that if *Troublesome Reign* were a bad quarto of Shakespeare's play, "we would expect to find many of his lines and phrases reproduced, badly perhaps, in T. R.—compare the treatment of the suicide soliloquy in the 'bad quarto' of *Hamlet*,—but none such has been detected" (302). In his analysis of source problems in Shakespeare's histories, Kenneth Muir wrote, "I think it incredible that hack writers who were so well acquainted with Shakespeare's play [*King John*] as to follow it scene by scene could reproduce none of the actual dialogue" ("Problems" 50).

Robert A. Law echoed this argument in a 1957 article on the date of *King John*. Citing half-a-dozen felicitous passages in *King John*, he compared them to the corresponding passages in *Troublesome Reign* and found Shakespeare's versions far superior. "Personally, I cannot conceive of any playwright's crossing out 'the Shakespearean passage' and substituting the bald language of [*Troublesome Reign*]" ("Date of *King John*" 122). Law also rejected Honigmann's claim that the Queen's Men pirated *King John*, and added that if *King John* were written and performed in 1591 or earlier, "…we are forced to conclude that the Queen's Players in 1591 ventured to duplicate in its characters, its setting, and practically its entire action a play that had just been given by a competing company" (120).

In 1964, Peter Alexander repeated his claim that *King John* preceded *Troublesome Reign* and identified the latter as an "imitation." There was "no known author," he wrote, who was capable of constructing "a series of scenes so skillfully devised that Shakespeare had only to take over his arrangement with little alteration" (*Shakespeare* 168). He also noted that "Heminge and Condell treated the publication of *The Troublesome Reign* as authorizing the printing of *King John*, a claim which could hardly have been maintained had *The Troublesome Reign* been an original play by an author other than Shakespeare" (171). But as Eric Sams and others have pointed out, the best explanation for what Hemings and Condell did is that they knew that *Troublesome Reign* was Shakespeare's first version of *King John*, and that the printing of the play had, in effect, already been authorized.

In his Penguin edition of 1974, R. A. Smallwood wrote:

> If *King John* is the earlier play, one must therefore imagine the author of *The Troublesome Reign* as a man capable of remembering, with meticulous care, the details of a plot from scene to scene throughout an entire play; capable also of getting by heart one or two lines and pieces of information of a rather precise kind; and with the ability, finally, to forget the whole of the rest of Shakespeare's language [ed. *King John* 368].

Summing up the case for the priority of *Troublesome Reign*, Marco Mincoff wrote that it was "a fairly simple matter" to derive *King John* from the anonymous play, but "the converse process would be a nerve-wracking work of reshuffling, mostly for no obvious purpose…" (52). He described Honigmann's arguments for Shakespeare's precedence as no more than a "plea" that they were no worse than those for the anonymous author.

These and other supporters of the precedence of *King John* appear to base their position on the improbability that there was any Elizabethan playwright capable of writing *Troublesome Reign* from scratch, so to speak, in 1591. Peter Alexander complained, "Yet we are asked to regard the author of *The Troublesome Reign* as capable of giving Shakespeare a lesson almost in his own specialty" (*Shakespeare* 168). There being no such man known, a pirate, copyist or imitator is proposed. A few editors continue to hold the notion that *Trou-*

*blesome Reign* was the later play. But the two most recent commenters, Vickers ("*The Troublesome Reign*") and Forker ("Intertextuality" 141–2), as well as nearly all modern critics and editors, agree that it not only preceded *King John*, but was Shakespeare's primary source.[8]

## Sources of the Plays

Since the mid-twentieth century, several scholars have attempted to trace the sources of *Troublesome Reign*, and have come to slightly different conclusions. The principal sources cited are John Foxe's *Acts and Monuments* (1563), Raphael Holinshed's *Chronicles of England*, published in 1577 and 1587, and John Bale's anti–Catholic interlude *King Johan*, in manuscript until 1838 (Pafford xxiv). John Elson points out that most of the material on King John in Holinshed appeared first in Foxe, and that the language and ideas in *Troublesome Reign* are more closely aligned to those in Foxe's account than to those in Holinshed's (186–9).

Among several details in *Acts and Monuments* that also appeared in *Troublesome Reign*, Elson mentions a woodcut in early editions of the work in which six panels depict scenes from the episode of John's alleged poisoning at Swinstead Abbey. In one of them, a monk is giving King John a cup of poison and saying "Wassail my Lige" (*sic*), a scene exactly duplicated in scene viii of *2 Troublesome Reign*. The same poisoning incident, which first appears in a chronicle more than a century after John's death, occurs in Bale's *King Johan*, another source of dozens of words, phrases and details in *Troublesome Reign* (B. Adams 32–3; Elson 191–4).

Other sources cited are Polydore Vergil's chronicle *Anglica Historia*, published in 1555, and the *Chronica Majora* of Matthew Paris, in manuscript until 1571. M. P. McDiarmid quotes Latin passages in Matthew Paris that are closely reproduced in *Troublesome Reign* (42–3). J. W. Sider cites a passage from Richard Grafton's *A Chronicle at Large* in which he finds sources of details in *Troublesome Reign*, but the connection is unconvincing.[9]

Certainty about sources is not possible because Foxe and the chroniclers routinely copied extensively from their predecessors. Also, during the last fifteen years of Bale's life, he and John Foxe worked closely together in the compilation of *Acts and Monuments*. As Foxe's mentor and collaborator, Bale researched and wrote several sections of the book, and had a profound influence on its arrangement and contents (Freeman, "Foxe, John"). Thus, the two major sources for *Troublesome Reign* were written by the two leading anti–Catholic polemicists of the time.

It is well-known that Shakespeare customarily studied several relevant chronicles before writing a history play. This was precisely the method used by the author of *Troublesome Reign*—additional evidence that he was Shakespeare. Evidence of Oxford's access to these sources is supplied below. Against his usual custom, it appears that Shakespeare wrote *King John* without recourse to any historical chronicle, and relied exclusively or nearly so on the research he did at the time of writing *Troublesome Reign*. Aside from a minor detail or two, all the historical material in *King John* appeared previously in *Troublesome Reign*.[10] This is further evidence that Shakespeare considered *Troublesome Reign*, and his research for it, his own property.

## *Relationships Between* Troublesome Reign *and* King John

In the present context, the most noticeable thing about *Troublesome Reign* is its remarkable similarity to Shakespeare's *King John*. Both plays tell the same story in the same sequence of events, with only minor variations. The same characters appear in both plays, except that in his revision Shakespeare added a single inconsequential character, James Gurney, and removed ten or so minor ones. *King John* contains the same scenes in the same order as *Troublesome Reign*, with the exception that Shakespeare deleted three and shortened several others. The plot adheres to the typical dynamic of almost all of Shakespeare's history plays—a feud within England's extended royal family combined with a rebellion against the king. The time period of both plays encompasses the entire reign of King John (1199–1216).

The long first scene in both plays exemplifies the comparable liberties that each playwright took with the historical record and how each introduced the same fictional material. In the opening scene of both plays, King John, accompanied by the identical four characters—his mother Eleanor of Aquitaine, and the Earls of Pembroke, Essex and Salisbury—greets the French ambassador, Chatillion, at the English court. John has just been crowned, following the death of his brother, Richard I. The French support the competing claim to the English throne of John's young nephew, Arthur of Brittany, who has come under the protection of the French King, Philip II. In both plays John refuses the French demand that he yield the throne to Arthur. In *Troublesome Reign*, Chatillion replies:

*Chatillion.*   I doo defie thee as an Enemie,
        And wish thee to prepare for bloodie warres.        *1 TR* 47–8[11]

In *King John*, he replies:

| Chat. | Then take my King's defiance from my mouth, |
|---|---|
| | The farthest limit of my embassy.     *King John* I.i.21–2[12] |

In *Troublesome Reign*, this unhistorical scene is interrupted by the Falconbridge brothers and their mother, who have a dispute among themselves that they are unable to resolve. (In *King John* their mother does not enter until the following scene.) Robert Falconbridge, son of a recently-deceased knight of the same name, claims that it is he, and not his older brother Philip, who should inherit his father's lands and wealth. He declares that Philip, though born of the same mother, was actually fathered by King Richard I while Sir Robert was away on a diplomatic mission in Germany. After first disputing this charge of bastardy, Philip acknowledges that he is King Richard's son, and relinquishes to Robert his father's inheritance. In both plays Philip's mother, Lady Falconbridge, at first vigorously denies the liaison with Richard, but finally admits it. King John observes that Philip resembles King Richard, pronounces him Richard's son, and knights him on the spot, renaming him Sir Richard Plantagenet.

In *King John*, Shakespeare handles the scene in a slightly different way, but the presentation of the situation and the interaction of the characters are identical. Both plays depart from the historical chronicles, which record that King John met directly with the French King Philip in Normandy, and that the Queen mother was elsewhere at the time (W. L. Warren 51–3). Nor is there any record of the Falconbridge family and the dispute between the brothers. There is mention in several chronicles that King Richard had a bastard son named Philip who avenged his father's death by killing the Viscount of Lymoges, occupant of the castle Richard was besieging when he was killed. But his paternity was apparently never in question and he had nothing to do with John's court or his campaign in France.[13]

In both plays, the fictional Philip the Bastard becomes King John's right hand man and plays essentially the same role throughout the play, even to the final scenes, which end with his patriotic speech containing nearly-identical lines about the need for England to remain united:

| Philip. | If *Englands* Peeres and people joyne in one, |
|---|---|
| | Nor Pope, nor *Fraunce*, nor *Spaine* can doo them wrong. |
| | *2 TR* 1195–6 |
| Bast. | Come the three corners of the world in arms, |
| | And we shall shock them. Nought shall make us rue, |
| | If England to itself do rest but true.     *King John* V.vii.116–18 |

As one recent editor wrote, "...the plays match so closely in the selection of characters, the sequence of events, and the management of scenes that they cannot have been written independently. Sometimes they parallel not just scene for scene but (substantially) speech for speech" (Beaurline, ed. *King John* 195).

This close similarity of structure and plot is all the more significant because neither play adheres to the historical order of events, and both attach the same results to historical events that did not cause them. Geoffrey Bullough pointed out the most drastic of these rearrangements: "...the plays make Arthur's death (in 1203) the immediate cause of the nobles' rebellion (1216) and both occur just before John surrenders his crown (1213)" (*Narrative* 4:10).

Further departures from the historical record in both plays occur in the descriptions and behavior of several characters. For instance, Hubert de Burgh was a high official under Richard I and became Justiciar of England late in John's reign (West), but in both plays he is presented as a person of much lower rank. Both playwrights conflate several papal representatives during John's reign into the single character, Pandulph, who describes himself as a "Cardinal of Milan." But the historical Pandulph was neither a Cardinal of Milan nor a Cardinal at all, as both plays have him, but a papal subdeacon and only one of several papal legates who visited John (Beaurline 61, 202). Similarly, both playwrights attach the title of Leopold V, first Archduke of Austria (1157–1194), to a different person—Vidomar, Viscount of Lymoges (d. 1200), and thus conveniently consolidate (as Lymoges, Duke of Austria) two enemies of Richard I and allow his bastard son Philip to avenge his death by killing them both at once (Stokes 198).

At least a dozen additional unhistorical characterizations and incidents have been inserted into *Troublesome Reign* by its author, and carried over into *King John* by Shakespeare. These additions to, and rearrangements of, the historical record were obviously undertaken by the anonymous playwright to create a logical story line, to improve the play's dramatic interest, and to support the motivation of its characters. Shakespeare's ready use of them suggests that he created them himself, and had no compunction about retaining them in his revision.

Further inaccurate or invented names and details throughout *Troublesome Reign* are repeated in Shakespeare's play: the use of the title "Dauphin" ("Dolphin" in *Troublesome Reign*) for the French King's son, a title that came into use only in the mid-fourteenth century; the confusion of the town of Poitiers with the province of Poitou; John's creation of Arthur as Earl of Richmond, an act that never took place; the anachronistic reference to cannons, which did not come into use for another one hundred years; and the suggestion by a "Citizen" of "Angiers" (modern Angers) that the two Kings' differences could be settled by a marriage between Lewis, the thirteen-year-old Dauphin, and the twelve-year-old Blanche of Castile, John's niece. Although this marriage actually took place, in 1200, both plays present it, unhistorically, as the arrangement that ended the simultaneous siege of "Angiers" by King John and King Philip (Sams, *The Real Shakespeare* 151).

## SHAKESPEARE'S MODIFICATIONS

Similarly, Shakespeare's modifications of the plot and characters' motivations are consistent with the scenario of a mature playwright revising an earlier play of his own making. As R. L. Smallwood observed, "…Shakespeare seems to have worked more closely with this play than with any other source he used…" (ed. *King John* 155). One type of modification that Shakespeare made was to compress his original play and give it a more concrete form. He reduced the period of the play's action from ten days, with intervals, in *Troublesome Reign* to seven days, with intervals, in *King John*. He also reduced the number of dramatic incidents and shortened the play by about three hundred lines. Besides pruning the cast list, he reduced the speaking parts from forty-odd to twenty-five.

One particular character deletion is noteworthy. In *Troublesome Reign*, Geoffrey Fitzpeter, Earl of Essex, appears as one of the nobles who is close to John, but then revolts against him after the death of Arthur, only to join him again near the end of his life. He is in the first group of characters on stage and appears in four additional scenes, speaking a total of over 120 lines. When John leaves England to fight in France, he places Essex in charge of the kingdom. Later in the play, Essex is the spokesman for the three nobles who discover the dead Arthur, and the first to call for John's deposition. But in *King John*, Shakespeare excised him almost entirely, giving him a mere three lines in the first scene, and dividing his role thereafter between the Earls of Pembroke and Salisbury. No other character of his importance has been deleted. This specific and deliberate revision might have been Shakespeare's response, political or personal, to the controversial Robert Devereux, second Earl of Essex (second creation) during the late 1570s, when Essex began to come under the influence of the faction headed by Robert Dudley, Earl of Leicester, a faction that clashed with that of Lord Burghley, with whom Oxford was associated.[14]

Of the several scenes and episodes that Shakespeare deleted, three are caustic, anti–Catholic depictions of the clergy. In the first, Philip the Bastard ransacks a monastery where friars and nuns are revealed to be buffoons and sexually promiscuous liars. Besides being crude and offensive, this scene is radically different from all others in the play in its satirical, Skeltonic lines, akin to doggerel, nearly all rhymed, and many including forced rhymes. Another deleted scene contains a discussion between a monk and an abbot about poisoning King John, and a third dramatizes his actual poisoning by the monk at Swinstead Abbey. Another deletion is the long discussion at St. Edmondsbury among a group of English nobles conspiring to unseat John and place the French Dauphin on the throne of England. In *King John*, Shakespeare alludes to all these events, but does not dramatize them.

Further revisions and excisions made by Shakespeare are as follows:

1. In the first scene, Lady Falconbridge is not present when both her sons accuse her of infidelity, as she is in *Troublesome Reign*.
2. An entire incident is deleted in which Philip the Bastard chases Lymoges, the Duke of Austria, takes King Richard's lion-skin from him, and then delivers a bombastic speech.
3. The role of Peter of Pomfret is reduced from thirty-four to a single line, and the description of his miracles is deleted.
4. The ceremony of the second coronation and the appearance of the five moons, which are dramatized in *Troublesome Reign*, are only briefly reported in *King John*.

In another category of revision are Shakespeare's slightly different view of the characters, and the depth and dimension he adds to them:

1. In *King John* the king is more decisive; he is less confused and less bombastic. But his character is less sympathetic and more ambiguous. His right to the crown is less clear.
2. Pandulph's role is expanded. He is less aggressive and abrupt, but more treacherous, and his machinations are subtler and more effective.
3. The role of Arthur's mother Constance is expanded in *King John*, and she is transformed from a single-minded scold into an articulate, even eloquent, figure of much sympathy.
4. Philip the Bastard is less peevish and confrontational, and more given to humor. He becomes a nobler figure and a more substantial character. His patriotism is more mature.
5. Although Shakespeare retained the basic dynamic of the Hubert/ Arthur confrontation, he converted Arthur from, in Bullough's words, "a moralizing young man" to "a small boy crying out in his innocence" (*Narrative* 4:15). Arthur's plea to Hubert, his would-be assassin, is no longer legalistic and theological, as it is in *Troublesome Reign*, but simple and eloquent, grounded in human compassion. Similarly, Hubert responds out of compassion, rather than his fear of damnation.

As is evident, none of these revisions adds or deletes a major character, nor does it change any character's fundamental nature. Some motivations are modified, but the characters relate to each other in the same way as in the earlier play. Certain dramatic details are deleted, and the few that are added tend to expand and sharpen the characters' roles. This detailed and comprehensive revision suggests that in writing *King John* Shakespeare worked from a copy of *Troublesome Reign*—rewriting the dialogue as he deleted and rearranged scenes, speeches and dramatic details.

However, some of Shakespeare's revisions cause confusion rather than add clarity. A. R. Braunmuller remarked that "The narrative organization of *The Troublesome Reign* is arguably clearer, certainly simpler, than *King John*..." (ed. *King John* 9). Bullough pointed out that numerous passages in *King John* "become clearer by reference to *The Raigne*—e.g. the reasons for the second coronation, the nobles' pilgrimage to St. Edmundsbury, the reasons for, and the method of, John's poisoning" (*Narrative* 4:22).[15] The poisoning incident is a source of confusion in *King John*. In the penultimate scene, after the French supply fleet has been lost at sea and the English barons have returned to John, Hubert suddenly announces that John has been poisoned by a monk. There has been no preparation or reason given for this incident. John Dover Wilson observed, "In *The Troublesome Reign*, on the other hand, the poisoning ... occurs as the natural outcome of that harrying of the monasteries which is so prominent a feature of the old play, but which Shakespeare almost entirely suppressed" (ed. *King John* xxi–xxii).

Another blunder in Shakespeare's revision is the confusion about what King John wants Hubert to do to Arthur, whose claim to the throne is a decided threat to him. In III.iii, John plainly indicates he wants him dead, but two scenes later Hubert confronts Arthur with hot irons and a warrant from the King to burn out his eyes. This discrepancy is never mentioned, explained or accounted for. But the issue is made clear in *Troublesome Reign*, where John admits that it is too dangerous to kill Arthur. Hubert's subsequent appearance with the warrant to blind Arthur, rather than kill him, is John's concession to political reality, but one that effectively ends Arthur's threat.

Other matters left unexplained in Shakespeare's revision, but fully accounted for in *Troublesome Reign*, are the Bastard's hostility to the Duke of Austria (he thought he had killed his father, Richard I) and his annoyance at the betrothal of Blanche to the Dauphin (he thought that he would marry her himself).[16] Honigmann calls these lapses "inconsistencies" and cites similar ones in other Shakespeare plays, and in *Troublesome Reign* itself, to support his view that *King John* preceded *Troublesome Reign*. But the hypothesis that best accounts for the motivations and explanations that were omitted from *King John* is that they were already in the play as Shakespeare originally conceived it and, in his wholesale rewriting of the entire dialogue, he neglected to include them. In the words of Samuel Johnson, "The omission of this incident, in the second draught, was natural. Shakespeare, having familiarised the story to his own imagination, forgot that it was obscure to his audience" (Bronson 150). This confusion worked in both directions. Beaurline remarked that both plays "contain their share of inconsistencies and puzzling contradictions that are clearer in the other" (ed. *King John* 195).

In his analysis of the garbled speech headings in both *Troublesome Reign* and *King John*, John Dover Wilson pointed out that in the Folio text of II.i in *King John* Shakespeare twice mistakenly identified the French King as "Lewis" (errors corrected by later editors). Wilson surmised that Shakespeare was revising a scene in *Troublesome Reign* from memory or from a manuscript, rather than the printed copy, which identified the King correctly as "Philip" (ed. *King John* xliv–xlv). Although Wilson did not draw the conclusion, this possible access to a manuscript carries an implication that it was in Shakespeare's possession because he wrote it.

Eric Sams commented that "Shakespeare ... not only treated *Troublesome Reign* exactly as if it was his own intellectual property to exploit as he pleased, but also shared idiosyncratic features and expressions with its author" ("Troublesome Wrangle" 43). Indeed, as some critics have observed, Shakespeare's re-use of the characters and plot of his old play seems to have caused him to write a poorer play than if he had started afresh (Ornstein 88–9).

R. A. Law pointed to important structural differences between Shakespeare's early history plays and *King John*, suggesting that the play suffered because of its reliance on *Troublesome Reign*. For instance, in *1 Henry VI, Richard III, Richard II* and *1 Henry IV*, the opening scene clearly establishes the dominant theme of the play and presents the conflicts that will inform the plot. But in the first scene of *King John*, after less than fifty lines that introduce the theme and plot of the play, the action shifts abruptly to the issue of the Bastard's paternity, where it remains until the end of the scene more than 200 lines later ("Date of *King John*" 124). This dispute within the Falconbridge family has no bearing on subsequent events and is irrelevant to the play, except as it vaguely reflects the question of John's legitimacy as king.

Another difference between Shakespeare's early history plays and *King John* is the scope of events that the author attempts to depict. In his early history plays Shakespeare compressed the action so as to focus on only one or two years in the king's reign, thus simplifying the story and maintaining a unity of action and motivation. But in *King John*, he attempted to encompass the whole of John's seventeen-year reign from his accession to his death, with the result that the play's dominant theme, if not obscured, is open to varying interpretations. *Troublesome Reign* suffers from the same fault—a loose, episodic structure incorporating the entire reign that weakens the play and muddies its message. This feature of *Troublesome Reign* marks a difference in compositional technique from Shakespeare's other early history plays—a difference probably due to its place in the earliest stratum of his dramatic work. It is obvious that his ability to select and compress the events of an entire reign improved over the years, and the best explanation for his departure from his usual custom in *King John* is that in rewriting the story, he took over the existing structure of *Troublesome Reign*, just as he took over its characters.

## LINGUISTIC SIMILARITIES

Nearly all commenters have found numerous instances of phrasing and vocabulary in *Troublesome Reign* that are repeated or echoed in *King John*. In his text of the anonymous play, Bullough found over ninety in Part 1 alone, and another thirty-five in Part 2. E. K. Chambers wrote that "in some 150 places [in *King John*] a few words from T. R. are picked up and used" (*William Shakespeare* 1:367). In his study of the two plays, Charles Forker listed twenty-two phrases and five nearly-identical stage directions in *Troublesome Reign* that are repeated nearly verbatim in *King John* ("Intertextuality" 137–42).[17] One stage direction in both plays is significant in that the character whom it directs to enter appears in the earlier play, but not in *King John*:

[S. D.]        Enter the Shrive, & whispers the Earle of Sals. in the eare.

*1 TR* 65.1

[S. D.]        *Enter a* SHERIFF [*and whispers Essex in the ear*]

*King John* I.i.43

In *Troublesome Reign*, the sheriff of Northamptonshire appears on stage, identifies himself, and delivers eight lines explaining the dispute among the Falconbridges, and is not heard from again. In *King John*, the sheriff enters, but doesn't speak and is not shown exiting. (The bracketed words have been added by later editors.) Several scholars have noted this anomaly and proposed various explanations, but the most reasonable is that Shakespeare, in rewriting *Troublesome Reign*, decided to delete the sheriff's dialogue, but neglected to delete the stage direction (Forker, "Intertextuality" 140; Thomas, "'Enter a sheriffe'").

Many of the verbal borrowings identified by scholars are distinctive or unusual words and phrases, such as Constance's use of the word *perjured* to describe King John; King Philip's claim that Englishmen have greeted him with shouts of *Vive le roy*; and Blanche's complaint that her wedding will be marred by warfare—*dreadful drums* in *Troublesome Reign*, *churlish drums* in *King John*. Most of the verbal parallels, however, are ordinary words and phrases, such as

Arthur's reference in both plays to his soul passing into heaven at his coming death, and the references in both plays to the tide at the Lincoln Wash that has destroyed John's baggage train. These similarities suggest that the words and ideas were not consciously appropriated, but were the natural expression and use of words by the same writer.

Of the many parallel phrases first pointed out by Geoffrey Bullough, one is a reference to Philip the Bastard made by the French Ambassador in both plays.

| *Chatillion.* | Next them a bastard of the King's deceast, | *1 TR* 490 |
| *Chat.* | With them a bastard of the king's deceas'd; | |
| | | *King John* II.i.65 |

In another example, King John addresses the men of Angiers with the same words in both plays:

| *John.* | You men of *Angiers,* and as I take it my loyall Subjects, | *TR* 613–14 |
| *K. John.* | You men of Angiers, and my loving subjects — | |
| | | *King John* II.i.204 |

In the preparations for the marriage of Blanche and Lewis the Dauphin, there are two instances of identical language in both plays. The amount of money in the dowry that King John promises will accompany his niece on her marriage to Lewis the Dauphin, and the location of the marriage is identical in both plays, but both are unhistorical

| *John.* | And thirtie thousand markes of stipend coyne. | *1 TR* 841 |
| *K. John.* | Full thirty thousand marks of English coin | *King John* II.i.530 |
| *John.* | Lets in and there prepare the mariage rytes Which in S. *Maries* Chappell presently Shallbe performed ere this Presence part. | *1 TR* 856–8 |
| *K. Phi.* | Let in that amity which you have made For at Saint Mary's Chapel presently The rites of marriage shall be solemnized. | |
| | | *King John* II.i.537–39[18] |

Another instance of identical language in the two plays:

John.          Brother of *Fraunce*, what say you to the Cardinall?

*1 TR* 1010

K. John.      Philip, what say'st thou to the Cardinal?

*King John* III.i.202

## PLAGIARISM OR REVISION?

Shakespeare is well-known for using other men's plots, usually classical or foreign authors, but in no case did he appropriate the precise plot and structure, as well as all the characters, from another writer's play or prose work. Moreover, no contemporary of Shakespeare, except possibly Robert Greene, ever accused him of plagiarism, not even the alleged author of *Troublesome Reign*.

Also weighing against the charge of plagiarism is the body of evidence linking Shakespeare to the Queen's Men, the company that is named on the 1591 and 1611 Quartos as having performed *Troublesome Reign*. There is no record of Shakespeare's involvement with any theatrical company before 1594, but the internal evidence for this association—from the Queen's Men's plays themselves—is strong. Scott McMillin and Sally-Beth MacLean have shown that of the nine plays that can be confirmed as belonging to the Queen's Men's repertory, four, including *Troublesome Reign*, have Shakespearean counterparts, that is, plays in the Shakespeare canon that resemble them in terms of plot, characters and verbal details. Thus, the Queen's Men's repertory is "the largest theatrical source of Shakespeare's plots..." (160–1).[19] This suggests that Shakespeare's use of *Troublesome Reign* as a source was not a theft, but part of a pattern of re-writing his previous work.

As pointed out in the Introduction, in recent years scholars have accepted the fact that Shakespeare was a persistent and meticulous reviser of his own work, especially his history plays. The evidence supplied above supports the conclusion that Shakespeare was revising his own play, not appropriating another playwright's plot and characters. The evidence in the following Sections strongly associates *Troublesome Reign* in numerous ways with the accepted Shakespeare canon.

## Troublesome Reign *and the Shakespeare Canon*

Editors and critics have found numerous parallels of vocabulary, imagery, ideas and conceits, and dramatic devices between *Troublesome Reign* and canonical Shakespeare plays. For example, in 2010 Charles Forker examined the relationship between *Troublesome Reign* and *Richard II*, and wrote the following: "I note some seventy verbal, thematic, thought-related, staging and situational links ... that ... suggest a considerable impact of *The Troublesome Reign* upon *Richard II*" ("Intertextuality" 128–9). Some of these are incorporated in the pages that follow, along with dozens of other parallels noticed, or unnoticed, by other scholars. In almost every case, Forker excepted, scholars charge the anonymous author with the borrowing, even though *Troublesome Reign* was printed before anything else by Shakespeare, and its crude style and simple dramaturgy suggest that it antedates the entire accepted canon.

## Words and Phrases

As part of his argument that the play is a "loose piracy" of *King John*, A. S. Cairncross (*Hamlet* 139) called attention to these lines from scene vi of 2 *Troublesome Reign* in which Philip the Bastard reports the flight of John's army from the French:

| | | |
|---|---|---|
| *Philip.* | Another moan, *to make the measure full.* | 2 TR 811 |
| | At last the rumour scal'd these ears of mine, | |
| | Who rather chose, as sacrifice for Mars, | |
| | Than ignominious *scandal by retire.* | |
| | I cheer'd the troops, as did the prince of Troy | |
| | His weary followers [apost]gainst the Myrmidons, | |
| | Crying aloud, "*Saint George, the day is ours!*" | |
| | But *fear* had *captivated* courage quite; | 2 TR 816–22 |
| | *Short tale to make*—myself among the rest, | |
| | Was fain to fly before the eager foe. | 2 TR 825–6 |
| | When in the morning our troupes did *gather head* ... | 2 TR 831 |
| | Cairncross's spelling, emphasis and omitted lines. | |

Citing the following lines from II.i of 3 *Henry VI*, Cairncross claimed that the passage from *Troublesome Reign* "echoes unmistakably the similar account related by Warwick of the defeat of St. Alban's" (*Hamlet* 138–9):

| | |
|---|---|
| *War.* | And now, to add *more measure* to your woes, |
| | I come to tell you things sith then befall'n. |

*3 Henry VI* II.i.105–6

|  |  |  |
|---|---|---|
| | *Short tale to make*, we at Saint Albons met, | 120 |
| | Or more than common *fear* of Clifford's rigour | |
| | Who thunders to his *captives* blood and death, | 126–7 |
| | So that we *fled*; the King unto the Queen; | |
| | Lord George your brother, Norfolk, and myself, | |
| | In haste, post-haste, are come to join with you; | |
| | For in the marches here we heard you were, | |
| | *Making another head* to fight again. | 137–41 |
| Rich. | 'Twas odds, belike, when valiant Warwick fled: | |
| | Oft have I heard his praises in pursuit, | |
| | But ne'er till now his *scandal of retire*. | 148–50 |
| Edw. | Then strike up drums: God and *Saint George for us!* | 204 |

Cairncross's spelling and emphasis.

Cairncross identified another line from *Troublesome Reign*: "Are marching hether-ward in good aray" (2 *TR* 643) as a borrowing from 2 *Henry VI*: "Is marching hitherward in proud array" (IV.ix.27). The similarity of words and phrases in these passages is clear enough, and Cairncross concluded that they had been copied from the *Henry VI* plays by the author of *Troublesome Reign*. However, these particular words, phrases and ideas (and several others from the same passage) were clearly part of Shakespeare's linguistic stock, and he used them all repeatedly in every period of his career. As regards the first phrase in the passage (not noted by Cairncross), Shakespeare frequently juxtaposed the words *moan* and *make*:

| | |
|---|---|
| Launce. | Now come I to my sis- |
| | ter; mark the moan she makes. |

*Two Gentlemen of Verona* II.iii.29–30

| | |
|---|---|
| Bass. | Nor do I now make moan to be abridg'd |

*The Merchant of Venice* I.i.126

He also used *full* to modify *measure*:

| | |
|---|---|
| Pet. | Carouse full measure to her maidenhead |

*The Taming of the Shrew* III.ii.225

| | |
|---|---|
| Bea. | the wedding, mannerly-modest, as |
| | a measure, full of state and ancientry; |

*Much Ado About Nothing* II.i.76–7

The use of *fled* as a past participle adjective in the passage from *Troublesome Reign* (not noted by Cairncross) is unusual:

*Philip.*        That *John* was fled, the King had left the field.        2 TR 815

This use is not recorded by the *Oxford English Dictionary* before 1621. But Shakespeare's use of it in *Much Ado About Nothing* is identical with that in *Troublesome Reign* in 1591:

*D. Pedro.*        Did he not say, my brother was fled?

                                                   *Much Ado About Nothing* V.i.204

The juxtaposition of *rumour* and *ear* (not noted by Cairncross) is also common in Shakespeare:

*Hel.*        That pitiful rumour may report my flight,

              To consolate thine ear. Come, night; end, day

                                                   *All's Well That Ends Well* III.ii.127–8

*Glou.*        That fill his ears with such dissentious rumors.

                                                   *Richard III* I.iii.46

So is the use of *retire* as a noun, accompanied by a pejorative noun or adjective:

*P. Cha.*        Our trumpets sound dishonor and retire

                                                   *Edward III* IV.vii.1

*Com.*        Breath you, my friends. Well fought; we are come off

              Like Romans, neither foolish in our stands

              Nor cowardly in retire.        *Coriolanus* I.vi.1–3

Shakespeare twice mentioned the Prince of Troy (Hector) in connection with Achilles' Myrmidons in *Troilus and Cressida*:

*Ulyss.*        Together with his mangled Myrmidons,

               That noseless, handless, hack'd and chipp'd, come to him,

               Crying on Hector.        *Troilus and Cressida* V.v.33–5

*Achil.*        On, Myrmidons, and cry you all amain,

               "Achilles hath the mighty Hector slain!"

                                                   *Troilus and Cressida* V.viii.13–14

As regards Cairncross's last example, at least half-a-dozen of Shakespeare's characters (Edward IV, John Talbot, Richard III, Richard II, Henry V, and Petruchio) invoke St. George in one form or another, usually at the start of a battle.

⚘

In *Hamlet*, Polonius uses the same formulaic expression, "short tale to make," that appeared in *Troublesome Reign*:

Pol.        And he repell'd, a short tale to make,

            Fell into a sadness, then into a fast,        *Hamlet* II.ii.146–7

The words and imagery in this couplet in *Troublesome Reign*:

Phil.       By this time night had shadowed all the earth,

            With sable curteines of the blackest hue,        *2 TR* 827–8

are replicated in both *Hamlet* and *Lucrece*:

Ham.       The rugged Pyrrhus, he whose sable arms,

            Black as his purpose, did the night resemble

                                                        *Hamlet* II.ii.452–3

            Till sable Night, mother of dread and fear,

            Upon the world dim darkness doth display,        *Lucrece* 117–18

Shakespeare referred to the goddess Juno more than twenty times throughout his plays, several times in connection with her jealousy and anger over Jove's attentions to Io:

Pis.        You made great Juno angry.        *Cymbeline* III.iv.164

Vol.        Leave this faint puling, and lament as I do,

            In anger, Juno-like. Come, come, come        *Coriolanus* IV.ii.52–3

He also used the phrase *gather head* in the same way as did the author of *Troublesome Reign*:

Aemil.      The Goths have gathered head, and with a power

            Of high-resolved men, bent to the spoil.

                                        *Titus Andronicus* IV.iv.63–4

Although Shakespeare never repeated the precise phrase "marching hitherward in proud array" after using it in *2 Henry VI*, he used its constituent phrases again in one of his last plays:

Mess.       The British pow'rs are marching hitherward.

                                        *King Lear* IV.iv.21

Edg.               ...    set not thy sweet heart on

            proud array. Tom's a-cold.        *King Lear* III.iv.82–3

Thus, every word and phrase claimed by Cairncross to have been copied from 2 and 3 *Henry VI*, and several additional ones, was used in the same way and in the same context by Shakespeare in later plays. Either the unknown author of *Troublesome Reign* anticipated these dozen phrases and ideas that Shakespeare used throughout his career, or that author was Shakespeare, and they were early formulations of his own that he retained in his vocabulary.

In his 1939 edition of *King Richard II*, John Dover Wilson noted several passages of "fatuous lines" and "jog-trot" couplets in Act V that to him represented "the very bankruptcy of rhyme-tagging" (lxx–lxxi). He also identified "fossil rhymes" in passages in Acts I and III. These anomalies suggested to him that portions of the play had been originally written in couplets, and that Shakespeare's *Richard II* was his adaptation of an older, crudely-written play by an anonymous playwright. He then observed that "couplets of an exactly similar stamp" could be found throughout *Troublesome Reign*. Quoting an exchange between Hubert and Arthur containing ten rhymed couplets, he noted its "clumsy manoeuvring for rhyme" and its "frequent sacrifice of sense and clarity to metrical considerations" (lxxiii). To explain these similarities, he suggested that a single author, a "learned historian, but a very indifferent poet," wrote both *Troublesome Reign* and the original *Richard II*.

In a 1940 article, William Wells asserted that Thomas Kyd was the author of *Edward III*, and "with slight reservations," of *Troublesome Reign* ("Thomas Kyd" 218–24). One reason he gave for rejecting Robert Greene's and George Peele's authorship of either play was that "Neither author paid serious attention to the verities of history" (218). On the other hand, "the author (or authors) of 'Edward III' and the 'Troublesome Reign' treated the facts of history with more respect. If strict accuracy was not always held in mind, nothing unhistorical in either play flouted probability or the laws of nature."[20] Wells also found words and phrases in *Troublesome Reign* that are echoed in Shakespeare's plays:

| | | |
|---|---|---|
| *Constance.* | I trouble now the fountaine of thy youth, | |
| | And make it moodie with my doles discourse, | *1 TR* 899–900 |
| | | |
| *Kath.* | A woman mov'd is like a fountain troubled, | |
| | Muddy, ill-seeming, thick, bereft of beauty, | |
| | | *The Taming of the Shrew* V.ii.142–3 |

\* \* \*

| | | |
|---|---|---|
| *Philip.* | I beg some instance whence I am extraught. | *1 TR* 341 |

*Mother.*     And when thou knowest from whence thou art extraught,

                                                                 *1 TR* 394

*Rich.*       Sham'st thou not, knowing whence thou art extraught,

                                                          *3 Henry VI* II.ii.14

                              \* \* \*

*Philip.*                                                    ... yet
              wil I abide all wrongs, before I once open my mouth to un-
              rippe the shamefull slaunder of my parents,          *1 TR* 86–8

*1. Mur.*     Unrip'st the bowels of thy sov'reign's son.

                                                          *Richard III* I.iv.207

                              \* \* \*

*John.*       *Arthur*, although thou troublest *Englands* peace,          *1 TR* 849

*Q. Mar.*     On thee, the troubler of the poor world's peace!

                                                          *Richard III* I.iii.220

                              \* \* \*

*John.*       Set downe, set downe the load not worth your pain,     *2 TR* 787

*Anne.*       Set down, set down your honourable load,          *Richard III* I.ii.1

In his 1961 Arden edition of *Titus Andronicus*, J. C. Maxwell quoted the
following lines from *Troublesome Reign*:

*John.*       How, what, when, and where, have I bestowd a day
              That tended not to some notorious ill?          *2 TR* 1060–1

He remarked that this passage "can hardly be independent of Aaron's speech"
(xxi):

*Aar.*        Even now I curse the day—and yet I think
              Few come within the compass of my curse—
              Wherein I did not some notorious ill:

                                                   *Titus Andronicus* V.i.125–7[21]

He also noticed a connection between the following passages, spoken over the bodies of Arthur in *Troublesome Reign* and Tamora in *Titus Andronicus*, respectively:

| | |
|---|---|
| *Pemb.* | But who is this? lo, Lords, the withered flowre, |
| | Who in his life shinde like the Mornings blush, |
| | Cast out a doore, denide his buriall right, |
| | A pray for birds and beasts to gorge upon.    2 TR 33–6 |

| | |
|---|---|
| *Luc.* | No funeral rite, nor man in mourning weed, |
| | No mournful bell shall ring her burial, |
| | But throw her forth to beasts and birds to prey: |
| | *Titus Andronicus* V.iii.196–8 |

Another parallel with *Titus Andronicus*:

| | |
|---|---|
| *John.* | Me thinks the Devill whispers in mine eares    2 TR 1049 |

| | |
|---|---|
| *Aar.* | Some devil whisper curses in my ear, |
| | *Titus Andronicus* V.iii.11 |

In his 1964 Arden edition of *3 Henry VI*, Cairncross (187) found additional words and phrases in it that were similar to those in *Troublesome Reign*:

| | |
|---|---|
| *Phil.* | The impartiall tyde deadly and inexorable, |
| | Came raging in with billowes threatning death, |
| | And swallowed up the most of all our men.    2 TR 833–6 |

| | |
|---|---|
| *K. Hen.* | The sun that sear'd the wings of my sweet boy, |
| | Thy brother Edward; and thyself the sea |
| | Whose envious gulf did swallow up his life. |
| | *3 Henry VI* V.vi.23–5 |

Despite these obvious parallels, and other indications of his authorship, none of these four editors—Cairncross, Wilson, Wells and Maxwell—fathomed that *Troublesome Reign* was the work of Shakespeare.

Most of the examples of further use by Shakespeare of words and phrases from *Troublesome Reign* come from the canonical history plays. In *Troublesome*

*Reign*, the word "latest" is used three times to mean "last" in the context of dying:

| K. Philip. | Ile fight it out unto the latest man. | *1 TR* 603 |
|---|---|---|

| Bast. | And with that word, the rope his latest friend | *2 TR* 163 |
|---|---|---|

| Bast. | And call on Christ, who is your latest friend. | *2 TR* 1073 |
|---|---|---|

This usage is echoed by Warwick in both *3 Henry VI*:

War.      Where your brave father breath'd his latest gasp

*3 Henry VI* II.i.108

and in *2 Henry IV*:

War.      And hear (I think) the very latest counsel
            That I shall ever breathe.      *2 Henry IV* IV.v.182–3

✍

When confronted by their presumed assassins, both Arthur in *Troublesome Reign* and Richard in *Richard II* respond in nearly-identical language:

Arthur.      Why how now sirs, what may this outrage meane?    *1 TR* 1337

K. Rich.      How now, what means death in this assault?

*Richard II* V.v.105

Further examples of the author's use of words and phrases identical to those later used by Shakespeare:

John.      I see I see a thousand thousand men      *2 TR* 1052

Cran.      Upon this land a thousand thousand blessings,

*Henry VIII* V.iv.19

| | | |
|---|---|---|
| *Clown.* | A thousand thousand sighs to save, | *Twelfth Night* II.iv.63 |
| | Would purchase thee a thousand thousand friends | |
| | | *Lucrece* 963 |

* * *

| | | |
|---|---|---|
| *Abb.* | For why the deede is meritorious. | *2 TR* 925 |
| *Suff.* | Seeing the deed is meritorious | *2 Henry VI* III.i.270 |

* * *

| | | |
|---|---|---|
| *Philip.* | And holds my right, as lineall in discent | *1 TR* 353 |
| *King.* | From whence you spring by lineal descent. | |
| | | *1 Henry VI* III.i.165 |

* * *

| | | |
|---|---|---|
| *John.* | Ile ceaze the lazie Abbey lubbers lands | |
| | Into my hands to pay my men of warre. | *1 TR* 309–10 |
| *K. Rich.* | Think what you will, we seize into our hands | |
| | His plate, his goods, his money and his lands. | |
| | | *Richard II* II.i.209–10 |

* * *

| | | |
|---|---|---|
| *Essex.* | What have you done my Lord? Was ever heard | |
| | A deede of more inhumane consequence? | *1 TR* 1671–2 |
| *Anne.* | Thy deeds inhuman and unnatural | |
| | Provoke this deluge most unnatural. | *Richard III* I.ii.60 |

* * *

| | | |
|---|---|---|
| *Philip.* | A boone O Kings, a boone doth *Philip* beg | |
| | Prostrate upon his knee: which knee shall cleave | |
| | Unto the superficies of the earth, | *1 TR* 918–20 |

| Aum. | For ever may my knees grow to this earth, |
| | My tongue cleave to my roof within my mouth, |

*Richard II* V.iii.30–1

| Duch. | Our knees still kneel till to the ground they grow. |

*Richard II* V.iii.106

\* \* \*

| Constance. | Poore helples boy, hopeles and helples too, | 1 TR 894 |
| Ege. | Hopeless and helpless doth Egeon wend, |
| | But to procrastinate his liveless end. |

*Comedy of Errors* I.i.157–8[22]

\* \* \*

| Fr. Lawrence. | To my conscience a clog to dye like a dog. | 1 TR 1284 |
| Percy. | With clog of conscience and sour melancholy |

*Richard II* V.vi.20

\* \* \*

| Mess. | So he and his environed with the tyde, |
| | On Lincolne washes all were overwhelmed, | 2 TR 968–9 |
| Tit. | For now I stand as one upon a rock |
| | Environ'd with a wilderness of sea |
| | Who marks the waxing tide grow wave by wave, |

*Titus Andronicus* III.i.93–5

\* \* \*

| John. | Peter, unsay thy foolish doting dreame, | 2 TR 130 |
| Bagot. | My Lord Aumerle, I know your daring tongue |
| | Scorns to unsay what once it hath delivered. |

*Richard II* IV.i.8–9

| Old L. | I'll have more, or else unsay't; and now, |
| | While 'tis hot, I'll put it to the issue. |

*Henry VIII* V.i.175–6[23]

The Earl of Essex uses the phrase "convey this body hence" twice in *Troublesome Reign*, referring to the body of Arthur, who has just jumped to his death. Two scenes later, the Earl of Salisbury uses a similar phrase over the body of the French nobleman Melun who, in a dying speech, has just warned the English of a French plot to attack them, and enabled them to avoid a defeat:

| | | |
|---|---|---|
| *Essex.* | Meane while let us conveigh this body hence | 2 *TR* 102 |
| *Essex.* | Then let us all convey the body hence. | 2 *TR* 109 |
| *Sals.* | Beare hence the bodie of this wretched man, | 2 *TR* 778 |

In a play written a decade later, and set 250 years later, *1 Henry VI*, John Talbot, Earl of Shrewsbury, uses a nearly-identical phrase over the dying Earl of Salisbury, who has just been shot during the fighting against the French at Orleans:

| | | |
|---|---|---|
| Tal. | Bear hence his body; I will help to bury it. | *1 Henry VI* I.iv.87 |

As Charles Forker remarks, "…verbal borrowings were often virtually subliminal—useful phrases from a probably unsorted store of theatrical utterances that had become commonplace in the minds of their users" ("Intertextuality" 136). But the "useful phrase" and the similar association with the Earl of Salisbury is more likely to have occurred in the mind of a single person—the author of both plays. Oxford would use similar language in similar situations in two later plays:

| | |
|---|---|
| *Gaunt.* | Convey me to my bed, and then to my grave; |

*Richard II* II.i.137

| | |
|---|---|
| *Prin.* | Bear hence this body and attend our will; |

*Romeo and Juliet* III.i.196

Forker cites two other instances of "verbal borrowings" from *Troublesome Reign* that reappear in Shakespeare plays, and that occur in similar contexts. Lewes the Dauphin has just defeated John's army in Kent, and is urged by Cardinal Pandulph to return to France now that John has finally submitted to the Pope. Lewes does not want to go:

| | | |
|---|---|---|
| *Lewes.* | But al's not done that *Lewes* came to doo | 2 *TR* 665 |

In *Henry V*, where once again the English and French are at war, this time at Agincourt, King Henry uses the identical phrase after his troops have routed the French:

*K. Hen.*     Well have we done, thrice valiant countrymen:

          But all's not done—yet keep the French the field.

Henry V IV.vi.1–2

In yet another example of an echo from *Troublesome Reign* in a canonical play, two loyal subjects react with alarm at the sight of their stricken monarchs. On King John's impending death by poison, Philip the Bastard exclaims:

*Bast.*      O piercing sight, he fumbleth in the mouth,

          His speech doth faile:              *2 TR* 1103–4

On the heath, near the end of *King Lear*, Edgar addresses his maddened King:

*Edg.*      O thou side-piercing sight!        *King Lear* IV.vi.85

Neither of these phrases—"But all's not done" and "piercing sight"—appears elsewhere in Tudor drama (Forker, "Intertextuality" 136).

While writing a scene in *2 Henry VI* in which Duke Humphrey rebukes his wife Eleanor, Shakespeare seems to have recalled language that Constance and Queen Elinor used against each other in *Troublesome Reign*. After she is captured by the French, Queen Elinor rages at Constance:

*Q. Elinor.*    Contemptuous dame unrev[er]ent Dutches thou,   *1 TR* 1063

In the scene in *2 Henry VI*, Humphrey, Duke of Gloucester, and his wife are alone on stage:

*Glou.*      Nay, Eleanor, then must I chide outright

          Presumptuous dame, ill-nurtur'd Eleanor,   *2 Henry VI* I.ii.41–2

In *Troublesome Reign*, Constance accuses Elinor of blocking her son's claim to the throne:

*Constance.*   I theres the griefe, confusion catch the braine,

          That hammers shifts to stop a Princes Reign.    *1 TR* 540–1

Duke Humphrey uses similar imagery to chide his wife:

*Glou.*      And wilt thou still be hammering treachery,

          To tumble down thy husband and thyself

2 Henry VI I.ii.47–8

In both quotations the verb *hammer* is used in the same sense: "to devise or contrive."

The kings in *Troublesome Reign* and *Richard II* each use the verb *undo* "in the context of royal displacement or deposition" (Forker, "*Troublesome Reign*" 130):

| John. | And *John* of *England* now is quite undone. | 2 TR 224 |
| K. Rich. | Now mark me how I will undo myself; | *Richard II* IV.i.203 |

One passage in particular, from the second scene of *Troublesome Reign*, yields several words that are found in similar association with each other later in the Shakespeare canon:

Bastard.　What words are these? how doo my sinews shake?
　　　　　My Fathers foe clad in my Fathers spoyle,
　　　　　A thousand furies kindle with revendge,
　　　　　This hart that *choller* keepes a consistorie,
　　　　　Searing my *inwards* with a brand of hate:
　　　　　How doth *Alecto* whisper in mine eares?
　　　　　Delay not Philip, kill the *villaine* straight,
　　　　　Disrobe him of the matchles moniment
　　　　　Thy Fathers triumph ore the Savages.
　　　　　Base heardgroome, coward, *peasant*, worse than a threshing *slave*,
　　　　　What makst thou with the Trophie of a King?
　　　　　Shamst thou not coystrell, loathsome *dunghill* swad,
　　　　　To grace thy carkasse with an ornament
　　　　　Too precious for a Monarch's coverture?　　　*1 TR* 556–69

Flu.　　　Alexander, God knows, and you know, in his rages,
　　　　　and his *furies*, and his wraths, and his *cholers*,

　　　　　　　　　　　　　　　　　　　　*Henry V* IV.vii.34–5

Iago.　　But partly led to diet my revenge,
　　　　　For that I suspect the lusty Moor
　　　　　Hath leap'd into my seat; the thought whereof
　　　　　Doth (like a poisonous mineral) gnaw my *inwards*;

　　　　　　　　　　　　　　　　　　　　*Othello* II.i. 294–7

Pist.　　Rouse up *revenge* from ebon den with fell *Alecto's* snake.

　　　　　　　　　　　　　　　　　　　　*2 Henry IV* V.v.37

| York. | Base *dunghill villain* and mechanical | *2 Henry VI* I.iii.193 |
| Ham. | O, what a rogue and *peasant slave* am I! | *Hamlet* II.ii.550 |
| Pist. | Shall *dunghill* curs confront the Helicons? | |
| | And shall good news be baffled? | |
| | Then, Pistol, lay thy head in *Furies'* lap. | |

*2 Henry IV* V.iii.104–6 (emphasis added)

This catalog of parallels of words and phrases between *Troublesome Reign* and plays in the subsequent Shakespeare canon, especially the early history plays, does not exhaust the examples. But it amply demonstrates that Shakespeare and the author of *Troublesome Reign* used a great many of the same words and phrases to convey similar ideas, often in an identical context.

## IMAGERY

The types of images used by a writer have long been recognized as keys to his particular experiences, thoughts and circumstances. Generally speaking, the patterns of an author's use of particular images remain with him throughout his life, and are thus useful in determining authorship. On the other hand, images are common property, so to speak, and those used to describe the human environment or illuminate human behavior are part of a common stock of language employed by every writer. The value of evidence based on imagery is therefore limited with respect to determining authorship, and is useful primarily in its corroborative and cumulative effect.

Shakespeare's use of imagery—pre-eminent among Elizabethan dramatists—has been the subject of numerous investigations. In her comprehensive *Shakespeare's Imagery and What It Tells Us*, Caroline Spurgeon counted the images in each of the Folio plays, plus *Pericles*—arriving at an average of about 180. The lowest number was sixty (*The Comedy of Errors*) and the highest, 340 (*Troilus and Cressida*). Among the early history plays (*1, 2* and *3 Henry VI, Richard II, Richard III*), the average was about 200 (361–2). As regards frequency, *Troublesome Reign*, with well over 200 images, fits easily in this group.

Spurgeon identified the most prevalent images in Shakespeare as coming from "nature (especially the weather, plants and gardening), animals (especially birds), and what we may call everyday and domestic, the body in health and sickness, indoor life, fire, light, food and cooking...."[24] The imagery in *Troublesome Reign* is in large part identical:

1. Images from the weather and the seasons—about twenty.
2. Imagery from plants and gardening—about fifteen.
3. Images using animals and birds—about thirty.
4. Imagery from the body and bodily functions—more than 110.
5. Images from domestic and indoor life—about thirty. There are only a few of food and cooking.

Spurgeon also mentioned Shakespeare's preference for images of the sun, stars and planets moving in their spheres (21). *Troublesome Reign* contains about a dozen images of this type, and an equal number referring to "heaven" or "heavens."

Among Shakespeare's five early history plays, Spurgeon noted many images expressing the idea of the nobility, especially the royal house, as a tree or plant, often one that suffers untimely cropping or cutting (216–22). Most of the plant and tree imagery in *Troublesome Reign* reflects the identical idea— with the words *root, plant, flower, crop, stock, branch*, etc., repeatedly used in reference to the extended royal family. Among the images in King John's last lines, is this prediction that a descendant will successfully defy the Pope (as did Henry VIII in the 1530s):

| | |
|---|---|
| *John.* | From out these loynes shall spring a Kingly braunch |
| | Whose armes shall reach unto the gates of *Rome*, |
| | And with his feete treade downe the Strumpets pride, |
| | That sits upon the chaire of *Babylon.*          2 *TR* 1084–7 |

In *3 Henry VI*, Gloucester evokes the same image of King Edward in the same language:

| | |
|---|---|
| *Glou.* | Ay, Edward will use women honourably. |
| | Would he were wasted, marrow, bones, and all, |
| | That from his loins no hopeful branch may spring, |
| | To cross me from the golden time I look for! |
| | *3 Henry VI* III.ii.124–7 |

On the other hand, Spurgeon noted that in the imagery of the twelve other dramatists she examined, she could find "not a trace of love or care for the plant, so characteristic of [Shakespeare]." Of first-hand gardening knowledge and observation, she could "find practically no sign...."[25]

The image of a cold wind or other malevolent force that "nips" a person's life or well-being is expressed twice in *Troublesome Reign*:

| K. Philip. | This bitter winde must nip some bodies spring | *1 TR* 487 |
|---|---|---|
| Lewes. | Only two crosses of contrary change | |
| | Do nip my heart, and vexe me with unrest. | *2 TR* 934–5 |

This image is found several times in the Shakespeare canon:

| Sat. | These tidings nip me, and I hang the head | |
|---|---|---|
| | As flowers with frost, or grass beat down with storms. | |
| | | *Titus Andronicus* IV.iv.70–1 |
| Prin. | If frosts and fasts, hard lodging and thin weeds | |
| | Nip not the gaudy blossoms of your love | |
| | | *Love's Labor's Lost* V.ii.801–2 |
| Wol. | The third day comes a frost, a killing frost, | |
| | And when he thinks, good easy man, full surely | |
| | His greatness is a-ripening, nips his root, | |
| | | *Henry VIII* III.ii.355–7 |

Although this was a well-known proverbial sentiment, Spurgeon remarked, "…I do not find in all my search of other dramatists, any single image of frosts and sharp winds nipping buds, which is so common with Shakespeare" (91).

E. K. Chambers also observed Shakespeare's "numerous similes and metaphors from natural history and country life," especially in the early plays and narrative poems. He added that he did not find these in any of the other dramatists of the time—Marlowe, Kyd, Peele, Greene, Lodge, Nashe and Drayton (*William Shakespeare* 1:287).

In his study of Shakespeare's imagery, W. H. Clemen noted that a main feature of his early style was "amplification," and "the endeavour to weave into the tissue of the play at every opportunity some sort of decorative device" (41). This tendency to amplify and decorate is obvious throughout *Troublesome Reign*, especially in the author's use of classical images:

| Philip. | This Madame, this, hath drove me from myselfe: | |
|---|---|---|
| | And here by heavens eternall lampes I sweare, | |
| | As cursed *Nero* with his mother did, | |
| | So I with you, if you resolve me not. | *1 TR* 368–71 |

| | |
|---|---|
| *John.* | O *John*, these troubles tyre thy wearyed soule, |
| | And like to *Luna* in a sad Eclipse, |
| | So are thy thoughts and passions for this newes.    2 *TR* 336–8 |

The reaction of Essex to the death of Arthur is another example:

| | |
|---|---|
| *Essex.* | If waterfloods could fetch his life againe, |
| | My eyes should conduit foorth a sea of teares, |
| | If sobbs would helpe, or sorrowes serve the turne, |
| | My heart should volie out deepe piercing plaints. |
| | But bootlesse weret to breathe as many sighes |
| | As might eclipse the brightest Sommers sunne,    2 *TR* 40–5 |

In another passage, the playwright decorates and amplifies a patriotic speech by the dying Frenchman Melun, who has defected to the English side. Melun exhorts the rebellious English barons not to be taken in by the French King's promises:

| | |
|---|---|
| *Mel.* | Lift up your swords, turne face against the French, |
| | Expell the yoke thats framed for your necks. |
| | Back warmen, back, imbowell not the clyme, |
| | Your seate, your nurse, your birthdayes breathing place, |
| | That bred you, beares you, brought you up in armes. |
| | Ah! be not so ingrate to digge your Mothers grave, |
| | Preserve your lambes and beate away the Wolfe.    2 *TR* 756–62 |

Bullough drew attention to a corresponding passage in *King John*, in which Philip the Bastard admonishes the same barons, whom he calls "revolts," with similar words:

| | |
|---|---|
| *Bast.* | And you degenerate, you ingrate revolts, |
| | You bloody Neroes, ripping up the womb |
| | Of our dear mother England, blush for shame; |

*King John* V.ii.151–3

Clemen also observed that "in the presence of death Shakespeare's characters always use metaphorical language" (43). This is certainly the case in all three of the scenes in *Troublesome Reign* in which a character is faced with death or serious injury. When Hubert comes to put out Arthur's eyes at the behest of King John, Arthur remonstrates with him, using metaphors of hell and damnation:

*Arthur.*      Ah *Hubert,* makes he thee his instrument

To sound the tromp that causeth hell triumph?      *1 TR* 1373–4

*Arthur.*      This seale, the warrant of the bodies blisse,

Ensureth Satan chieftaine of thy soule:      *1 TR* 1381–2

In his dying speech to the English barons, Lord Melun invokes the Romans' god of war and goddess of the earth to metaphorically describe his wounds and his impending death:

*Mel.*      Behold these scarres, the dole of bloudie *Mars*

Are harbingers from natures common foe,

Cyting this trunke to *Tellus* prison house?      *2 TR* 726–8

As he succumbs to poison, King John unleashes the grandly jumbled image of the destruction of the Church (already quoted above):

*John.*      From out these loynes shall spring a Kingly braunch

Whose armes shall reach unto the gates of *Rome,*

And with his feete treade downe the Strumpets pride,

That sits upon the chaire of *Babylon.*      *2 TR* 1084–7

The absence of certain types of images from the Shakespeare canon is also significant. Spurgeon noted the paucity of images from "town life and scenes—taverns, shops, streets, marts, pageants and crowds." Literary references, other than classical or Biblical, are also comparatively infrequent in the Shakespeare canon (45). The absence of this same range of images from town life and scenes is apparent in *Troublesome Reign.* Moreover, all but one of the two dozen literary references in the play are to classical or Biblical figures, and all but two (Mors and Morpheus) are mentioned in later Shakespeare plays. All the saints alluded to in *Troublesome Reign,* including the two who are unhistorical (St. Withold and St. Charitie), are also mentioned in later Shakespeare plays (Sider 198; Onions 33).

As to the literary sources to which Shakespeare turned for his images, references and quotations from classical mythology, it is well known that the overwhelming majority of them are from the works of Ovid, and nearly all the remainder from Vergil (Root 3). The author of *Troublesome Reign* was similarly inclined. Of the twenty such allusions and quotations in the play, all but one (Luna) appear in the works of Ovid or Vergil.

This accumulation of parallel imagery between *Troublesome Reign* and numerous Shakespeare plays is further evidence that the anonymous author and Shakespeare were the same person, and that in this early play he used many of the images he would return to throughout his life.

## IDEAS AND CONCEITS

Closely related to imagery are the ideas and conceits that a writer employs to illustrate and animate his dialogue. Here again, many of those found several times in the Shakespeare canon appeared first in *Troublesome Reign*. One such idea is the bold face-to-face defiance of a king. In the first scene of *Troublesome Reign*, after the French King Philip challenges him to a "set battle," King John replies:

| | | |
|---|---|---|
| *K. John.* | I accept the challenge, and turne the defiance | |
| | to thy throate. | *1 TR* 654–5 |

Shakespeare returned to this idea in three early history plays:

| | | |
|---|---|---|
| *Douglas.* | Arm, gentlemen, to arms! for I have thrown | |
| | A brave defiance in King Henry's teeth | *1 Henry IV* V.ii.41–2 |
| *King.* | Yea, for my sake, even to the eyes of Richard | |
| | Gave him defiance. | *2 Henry IV* III.i.64–5 |

In *Edward III*, the Duke of Lorraine and Edward the Black Prince address each other in the same way:

| | |
|---|---|
| *Lorraine.* | Then, Edward, here, in spite of all thy lords, |
| | I do pronounce defiance to thy face. |
| *Prince* | Defiance, Frenchman! we rebound it back |
| *Edward.* | Even to the bottom of thy master's throat, |

Edward III I.i.87–90

Later in the play, the Black Prince's message to the French King is the same:

| | | |
|---|---|---|
| *Prince* | Return him my defiance in his face. | *Edward III* IV.iv.86 |
| *Edward.* | | |

Thus, the simple idea, first expressed in a single line in *Troublesome Reign*, is repeated in three of Shakespeare's subsequent history plays.

The idea of the blood of the wounded or the dead spilling into a personified earth, found in Greek and Roman tragedy, as well as in Genesis, appears in *Troublesome Reign*. Constance uses it to complain about a wedding that has ended a war that might have brought her son Arthur to the throne:

*Constance.*  Is all the bloud yspilt on either part,

Closing the cranies of the thirstie earth,

Growne to a lovegame and a Bridall feast?          *1 TR* 890–2

Shakespeare was sufficiently drawn to the idea to elaborate on it in several subsequent plays:

*Rich.*          Thy brother's blood the thirsty earth hath drunk,

*3 Henry VI* II.iii.15

*War.*          Then let the earth be drunken with our blood!

*3 Henry VI* II.iii.23

*Tit.*          Let my tears staunch the earth's dry appetite,

My sons' sweet blood will make it shame and blush.

*Titus Andronicus* III.i.14–15

*Anne.*          O earth! which this blood drink'st, revenge his death!

*Richard III* I.ii.63

*King.*          No more the thirsty entrance of this soil

Shall daub her lips with her own children's blood,

*1 Henry IV* I.i.5–6

The figurative use of the contrast between shadow and substance is one of Shakespeare's favorite formulations. In *Troublesome Reign*, Constance used the two words to contrast her son Arthur's legitimate claim to the throne with John's illegal possession:

*Constance.*  *Arthur* my Sonne, heire to thy elder Brother,

Without ambiguous shadow of discent,

Is Sovereign to the substance thou withholdst.          *1 TR* 512–14

Of the more than a dozen instances of this idea in the Shakespeare canon, two occur in early plays:

*Marc.*          Alas, poor man, grief has so wrought on him,

He takes false shadows for true substances.

*Titus Andronicus* III.ii.79–80

*Bushy.*          Each substance of a grief hath twenty shadows,

Which shows like grief itself, but is not so;

*Richard II* II.ii.14–15

In another early play, Shakespeare also used the word *shadow* in connection with a king's legitimacy. As Warwick removes the captured King Edward's crown in *3 Henry VI*, he declares:

*War.*        But Henry now shall wear the English crown,

          And be true king indeed, thou but the shadow.

*3 Henry VI* IV.iii.49–50

Another distinctive idea in *Troublesome Reign* is a request made to a dying man that he raise his hand as a signal of agreement. As King John is dying, Cardinal Pandulph asks him to raise his hand if he forgives the assembled barons for their revolt against him:

*Pand.*        Then good my Lord, if you forgive them all,

          Lift up your hand in token you forgive.          *2 TR* 1115–16

The idea is repeated in a similar scene in *2 Henry VI*, in which the King addresses the dying Cardinal Beaufort:

*King.*        Lord Card'nal, if thou think'st on heaven's bliss,

          Hold up thy hand, make signal of thy hope.

*2 Henry VI* III.iii.27–8

The author of *Troublesome Reign* also demonstrated an acute interest in language and how it is communicated, another trait that Shakespeare exhibited throughout the entire canon. Jane Donawerth made a count of the words Shakespeare used relating to "ideas about language"—words such as *speak, speech, language, name, voice, tongue, mouth, throat, ear, breath, pen, paper, ink* and *parchment*. The frequent use of these words is characteristically Shakespearean, and every play is replete with them. Donawerth found that in the early plays these words are used at the rate of once in every twenty-four lines, and for the entire canon, once in twenty-six.[26] The frequency of these words in *Troublesome Reign* is higher still—127, once in every twenty-three lines.

The idea of the multitude as a vulgar mob is common in Shakespeare. In his two dozen uses of the word, he attached such adjectives to it as *barbarous, rude, giddy, ragged, fool, distracted,* and *bisson* (purblind). One particular variation of this idea—that a multitude is many-headed—is first presented in *Troublesome Reign*:

*John.*        The multitude (a beast of many heads)

          Doo wish confusion to their Soveraigne;          *2 TR* 233–4

Shakespeare returned to the idea in *2 Henry IV*:

*Rumor.*　　　　　　　　　　　　　Rumor is a pipe

　　　Blown by surmises, jealousies, conjectures,

　　　And of so easy and so plain a stop

　　　That the blunt monster with uncounted heads,

　　　The still-discordant wav'ring multitude,

　　　Can play upon it.　　　　　　　*2 Henry IV* Ind. 15–20

And again in his last Roman play:

*1. Cit.*　　　for once we stood up about the

　　　corn, he himself stuck not to call us the many-headed

　　　multitude.　　　　　　　　*Coriolanus* II.iii.15–17

These examples, far from exhaustive, are further evidence that Shakespeare and the author of *Troublesome Reign* shared many similar ideas and conceits, as well as a similar interest in language and communication.

## Vocabulary and Style

As pointed out in Chapter II, Shakespeare is well-known for his verbal inventiveness. Alfred Hart's research has shown that all his works contain a high proportion of new or rare words.[27] His average is about fifty per play, far more than any other writer (Schäfer 83). The author of *Troublesome Reign* was also unusually inventive—adding more than forty-five new words to the language in this play alone. He was also creative in his use of existing words in different senses or meanings. Besides the new words he introduced, he used more than one hundred additional words in senses or meanings that are described by the *OED* as first used in *Troublesome Reign* in 1591 or subsequently by another writer. For most of the words in these two categories, that writer was Shakespeare. More than 260 additional unusual words and meanings in *Troublesome Reign* also appear in later Shakespeare plays. At least a dozen usages in the play have not yet been defined by the *OED*.

Shakespeare also excelled in another aspect of verbal facility—the number of different words he used in each play. In 1943, Alfred Hart published his count of the number of different words in each of the plays in the First Folio, adding *Pericles*. Although the individual play count ranged from 2037 different words in *The Comedy of Errors* to 3882 in *Hamlet*, most fell within the 2500–3100-word range, the average being 2800 different words per play.[28] Using Hart's methodology, a count of the different words in *Troublesome Reign* yields a total of 2952. In *King John*, Shakespeare used 2901 different words. By comparison, Hart's count of different words in Marlowe's plays showed that in no play did he use more than about 2500 different words, and his average, excluding the short *The Massacre at Paris*, was 2280 ("Vocabularies" 138).

A more refined measure of lexical variety is the ratio of different words to total lines. Among Shakespeare's ten English history plays, the ratio is one different word per line (Hart "Vocabularies" 132, Table I). The author of *Troublesome Reign* used different words at the same rate—one per line.

In the course of compiling his Concordance in the late 1960s, Marvin Spevack extracted a group of 335 words that occurred in each of the thirty-six plays of the Folio, plus *Pericles* and *The Two Noble Kinsmen* (108–113). With the exception of two, all 335 words appear in *Troublesome Reign*. In 2005, Ben Crystal and David Crystal compiled a list of one hundred content-carrying words that are frequently encountered in the Shakespeare canon (xxi–xxvii). More than half of these words can be found in *Troublesome Reign*.

*Troublesome Reign* is also strikingly similar to Shakespeare's plays in another aspect of vocabulary usage—the incidence of words beginning with certain prefixes. Hart examined six of Shakespeare's history plays and counted the number of different words beginning with seventeen prefixes: *ad, be, con, de, dis, en, ex, for, in, out, over, per, pre, pro, re, sub* and *un*. The number of such prefixes in the six plays averaged 516 (*Homilies* 227). The number of different words with these same prefixes in *Troublesome Reign* is 494. By contrast, Hart found an average of only 382 such prefixes in three plays of Marlowe (*Homilies* 227). Shakespeare was so fond of the prefix *un* that he used it more than 170 times to coin new words or meanings (Schäfer 130–4). Hart could find only four such coinages using the prefix *un* in seven plays of Marlowe, and three each in the plays and poems of Robert Greene and George Peele (*Homilies* 229). The author of *Troublesome Reign* used more than forty words with an *un* prefix, and is credited by the *OED* with coining two new words prefixed by *un*, *unfitted* and *unhallowed*. Both of these coinages subsequently appeared in the Shakespeare canon.

*Troublesome Reign* also comports with Shakespeare's history plays in its liberal use of the words *thou, thee, thy* and *thine*. In his study of his use of these words, Jonathan Hope compiled an index that reflected their use in each play. (See "*True Tragedy* and Other Canonical Plays" in Chapter II.) For the nine history plays (excepting the late *Henry VIII*), the average index is fourteen (62–3). A similar calculation for *Troublesome Reign* reveals an index of seventeen.

Another notable feature of Shakespeare's plays is their unusual length. Of the principal Elizabethan playwrights, only Jonson and Dekker exceeded Shakespeare's average play length of about 2750 lines. At 2936 lines, *Troublesome*

*Reign* is near the average of Shakespeare's history plays (3080), somewhat longer than *King John* (2570), and hundreds of lines longer than the average play by Peele, Greene, Kyd or Marlowe (Hart, "Length" 149).

It has been observed by various scholars that Shakespeare preferred certain spellings and usages over others. As pointed out in Chapter II, David Lake wrote: "Through all his work, Shakespeare prefers *them* to *'em* and *hath* to *has*; he makes very little use of *I'm* ... or of *'Has* for *he has*..." (281). The author of *Troublesome Reign* used *them* sixty times, *'em* never. He used *hath* fifty-six times, *hast* fifteen times, and *has* never. Neither *I'm* nor *'Has* for *he has* appears in the play at all. In addition to preferring *hath* to *has*, Shakespeare, at least in his first twenty plays or so, preferred *doth* to *does*, rarely using the latter (Jackson, 56). Similarly, the author of *Troublesome Reign* used *doth* thirty-four times, *does* never. Thus, the verbal creativity and diversity, and the verbal habits and preferences, of the author of *Troublesome Reign* comport almost exactly with those of Shakespeare, especially in his early plays.

## DRAMATIC DEVICES

"Shakespeare's habit of recycling his favorite dramatic devices is generally recognized." This is the opening sentence of an article by E. A. J. Honigmann in which he described a collection of ten "self-repetitions" in *King John* that appeared in previous and subsequent Shakespeare plays. He suggested that "such self-repetitions, when of sufficient quality and quantity, can serve as an authorial finger-print..." ("Self-Repetitions" 175). The most notable of these is the cluster of "character stereotypes" that appeared in both *King John* and *Troublesome Reign*. These include "scolding, aggressive and bitter women" who "revile their enemies and/or utter long-winded lamentations." Both Queen Elinor and Constance in *Troublesome Reign* fit this description, as do Joan of Arc in *1 Henry VI*; the Duchesses of Gloucester and York, and Queen Elizabeth in *2* and *3 Henry VI*; Lady Macbeth; Cleopatra; Volumnia in *Coriolanus*; and Paulina in *The Winter's Tale*.

Honigmann also points to the childlike Arthur of Brittany—a "prattling" and "pathetic" boy who is threatened with death—who is the person around whom the plot of *Troublesome Reign* revolves. This character type reappears as the Earl of Rutland in *3 Henry VI*, the princes in the Tower in *Richard III*, and Macduff's son in *Macbeth*. Cardinal Pandulph, a Machiavellian churchman in *Troublesome Reign* who is preoccupied with temporal rather than spiritual affairs, is recreated in Cardinal Beaufort in *1* and *2 Henry VI*, Cardinal Bourchier in *Richard III*, the Archbishop of Canterbury in *Henry V*, and Cardinal Wolsey in *Henry VIII*. Blanche of Castile, a princess who "becomes a pawn in the dynastic power-game" in *Troublesome Reign*, may be compared to Princess Bona in *3 Henry VI*, Lady Anne in *Richard III*, and Katherine in *Henry V*.

Honigmann calls the Bastard Falconbridge in *King John* "one of Shakespeare's undisputed successes." He is plainly one of a group of "high-spirited men, mostly youthful, who may be either villains (Aaron, Richard III, Iago, Edmund) or boisterous but not evil (Petruchio, Mercutio, Graziano, Hotspur)" ("Self-Repetitions" 177)." The comparison with Richard III is arresting. Both he and Falconbridge are humorous and impudent; they mock conventional lovers and taunt their enemies; each displays a sadistic streak and ridicules "the simplicity of others." "Each is a keen analyst of motives, including his own," and neither has much "respect for his superiors" and offers them unrequested advice. Each admires his father, vows to revenge his death, casts doubt on his mother's chastity, and is rebuked by her. "Who, except Shakespeare," Honigmann asked, "could have *imagined* the Bastard, the crowning glory of the play, so closely related as he is to Richard III...."[29] Although the Falconbridge in *Troublesome Reign* is a paler and less-substantial character than his namesake in *King John*, these remarks apply almost equally to him. In the same category is Harold Bloom's pronouncement that the Falconbridge in *King John* "...inaugurates Shakespeare's invention of the human" (52).

In addition to his resemblance to Richard III, the Bastard Falconbridge in *Troublesome Reign* introduces a major theme that flourished in the Shakespeare canon—bastards and bastardy. The Falconbridges of *Troublesome Reign* and *King John* are the clear predecessors of such notable bastards as Edmund in *King Lear* and Thersites in *Troilus and Cressida*. In her study of bastards in Renaissance drama, Alison Findlay found that during the two decades between 1590 and 1611, of the thirty-three plays with parts for bastards or characters threatened with bastardy, eight are by Shakespeare.[30]

Another of Shakespeare's "self-repetitions" cited by Honigmann is the "heroic or idealized figure from the immediate past" who both overshadows and serves as a yardstick for the next generation. This describes the recently-deceased Richard I in both *Troublesome Reign* and *King John*, as well as Henry VI in *1, 2* and *3 Henry VI*, Hamlet's father, Julius Caesar in *Antony and Cleopatra*, and the dead fathers in *All's Well That Ends Well*. Another repeated dramatic device identified by Honigmann is a plot "structured around a voluntary abdication or a deposition." In this category, with *Troublesome Reign* and *King John*, are *3 Henry VI*, *Richard II*, *King Lear* and, "in modified form," *Titus Andronicus* (I.i.187ff), *Measure for Measure* (I.i.13ff), *Pericles*, *The Winter's Tale* and *The Tempest*.

Additional examples include the instance of an ambiguous prophecy being understood too late (repeated in *2 Henry VI* and *Richard III*), and the siege of a city serving as a "focal point for a sequence of scenes" (found also in *1 Henry VI, Henry V* and *Coriolanus*) ("Self-Repetitions" 176). What is significant about the ten "self-repetitions" in *King John* that Honigmann found repeated in other Shakespeare plays is that nine of them appeared earlier in *Troublesome Reign*.

Two dramatic devices common to *Troublesome Reign* and other Shakespeare plays that Honigmann failed to mention have been pointed out by other scholars. In her study of bit parts in Shakespeare's plays, Molly M. Mahood wrote: "The most notable feature of Shakespeare's pairs or trios of hired assassins is that almost invariably one man among them shows reluctance before or remorse after the deed" (49). She cited two well-known examples—the Second Murderer of Duke Humphrey in *2 Henry VI*:

> 2 Mur.    O that it were to do! What have we done?
>
> Didst ever hear a man so penitent?    *2 Henry VI* III.ii.3–4

and the two assassins in *Richard III*:

> 2. Mur.    The urging of that word "judgment" hath
> bred a kind of remorse in me.
>
> 1. Mur.    What? art thou afraid?
>
> 2. Mur.    Not to kill him, having a warrant, but to
> be damned for killing him, from which no warrant
> can defend me.    *Richard III* I.iv.107–112

In *Troublesome Reign*, King John orders Hubert de Burgh to put out the eyes of Prince Arthur. (In *King John*, his order is to kill him.) Three men accompany Hubert, who instructs them to wait outside, remarking "I would the King had made choice of some other executioner." They are also reluctant, and reply "We go, though loath" (*1 TR* 1317, 1325). Hubert and Arthur then engage in a lengthy dialogue about the morality of the act, and Hubert confesses to the same fear as the Second Murderer in *Richard III*, even using the same word—*warrant*:

> Hubert.    I faint, I feare, my conscience bids desist:
> Faint did I say, feare was it that I named?
> My King commaunds, that warrant sets me free:
> But God forbids, and he commaundeth Kings.    *1 TR* 1433–6

Another example from the same two plays is the exchange between the victims, Arthur and Clarence, and those who come to harm them. Both Hubert in *Troublesome Reign* and the murderers in *Richard III* assert that they have been commanded by royal authority to commit their acts:

| | |
|---|---|
| *Hubert.* | My Lord, a subject dwelling in the land |
| | Is tyed to execute the King's commaund.    *1 TR* 1391–2 |
| *1. Mur.* | What we will do, we do upon command. |
| *2. Mur.* | And he that hath commanded is our King |
| | *Richard III* I.iv.193–4 |

Both Arthur and Clarence respond sharply with the same argument:

| | |
|---|---|
| *Arthur.* | Yet God commands, whose power reacheth further, |
| | That no commaund should stand in force to murther. |
| | *1 TR* 1393–4 |
| *Clar.* | Erroneous vassals, the great King of kings |
| | Hath in the table of his law commanded |
| | That thou shalt do no murther. Will you then |
| | Spurn at his edict, and fulfill a man's?    *Richard III* I.iv.195–8 |

The murderers in *Richard III* carry out their mission, but Hubert doesn't—thus introducing a recurring Shakespearean character, the faithful, but conscience-stricken, servant who is virtuously disobedient. This character-type appears again as Pisanio in *Cymbeline*, Antony's servant Eros in *Antony and Cleopatra*, and the servant in *King Lear* who resists Cornwall's assault on Gloucester.

Another Shakespearean dramatic device is the frequent use of messengers to move the plot along, especially in the history plays. Several scholars have pointed out that both formal and informal messengers appear more often in Shakespeare's plays than in those of other playwrights. For instance, Bernard Beckerman, who called the messenger "a unique figure peculiar to Shakespeare," calculated that an average of five messengers appeared in each of Shakespeare's fifteen Globe plays, but an average of only one in each of the non–Shakespearean Globe plays (205; also Mahood 52–3.) In five of Shakespeare's early history plays, the average number of formal messengers alone is also five. Here again, Shakespeare's practice, at the beginning of his career and at the end, was prefigured by the author of *Troublesome Reign*, who used nine formal, and half-a-dozen informal, messengers in his play.

Although Honigmann acknowledged the unusual number of identical dramatic devices used in both *Troublesome Reign* and in later Shakespeare plays, he rejected the idea that a single author was responsible. He offered the expla-

nation that the author of *Troublesome Reign* had acted in *King John*, and that
the language, characters and dramatic devices common to both plays, as well
as the many other echoes from plays by Marlowe, Peele, Kyd and Shakespeare
that appeared in *Troublesome Reign*, were the result of its author recollecting
material from these playwrights' works in which he had acted ("Self-Repetitions" 180). But the sheer volume and consistency of these similarities and
echoes weighs against this explanation. Indeed, Honigmann himself asks if this
author "anticipated so many of Shakespeare's dramaturgic characteristics and
felicities that we have to see him as, to all intents, another Shakespeare?" ("Self-
Repetitions" 177–8.)

But it is not necessary to imagine another Shakespeare (an actor/play-
wright who is otherwise absent from Elizabethan drama) to account for this
phenomenon. The external evidence of the publication and ascription of *Troublesome Reign* agrees with the substantial internal evidence that the play preceded Shakespeare's *King John*, as well as the numerous other plays by
Shakespeare and other dramatists who echoed its material. The close relationship of the two *King John* plays, and the very obvious similarities between their
authors' habits of stagecraft, style and vocabulary, their use of the same character types, and their reliance on similar dramatic devices, all lead to the conclusion that they were created by the same person—Edward de Vere, the real
Shakespeare.

## A Mistaken Ascription to George Peele

In a paper published in 2004, Brian Vickers asserted, on the basis of internal evidence, that George Peele was the author of *Troublesome Reign*, and suggested that Shakespeare took over the structural outline of the play in the
mid–1590s, "totally transforming its language and characterization, and fully
realizing the dramatic potential of the story" (111). This attribution to Peele
was endorsed by Hugh Craig in his review of Vickers' paper, by Charles Forker
in his edition of *Troublesome Reign*, and by Charles Whitworth in his review
of Forker's edition in *Cahiers Élisabéthains*. However, an analysis of Vicker's
evidence reveals that although the language, themes and dramatic devices in
*Troublesome Reign* have some similarity to those in Peele's plays, the more striking similarity is to those in Shakespeare's. Furthermore, as shown above, there
is substantial external evidence for Shakespeare's authorship of the play, but
none for Peele's.

An active poet and playwright for about fifteen years, Peele composed
five, possibly six, plays, four long poems, several mayoral pageants, and mis-

cellaneous occasional poetry before his death at forty in 1596. Peele signed most of his poems and one of his plays (*Edward I*), describing himself as "Maister of Artes in Oxenford" (Hook, ed. *Edward I*, 1). He is identified as the author on the title pages of two others—*The Old Wives Tale* and *David and Bethsabe*. He has become a magnet for the authorship of anonymous plays. More than a dozen, from *Clyomon and Clamydes* (c. 1570) to *Alphonsus, Emperor of Germany* (printed 1654) have been ascribed to him.[31]

The evidence Vickers cited consists almost entirely of similarities of language, themes and dramatic devices between Peele's works and *Troublesome Reign*. These are analyzed below.

PARALLELS OF VOCABULARY AND
LONGER SEQUENCES OF THOUGHT

With respect to parallels of vocabulary, Vickers cited seven uncommon words and phrases—*remunerate, gratify, pheere* or *fere, Mother Queen, Acon* for *Acre, Palestine,* and *Albion*, that are used in *Troublesome Reign* and that also appear in Peele's work (79–82). All seven are used in other Elizabethan plays and five of the seven appear in canonical Shakespeare plays

*Men.*      To gratify his noble service that

Hath thus stood for his country; therefore to please you,

*Coriolanus* II.ii.40–1

*Pal.*                    This anatomy

Had by his young fair fere a boy, and I

Believed it was his,      *The Two Noble Kinsmen* V.i.115–17

*Chat.*      With him along is come the mother-queen,      *King John* II.i.62

*Emil.*      I know a lady in Venice would have walked

barefoot to Palestine for a touch of his nether lip.

*Othello* IV.iii.38–9

*Brit.*      In that nook-shotten isle of Albion      *Henry V* III.v.14

Although Shakespeare never used the precise word *remunerate* (*remunerated* in *Troublesome Reign*), his spirited repetition of *remuneration* five times in a single speech in *Love's Labor's Lost* (III.i.136–42) is sufficient to show that the word was part of his vocabulary. Besides Peele and the author of *Troublesome Reign*, both Anthony Munday and Michael Drayton used *Acon* for *Acre*, but neither word appears in the Shakespeare canon. In sum, these uncommon words and phrases in *Troublesome Reign* are not peculiar to Peele, and all but two of them appear in Shakespeare's plays.

Vickers also refers to "a number of convincing parallels between *Troublesome Reign* and Peele's works involving longer sequences of thought and language" (80–1). Almost all of these particular sequences can also be found in the Shakespeare canon, especially in the early history plays, and in several cases Shakespeare's development of the thought is closer to its use in *Troublesome Reign* than is Peele's. One example is the speech of the dying Arthur, after he has jumped from the walls of his prison. In this case Arthur seems more concerned "with the grief that his death will cause his mother, rather than his own sensations or sufferings":

> Arthur.    My fall, my fall, hath kilde my Mother's Sonne.
>
> How will she weepe at tidings of my death?
>
> [My death indeed, O God my bones are burst.]
>
> Sweet Jesu save my soule, forgive my rash attempt,
>
> Comfort my Mother, shield her from despaire,        2 *TR* 17–21

In a similar speech by the dying Absalon in Peele's biblical tragedy *David and Bethsabe*, he "harps upon the thought of the sorrow that his death will bring to David" (Vickers 80–1):

> Absalon.    O my deere father, that thy melting eyes
>
> Might pierce this thicket to behold thy sonne,
>
> Thy deerest sonne gor'de with a mortall dart:
>
> Yet Joab pittie me, pittie my father, Joab,
>
> Pittie his soules distresse that mournes my life,
>
> And will be dead I know to heare my death.
>
> *David and Bethsabe* 1533–38[32]

It is true that the two passages express a similar thought, but it is not an unusual one, especially when the dying speaker is a young person referring to a parent. Shakespeare deleted this particular idea from Arthur's dying speech in the corresponding scene in *King John*, but he has Arthur express it clearly one act earlier, just after King John's troops have captured him:

> Arth.    O, this will make my mother die with grief!    *King John* III.iii.4

Moreover, Shakespeare used the phrase "my mother's son" several times in later plays:

| *Pet.* | Now, by my mother's son, and that's myself, | |
|---|---|---|
| | | *The Taming of the Shrew* IV.v.6 |
| *Shad.* | My mother's son, sir | *2 Henry IV* III.ii.127 |

He also used it in the first scene of *King John*:

| *Rob.* | That this my mother's son was none of his | *King John* I.i.111 |
|---|---|---|
| *K. John.* | My mother's son did get your father's heir. | *King John* I.i.128 |

The line that Vickers omitted from the quotation (in brackets)

| *Arthur.* | My death indeed, O God my bones are burst. | *2 TR* 19 |
|---|---|---|

is even more striking in its similarity to the line in *King John* uttered in the same context. When Arthur has jumped from the wall, he declares:

| *Arth.* | Heaven take my soul, and England keep my bones! | |
|---|---|---|
| | | *King John* IV.iii.10 |

The stage direction in *Troublesome Reign* that divides Arthur's speech in half also contains a reference to bones:

| [*S. D.*] | He leapes, and brusing his bones, after he was [wakes?] | |
|---|---|---|
| | from his traunce, speakes thus: | *2 TR*, following 11 |

Further, the phrase *How will* in the lines from Arthur's speech:

| *Arthur.* | My fall, my fall, hath kilde my Mother's Sonne. | |
|---|---|---|
| | How will she weepe at tidings of my death? | *2 TR* 17–18 |

is used in the identical context in the well-known scene in *3 Henry VI*:

| *Son.* | How will my mother for a father's death | |
|---|---|---|
| | Take on with me, and ne'er be satisfied! | |
| *Father.* | How will my wife for slaughter of my son | |
| | Shed seas of tears, and ne'er be satisfied! | |
| *K. Hen.* | How will the country for these woeful chances | |
| | Misthink the king, and not be satisfied! | *3 Henry VI* II.v.103–108 |

The imagery in another line from Arthur's speech—

*Arthur.*     My heart controules the office of my toong,          *2 TR* 23

is echoed in two of Shakespeare's history plays:

*Bull.*     When the tongue's office should be prodigal
            To breathe the abundant dolor of the heart.   *Richard II* I.iii.256-7

*North.*    Hath but a losing office, and his tongue
            Sounds ever after as a sullen bell.          *2 Henry IV* I.i.101-2

A simple count reveals over 900 occurrences of *heart* and more than 500 of *tongue* in the Shakespeare canon. Further, there are more than thirty occurrences of *control* and its variants in Shakespeare's plays and poems. In sum, the language in this five-line example from *Troublesome Reign* is more closely linked to language in *King John* and in other Shakespeare plays than to the passage in Peele's *David and Bethsabe.*

Vickers also cited three other examples from Sykes of "distinctive phraseology" that is shared by *Troublesome Reign* and Peele's plays and poetry:

*Queene*    Though God and Fortune have bereft from us
*Elinor.*   Victorious *Richard* scourge of Infidels,
            And clad this Land in stole of dismall hieu          *1 TR* 2-5

*Mercury.*  Melpomene, the muse of tragicke songes,
            With moornfull tunes in stole of dismall hue

                              *The Arraignment of Paris* 610–11[33]

The last four words in these passages are clearly identical, but both *dismal* and *hue* appear in the Shakespeare canon about two dozen times in their ordinary meanings, such as in the following:

*Nur.*     A joyless, dismal, black, and sorrowful issue!

                                      *Titus Andronicus* IV.i.66

*Bot.*     The woosel cock so black of hue,

                              *A Midsummer Night's Dream* III.i.125

The notion of a landscape being clad in a particular color is similarly expressed in *Hamlet*:

*Hor.*     But, look, the morn, in russet mantle clad,       *Hamlet* I.i.166

Other uses of *bereft* as a transitive verb in Shakespeare:

| | | |
|---|---|---|
| *Glou.* | He that bereft thee, lady, of thy husband, | *Richard III* I.ii.138 |
| *Fath.* | And hath bereft thee of thy life too late. | *3 Henry VI* II.v.93 |

Even more significant are the following lines from *2 Henry VI*, where both *dismal* and *bereft* are used in the same way as in the passage from *Troublesome Reign*:

| | | |
|---|---|---|
| *King.* | Came he right now to sing a raven's note, | |
| | Whose dismal tune bereft my vital pow'rs; | *2 Henry VI* III.ii.40–1 |

In a second pair of examples, these couplets from *Troublesome Reign*:

| | | |
|---|---|---|
| *Mother.* | Or if thy knewst what sutes, what threates, what feares, | |
| | To moove by love, or massacre by death, | *1 TR* 395–6 |
| *Constance.* | What joy, what ease, what rest can lodge in me, | |
| | With whom all hope and hap doth disagree? | *1 TR* 870–71 |

are compared with these lines in *David and Bethsabe*:

| | |
|---|---|
| *David.* | What tunes, what words, what looks, what wonders pierce |
| | My soule, incensed with suddain fire? |
| | What tree, what shade, what spring, what paradise |
| | Enjoyes the beautie of so faire a dame? *David and Bethsabe* 49–52 |

This simple use of *epanaphora*, the repetition of the same word at the beginning of successive sentences or phrases, is common throughout Shakespeare, such as:

| | |
|---|---|
| *Ulyss.* | What plagues and what portents, what mutiny! |
| | What raging of the sea, shaking of earth! |
| | *Troilus and Cressida* I.iii.96–7 |
| | Some glory in their birth, some in their skill, |
| | Some in their wealth, some in their body's force, |
| | Some in their garments, though new-fangled ill, |
| | Some in their hawks and hounds, some in their horse; |
| | Sonnet 91.1–4 |

Another parallel offered by Vickers is the phrase *withered flowre* in *Troublesome Reign*, which Peele had used in a poem he wrote in the 1580s:

| | | |
|---|---|---|
| *Pemb.* | But who is this? lo Lords the withered flowre | |
| | Who in his life shinde like the Mornings blush, | |
| | Cast out a doore, denide his buriall right, | *2 TR* 33–5 |

Loe now at last the Greekes have home againe,

With losse of many a Greeke and Troyans life

Their wither'd flower, King Menelaus' wife.

*The Tale of Troy* 475–8[34]

In *Troublesome Reign* the phrase *withered flower* is used to describe the dead boy, Arthur. In Peele's *The Tale of Troy* it describes the tarnished and penitent Helen being brought back to Sparta by her husband. Shakespeare used the image of a person as a withered flower in *Richard II*:

Gaunt.      To crop at once a too long withered flower.     *Richard II* II.i.134

He also used *withered* to describe a dead person in *1 Henry VI*, where the French General predicts how Talbot will look within the hour:

Gen.      These eyes that see thee now well colored,

        Shall see thee withered, bloody, pale and dead.

*1 Henry VI* IV.ii.37–8

In *Cymbeline*, Belarius invokes the image of withered flowers to describe the dead Cloten:

Bel.      You were as flow'rs, now wither'd:      *Cymbeline* IV.ii.286

Thus, the "withered flower" phrase in *Troublesome Reign* matches more closely with Shakespeare's later usage than it does with Peele's in *The Tale of Troy*.

SIMILAR VERBAL MANNERISMS

As examples of Peele's "verbal mannerisms" in *Troublesome Reign*, Vickers (84) cited (from Sykes) these quotations from *Troublesome Reign* in which the author "omits the pronoun 'I' before 'dare' in the present tense":

Q. Elinor.   Dare lay my hand that *Elinor* can gesse

        Whereto this weightie Embassade doth tend          *1 TR* 19–20

Abb.      Dare lay my life heel kill me for my place          *2 TR* 892

He noted that this mannerism occurs in four places in Peele's *The Arraignment of Paris*:

Paris.      Thou hast a soret of pretie tales in stoore,

        Dare saye no Nymphes in Ida woods hath more:          236–7

| | | |
|---|---|---|
| *Oenone.* | For thou hast harde my stoore long since, dare say, | 251 |
| *Juno.* | Dare saie for him a never strayed so wyde: | 333 |
| *Mercury.* | Dare wage my winges the lasse doth love, she lookes so bleak and thin, | 605 |

While the pronoun is absent in all six examples, in three of the four from *The Arraignment of Paris*, the phrase *dare say* is an ordinary "discourse marker" and has no meaning. The phrase *dare lay* in both *Troublesome Reign* quotations refers to the placing of a bet, as it does in an identical usage in *Twelfth Night*:

| | | |
|---|---|---|
| *Sir T.* | I dare lay any money 'twill be nothing yet. | *Twelfth Night* III.iv.396 |

As for the omitted *I*, there are many examples in the Shakespeare canon:

| | | |
|---|---|---|
| *1. Cit.* | Give you good morrow, sir | *Richard III* II.iii.6 |
| *Mir.* | Beseech you, father. | *The Tempest* I.ii.474 |
| *Gon.* | Beseech you sir, be merry; | *The Tempest* II.i.1 |

Vickers also cited several examples of "symmetrical phrases in the form *aba*," which he finds "plentiful" in *Troublesome Reign* (84). This is the rhetorical device *ploce*, the repetition of a word within the same phrase or line:

| | | |
|---|---|---|
| *Philip.* | Come Madame come, you neede not be so loth | *1 TR* 385 |
| *Q. Elinor.* | I tell thee I, not envie to thy Son, | *1 TR* 544 |
| *John.* | Griefe upon griefe, yet none so great a griefe | *2 TR* 839 |
| *John.* | As I, poore I, a triumph for despight. | *2 TR* 843 |

This same formulation is found throughout Peele's plays:

| | |
|---|---|
| *Oenone.* | Then had not I poore I bin unhappie |
| | *The Arraignment of Paris* 657 |
| *Muly Mah. S.* | As death, plae [*sic*] death with fatall shaft hath giuen. |
| | *The Battle of Alcazar* 122 |
| *Jethray.* | Go madame goe, away, you must be gone, |
| | *David and Bethsabe* 318 |
| *Lluel.* | Come Potter come and welcome to,    *Edward I* 1287[35] |

However, the use of *ploce* is common in English poetry from Chaucer to Pope, especially in Shakespeare:

K. Hen.      Woe above woe! grief more than common grief!

*3 Henry VI* II.v.94

Stan.      Come, madam, come, I in all haste was sent.   *Richard III* IV.i.56

Doll.      Come, you rogue, come bring me to a justice.

*2 Henry IV* V.iv.26

Cade.      Stand, villain, stand, or I'll fell thee down    *2 Henry VI* IV.ii.115

The frequent use of self-address or self-naming is another verbal mannerism in *Troublesome Reign* that Vickers found in Peele's works. However, this is not peculiar to Peele, nor to the author of *Troublesome Reign*. In her study of self-naming in Shakespeare's plays, Deborah Curren-Aquino found it to be "prevalent" in the early plays and "still important" in several middle plays (160). Moreover, in her cursory survey of plays by Shakespeare's early contemporaries, she found a "high frequency" of the technique in plays by Kyd, Greene and Marlowe, as well as Peele (163, n. 14).

Vickers also cited the excessive use of vocatives, i.e., adjectives used to call or address someone, especially those followed by an imperative, as "another verbal detail that links *The Troublesome Reign* to Peele's canon" (86). He supplied the following data for *Troublesome Reign* and two of Peele's plays:

| | Vocatives alone | Vocatives with imperatives | Total Vocatives | Frequency every × lines |
|---|---|---|---|---|
| *Troublesome Reign* (2936 lines) | 372 | | | 7.9 |
| | | 140 | | 21. |
| | | | 512 | 5.7 |
| *Edward I* (2685 lines) | 526 | | | 5.1 |
| | | 102 | | 26.3 |
| | | | 628 | 4.3 |
| *The Battle of Alcazar* (1278 lines) | 111 | | | 11.5 |
| | | 78 | | 16.4 |
| | | | 189 | 6.8 |

This rather limited comparison indicates that Peele used vocatives more often in *Edward I* and less often in *The Battle of Alcazar* than did the author of *Troublesome Reign*. In all three plays, the use of vocatives is higher than in most plays of the period. However, in two of his early history plays, *2 Henry VI* and *3 Henry VI*, Shakespeare used vocatives at almost the same rate as the author of *Troublesome Reign.*

| | Vocatives alone | Vocatives with imperatives | Total Vocatives | Frequency every × lines |
|---|---|---|---|---|
| 2 Henry VI | 263 | | | 12. |
| (3161 lines) | | 149 | | 21.2 |
| | | | 412 | 7.6 |
| 3 Henry VI | 242 | | | 12. |
| (2902 lines) | | 182 | | 16. |
| | | | 424 | 6.8 |

Vickers also cited the high number of vocatives in the first 150 lines of *Troublesome Reign*—fifteen—as further evidence that Peele was its author. However, Shakespeare used seventeen vocatives in the first 150 lines of *2 Henry VI* and thirty-one in the first 150 lines of *3 Henry VI*. Thus, the frequency of the use of vocatives by the author of *Troublesome Reign* comports well with Shakespeare's use of them in some of his early history plays, and does little to support Peele's authorship.

## Similar Excessive Use of Alliteration

A fondness for various types of alliteration is another verbal characteristic that Vickers cited as common to Peele and the author of *Troublesome Reign*. He described the frequency of alliteration in *Troublesome Reign* as "strikingly similar" to that in Peele's *The Battle of Alcazar* (95). One example is three alliterative doublets—*mounting mind, wreak wrongs* and *damned deed*—that appear in *Troublesome Reign* and in *Alcazar*, as well as in other Peele plays. Peele seems to be the only Elizabethan playwright to use all three, but Vickers acknowledged that Shakespeare used the first two in later plays. And although he never used *damned deed*, the phrase *damned despair* in *Venus and Adonis* (743) and the great variety of alliterative doublets scattered over the entire canon attest to his partiality to the device.

The following table displays Vickers' counts of alliteration and its frequency per line in *Troublesome Reign* and three of Peele's plays, and my count of the same in the first two acts of *3 Henry VI*. (Vickers didn't supply counts of total alliteration in *Edward I* and *David and Bethsabe*.) He counted 507 instances of all types of alliteration in *The Battle of Alcazar*—a play of 1452 lines, but calculated an incorrect frequency of one in every 3.9 lines (95). (The correct frequency is one in every 2.8 lines.)

|  | All Alliteration | Triple Alliteration | Frequency Every × Lines |
|---|---|---|---|
| *Troublesome Reign* | 904 | | 3.2 |
| | | 109 | 26.9 |
| *The Battle of Alcazar* | 507 | | 2.8 |
| | | 69 | 21. |
| *Edward I* | | 96 | 27.9 |
| *David and Bethsabe* | | 69 | 27.8 |
| *3 Henry VI* (Acts I & II) | 700 | | 1.83 |
| | | 130 | 9.8 |

It is obvious that Peele and the author of *Troublesome Reign* were excessively fond of both simple and multiple alliteration. Of all the rhetorical devices involving repetition, alliteration is among the oldest and most common. Every Elizabethan playwright used it, some excessively, and Shakespeare was no exception, especially in his early history plays, where he was every bit as prodigal as Peele. Vickers cited the "amazing coincidence" of the nearly-identical frequency of triple alliteration in *Troublesome Reign, Edward I* and *David and Bethsabe,* and called it "almost enough to place *The Troublesome Raigne* firmly in Peele's canon" (97). But in the first two acts alone of *3 Henry VI*, Shakespeare employed all types of alliteration about 700 times in 1284 lines—once in every 1.83 lines, and triple alliteration 130 times, or once in every 9.8 lines. The balance of the play is similarly peppered with excessive alliteration, including dozens of complex alliterative patterns involving five words or more. Shakespeare never abandoned alliteration, but scaled back his use of it over the course of his career. Thus, the alliterative excesses of *Troublesome Reign* are not peculiar to Peele's style. They fit comfortably within the parameters of Shakespeare's practice.

## SIMILAR FREQUENCY OF FEMININE ENDINGS

Another linguistic characteristic that Vickers identified as common to Peele and the author of *Troublesome Reign* is the infrequent use of feminine endings. In the earliest English dramatic poetry, scant use was made of feminine endings, but during the late 1580s and early 1590s dramatists employed it with steadily increasing frequency. As Vickers pointed out, the percentage of feminine endings in *Troublesome Reign* (1.6 percent) falls within the range (0.5 to 1.8 percent) of four of Peele's plays (103). But Peele was not consistent. In a fifth play, *The Old Wives Tale* (not mentioned by Vickers), Peele used feminine endings 5.4 percent of the time, or ten times more often than in *The Arraignment of Paris* (0.5 percent).[36]

In the Shakespeare canon, the percentage of feminine endings trended upward, generally speaking, during the author's writing career, from figures as low as 5 percent or 6 percent (*A Midsummer Night's Dream, 1 Henry IV*) to as high as

33 percent in some later plays (*The Winter's Tale, Cymbeline, The Tempest*).[37] This is also true of several other playwrights of the period: the range in Kyd's plays is 1.2 to 10.2 percent, in Marlowe's 0.4 to 3.7 percent, in Peele's 0.5 to 5.4 percent. Greene's range was much more limited—0.1 to 1.6 percent, and the percentage never exceeds 1 percent in the few plays of Lyly, Nashe and Lodge (Timberlake 117, 121–2).

Thus, for most of the playwrights of the period there was a wide variation in their use of feminine endings, and the percentage of feminine endings in *Troublesome Reign* falls within the range of their use by Kyd, Marlowe and Greene, as well as by Peele, and is very close to their use by Lyly, Nashe and Lodge. Although the evidence of feminine endings does nothing to support Shakespeare's authorship of *Troublesome Reign*, it does little to support Peele's.

## Verbal Parallels between *Troublesome Reign* and Peele's *Edward I*

As further evidence of Peele's authorship of *Troublesome Reign*, Vickers cited an article by Rupert Taylor in which he found more than twenty examples of parallel language in *Troublesome Reign* and *The Massacre at Paris* and fifteen word and phrase parallels in *Troublesome Reign* and Peele's *Edward I*. Taylor judged the author of *Troublesome Reign* to be the borrower, but Vickers adduced the parallels as evidence that Peele wrote *Troublesome Reign* (82–3).

Vickers cited (from Taylor) the following fifteen verbal parallels between *Troublesome Reign* and *Edward I*, to which I append lines from Shakespeare's plays and poems:

**1.**

| | | |
|---|---|---|
| *John.* | This is my doome, and this my doome shall stand | |
| | Irrevocable, as I am King of England | *1 TR* 209–10 |
| *Long.* | Since what I do shall rest inrevocable [*sic*], | *Edward I* 668 |
| *Friar.* | ... and this sentence is irrevocable con- | |
| | firmed by our Lord Lluellen Prince of Wales, | |
| | | *Edward I* 1852–3 |
| *Duke F.* | Firm and irrevocable is my doom | |
| | Which I have pass'd upon her; she is banish'd. | |
| | | *As You Like It* I.iii.83–4 |
| *King.* | Had I but said I would have kept my word | |
| | But when I swear, it is irrevocable | *2 Henry VI* III.ii.293–4 |

**2.**

| Q. Elinor. | Misgovernd Gossip, staine to this resort, | *1 TR* 515 |
|---|---|---|
| Mort. | ... and receave the reward of | |
| | monstruous treasons and villanye, staine to the name and | |
| | honour of his noble countrey, | *Edward I* 2148–50 |

Shakespeare used *stain* in this sense more than a hundred times:

| Duke. | redeem your brother from the angry | |
|---|---|---|
| | law; do no stain to your own gracious person; | |
| | | *Measure for Measure* III.i.201–2 |
| King. | Stain to thy countrymen, thou hear'st thy doom! | |
| | | *1 Henry VI* IV.i.45 |

**3.**

| Constance. | Send fell contagion to infect this Clyme, | *1 TR* 876 |
|---|---|---|
| Q. Eli. | This climat orelowring with blacke congealed clouds, | |
| | That takes their swelling from the marrish soile, | |
| | Fraught with infectious fogges and misty dampes, | |
| | | *Edward I* 1040–42 |
| Ham. | 'Tis now the very witching time of night, | |
| | When churchyards yawn and hell itself [breathes] out | |
| | Contagion to this world: | *Hamlet* III.ii.388–90 |
| Gard. | A most arch-heretic, a pestilence | |
| | That does infect the land; | *Henry VIII* V.i.45–6 |

Shakespeare used *infect* more than seventy times, nearly always in its negative sense.

**4.**

| Bastard. | And leave thy bodie to fowles for food. | *1 TR* 1056 |
|---|---|---|
| Bali40ll. | Hang in the aire for fowles to feede uppon | *Edward I* 2066 |
| Iden. | Leaving thy trunk for crows to feed upon. | *2 Henry VI* IV.x.84 |

**5.**

| | | |
|---|---|---|
| *Philip.* | Come on, sir Frier, pick the locke, this geere dooth cotton hansome, | *1 TR* 1254 |

*Lluel.*     Why so, now it cottens, now the game beginnes.

*Edward I* 1385

*Tit.*      Come, to this gear. You are a good archer, Marcus;

*Titus Andronicus* IV.iii.53

*2. Mur.*    Come, shall we to this gear?     *Richard III* I.iv.153 (Q1–6)

Shakespeare used *gear* several times in this sense. He apparently never used *cotton.*

**6.**

*Philip.*    How now, a Prophet? Sir prophet whence are ye?     *1 TR* 1303

*Friar.*     What? not Morgain Pigot, our good welsh prophet, *Edward I* 469

*K. Rich.*   How chance the prophet could not at that time
Have told me, I being by, that I should kill him?

*Richard III* IV.ii.100–1

*Mrs. Page*   How now, Sir Hugh, no school to-day?

*The Merry Wives of Windsor* IV.i.10

**7.**

*John.*      My word is past, receive your boone my Lords.     *1 TR* 1567

*Long.*      My word is past, I am well agreede,     *Edward I* 1656

*Clo. [Feste]*  but he will not pass his word for
twopence that you are no fool.     *Twelfth Night* I.v.80–1

In these examples, *past* and *pass* are used in the sense of given in pledge.

**8.**

*Pembrooke.*  The heavens frowne upon the sinfull earth,     *1 TR* 1598

*Lluel.*     The angry Heavens frowne on Brittains     *Edward I* 2109

*Tro.*       Frown on, you heavens, effect your rage with speed!

*Troilus and Cressida* V.x.6

Poor soul, the centre of my sinful earth     Sonnet 146.1

**9.**

*John.*      Decide in cyphering what these five Moones
             Portend this Clyme, if they presage at all.        *1 TR* 1611–12

*Edward.*    O Heavens, what maie these miracles portend?
                                                                *Edward I* 2321

*Glou.*      These late eclipses in the sun and moon portend
             no good to us:                          *King Lear* I.ii.103–4

**10.**

*John.*      Confound my wits, and dull my senses so,          *2 TR* 113

*Edward.*    Halloe Edward how are thy senses confounded,   *Edward I* 1886

*Ham.*       Confound the ignorant, and amaze indeed
             The very faculties of eyes and ears.        *Hamlet* II.ii.565–6

*Cor.*                        Those she has
             Will stupefy and dull the sense awhile,     *Cymbeline* I.v.36–7

**11.**

*John.*      To make thee great, and greatest of thy kin.         *2 TR* 132

*Lluel.*     Followe the man that meanes to make you great:
                                                              *Edward I* 269

*Harper.*                          must
             needes bee advaunced to bee highest of your kinne.
                                                            *Edward I* 554–55

*Friar.*                    And be the highest of his kinne;     *Edward I* 2387

*Const.*     Nature and Fortune join'd to make thee great. *King John* III.i.52

*Macd.*      By this great clatter, one of greatest note
             Seems bruited.                          *Macbeth* V.vii.21–2

*Sat.*       Sly frantic wretch, that holp'st to make me great,
                                                     *Titus Andronicus* IV.iv.59

*Fal.*       Fear not your advancements. I will be the man yet that shall
             make you great.                         *2 Henry IV* V.v.78–80

**12.**

| | | |
|---|---|---|
| *John.* | There let him hang, and be the Ravens food, | 2 TR 165 |
| *Baliol.* | Hang in the aire for fowles to feed uppon, | *Edward I* 2066 |
| *Pist.* | Young ravens must have food | |
| | | *The Merry Wives of Windsor* I.iii.35 |
| *Adam.* | Take that, and He that doth the ravens feed, | |
| | | *As You Like It* II.iii.43 |
| *Bast* | and vast confusion waits | |
| | As doth a raven on a sick-fall'n beast, | *King John* IV.iii.152–3 |

**13.**

| | | |
|---|---|---|
| *Pand.* | Thy forwardnes to fight for holy *Rome* | |
| | Shall be remunerated to the full: | 2 TR 657–8 |
| *Long.* | That Nobles strive who shall remunerate, | *Edward I* 140 |
| *Baliol.* | We will remunerate his resolution, | *Edward I* 2036 |
| *Cost.* | Now I will look to his remuneration. Remuneration! | |
| | | *Love's Labor's Lost* III.i.136 |
| *Duch.* | We'll see these things effected to the full | 2 *Henry VI* I.ii.84 |

**14.**

| | | |
|---|---|---|
| *Abb.* | And seeke some meanes for to pastime the King. | 2 TR 888 |
| *Lluel.* | Let us like friends pastime us on the sands, | *Edward I* 311 |
| *Ber.* | We will with some strange pastime solace them, | |
| | | *Love's Labor's Lost* IV.iii.374 |
| *Clo.* | Make | |
| | pastime with us a day or two, or longer | *Cymbeline* III.i.77–8 |
| *Rom.* | Bid her devise | |
| | Some means to come to shrift his afternoon, | |
| | | *Romeo and Juliet* II.iv.179–80 |

**15.**

| | | |
|---|---|---|
| *John.* | My tongue doth falter: *Philip*, I tell thee man, | *2 TR* 1074 |
| *Q. Eliz.* | That while this faultring engine of my speech | *Edward I* 2400 |
| *Suf.* | My tongue should stumble in mine earnest words | |

2 Henry VI III.ii.316

| | |
|---|---|
| *Duch.* | That my woe-wearied tongue is still and mute. |

Richard III IV.iv.18

According to Vickers, "these parallels are too frequent, and too ordinary in their phraseology, to be dismissed as imitations" (83). A questionable claim. Frequency and ordinariness need not disqualify parallels as imitations. What is more apparent is that the thoughts, words and phrases selected by Taylor from *Troublesome Reign* (occasionally only a single word) have more convincing parallels and stronger echoes in the plays and poems of Shakespeare than in *Edward I* and, as shown above, there are many more of them.

Vickers also cited the Novice's line in *Edward I*, "Mightie is love and will prevaile" (329) as an echo of Friar Laurence's line in *Troublesome Reign*, "*Amor vincit omnia*, so Cato affirmeth" (*1 TR* 1262). However, the connection is unconvincing. The editor of *Edward I* glossed the line as an echo of "for mightie is truth and will prevaile" from Peele's own poem, "Descensus Astraeae," published in 1591 (Hook, ed. *Edward I* 176).

Although the composition date of neither play can be securely fixed, the available facts of publication and performance indicate that *Troublesome Reign* was written at least a year or two earlier than *Edward I*. This evidence suggests that Peele was the borrower from *Troublesome Reign*, not the author.

## SIMILAR ANTI-CATHOLICISM

Vickers also pointed to the similar mixture of Latin and English phrases to satirize monastic abuses in Scene xi of *1 Troublesome Reign* and in Peele's *Edward I* as further evidence of their identical authorship (100–103). Both plays contain ten or so scattered Latin phrases from the Bible or Catholic ritual that are used to satirize the behavior of friars, and in both plays these are mixed and sometimes rhymed with English phrases. But there is a significant difference in the form and method of the satire. The scene cited in *Troublesome Reign* is a comic interlude of 120 lines that depicts three friars and a nun as essentially corrupt and mendacious clowns, whom Philip the Bastard confronts in their monastery and then orders hanged for their avarice and venality.

In contrast, Friar Hugh ap David ("Friar Tuck") in *Edward I* is a standard comic character derived from the May Day plays and the Robin Hood story of traditional folk literature (Hook, ed. *Edward I* 18). He interacts with the other characters, speaking more than 240 lines in seven scenes, and is given to punctuating his conversation with occasional Latin phrases from the law, the Bible and the Mass. Although he is teased about his "wench," he is neither ostracized nor punished, and at the end of the play he and his Novice are part of the group that leads the Welsh rebel David of Brecknock to his execution. The satire in *Edward I* is casual and genial; Vickers calls it "making good-natured fun" (103). But in *Troublesome Reign* it is mocking and derisive. Although both plays depict the Catholic clergy as venal and dishonest, the friar in *Edward I* is an integral part of the cast, while the friars and nuns in *Troublesome Reign* are cardboard figures inserted briefly into the plot for comic relief based on ridicule of Catholics.

In fact, the anti–Catholic material in *Troublesome Reign*, and what is retained of it in *King John*, tend to support the other evidence that the two plays came from the same pen. *King John* contains some of the strongest anti–Catholic passages in the entire canon.[38] In the pivotal first scene of Act III, just before he is excommunicated, John refers to the church's "juggling witchcraft," calls Pandulph a "meddling priest," and derides the Pope:

> K. *John.*    Thou canst not, Cardinal, devise a name
>
> So slight, unworthy, and ridiculous,
>
> To charge me to an answer, as the Pope.
>
> Tell him this tale, and from the mouth of England
>
> Add thus much more, that no Italian priest
>
> Shall tithe or toll in our dominions     *King John* III.i.149–54

The last three lines of this passage are an obvious paraphrase of these lines in *Troublesome Reign*:

> *John.*                                      Tell
>
> thy Maister so from me, and say, *John of England* said it, that
>
> never an Italian Priest of them all, shall either have tythe,
>
> tole, or poling penie out of *England*          *1 TR* 978–81

In his revision, Shakespeare did not retain the coarse monastery scene, nor the scenes in which the monks plot John's murder and then poison him. But he did include the report that John had been poisoned by a monk, "a resolved villain," as Hubert describes him (V.vi.29). He did not moderate John's criticism and ridicule of Cardinal Pandulph, the Pope, and the Catholic church. Nor did he mitigate the role that Pandulph plays in prodding the French to attack England. And in *King John*, he retained the contempt that both Blanche and Constance also express for the Pope and the church.

Although Vickers identified several uncommon words, turns of phrase and stylistic habits that Peele shared with the author of *Troublesome Reign*, the sum of his evidence does not support his conclusion that Peele wrote the play. He acknowledged that it was Shakespeare's "main source" (78), but nowhere in his thirty-nine page paper did he address the idea that Shakespeare may have written it himself. Of the more than a dozen critics and editors who have made a serious attempt to identify the author of *Troublesome Reign*, only Vickers, H. Dugdale Sykes (*Sidelights* 99–125), and possibly John Dover Wilson (ed. *King John* xvii) ascribe it to Peele alone.

## TROUBLESOME REIGN AND EDWARD I COMPARED

In that it depicts an English king and his court in the thirteenth century, *Edward I* is the only play of Peele's that bears any resemblance to *Troublesome Reign* and, as such, is the best candidate for a comparison. But aside from the scattered similarities already mentioned, *Troublesome Reign* is a totally different approach to the English history play, and a decidedly superior treatment of the reign of an English king. As noted above, William Wells disparaged Peele's attitude toward history, called *Edward I* a "farrago of tomfoolery," and found it "difficult to see how he could have written so, on the whole, well-constructed a play as the '*Reign*' some two years before *Edward I*" ("Thomas Kyd" 222). He also found such similarities between *Troublesome Reign* and Shakespeare's *Edward III* that he thought they were by the same author.

Wells' opinion is not unique. In fact, it would be hard to find a purported chronicle history play by a major dramatist of the time that has less respect among critics than Peele's *Edward I*. According to Irving Ribner, the "romantic folklore" of *Edward I*, "bearing no relation to any historical purposes" is easily distinguished from "the serious treatment of history which we have noted in *The Troublesome Reign*" (89). Alfred Hart wrote that "*Edward I* is an incoherent travesty of historical facts mixed with fable and dull comedy" (*Stolne* 467). In his introduction to his 1961 edition of *Edward I*, Frank Hook commented that "The play is marked throughout by a shallowness of political and historical sense" (16). As for its plot, Hook wrote that "The structure of the play as a whole is an utter failure" (47).

In recent decades, this judgment has not changed. In the opinion of the latest commentator, the play is "a rambling and confusing narrative without memorable characters or language. Its story line is shot through with ludicrous and bizarre events…" (Egan, ed. *Richard II, Part One* 1:14–15). Moreover, in contrast to the rich imagery and vigorous verse of *Troublesome Reign*, the verse in *Edward I* is described by its editor as "generally pedestrian." He adds that there is "little imagery—an occasional personification, simile, or metaphor, but seldom a really striking figure" (Hook, ed. *Edward I* 52).

The most recent theory about the authorship of *Troublesome Reign*—proposed by Michael Egan—is that it was a collaboration between Peele and Shakespeare. Citing Vickers' attribution to Peele as the basis of his theory, Egan has Shakespeare outlining the plot and creating the characters of *Troublesome Reign*, and Peele writing the verse. Shakespeare subsequently rewrote the play, discarding most of his partner's verse and several objectionable scenes (Egan, "King John" 170). But this hypothesis suffers from the same defects as Vickers' theory of Peele's sole authorship. There is nothing in *Troublesome Reign* that is peculiar to Peele, and very little that is characteristic of him. Egan's theory would explain the distinctive characterization, the solid construction, and the logical movement of *Troublesome Reign*. But it does not explain its vigorous language, its frequent and powerful images, and its verbal inventiveness.[39]

As shown above, those most familiar with Peele's verse, especially that in *Edward I*, find it pedestrian, flat and lacking in imagery. Commenters on his other plays echo these opinions. His blank verse in *The Battle of Alcazar* has been described as "jerky and monotonous, with little attempt to utilize such devices as feminine endings, run-on lines, and variation in the caesural pause" (Horne, ed. *Dramatic Works* 1:78). The same editor remarked about *The Old Wives Tale* that "there is no disputing the mediocrity of its characterization and verse" (1:90). Peele is most often praised, rightly, for his skill with spectacle and pageantry rather than for his dramaturgy. Assigning the verse of *Troublesome Reign* to him ignores and trivializes the strong connections, notably of language and imagery, it has to Shakespeare's *King John* and to his early history plays, as well as to several of his later works, many of which are noted above.

Another objection to this theory is the unusual nature of the supposed collaboration. All the important cases of dual authorship by Shakespeare and other writers that have been alleged by scholars assign the collaboration to the different authors by acts and scenes, rather than by plot and characters. A scheme by which one author created the plot and characters and the other the verse would not only be unusual, but difficult to carry out in practice.[40]

## *The King John Plays and Edward de Vere*

The considerable evidence that the Earl of Oxford was the author of the Shakespeare canon, and therefore of *Troublesome Reign*, is further supported by events and circumstances in his own life. The plot of the anonymous play contains the most striking of those connections.

As recounted above, the author of *Troublesome Reign* inserted the fictional Falconbridge family and their dispute into his dramatic narrative of the reign of King John. Robert Falconbridge, younger son of Sir Robert Falconbridge, asserts that his older brother Philip is the child of an adulterous liaison between their mother and King Richard I, and that he, Robert, is the legitimate heir to the lands and wealth of their recently-deceased father. The matter is brought to the King's attention during a diplomatic conference at John's court within minutes of the opening of the play.

This accusation is nearly identical to that made by Katherine de Vere, Oxford's older half-sister, and her husband, Edward, Lord Windsor, in a petition to the Archbishop of Canterbury in June 1563, just ten months after the death of the sixteenth Earl of Oxford. The petition is said to have alleged that the sixteenth Earl's marriage in 1548 to Margery Golding, mother of Edward and his younger sister Mary, was bigamous because he was married at the time to anther woman.[41] Had the accusation been sustained, Oxford would have been declared illegitimate and forfeited the earldom and the wealth and lands of his father. Fortunately for him, the petition was ultimately unsuccessful, but the threat of bastardy, poverty and disgrace most certainly had a profound effect on the thirteen-year-old, who had, only nine months earlier, been removed, as a ward of the court, to the household of William Cecil in London after the death of his father.

It is apparent that Oxford, in *Troublesome Reign*, portrayed himself as Philip Falconbridge, a young man who was accused of bastardy by his half-brother. But he transformed this painful incident in his life into a triumphant one in the life of his fictional counterpart. After first denying the charge, Philip embraces it, reveling in his new identity as a bastard of Richard I. His mother, as well, after denying the liaison in the most vigorous terms—"What head-strong furie doth enchaunt my sonne?"—finally admits that she was overcome by King Richard's "mightenes," and compares herself to the unfortunate Lucrece of Roman tradition. Philip agrees to forfeit the lands and wealth of his deceased father to his younger half-brother, and declares:

Philip.    It will not out, I cannot for my life

Say I am Sonne unto a *Fauconbridge.*

Let land and living goe, tis honor's fire

That makes me sweare King *Richard* was my Sire.

Base to a King addes title of more State,

Than Knight's begotten, though legittimate.

Please it your Grace, I am King *Richard's* Sonne       *1 TR 273–9*

King John quickly supports Philip's new identity—"I never saw so lively counterfet / Of Richard Cordelion, as in him," and immediately knights him, renaming him "Sir Richard Plantagenet" (*1 TR* 102–3). The fictional Philip the Bastard becomes King John's most competent and trusted courtier, and dominates the action for the balance of the play. His nearly ninety speeches contain only a few lines less than those of King John himself. Furthermore, Oxford portrays Philip as a model of character and behavior, and the soul of wit. He is also a mediator and a leader, and is repeatedly presented as brave, clever, loyal and patriotic. It is clear that Oxford transformed this humiliating threat to his wealth and nobility into an episode of dramatic art and recreated it in the most positive terms he could imagine.

Oxford included the identical fictional episode involving the Falconbridge family when he rewrote *Troublesome Reign* years later and produced the *King John* that appeared in the First Folio. The same accusation of bastardy is leveled against Philip. His mother and King John react in the same way, and Philip is portrayed nearly-identically during the balance of the play. The retention of this unhistorical episode and the portrayal of Philip Falconbridge in the two plays are further indications that they were by the same person.

Another example of Oxford's strong reaction to this threat is found in a poem that he wrote about the same time. In the early 1560s, the poet and playwright Richard Edwards assembled a group of nearly one hundred poems that was later published under the title *The Paradyse of Dainty Devices.* Among the eight poems in the collection signed by or attributed to the Earl of Oxford is one titled "His Good Name Being Blemished, He Bewaileth." The first of the three verses announces the poem's message:

Fram'd in the front of forlorn hope, past all recovery
I stayless stand, to abide the shock of shame and infamy.
My life, though ling'ring long, is lodg'd in lair of loathsome ways,
My death delay'd to keep from life the harm of hapless days:
My sprites, my heart, my wit and force in deep distress are drown'd,
The only loss of my good name, is of these griefs the ground.[42]

This is further evidence that he was deeply disturbed by the accusation, and that one way he dealt with it was to express himself in poetry and drama.

Another connection between *Troublesome Reign* and Edward de Vere lies in the strong probability that he saw a performance of *King Johan*, one of its main sources, and that he was acquainted with that play's author, the Protestant polemicist John Bale (1495–1563). After ordination as a Carmelite priest, Bale served in several positions for six years until 1536, when he renounced his clerical vows and left his post at Thorndon in Suffolk (King, "Bale, John"). Between 1534 and 1540, he wrote more than twenty plays, and obtained the patronage of both Thomas Cranmer, Archbishop of Canterbury, and John de Vere, fifteenth Earl of Oxford. Among those he wrote for de Vere during this period, and the one for which he is best known, was the strongly anti–Catholic *King Johan* (Harris 71–7).

The single surviving manuscript of the play (now in the Huntington Library) surfaced in Ipswich in 1838, when it was sold to the Duke of Devonshire by an Ipswich manuscript collector. Although confirmation is lacking, those familiar with the transaction report that they were told that the manuscript had been found "among some old papers probably belonging to the Corporation of Ipswich" (Pafford v). The manuscript is a revision of the original play, with a prayer for Queen Elizabeth inserted after the final scene. This has led scholars to surmise that Bale revised the play at some time after the accession of Queen Elizabeth in November 1558, and that it was performed at Ipswich at the time of her visit to the city early in August 1561 (Pafford v–xxiii; Chambers, *Mediaeval Stage* 2:450).

According to Chambers, it is "probable" that the company performing in Ipswich in 1561 was the Earl of Oxford's men (*Elizabethan Stage* 2:99–100). The Queen then stopped at Hedingham Castle between August 14th and 19th (Chambers, *Elizabethan Stage* 4:79 and n. 12). There can be no doubt that young Edward was residing at Hedingham Castle, or was called home from wherever he was living, at the time of the Queen's visit. Bale's association with the de Vere household and his recent revision of *King Johan* make it likely that Edward was present at the conjectured performance in Ipswich, and that Bale and de Vere met at some time during the summer of 1561. De Vere might have had access to the manuscript, and might have discussed the play with its author.

John Foxe, the author of *Acts and Monuments*, his collaborator, John Bale, and the printer, John Day, were all favored and supported by William Cecil, one of the leading book and manuscript collectors in Elizabethan England. We may assume that a copy of the book was delivered to the Cecil household when it was published in March 1563, just six months after the arrival of Edward de Vere.

## Dates of the King John Plays

As recounted in the previous chapter, the five plays treated in this book, except *King Leir*, must be assigned to Edward de Vere's teen years. The absence of legal issues and legal terms in four of them strongly suggests that he wrote them between the fall of 1562, when he arrived in London, and the spring of 1567, after which he became immersed in the law and the language of the law. The evidence in the previous Section supports a composition date of *Troublesome Reign* between the summer of 1563 and the spring of 1567. Because of the poor quality of the verse and the confused dramaturgy, it is most likely that Oxford wrote the play early in this period, probably before he was fifteen.

## Conclusion

From the evidence presented above, it is clear that Shakespeare himself wrote *Troublesome Reign*, and did so very early in his career. If not Shakespeare, the author was an unknown dramatist who shared his linguistic habits, his fondness for new and unusual words, and his ability to interpret and organize numerous historical events over a lengthy reign into a coherent dramatic narrative. No other dramatist of the time, including George Peele, shared these characteristics.

Although *Troublesome Reign*'s editor could not accept Shakespeare as its author, he could not help speculating that it might have been his apprentice work: "Yet what he did with his first play makes fascinating conjecture; unless he sprang to poetic life almost full-grown, the *Reign* might reflect his development about 1587" (Sider, ed. *Troublesome Raigne* liii).

*Troublesome Reign* is a rightful example of Shakespearean juvenilia, antedating his earliest published play, *Titus Andronicus* (1594), and also by two years his first printed work—*Venus and Adonis* (1593). The three thousand lines of Shakespearean verse in *Troublesome Reign*, supply another important example of his earliest endeavors to bring English history to the stage.

# IV

## *The Taming of a Shrew* and *The Taming of the Shrew*

For more than 400 years the two *Shrew* plays, one anonymous, the other in the Shakespeare canon, have been entangled with each other in scholarly disagreements about who wrote them, which was written first, and how they relate to each other. Even today, there is consensus on only one of these questions—that it was Shakespeare alone who wrote *The Shrew* that appeared in the Folio. It is, as John Dover Wilson wrote, "one of the most difficult cruxes in the Shakespearian Canon" (Quiller-Couch, ed. *Taming* vii).

An objective review of the literary and external evidence, however, supplies a solution to the puzzle. It confirms that the two *Shrew* plays were written in the order in which they appeared in the record, *The Shrew* being a major revision of the earlier play, and that they were by the same author—Edward de Vere, seventeenth Earl of Oxford. Events in Oxford's sixteenth year and his travels in the 1570s support composition dates for both plays before 1580. These conclusions also reveal the playwright's progress and development from a teenager learning to write for the stage to a journeyman dramatist in his twenties. De Vere's extended tour of France and Italy, as well as his maturation as a poet, stimulated him to rewrite his earlier effort and produce a comedy that continues to entertain centuries later.

The first appearance of any *Shrew* play was the Quarto of *A plesant Conceyted historie called the Tayminge of a Shrowe* that Peter Short registered on May 2, 1594 (Arber, ed. *Transcript* 2:648) and printed later the same year. Only a single copy survives from the stock of the bookseller Cuthbert Burby, who later published several canonical plays. Neither the Stationers' Register entry nor the title page named an author. According to the title page, the play had been performed by the Earl of Pembroke's Men, a company for which no record exists before 1592. During the next year, they sold several plays to booksellers, including *A Shrew* and *Titus Andronicus* (Chambers, *Elizabethan Stage* 2:128–30).

In his Diary, Philip Henslowe subsequently recorded a group of plays performed by "my Lord Admerall men and my Lorde Chamberlen men" in the playhouse at Newington Butts in June 1594. Onstage, just a few days apart, were *Hamlet,* "Andronicous," "*the Tamynge of A Shrowe*" and four other plays (Chambers, *William Shakespeare* 2:319). By coincidence, perhaps, two acknowledged Shakespeare plays were published in the same year—*Titus Andronicus* and *The First Part of the Contention.*

Peter Short printed Quarto 2 of *A Shrew* in 1596. When he died in 1603, ownership passed to Nicholas Ling, who registered the play again in January 1607, along with *Romeo and Juliet* and *Love's Labor's Lost* (Arber, ed. *Transcript* 3:337). Ling had a third Quarto printed within a few months, with minor variations from the first two. Ling died in April 1607, and ownership of these three plays, plus "A booke called *Hamlett*" and fourteen other works by other authors, was transferred from Ling's widow to publisher and bookseller John Smethwick in the following November (Arber, ed. *Transcript* 3:365). It appears that these four plays were Smethwick's contribution when he and his colleagues published the First Folio in 1623. There is only one other mention of *A Shrew* in this period. In his *Metamorphosis of Ajax* (1596), Sir John Harington made an isolated reference to "the book of Taming a Shrew" (153).[1] The play was not printed again until 1779 (Boas, ed. *Shrew* x–xi).

The first probable citation of the canonical *The Taming of the Shrew* was by the satirist Samuel Rowlands in a so-called "gossip pamphlet," *A whole crew of kind Gossips, all met to be merry,* published in 1609:

> The chiefest Art I have I will bestow
>
> About a work cald taming of the Shrow         Rowlands 2:33[2]

Shakespeare's name was not associated with any *Shrew* play until the initial printing of *The Taming of the Shrew* in the First Folio. *The Shrew* was not among the twelve Shakespeare plays that Francis Meres listed in his *Palladis Tamia* in 1598 (282). Nor was any *Shrew* play included in the list of plays in the Stationers' Register entry for the Folio by Edward Blount and William Jaggard in November 1623, a list containing only those plays "not formerly entred to other men" (Arber, ed. *Transcript* 4:107). John Smethwick's acquisition of the rights to *A Shrew* in 1607 apparently sufficed to allow the printing of *The Shrew* in the Folio. In this respect, *The Shrew* was treated in the same way as *King John* (See Chapter III). Smethwick published a Quarto of *The Shrew* in 1631, using the Folio text. In the words of E. K. Chambers, "The bibliographical *data* [*sic*]

A

# Pleafant Conceited

Hiftorie, called The taming
of a Shrew.

As it was fundry times acted by the
*Right honorable the Earle of*
Pembrook his feruants.

Printed at London by Peter Short and
*are to be fold by Cutbert Burbie*, at his
fhop at the Royall Exchange.
1594.

Title page of the anonymous *The Taming of a Shrew*. 1594. There is a record of its performance at Philip Henslowe's theater at Newington Butts in June of 1594. It was reprinted in 1596 and 1607. Shakespeare's name was not associated with any *Shrew* play until the initial printing of *The Taming of the Shrew* in the First Folio (© Huntington Art Collections, San Marino, California).

up to 1607 relate to *The Taming of A Shrew*, but it is clear that *A Shrew* and *The Shrew* were regarded as commercially the same, and that the copyright acquired by Smethwick in 1607 [for *A Shrew*] covered both F1 and the Q of 1631..." (*William Shakespeare* 1:323).

Thus, the bibliographical evidence associates *A Shrew* with canonical Shakespeare plays in four different contexts—as part of a sale (1593), on the same weekly playbill (1594), in a group of plays registered together (1607), and in a group of eighteen plays transferred to one of the publishers of the First Folio (1607). In the face of this array of documentary and interpretative evidence, it is hard to understand why nearly all modern scholars deny that Shakespeare wrote any part of *The Taming of a Shrew*, and insist that it was the work of another playwright, whom they are unable to identify. Some even claim that it is an imitation of Shakespeare's play. Such was not always the case.

The earliest commentators on the authorship of *A Shrew*—Alexander Pope and several German scholars—assigned it to Shakespeare. Pope considered it an "alternative version" of *The Shrew*, and even introduced scenes from it, including the final dialogue between Sly and the tapster, into the text of the play in his edition of Shakespeare's plays in 1723. Other early editors of the collected plays, such as Lewis Theobald (1733), Thomas Hanmer (1744), William Warburton (1747), Samuel Johnson (1765), and Edward Capell (1768), included some or all of the Sly passages in their versions of the canonical *Shrew*. However, in his edition of 1790, Edmund Malone asserted that Shakespeare did not write *A Shrew*, but used it as a source for *The Shrew*.

The view that the anonymous *Shrew* preceded Shakespeare's play prevailed until 1926, when Glasgow University Lecturer Peter Alexander argued that *A Shrew* was a "bad quarto" that had been reconstructed from *The Shrew* by a pirate ("The Taming of a Shrew" 614). The opposing views about the order of the plays among editors and critics at that time are plainly apparent in the 1928 New Cambridge *The Taming of the Shrew*, edited by Sir Arthur Quiller-Couch and John Dover Wilson—"*A Shrew* ... is demonstrably based upon the Shakespearian play," wrote Wilson (126). But his co-editor Quiller-Couch was not so sure, and leaned to the "inherent probability" that it was Shakespeare's play—an adaptation of the anonymous *Shrew*—that was performed at Henslowe's theater in 1594 (xxiii).

The view that the canonical *Shrew* was the earlier play was rejected over the next several decades by such editors and scholars as E. K. Chambers (*William Shakespeare* 1:327), G. B. Harrison (*Complete Works* 328), and Geoffrey Bullough (*Narrative* 1:57–8). In most editions, texts, and standard works of reference, *A Shrew* continued to be regarded as the earlier play.

Beginning in the 1960s, however, Alexander's theory was resurrected, and a majority of editors and commentators agreed that the 1594 quarto of *A Shrew* was a "piracy," a "derivative," an "imitation," a "plagiarism," or simply a "bad quarto" produced by one or more actors, pirates or stenographers. Recent editors—Miller (of *A Shrew*, 10–11) and Morris (of *The Shrew*, 32)—refuse to assign an author to *A Shrew*, and instead call the play the product of an "adapter" or a "compiler." To explain the extraordinary similarities between the two *Shrew* plays, some critics resorted to a second theory first proposed by Charles Knight, in 1842—that yet another anonymous play, an *Ur-Shrew*, now lost, was the common source of both extant *Shrew* plays (2:119–120).

Despite these rather implausible explanations, the opinion of the earliest commentators—-that *A Shrew* was Shakespeare's first version of the story—has persisted. In the nineteenth century, such prominent scholars as Albert W. Frey (37–8) and Sir Walter A. Raleigh assigned it wholly to him, the latter commenting that "The play is nevertheless a work of comic genius; and contains, without exception, all the ludicrous situations which are the making of Shakespeare's comedy" (110). The respected nineteenth century scholar and poet William Courthope described the play as "the first rude sketch of the philosophical idea of life which characterises all Shakespeare's mature creations" (4:75). In the first Arden edition of *The Shrew*, R. W. Bond substantially agreed, writing about the anonymous *Shrew* that "...I feel the Induction to be so vigorous and natural a piece of imaginative work, and the conception of Kate and Ferando so powerful and humorous ... that one knows not to whom to attribute these creations if not to Shakespeare" (ed. *Taming* xlii). Throughout the twentieth century, respected editors and critics, such as Geoffrey Bullough (1:58), and Eric Sams recognized Shakespeare's distinctive hand in *A Shrew*, albeit an early and undisciplined one, in the ingenious plotting, the exuberant action, and even the irregular and bombastic verse.[3]

## *The Anonymous* Shrew

The anonymous *Shrew* of 1594 consists of 1520 lines of mixed verse and prose printed continuously without act or scene divisions, and without a list of characters. Later editors added a cast list and scene divisions, the most logical being an arrangement in fifteen scenes, including the two "Induction" scenes, such as in Steven Roy Miller's New Cambridge edition (1998). The numerous, but incomplete, stage directions have been amended by modern editors. A doubling chart suggests that ten men and four boys would be needed to stage the play (Miller 146).

In the plotting and structure of *A Shrew*, the playwright demonstrated an exceptional competence. In the words of a modern editor, "The structural and thematic sophistication of *A Shrew* (which contains all three of the plot-strands of *The Shrew*) is … outstanding…" (Thompson 9). Frederick Boas remarked that the "author shows a true instinct for dramatic technique" (ed. *Shrew* xxvi). The playwright's skillful handling of a three-plot play is admitted by nearly all commentators, and has been termed "without parallel in Elizabethan drama" (Hosley 294). This unusual feature has led a few modern editors to the conclusion that *A Shrew* was an early Shakespeare play. In the words of Geoffrey Bullough, "*A Shrew* may not be so much the source-play as Shakespeare's first shot at the theme" (*Narrative* 1:58).

Most modern editors of *The Shrew* print as "additional passages" the five short scenes of the "Sly Frame" that appear in the anonymous *Shrew*, but not in the Folio text. Besides the additional scenes from the "Sly Frame," Ann Thompson, in her New Cambridge edition (1984), printed another 46-line scene from *A Shrew* "which I believe may similarly relate to a Shakespearean scene missing from the Folio text" (175).

The publication and performance details of *A Shrew* are similar to those of *Titus Andronicus* and the second and third parts of *Henry VI*, each of which has been, in modern times, accepted as a genuine Shakespeare play, although some consider them collaborations. But as Leah Marcus observes, "…*A Shrew* remains in a curious limbo. It is too regular and original to be a 'bad quarto,' yet somehow too derivative and uncouth to be acceptable Shakespeare" (181).

*A Shrew* is notable for two dozen phrases and lines that are identical or nearly so to those in other literary works of the period, notably Christopher Marlowe's two *Tamburlaine* plays and *Doctor Faustus*, and Robert Greene's *Menaphon*. There are also ten lines in scene 14 that are very similar in wording to lines in the first section, the *Premiere Sepmaine*, of the long poem *La Création du Monde* published in 1578 by the French poet Guillaume, Sieur Salluste du Bartas. These are discussed in "Dates of the Two Shrews," below.

## *The Canonical* Shrew

Of the 2597 lines in *The Shrew* of the Folio, approximately 22 percent are in prose, 72 percent in blank verse and 6 percent rhymed verse. The eccentric act division in the Folio has been reorganized by later editors, the most common arrangement being in fourteen scenes, including the Induction, spread over five acts (Evans, et al., eds. *Riverside*).

*The Shrew* is generally thought to be one of the earliest plays in the canon. It has many stylistic and technical affinities with *The Comedy of Errors*, such as the device of mistaken identities, the treatment of the husband/wife relationship, and the unusually detailed stage directions relating to location, property, costume and action.[4] By comparing style, workmanship, complexity and the use of classical imagery, Marco Mincoff made a strong case that *The Shrew* predated *Errors* and was Shakespeare's first comedy. Orthodox scholars propose dates of composition ranging from 1588 to 1598 (Morris 57–65; Parrott 56).

The structure, characterization and verse of *The Shrew* are of such uneven quality that until the mid-twentieth century many scholars considered it to be only partially by Shakespeare, and some proposed another author entirely. In 1857, Grant White suggested that Shakespeare had two collaborators and had nothing to do with the underplot (4:390). In his analysis of the play in the 1870s, F. G. Fleay complained of numerous "metrical peculiarities," "doggerel," and inappropriate classical allusions, and proposed that it was a reworking of *A Shrew*, which had been written by Shakespeare and Marlowe for Pembroke's Men (*Shakespeare Manual* 186). Chapman and Greene have also been suggested as Shakespeare's collaborators.

E. K. Chambers assigned only three-fifths of the play to Shakespeare, and the subplot to an unknown collaborator. He complained that the writer of the subplot was "much less vigorous" than Shakespeare, and that he wrote "many awkward lines which disregard stress or contain unmanageable trisyllabic feet.... The numerous scraps of Latin and Italian and the doggerel belong to his part" (*William Shakespeare* 1:324). Later editors (Quiller-Couch and Wilson 124–6; Hodgdon 313–316) have pointed out puzzling remarks by Hortensio, who does not exist in the source play, and noted the author's confusion about his place in the plot.

But the view that Shakespeare alone was responsible for *The Shrew* has had advocates throughout the twentieth century. Brandes in 1898 (113–116), Raleigh in 1907 (110), Boas in 1908 (ed. *Taming* xxxix), and Quiller-Couch and Wilson in 1928 (vii–xii) all argued for his single authorship. More recently, scholars have assembled credible evidence of Shakespeare's responsibility for the entire play. In 1925, Kuhl found a unity of structure, characterization and mood throughout the play. In 1954, Wentersdorf concluded that "the imagery indicates that the play was the work of but one playwright, and that this playwright was Shakespeare" ("Authenticity" 31–2). On the basis of both simple and complex allusions to music and musical instruments, Waldo and Herbert asserted that it was Shakespeare's work throughout. Today most scholars assign the entire play to Shakespeare.

## Sources of the Plays

As mentioned above, there are roughly two schools of thought about the relationship between the two *Shrew* plays—one, that the "compiler" of the anonymous *Shrew* obtained a manuscript of the canonical *Shrew* and used it as a model and a source; the other, that the anonymous *Shrew* was written first, and used by Shakespeare as a template for the play in the Folio. It is the latter scenario that is adopted and defended in this book, the same scenario that obtains in the other four pairs of plays making up Shakespeare's apprenticeship. In this case, the evidence supports the finding that the direct source of the Folio *Shrew* was the anonymous *Shrew*, and that the sources of the latter can be found in contemporary folklore, and in a third play recently-translated from the Italian. Another theory is that each author used the same version of the lost play as a source for his own. Some critics speculate that this lost play was by Shakespeare himself, others that it was written by an unknown playwright.

The main taming plot was apparently derived from a folk tale group, a "Shrew-taming complex," consisting of more than 400 oral and written versions that have been identified in the folklore of various countries from Ireland to India (Miller 12–16). Folklorist Jan Harold Brunvand found more than a dozen elements in the folkloric versions of the taming plot that appeared in both *Shrew* plays, as well as others that appeared in one play, but not the other (*Comparative* 188–9). In many cases, elements from the traditional tales that are common to both plays are presented more rationally and handled with greater skill in *The Shrew*.[5]

The origin of the subplot in both plays, which involves a visiting student and the sister(s) of the shrew, lies in the Italian comedy *I Suppositi*, written by Ludovico Ariosto in the first decade of the sixteenth century in imitation of the Roman comedies of Plautus and Terence. It was published in prose in 1524, and rewritten in verse and published again in 1551. It was translated into English prose as *Supposes* by George Gascoigne for the revels at Gray's Inn late in 1566, and published in 1573. The subplot of each *Shrew* play contains characters, incidents and dramatic devices based on *Supposes*, and each play contains incidents from it that do not appear in the other. Gascoigne's *Supposes*, which has been called "the first comedy in the English tongue" (Gayley 1:lxxxiv), was also a source for circumstances and dramatic devices in *Comedy of Errors* (Salingar 207–8). Another work of Gascoigne's, an untitled mask written for a double wedding in 1572, has been shown to be a source for details in *A Midsummer Night's Dream* and *Romeo and Juliet*.[6]

Several editors have noted that two characters in *The Shrew*, Tranio, servant to Lucentio, and Grumio, servant to Petruchio, have the same names as two similar characters in Plautus's *Mostellaria*— "The Haunted House." Edwin W. Fay found further similarities in the roles and behavior of the two servants in that in both *The Shrew* and *Mostellaria* Tranio tempts his young master to misbehave, and Grumio sustains a beating—by Tranio in *Mostellaria*, and by Petruchio in *The Shrew* (245–8).

There are further connections between the *Shrew* plays and *Mostellaria*. Both *A Shrew* and *Mostellaria* are set in Athens. The young masters in each of the three plays, Philolaches in *Mostellaria*, Aurelius in *A Shrew*, and Lucentio in *The Shrew*, are "model young men" who suddenly fall in love with the woman they have just met—Philematio in *Mostellaria*, Philema in *A Shrew* (the similarity in names is clear), and Bianca in *The Shrew*. The Lord in the Induction scenes of *A Shrew* calls himself "Simon," a name that Christopher Sly shortens to "Sim." The names are very close to that of Simo, an old man in *Mostellaria* who complains about his wife in the same way that Sly complains about his (Harrold 191–2). Moreover, as Fernando Cioni points out, in the Italian translation of *Mostellaria*, published in Venice in 1530, the speech prefix for Simo is "Sim" (123).

Besides the similarity of names, Harrold, Cioni, and a third scholar, Albert H. Tolman, have, among them, identified some fifteen plot elements and circumstances in *Mostellaria* that reappear in one or both of the *Shrew* plays. These include such things as the servant-beating-servant motif, a knocking at a gate, a banquet, and others. This has led some critics to posit yet another play, a "lost" version of the story on which Shakespeare relied in composing *The Shrew*, as did the author of *A Shrew*. But a non-existent play and an unknown author are not a credible explanation for these relationships found between the two *Shrew* plays. The most economical and sensible scenario is that a young Shakespeare composed the anonymous *A Shrew*, using folkloric sources, the *Supposes* of George Gascoigne, and elements and ideas from Plautus' *Mostellaria*. A decade or so later, during or just after his visit to Italy, he revised this play, returning to both *Supposes* and *Mostellaria* for material, and produced the *Shrew* we find in the Folio. This scenario is explicated further in "The Two Shrews and Edward de Vere," below.

The source or sources of the "framing plot" are more obscure. The story of a sleeping drunkard, or a "dreaming man," who awakes to find himself a wealthy noble is a staple of traditional folklore. A more specific source, a collection of short comic stories in prose made by Richard Edwards and allegedly printed in 1570, has been cited by several critics. Although this book has never been found, the pages containing one of the stories, "The Waking Man's Dream," turned up in the mid-nineteenth century and were printed by the Shakspere Society (Mish). Another possible source, an anonymous and undated ballad called "The Frolicksome Duke or The Tinker's Good Fortune," has been suggested by Derran Charlton (114–116). In twelve verses, the ballad describes an episode that is nearly identical to that in both plays. The play is not mentioned in the ballad, so it is possible that the ballad preceded the play, and that the playwright was familiar with it.

## Relationships Between the Two Shrews

The plot in both *Shrew* plays is an extended farce, set in Athens in *A Shrew*, and in Padua in *The Shrew,* that involves the courtship and marriage of the three daughters of an Athenian merchant (Alfonso) in *A Shrew*, and the two daughters of a wealthy citizen of Padua (Baptista) in *The Shrew*. Each of the main characters, except Gremio, and several minor ones has a counterpart in the same role in the other play. But except for Sly and Kate/Katherina, their names are different. In each play the eldest daughter Kate/Katherina is a scold and a shrew who her father demands must be the first to marry.

The two plays agree in theme, plot and subplot, and in dozens of details of characterization, action and language. Of the fifteen scenes in *A Shrew*, all but three occur in *The Shrew*. If the Sly epilogue in *A Shrew* is set aside (it is absent from the Folio text), both plays divide into fourteen scenes, the first two and the last three of which are "roughly equivalent" (Miller 23).

*A Shrew* is the shorter and simpler play, the characters are less well-rounded, and their motivations less clear than in *The Shrew*. In *A Shrew*, three young men each court a different daughter of the merchant Alfonso, one of whom is the shrew. In *The Shrew*, one man courts the shrew, and three other men, including one much older (Gremio), court the shrew's only sister Bianca. In the fourth act, one abandons his courtship of Bianca and transfers it to an unnamed Widow.

The three structural components in each play—the main "taming" story, the subplot of the wooing of the shrew's sister(s), and the frame in which a lord plays tricks on a sleeping drunkard, Sly—are similar, and are arranged with each other in the same way. On the other hand, there are noteworthy differences in the casts of the two plays, in the interactions among the characters, and in the sequence of events in each subplot.

### THE "SLY FRAME"

Much critical attention has been devoted to the "Sly Frame" that is present in both plays. It encloses the entire plot and subplot of the anonymous *Shrew*, but in *The Shrew* Sly and the others disappear after the second Induction scene. In *A Shrew*, Sly and the lord are part of the extended dramatic framework, and reappear throughout the play, and in the twenty three-line closing scene.

The two opening scenes in both plays are the most nearly alike of all the scenes in the two plays. There are more than thirty details of action, characterization and language that are virtually identical. The most obvious are the following.

The first scene in *both* plays opens with a drunkard named Sly exiting a tavern after quarreling with the tapster/hostess, and then falling asleep. A lord who has been hunting enters with his men, and tells his servants to attend to his dogs. He regards the sleeping Sly with disgust, but then orders him taken to a luxurious setting in his own house. He instructs his servants to address, and to treat, Sly as "Lord" when he awakes. He also arranges for a boy to pretend to be a woman who is Sly's wife, and instructs him at length in the seductive behavior he is to use to charm him. A servant announces that the lord's players have arrived. The lord welcomes them and arranges for them to put on a play that evening before the "Lord" Sly. He orders his servants to see that the players are given food and whatever else they need.

In the first scene of *A Shrew*, the lord asks the players, "Now sirs, what store of plays have you? A player answers, "Marry my lord, you may have a 'tragical' or a 'commodity' or what you will" (1.57–8).[7] In *The Shrew* the malapropism comes from the mouth of Sly, who confuses "comedy" and "comonty":

Sly.       Marry, I will, let them play it. Is not a

           comonty a Christmas gambold, or a tumbling trick?

                                                          Ind.ii.137–8

In the second scene in *both* plays, music is playing when Sly awakes; he is dressed in luxurious garments, and a banquet set before him. He calls for ale; servants offer him wine and refer to his horses and dogs. The lord presents himself as a commoner and addresses Sly as if *he* were a lord, suggesting a variety of activities as if he were a wealthy nobleman. Sly asks, "Am I a lord?" The servant boy enters, disguised as Sly's wife, and presents herself to him. Sly suggests that he and she will go to bed shortly, but the boy puts him off. The players are announced, and the group prepares to watch.

The first two scenes of *The Shrew* contain about twice as many lines as the same two scenes in *A Shrew*. While they also contain the same elements, the dialogue is drawn out and elaborated. Except for a five-line exchange between Sly and the lord after the first scene in Padua (I.i), the characters in the first two scenes of *The Shrew* do not appear again. However, in *A Shrew* Sly and the lord or the tapster reappear five more times, and the final scene (15) consists entirely of a 23-line dialogue between Sly and the tapster. In each of these short reappearances, Sly and the lord maintain their reversed relationship, and actually comment on the progress of the play. In the last scene Sly awakens in his previous state, and exclaims to the tapster that he has had a wonderful dream, and that now he knows "how to tame a shrew."

It is clear that the author of the Folio *Shrew* has simply taken over the situation and characters in the "Sly frame" in *A Shrew* and rewritten the dialogue.

## The Subplot

In the third scene of both plays, the action of the subplot begins with the arrival in Athens/Padua of Aurelius/Lucentio, a well-to-do young man who is accompanied by his servant Valeria/Tranio. In the Folio play Lucentio has an additional servant, Biondello, a boy. The subplots of *both plays* contain more than a dozen identical elements:

- Aurelius/Lucentio arrives in a university town to study. In *A Shrew* he is the son of the Duke of Sestos; in *The Shrew* he is the son of a Pisan merchant "of incomparable wealth." He promptly falls in love with Phylema/Bianca, the younger sister of Kate/Katherina, the shrew.
- He learns that her wealthy father, Alfonso in *A Shrew*, Baptista in *The Shrew*, requires that his oldest daughter, the shrew, be the first daughter to marry.
- In order to gain access to Phylema/Bianca and to court her more effectively, the student disguises himself as a person of lower rank by exchanging identities with his servant.
- He is encouraged when the tamer (Ferando/Petruchio) appears as a suitor for the shrew.
- Music lessons for the shrew are attempted by a disguised music instructor, who makes sexual advances toward her. She rejects him, and the lesson ends badly.
- After the wedding of the tamer and the shrew is arranged, her father agrees to the marriage of Aurelius/Lucentio to his younger daughter Phylema/Bianca if the groom's father will vouch for her dowry.
- The servant disguised as Aurelius/Lucentio recruits a man to pretend to be the father of Aurelius/Lucentio.
- The scheme is successful, and the wedding is arranged.
- The true father of Aurelius/Lucentio arrives in Athens/Padua and meets the tamer and the shrew.

- The true father encounters his and his son's impersonators, berates them both, and threatens them with prison.
- After explanations and apologies all around, the true father of Aurelius/ Lucentio agrees to his marriage to Phylema/Bianca.
- Each of the new husbands wagers the others that his wife is the most obedient.

Thus, aside from the rearrangement of suitors and daughters, the subplots of the two plays are identical. But the verse has been entirely rewritten. Scholars have noted that in both subplots events are dramatized that are only narrated in the source, Gascoigne's *Supposes*, and there are circumstances and details in both that do not appear in the source at all. According to *A Shrew*'s latest editor, the two *Shrew* plays "have more in common with each other than either has with *Supposes*," supplying further evidence that "one must derive from the other" (Miller 16–17).

## The "Taming" Plot

Once the characters of the subplot have been introduced in both plays, those in the taming plot, Ferando/Petruchio and his servant Sander/Grumio, join them in Athens/Padua. The tamer is in search of a wife. The following identical details of plot and action in the taming component, upwards of thirty, appear in *both* plays:

- The tamer hears of the shrew, Kate/Katherina, and her wealthy father Alfonso/Baptista.
- Before he even meets Kate/Katherina, the tamer arranges for a large cash payment from her father upon their marriage.
- The tamer flirts with the shrew in a bantering way. She rebuffs him with witty and scornful replies.
- After a display of erratic behavior by both the tamer and the shrew, the tamer announces their wedding, with the assent of her father.
- The wedding is delayed because Ferando/Petruchio arrives late. The bride's father and the other guests are dismayed by his "base attire" in *A Shrew*, "unreverent robes" in *The Shrew*. They try to persuade him to change into more suitable clothes, but he refuses.
- The tamer behaves like a boor at the wedding. Doubts about the success of the marriage are expressed by several characters.
- After the wedding, Ferando/Petruchio announces that he and his bride will depart immediately and not join the other guests at dinner. As

Kate/Katherina and the others entreat him to stay, he calls for his horse and the two of them leave.

- When they arrive at home, Ferando/Petruchio berates his servants, rejects the meat they bring them, and strikes several of them.

- The tamer departs with the shrew, but then returns to explain to the audience that he will tame his "headstrong" wife in the same way that men tame wild birds—by denying her food and sleep.

- Mention is made of a "taming school" where Ferando/Petruchio is the master.

- In similar scenes of approximately fifty lines each, Kate/Katherina asks the tamer's servant, Sander in *The Shrew*, Grumio in *The Shrew*, to bring her food. He brings her beef and mustard and two other dishes, but as soon as she displays interest, he finds a reason to withdraw each one. Finally, beset with anger and frustration, she "beats him."

- A haberdasher and a tailor are brought in to furnish Kate/Katherina with a hat and a gown, but the tamer rejects them immediately, even though she thinks them fashionable and wishes to wear them.

- On the tamer's demand, the shrew agrees to call the sun the moon, pretends that an old man is a woman, etc.

- In the outcome of the wager scene, Kate/Katherina comes to her husband when commanded by him, after the other two wives have refused.

- At the tamer's command, Kate/Katherina throws down her cap and then fetches the other two wives.

- At the tamer's command, Kate/Katherina exhorts the other two wives to love and obey their husbands. As an example, she offers to place her hand under her husband's feet.

As this catalog reveals, Shakespeare appears to have appropriated all three elements of *A Shrew's* plot, nearly all of its characters, and dozens of its details of plot and action. This juxtaposition of the two *Shrews*, and their undoubted correspondences, are identical with those of the four other pairs of plays treated in this book—in which Shakespeare rewrote his earlier play, and both were then subsequently published, the first anonymously, the second under his pseudonym.

Another significant similarity between the two plays is the modification of a basic assumption in the Shrew-taming folk tale complex—that a shrew can be tamed by violence. In both plays the tamer manipulates and humiliates the shrew, but does so without violence, a "revolutionary" alteration of the method used in the folk tale complex. But although the tamer's actions in both plays are roughly similar, in *The Shrew* Shakespeare offers a rationale for them—that they are done in "reverend care" of her health and well-being—that is absent from *A Shrew* (Miller 14–15).

Despite these similarities in the taming plots of both plays, there are noticeable differences. Ferando is clearly less demeaning toward Kate in *A Shrew*, and his taming techniques are less effective. Also, in *A Shrew*, "Kate appeals to wives to obey because their husbands need their assistance," but in *The Shrew*, "the rationale is precisely reversed: women are presented as helpless, passive, creatures of the household" (Marcus 187).

## STYLE AND VOCABULARY

As both *Shrew* plays share the same farcical plot and characters, their styles are similar, and share numerous comedic characteristics, such as puns, ribald word play and racy vernacular. *A Shrew* is shorter, faster-moving and less complicated than *The Shrew*, and plainer in style. Its poetry is less polished and less refined than that in *The Shrew*, and more exaggerated and bombastic. Both plays contain similar rhetorical devices, such as repetition and alliteration, and both contain numerous compound adjectives and irregular inflections of verbs.

Many passages in *A Shrew* closely resemble corresponding passages in *The Shrew*, but the verse has been entirely rewritten. Eric Sams found "over 100 phraseological parallels" in the two *Shrew* plays and more than a dozen exact repetitions or "verbatim echoes" (*Real Shakespeare* 142–3). Moreover, in *A Shrew* we find images, metaphors and allusions to birds and falconry, dogs, music, and classical and mythological names in the same profusion that we find them in *The Shrew*, and throughout the Shakespeare canon. One exception is the use of legal terms, which are virtually absent from *A Shrew*, as mentioned below, but frequent in the Folio *Shrew*.

The author of *A Shrew* proved himself prolific in the creation of new words and new meanings of words, in the same way that Shakespeare was, and the *Oxford English Dictionary* cites at least six words in the play as the first use or new usage in the language. Another thirty words that appear in *A Shrew* are listed in error in the *OED* as new words or usages introduced by other authors, but in works published after 1594, the publication date of *A Shrew*. Half of those works are canonical Shakespeare plays. The particular usages of seven additional new words in *A Shrew* are not listed in the *OED*.

As recounted in Chapter III ("Ideas and Conceits"), Shakespeare made abundant use of words about language—such as *speak, speech, language, name, voice, tongue, mouth, throat, ear, breath, pen, paper, ink,* and *parchment*—and every canonical play is replete with them. In the early plays he used these words at the rate of once every twenty-four lines, and for the entire canon, once every twenty-six lines (Donawerth 141, 161). In *A Shrew*, they are used sixty times, once every twenty-five lines. Curiously, the language-related word ratio for *The Shrew* is among the lowest in all the canonical plays, once every thirty lines.

## A Shrew *and the Shakespeare Canon*

Despite its shortcomings when compared to the Folio *Shrew*, the anonymous *Shrew* exhibits unmistakable characteristics that are evident throughout the canonical plays—structural competence, thematic unity, multiple plots, specific dramatic devices, farcical humor and innovative vocabulary.

One shared dramatic device is the play or the scene within the play, a common feature in Elizabethan dramaturgy, but especially prominent in the Shakespeare canon. It is found in *1 Henry IV, A Midsummer Night's Dream, Hamlet, Love's Labor's Lost, The Tempest* and *Henry VIII*. In *A Shrew* this device is carried to the extreme, the entire play being enclosed in the Sly framing story.

In several canonical plays, the inserted play is offered by a company of players that arrives on stage in the same way as they do in *A Shrew*. In three of them, *A Midsummer Night's Dream, Hamlet* and *The Tempest*, the inserted play illustrates, in Frederick Boas' words, "the eternal problem of shadow and substance, appearance and reality," just as it does in *A Shrew* ("Play" 154–5).

On arriving in Athens, Aurelius, the student in *A Shrew*, falls in love at first sight with Alfonso's daughter Phylema, whom he describes as:

*Aurelius.*     The image of honour and nobility,

In whose sweet person is comprised the sum

Of nature's skill and heavenly majesty.          *A Shrew* 3.62–4

He has this in common with Antipholus of Syracuse in *Comedy of Errors*, and Valentine and Proteus in *Two Gentlemen of Verona*, all of whom are similarly smitten on arriving in a strange city. The courtiers in *Love's Labor's Lost* are similarly affected.

Particular parallels of language, thought and situation in *A Shrew* have been identified in a dozen Shakespeare plays, especially *A Midsummer Night's Dream, Love's Labor's Lost* and *Hamlet*.

### *A Midsummer Night's Dream*

- The initial scene in *A Shrew*, in which the lord and his hunting dogs enter to find Sly asleep is echoed in the first scene in Act IV, when

Theseus and his hunting dogs enter to find the four lovers and Bottom asleep. The verb *couple*, referring to the leashing together of two dogs, is used in both passages, as well as in *The Shrew*, where the conversation about the dogs is extended, as in the episode in *A Midsummer Night's Dream*.

- The inverted syntax of Ferando's comment about himself and Kate, "Not lambs to lions never was so tame" (4.121) is echoed in a similar context by Pyramus and Thisbe:

Pyr.       Not Shafalus to Procrus was so true.

This.      As Shafalus to Procrus, I to you.

*A Midsummer Night's Dream* V.i.198–9

- When Sly awakes for the last time in the final scene of *A Shrew*, he says to the tapster:

Sly.       Who's this? Tapster? O Lord, sirrah,

           I have had the bravest dream tonight

           That ever thou heardest in all thy life.        *A Shrew* 15.11–13

This anticipates the account of a dream that Bottom begins in *A Midsummer Night's Dream* (IV.i.204ff) by saying "I have had a most rare vision. I have had a dream, past the wit of man to say what dream it was...."

- "Sly's suggestion that "we'll flout the players out of their coats" (*A Shrew* 2.53–4) is an early example of situations in the canon where characters interrupt others who are performing, as the lovers do in *A Midsummer Night's Dream* and *Love's Labor's Lost*, and as Hamlet does.

### Love's Labor's Lost

In scene 13 of *A Shrew*, Sly says "That's flat!" (13.48), which is defined in the *OED* as "A defiant expression of one's final resolve" (*flat*. II 6b). The identical phrase appears in *Love's Labor's Lost* at III.i.101 and twice in *1 Henry IV*, at I.iii.218 and IV.ii.39 with a similar meaning—that's the unquestionable and absolute truth.

The student Polidor courts Emelia in scene 4 of *A Shrew*, and praises her in an extravagant passage:

Polidor.      Come, fair Emelia, my lovely love,

Brighter than the burnished palace of the sun,

The eye-sight of the glorious firmament

In whose bright looks sparkles the radiant fire

Wily Prometheus slyly stole from Jove,

Infusing breath, life, motion, soul,

To every object stricken by thine eyes.      *A Shrew* 4.56–62

A passage using similar language appears in Act IV of *Love's Labor's Lost,* in which Biron scolds the courtiers:

Biron.      From women's eyes this doctrine I derive:

They sparkle still the right Promethean fire;

*Love's Labor's Lost* IV.iii. 347–8

In both passages, the beams that were thought to shoot from the eyes are compared to the fire that Prometheus stole from Zeus. The words *eye(s), sparkle, fire* and *Prometheus* or *Promethean* occur in both passages.

The two long conversations between Polidor's clever boy servant and Sander, a swaggering, sharp-tongued clown, at 3.209–51 and 5.1–46 in *A Shrew* are not carried over into *The Shrew,* but are similar to several such exchanges in the canon, most notably the badinage between Don Armado and Moth in I.ii and III.i in *Love's Labor's Lost.*

In *A Shrew,* Sly asks, "Why Sim, am not I Don Christo Vary?" (13.49). The same jocular title *Don* or *Dan* is used in *Much Ado About Nothing* (Don Worm), and in *Love's Labor's Lost* (Dan Cupid).

## Hamlet

In scene 1 of *A Shrew,* a messenger announces that the lord's players have arrived and are prepared to entertain him. The lord orders them to be prepared to play before Sly the same night, and advises them not to be disconcerted by what Sly says. As mentioned above, he also arranges for a boy to pretend to be a woman who is Sly's wife. He calls on his servants to see that the players "want nothing" (1.64–85).

This episode is echoed in Act II of *Hamlet,* where a group of players arrives at the court and Hamlet welcomes them as familiar friends. He addresses a boy among them as a woman and then demands that Polonius treat the players well

(II.ii.521–33). Two scenes later, he instructs the players at length on how they should perform—"Speak the speech, I pray you, as I pronounc'd it to you" (III.i.1–2).

In scene 13 of *A Shrew*, Polidor addresses the Duke of Sestos: "Taint not your princely mind with grief my Lord," (13.97). Similarly, in Act I of *Hamlet*, the Ghost adjures Hamlet: "But howsomever thou pursues this act, / Taint not thy mind…" (I.v.84–5). The *OED* erroneously records a line in *Twelfth Night*— "…for sure the man is tainted in's wits." (III.iv.13) as the first use of this sense of "taint."

## OTHER CANONICAL PLAYS

In scene 4 of *A Shrew*, Alfonso says "I cared not I, what cost he did bestow" (4.103). This formulation, 'I care not' with an extra 'I' is also used in *Two Gentlemen of Verona*: "Sir Valentine, I care not for her, I" (V.iv.132) and in *Titus Andronicus*: I care not, I, knew she and all the world" (II.i.71).

In scene 4 of *A Shrew*, Valeria, disguised as a music teacher and carrying a lute, reminds Kate that trees have been moved and savage beasts have hung their heads to the sound of "pleasant tuned strings" (4.1–4). In the last act of *The Merchant of Venice*, Lorenzo presents the identical idea to Jessica as music is playing (V.i.70–8). Lorenzo continues the thought by citing Ovid's description in *Metamorphoses* (X.86–116) of the power of Orpheus over "trees, stones and floods." Later in *A Shrew*, Emelia refers to the calming power of the music of Orpheus as she promises to entreat Pluto to leave Polidor harmless (11.28–34), just as the servant of Queen Katherine comforts her in *Henry VIII* with her song about the lute of Orpheus "Killing care and grief of heart" (III.i.3–14).

# *The Two* Shrews *and Edward de Vere*

In addition to the overall evidence that Edward de Vere was the playwright of the Shakespeare canon, the facts surrounding the two *Shrew* plays further support his authorship of both of them.

It is highly likely that he had access to several of the sources of both plays. As noted above, the ultimate source of certain names and plot elements in both plays was Plautus's *Mostellaria*. During the middle to late 1500s, comedies by Plautus and Terence were performed often at Cambridge University, those of Plautus, including *Mostellaria*, occurring about every other year (Hosley 131). According to University records, *Mostellaria* was performed at Trinity College in the 1559/60 school year (G. Smith 106). Although we do not know how long he remained at Cambridge, Oxford's matriculation at St. John's College in 1558, just across the river from Trinity, suggests that he might have seen *Mostellaria* when it was performed there a year later.

The source for the subplot of both plays, Gascoigne's *Supposes*, was performed at Gray's Inn late in 1566, just a few months before Oxford began his studies there. Given de Vere's early interest in the drama (he had inherited his father's playing company in 1562), and the fact that Gray's Inn was only a mile from his home at Cecil House, he might have attended the performance of *Supposes* in 1566, and quite possibly had access to the manuscript at that time, or soon afterward.[8]

What is more important is that Oxford visited Padua, the setting of the Folio *Shrew*, in November 1575, during his extended tour of France and Italy (Anderson 98). The anonymous *Shrew* is set in Athens, and most of its characters' names can be associated with classical Greece or Rome. The Folio *Shrew* is set in Padua, the characters have Italian names, and it contains a wealth of details that reveal a first-hand knowledge of the customs, geography and language of sixteenth century Italy. This suggests a scenario in which the dramatist, perhaps as early as 1567, set the first version of his comedy in Athens, the location of *Mostellaria*, one of his source plays. He gave the characters modern Italian names and introduced Italian phrases and references to Italian customs and art.

There is substantial evidence that the author of the canonical *Shrew* must have traveled in northern Italy and visited specific cities. In *The Shakespeare Guide to Italy*, Richard Roe examined several locations mentioned in *The Shrew*, as well as a number of phrases that have been erroneously explained or emended by editors. By associating clues in the text with historical information about travel in northern Italy in the sixteenth century, Roe located the precise spot described in the first scene of the play—the landing place of Lucentio and Tranio on Padua's interior canal in front of Baptista Minola's house. He also identified the adjacent bridge and hostelry that they spoke about, and the nearby parish church, the Chiesa di San Luca, dating from well before 1350, in which Lucentio and Bianca were to be married (96–105). Roe also enumerated details in *The Shrew* that conform to facts and practices in sixteenth century Italy that would be unknown to an Englishman, unless he had traveled there. These include mention of the Duke of Mantua's sea-going ships, and the sail makers in land-locked Bergamo (106–113).

As de Vere biographer Mark Anderson points out (xxx), Oxford also knew that Padua was the "nursery of arts" (*The Shrew* I.i.2). Thus, it is appropriate that Hortensio, one of the few natives of Padua in the play, proposes that he disguise himself as a music teacher (I.ii.131–4). Later in the play, the Pedant remarks that he has "bills for money by exchange / From Florence and must here deliver them" (IV.ii.89–90), suggesting that the author was aware that Florence was a banking center (Draper 288). Moreover, these observations are made in a natural and unobtrusive way, and are entirely appropriate in their context. Critics have observed that in plays by certain other dramatists, such as Jonson and Webster, such details are intrusive and unsubtle, as if they were taken from books (C. Brown 109; Elze 270–7).

Another salient fact persuasive of personal knowledge of Italy is that the original Italian paintings that inspired the three "wanton pictures" described in *The Shrew* (Ind. ii. 48–60) have been identified and located with a high degree of certainty. During the 1570s, they could be seen at three places on Oxford's itinerary—Florence, Mantua and Fontainebleau (Magri, "Shakespeare and Italian Renaissance Painting" 4–12).

A further circumstantial detail that links de Vere to *The Shrew* is the name of Katherina's father, Baptista Minola, a name that appears to be drawn from the names of several Italians with whom de Vere had financial dealings while in France and Italy. In his letter of September 24, 1575, to William Cecil, de Vere wrote that he had obtained a loan of 500 crowns from one Baptisto Nigrone, presumably in Venice, where de Vere was recovering from a fever (Chiljan, *Letters* 19–20). Other documents record that Cecil had arranged, through an Italian merchant in London, Benedetto Spinola, for de Vere to receive "bills of credit" during his trip (Chiljan, *Letters* 17). Moreover, John T. Looney proposed that the loan of "crowns" that Oxford obtained may have led him to use the word more than half-a-dozen times in *The Shrew*, more than in any other play.[9]

Arriving in Venice in the spring of 1575, Oxford, by now an experienced playwright, would have soon become immersed in the language and culture of Italy, and exposed to its theaters and dramatic productions. It is likely that he was stimulated to set his next play in Italy. But rather than create an entirely new play, he chose to rewrite one that he had composed nearly a decade earlier. Since the subplot of *A Shrew* was based on an old Italian play, relocating the entire play from Athens to Padua made perfect sense. This allowed him to apply his considerably improved poetic talent to a familiar plot and set of characters, and situate the story in a city with which he was now acquainting himself.

The characters in the Induction in both plays suggest another connection to de Vere. The players who arrive while the lord is contemplating the sleeping Sly appear to be sponsored or supported by the lord himself. In *A Shrew*, the messenger who announces them says "your players be come / And do attend your honour's pleasure here" (1.50–1). In *The Shrew*, it is clear that the lord is acquainted with them already; he recalls a previous performance in which one of them had "play'd a farmer's eldest son" (Ind. i.84). De Vere's lifelong association with players, playing companies and theaters is well-known, and is detailed in "The Author of the Canon."

Lastly, the activities of Cuthbert Burby, the publisher of the early quartos of *A Shrew* in 1594 and 1596, reveal links to works in the Shakespeare canon and to Edward de Vere. In May 1592, Burby published a translation of *Axiochus*, an alleged dialogue of Plato that he described as "translated out of Greek by Edw. [*sic*] Spenser." The title page of the *Axiochus* bore the words "Heereto is annexed a sweet speech or Oration, spoken at the triumphe at White-Hall before her Majestie, by the page to the right noble Earle of Oxenforde." The occasion for the recitation by the page was a tournament at Whitehall on January 22, 1581, a tournament at which Oxford was awarded the victor's prize (Swan 166–68).

Scholars disagree about the actual identity of the translator and the author of the page's speech, but the prevalent opinion is that the speech, and probably the *Axiochus* translation, are the work of Anthony Munday, a poet, translator, and writer of plays and romances who had entered Oxford's service in 1578 (Swan 170–2). The prolific Munday produced a poem or prose work nearly every year during the 1580s and 1590s, and dedicated many of them to Oxford. Several of them were published by William Wright, to whom Burby had been apprenticed until he gained his freedom in 1592.

Besides the two *A Shrew* Quartos and the *Axiochus*, Burby published several of Munday's works during the 1590s, and issued three of the earliest Shakespeare plays to reach print—two Quartos of *Edward III* in 1596 and 1599, Q1 of *Love's Labor's Lost* in 1598, and Q2, the "good Quarto," of *Romeo and Juliet* in 1599. Three of the four quartos were anonymous. The title page of Q1 of *Love's Labor's Lost* bore the phrase "Newly corrected and augmented by W. Shakespere." Thus, it appears that Munday was a likely conduit for the movement of manuscripts from Oxford's household to Burby, the earliest publisher of the anonymous *Shrew*.[10]

## Dates of the Two Shrews

The evidence of Oxford's authorship of both Shrew plays and the fact that he toured France and Italy between February 1575 and April 1576 establish parameters for dating *A Shrew* before 1575 and *The Shrew* in 1576, or slightly later. The fact that there are no legal terms, as such, in *A Shrew* and some twenty-three in *The Shrew* (Sokol 483; Sherbo 114), suggests that a further refinement of the composition dates can be made, that is, that Oxford probably wrote *A Shrew* early in 1567, before, or very early after, his admittance to Gray's Inn, and rewrote it entirely at some time during his visit to Italy, or soon after he returned to England in 1576.

Supporting evidence for the composition of *The Shrew* at this early date lies in several images and phrases in John Lyly's *Euphues, The Anatomy of Wit*, published in 1578, that have been shown by Katherine Chiljan to have been borrowed from the text of *The Shrew* (*Suppressed* 345–6). Four years older than Lyly, Oxford hired him as his secretary in 1578 or earlier, probably on the recommendation of Lord Burghley, to whom Lyly was related by marriage (Bond, ed. *Lyly* 1:17–18). His subsequent interactions with Oxford, both literary and personal, are manifold and well-known. In *Euphues*, Lyly copied freely from Pliny, Plutarch and Erasmus, among others, and in his employment with Oxford probably made the same use of the manuscript of *The Shrew*. In 1580 he dedicated to Oxford *Euphues and his England*, the sequel to *Euphues*, and later portrayed him as Endimion in his play of that name (J. Bennett 362–69).

Thus, it appears that there were two different *Shrew* manuscripts in existence before 1580, but the sketchy theatrical documentation remaining from this period does not record a performance of either until 1594. The flux of actors, playing companies and manuscripts during the 1590s makes it difficult to trace the history of a manuscript and its variations from composition to performance to print, but there are a few clues on which to base a probable path.

Because of the phrases and lines in *A Shrew* that are identical, or nearly so, to those in Marlowe's *Tamburlaine* plays and *Doctor Faustus*, E. K. Chambers speculated that it was staged c. 1589, within a year or two of performances of those plays—most likely by the Admiral's Men. Chambers further suggested that "Probably Pembroke's in their turn got the play from the earlier Admiral's or Strange's" (*Elizabethan Stage* 4:48).

There is evidence that the text of *A Shrew* was changed by someone connected to the Pembroke company before the play was sold to Cuthbert Burby in 1594. The names of four of the play's characters—Sly, Simon, Sander and Tom, can be associated with actors or sharers in Pembroke's Men—William Sly, Simon Jewell (sharer), Alexander Cooke and Thomas Goodale (George 312–13). All four appear in the Induction; Simon also appears, as Alfonso, in the subplot, and Sander in the taming plot. Tom and Sander also appear in *The First Part of the Contention* (printed 1594), another Pembroke play that is considered either a precursor or a reconstruction of *2 Henry VI*.

If it is correct that Oxford wrote both plays before 1580, the names of the four actors in the Pembroke company in the early 1590s cannot have been in the original manuscript of either play. They would have been added to the manuscript of *A Shrew* at the time that the company performed the play, and remained in the text when it was printed in 1594, and again in 1596 and 1607. It is likely that the phrases and lines from the Marlowe plays were inserted at the same time. The same reasoning applies to the image from Greene's *Menaphon* (printed 1589), and the passage from du Bartas mentioned above. The *Premiere Sepmaine* of du Bartas' poem was published, in French, in 1578, and various translations into English were made during the 1580s and 1590s.

On the basis of this information, it is probable that the *Shrew* play performed at Newington Butts in June 1594, as recorded by Henslowe, was the anonymous *Shrew*, and that it contained the additions made by the Pembroke company, but it is impossible to be sure. It appears that at some time during the ensuing years, the Chamberlain's Men acquired and performed the Folio *Shrew*, which Chambers calls "Shakespeare's revision" (*Elizabethan Stage* 4:48). The fact that the actor William Sly moved to the newly-formed Chamberlain's Men in 1594 (Chambers, *Elizabethan Stage* 2:340) and the appearance of the same character "Sly" in the Folio text of *The Shrew*, tend to confirm this scenario. In addition, an actor's name, Sincklo, is listed as one of the lord's players in the first scene in the Folio text. A John Sincler or Sincklo was an actor with both Lord Strange's and the Lord Chamberlain's Men during the 1590s (Chambers, *Elizabethan Stage* 2:339).

## Contrary Evidence

None of the editors and critics who are confident that Shakespeare had nothing to do with the anonymous *A Shrew*, not even those who propose that a "compiler" or "adapter" produced the play, has advanced a serious argument on behalf of any other playwright. John Dover Wilson toyed with the idea that Marlowe, with perhaps a few "kindred spirits," wrote it in the last year of his life, but was unwilling to express a confident opinion (Quiller-Couch, ed. *Taming* xxii–xxiv). After considering, and rejecting, the arguments for Kyd, Greene and Shakespeare, Boas concluded that "Its [*A Shrew's*] provenance ... is likely to remain one of the insoluble enigmas of Elizabethan dramatic history" (ed. *Shrew* xxxvii).

Those scholars who deny that Shakespeare wrote *A Shrew* routinely associate it with the other apprenticeship plays treated in this book. E. A. J. Honigmann, who once called Shakespeare a "reviser of genius," described the *Shrew* plays as "the non-identical twins whose relationship so strangely resembles that of KJ [*King John*] and TR [*Troublesome Reign*]" and speculated that the authors of *A Shrew* and *Troublesome Reign* were "perhaps one and the same man" ("King John" 124–5). Stanley Wells and Gary Taylor are "entirely confident that (despite claims to the contrary from Sams and Everitt) Shakespeare wrote neither" *A Shrew* nor *Troublesome Reign*. In their opinion, "[b]oth plays resemble 'bad quartos' less than they do plays like *King Leir* and *The Famous Victories of Henry the Fifth*, which served as sources for plays by Shakespeare" (*Textual* 85). Such statements tend to confirm the special nature of these four anonymous plays that, with *The True Tragedy of Richard the Third*, constitute a unique group of preliminary treatments that the author rewrote as early as ten and as late as thirty years after he first composed them.

The only internal evidence that appears to conflict with Oxford's authorship of *The Shrew* are several proper names mentioned in the Induction that orthodox scholars assert are references to people and places in the vicinity of Stratford-upon-Avon. In scene ii of the Induction, Sly has awakened and is addressed as "lordship." This is his response:

> Sly.          What, would you make me mad? Am not
>
> I Christopher Sly, old Sly's son of Burton-heath,
>
> by birth a pedlar, by education a cardmaker, by
>
> transmutation a bear-herd, and now by present
>
> profession a tinker? Ask Marian Hacket, the fat
>
> ale-wife of Wincot, if she know me not. *The Shrew* Ind. ii.17–22

Editors of the play claim that these allusions confirm that it was written by the Stratfordian William Shakspere because they refer to locations near his birthplace. But further investigation reveals that they do nothing of the kind, and actually support the other evidence that the author of the play was the Earl of Oxford.

For example, it is true that the "Wincot" mentioned by Sly might be construed as a reference to the village of Wilmcote, about three miles from Stratford, as orthodox scholars claim, or to Wincot Farm, two miles farther away to the southwest. But it is more likely that it is a reference to Wilnecote, pronounced "Wincot," a village in Staffordshire astride the ancient Watling Street, along which are found numerous other towns mentioned in Shakespeare's history plays, such as Shrewsbury, Tamworth, Stony Stratford and Hinckley. Moreover, there were five inns or ale-houses in Wilnecote in the late sixteenth century, and one has been associated with a Hacket family—a common name in the area, and one explicitly mentioned by Christopher Sly (Ind. ii.18).[11]

Lastly, Sly's description of himself as "old Sly's son of Burton-heath" is probably not a reference to Barton-on-the-Heath, a village fifteen miles south of Stratford, as orthodox scholars claim, but more likely a reference to Bourton Heath, a village on Dunsmore Heath, just west of Rugby and about twenty miles north of Stratford. An extensive tract of open, uncultivated ground, Dunsmore Heath is one of England's many upland moors, and has the distinction of not only being mentioned in a Shakespeare play—*3 Henry VI*—but identified as the location of a host of soldiers marching toward Coventry under the leadership of John de Vere, thirteenth Earl of Oxford. In Act V.i, Richard Neville, Earl of Warwick, is under siege inside the walls of Coventry, anxiously awaiting reinforcements from the direction of London:

| | |
|---|---|
| *War.* | Where is the post [messenger] that came from valiant Oxford? |
| | How far hence is thy lord, mine honest fellow? |
| *1 Mess.* | By this [time] at Dunsmore, marching hitherward. |

*3 Henry VI* V.i.1–3

The location of both Sly's birthplace and the troops of the thirteenth Earl of Oxford west of Rugby are best explained by Edward de Vere's connection to the area. It is well-established that the manor of Bilton Hall in the Avon River Valley, a few miles west of Rugby, was in de Vere's possession until well into Elizabeth's reign, perhaps as late as 1580. It is also well-known that Oxford was an important participant in the festivities arranged for Queen Elizabeth's visit to Warwick Castle, about sixteen miles west of Rugby, in August 1572.[12]

Thus, the purported references to places in the vicinity of Stratford-upon-Avon are actually references to places on or near the ancient road that Shakespeare's characters travelled, or to places that Oxford owned and/or visited before 1580. It is telling that Stratford-upon-Avon is nowhere mentioned in the Shakespeare canon.

## Conclusion

In every category of evidence—the dates that it was cited and printed, its stylistic deficiencies, its one-dimensional characters, its startling similarities to the Folio *Shrew*, and the treatment of the rights to print it—the facts surrounding *The Taming of a Shrew* all point to a single, simple conclusion—it was written, before he was twenty, by the man who was Shakespeare, and was probably his first comedy. The evidence indicates that he alone was the originator of this unusual comedy in which two different narratives are woven into a single story, set in a Mediterranean country, and then enclosed by a traditional folktale set in feudal England. After what was a lengthy and surely life-changing tour of France and Italy, he rewrote it completely, perhaps for some festive occasion. But in terms of plot, characters and action, his second version follows his first much more closely than his canonical plays follow their sources.

None of the claims to the contrary is sufficient to refute the evidence that *A Shrew* was the earlier play, and served as a template on which Oxford based the canonical *Shrew*. In the words of R. W. Bond, the first Arden editor of *The Shrew*, the theory that *The Shrew* was the model for *A Shrew* "is one which it is difficult to believe can have commended itself to anybody, so much more fully developed and finished is our play, so far does it surpass the other in fluency and naturalness of dialogue, in the handling of the plot, and in small but telling points of characterisation; while in diction too, and partly in versification, *A Shrew* represents an earlier style" (ed. *Shrew* xv).

The external evidence given above also supports Edward de Vere as the author of *A Shrew*. It is highly likely that he had access to the translation and production of *Supposes*, one of its main sources. Other details, such as the similarity of his activities and background to those of the lord in *A Shrew*, and the close connection between Cuthbert Burby, the original publisher of *A Shrew*, and Anthony Munday, a writer and translator who entered de Vere's service in 1578, are additional details that tend to confirm de Vere's authorship. Lastly, the allusions in *The Shrew* to the language, customs and geography of Italy, and the circumstances and facts of de Vere's tour of the country, strongly confirm the conclusion that after visiting Padua in 1575 he completely rewrote his original version, *A Shrew*, and the result was *The Taming of the Shrew* found in the First Folio.

# V

# The True Chronicle History
# of King Leir and The Tragedy
# of King Lear

The anonymous *King Leir* and the canonical *King Lear* are perhaps the clearest example of Shakespeare's transformation of a simple and thinly-drawn apprenticeship play into one of the masterpieces of the canon. In none of his four other wholesale revisions of his earliest plays did he so completely rethink and rewrite a play so as to change its genre, its message and its outcome. Although the legend of the British king who elected to resign his throne and divide his kingdom among his three daughters had been known in England for hundreds of years, the young Earl of Oxford, probably not yet twenty, was the first to dramatize it. The details surrounding the performance, registration and publication of the anonymous *King Leir* supply the first hints that it was a Shakespeare play.

The first mention of either play was by Philip Henslowe, who recorded in his Diary two performances of a *kinge leare* in his Rose Theater in April 1594, during the tenancy of the Queen's Men and the Earl of Sussex's Men (21).[1] In the next month, the following title was entered in the Stationers' Register: *The moste famous Chronicle Historye of LEIRE kinge of England and his Three Daughters* (Arber, ed. *Transcript* 2:649). This play was most probably the same *kinge leare* that Henslowe recorded in his Diary. The entry was made by Edward White, the co-publisher of Q1 of *Titus Andronicus* earlier in the year. There is no extant copy of a quarto proceeding from this entry, and it is likely that none was printed. Both E. K. Chambers (*William Shakespeare* 1:304) and W. W. Greg ("Date" 378) assert that it was not a new play at that time, but neither gives a reason for thinking so.

A second entry appeared in the Stationers' Register eleven years later, on May 8, 1605. This was called: *The Tragecall historie: of kinge LEIR and his Three Daughters* and was published by John Wright later in the year under the title: *The True Chronicle History of King LEIR and his three daughters, Gonorill, Ragan, and Cordella*. The printer, Simon Stafford, had previously printed Q2 of *1 Henry IV* ("Newly corrected by W. Shake-speare") and *Edward III* (anonymous), both in 1599, and would print Q3 of *Pericles* "By William Shakespeare" in 1611 (Bartlett 26, 42, 60). The publisher, John Wright, had been, until 1602, apprenticed to Edward White, the publisher who had registered the play in 1594 (Greg "Date" 378–9).[2] Neither of the Stationers' Register entries nor the title page of the 1605 Quarto listed an author. The latter indicated that the play had been "diverse and sundry times lately acted," suggesting that the play had been revived almost ten years after its reported performances in the Rose Theater in 1594. Of the five copies that survive, one was edited and published in facsimile by John S. Farmer in 1910 (British Museum Press Mark C. 34, l. 11). In his introduction, he wrote, "The traces (almost obliterated) of writing on the title page are ... 'first written by Mr. William Shakespeare.'" He added, "This note is devoid of authority," but offered no reason or explanation. The play was not reprinted until 1779, nor again until 1875 (Michie 51, 62).

It was not until November 1607 that the canonical *King Lear* was registered by Nathaniel Butter and John Busby as: *Master William Shakespeare his historye of Kinge Lear, as yt was played before the Kinges maiestie at Whitehall uppon Sainct Stephens night at Christmas Last, by his maiesties servantes playing usually at the Globe on the Banksyde vj$^d$* (Arber, *Transcript* 2:366). It was then printed in 1608 "for Nathaniel Butter" with the title: *M. William Shake-speare: His True Chronicle Historie of the life and death of King Lear and his three Daughters. With the unfortunate life of Edgar, sonne and heire to the Earl of Gloster, and his sullen and assumed humor of Tom of Bedlam.*

The subtitle contained the same statement about the venue, the audience and "Saint Stephens night" (Dec. 26, 1606) as the registration entry. *King Lear* was the fifth of Shakespeare's plays to bear the spelling "Shak-speare" or "Shake-speare" on its title page, there being more than twenty such quartos in all.[3] Of this edition, which has come to be known as the "Pied Bull" Quarto, twelve copies have survived, each of them slightly different, since corrections were introduced during the printing. A second Quarto, nearly identical to the first, was printed "for Nathaniel Butter" by William Jaggard in 1619, but with a title page dated 1608. "Butter must have sold the publishers of the First Folio and the Second Folio the right to print the play" (Kirschbaum 247). On the "A Catalogue" page of the First Folio, it is listed simply as *King Lear*

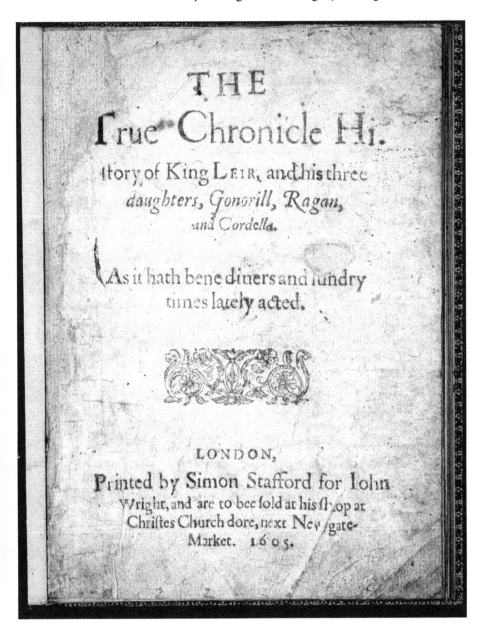

Title page of the anonymous *King Leir.* 1605. There is a record of its performance at Philip Henslowe's Rose Theater in April 1594 and of its registration in the following month. The canonical *King Lear* was not registered until 1607, and was first printed in 1608 (© Huntington Art Collections, San Marino, California).

under the "Tragedies" heading, but the running title is *The Tragedie of King Lear.*

During the nineteenth century and earlier, it was routinely claimed that Stafford's 1605 edition of the anonymous *King Leir* was an attempt to take advantage of presumed performances of Shakespeare's *King Lear* in the same year. Stafford's edition was registered as a *"Tragecall historie,"* but the play ends happily, although it contains tragic events and circumstances. Stafford, however, then published it as a *"True Chronicle History,"* with the names of the three daughters added. The canonical *King Lear* was registered in 1607 as a *"historye"* and then published in 1608 as a *"True Chronicle Historie,"* although it is certainly a tragedy. Thus, it is unclear, from the adjectives attached to the plays by the publishers, that there was an intent by Stafford to capitalize on Shakespeare's play.

A more likely stimulus for the publication of *King Leir* in 1605 was the publicity surrounding the case of Brian Annesley, who had been one of Queen Elizabeth's Gentlemen Pensioners for forty years, and became involved in a dispute with one of his three daughters. In brief, Annesley, a wealthy landowner, made a will in 1600 that greatly favored his youngest daughter Cordell. Three years later, he became senile, and his oldest daughter Grace and her husband tried to have him declared unfit to manage his affairs, with the intent of controlling his assets. But Cordell Annesley vigorously protested to Secretary of State Robert Cecil that this was unjust treatment of a long-time servant of the Queen, with the result that in October 1603 Cecil sent his own representatives to take charge of Annesley's affairs. When Annesley died in July 1604, Grace and her husband disputed the will and Cordell's appointment as executrix. In December 1604, the Prerogative Court ruled all matters in Cordell's favor (Bullough, "Annesley").[4] The Annesley case has been mentioned as possibly prompting Shakespeare to dramatize the King Lear story but, considering the dates of Cecil's intervention and Annesley's death, it is extremely unlikely. (See "Dates of the Two *Lears*," below.)

Another aspect of the case has been noticed by Shakespeare scholars. One of the men named by Brian Annesley as an overseer of his will in 1600 was the naval officer Sir William Hervey, who at the time was the third husband of Mary, Dowager Countess of Southampton, mother of Henry Wriothesley. After her death in 1607, Hervey took Cordell Annesley as his second wife. In 1922, Charlotte C. Stopes suggested that Hervey was the "Mr. W. H." to whom Thomas Thorpe dedicated his edition of *Shake-speare's Sonnets* in 1609, and that his wishes for the dedicatee's "all happiness and that eternity promised by our ever-living poet" were felicitations on Hervey's marriage to Cordell in the previous year (343–4). This suggestion has garnered little support.[5]

## *The Anonymous* Leir

By the late sixteenth century, more than fifty chroniclers and poets had produced versions of the fable that first appeared in Geoffrey of Monmouth's twelfth century *Historia Regum Britanniae—History of the Kings of Britain.* In dramatizing the tale of the legendary British king and his three daughters, the playwright adhered generally to the traditional story, except that he scrapped the defeat and death of Leir and his youngest daughter Cordella, which is the outcome in every previous version, in favor of a happy ending in which she survives and Leir is restored to his throne.[6] He converted a tragedy into a romance in which goodness is rewarded and wickedness punished.

Geoffrey Bullough places *King Leir* in the category of plays "using chronicle material together with romantic or comic ingredients," such as *A Knack to Know a Knave* and *Cymbeline.*[7] Other critics agree, calling the play a romantic comedy with strong religious overtones and no historical pretensions (Ribner 247–8; Bevington, *Tudor Drama* 343, n. 13). The conventional plot contrasts "parental unkindness and filial ingratitude, sins against natural and divine law," with "loyalty, truth and piety" (Bullough, *Narrative* 7:281). The hazards of heeding flattery at the expense of candid, if blunt, speaking is an explicit message. There are sixteen uses of "flatter" and "flattery" throughout the play.

The playwright added detail and complexity, and half-a-dozen new characters, to a simple legend, expanding Geoffrey's 1800-word tale into a drama of 2567 lines in thirty-two scenes. It is longer than most Elizabethan plays, but only four fifths the length of its descendant, the 1608 Quarto of *King Lear.* The play's strengths are the construction and movement of its tightly-knit plot, with its detailed exposition and logical development. According to its latest editor, "the playwright has left no loose ends or incomplete lines of action, and only a single scene could be eliminated without violating the play's unity" (Michie 43–4). Aside from the single phrase "ACTUS 1" on the first page, there are no act or scene divisions, and there is no subplot.

But with the possible exception of Cordella and Mumford, the play's characters are conventional and shallow, and little more than the abstractions commonly found in Morality plays. Skalliger is the evil counselor who suggests the love test, and then betrays the plan to Gonorill and Ragan. Subsequently, he incites Gonorill, whom he despises, to terminate Leir's allowance. The foil to Skalliger is Perillus, the traditional "faithful friend," who warns Leir against the love test, and later supports and encourages him. King Leir himself is a thinly-drawn and disappointing protagonist. After his initial denunciation of Cordella, he becomes passive and weak, and given to rambling and pedestrian speeches.

By the end of the play, he has aroused little concern in the reader, and has become merely pitiable.

Cordella is the most fully realized character in the play, personifying goodness and grace, candor and simplicity. She never waivers in her love for her father, and readily forgives him for his treatment of her. She is also effusive in her declaration of love for the disguised King of Gaul. Her sisters Gonorill and Ragan are vices in regal clothes, but reveal somewhat different personalities, Gonorill being the bolder and more outspoken. It is she who engages in a verbal duel with the French ambassador, and it is she who arranges with the Messenger to murder her father and Perillus.

The King of Gaul's companion Mumford is one of the characters added by the author to the original story. His conversations with the King enable the playwright to set the stage for their chance meeting with Cordella and her subsequent marriage to the King. Mumford adds a vein of humor, usually sexual humor, to the rather pedestrian dialogue, but his bawdy wisecracks about the charms of British women, even to the person of Cordella, become tiresome. His frequent sexual puns induce his companions to reply in kind, and in one forgettable exchange, Cordella and the King of Gaul tease him about the fidelity of his British "wench" (V.i.11–40). Mumford's name is a variant of the more familiar Mountfort or Mountford. His strange remark about it—"I am kin to the Blunts, and I think the bluntest of all my kindred; therefore if I be too blunt with you, thank yourself for praying me to be so" (II.i.44–47)—is a possible allusion to the Elizabethan family of the Blounts, one branch of which was the Lords Mountjoy, who were distantly related by marriage to Oxford. On the other hand, it may be just another lame pun.[8]

*King Leir* is written primarily in end-stopped blank verse, but contains 250 rhymed couplets and several other rhyming schemes, as well as double rhyme, internal rhyme and identical rhyme, as if the author were experimenting. In some speeches, he combines blank verse and rhyming couplets or alternative rhyming. There are many examples of forced rhyme, such as *much/church, chance/presence, residence/prince, surprise/ease,* etc., and many classical and Biblical allusions. There is little variation in the monotony of the meter, regardless of the emotion being expressed by the speaker. The verse has been described as sober, plain and sturdy, but more often as wooden, pedestrian and repetitive.

Another characteristic is the repeated references to the action by the characters. In several scenes (III.i, III.iv, IV.i, IV.vii, V.iv and V.v), speakers report actions that have taken place, make comments on them, and then reveal what they plan to do. This is precisely what occurs in V.iv, in which Leir recites the action of the entire play until then to a young woman who he does not know is Cordella. He then admits that he is seeking the daughter whom he mistreated, and hopes that she will forgive him, etc. A dozen monologues and more than thirty speeches to the audience also suggest a beginning dramatist. None of these deficiencies bothered Leo Tolstoy, who preferred the anonymous play to Shakespeare's revision. "However strange this opinion may seem to worshipers of Shakespeare, yet the whole of this old drama is incomparably and in every respect superior to Shakespeare's adaptation" (43).

The author of *King Leir* has also been praised for his "experimentation with words" (Everitt 14). He was prolific in the creation of new words, and new meanings of words, in the same way that Shakespeare was. The *Oxford English Dictionary* lists at least twenty new words or new usages in the 1605 Quarto. More than thirty additional words that appear in *King Leir* are listed in the *OED* as new words or usages introduced by other authors, but in works published after 1575, the latest date of composition of *King Leir*. (See "The Two Lears and Edward de Vere," below). The particular usages of fourteen additional words in *King Leir*, such as *afterwishes, safe-seated, tongue-whip* and *true-adopted* are not listed in the *OED*. The text is also replete with stage directions for sounds (drums, trumpets, thunder), properties (table, bags of money, swords and daggers), as well as the entrances and exits of actors, etc. In this characteristic, it is similar to the other apprenticeship plays, notably *The Taming of a Shrew*.

In the decades after the printing of *King Leir* in 1605, the right to reprint the play passed by inheritance and transfer through several hands until 1640, when Richard Oulton recorded his ownership of twenty plays, including *Lear and his 3 daughters*, "which lately did belong to Mistris Aldee his mother in Law deceased" (Arber, ed. *Transcript* 4:507). As Kirschbaum remarks, "Note the change of spelling in the assignment of the source play: *Leir* has become *Lear*. In the registers the sole distinguishing feature between the old play and Shakespeare's revision had been the spelling of the king's name. This distinction has now been obliterated" (248).

At some time in the next fifteen years, a publisher named Jane Bell came into possession of the twenty plays recorded by Oulton, presumably on his death. In one of the most peculiar episodes in the annals of Elizabethan printing, Jane Bell then printed a third Quarto of the canonical *King Lear* in 1655, based on the Quarto published by William Jaggard in 1619 (Kirschbaum 247–9). What we don't know is whether Jane Bell genuinely thought that she had the right to print *King Lear* because she had the printing rights to *King Leir*, or whether she simply thought she could get away with it. This scenario suggests that there was confusion about the identity of the two plays, and that they might have been thought of as two versions of the same play.

## *The Canonical* Lear

The printing history of Shakespeare's *Lear* presents one of the more interesting textual issues in the entire canon in that the Folio text of 1623 differs from the first Quarto text (1608) in several substantial ways. It contains 100 lines that are not in the Quarto, and the latter contains 300 lines, including one entire scene and two significant passages, that are not in the Folio. There are also some 850 changes of words, phrases and speech headings. The Quarto has been described as "bad," as "good," as a copy made by a stenographer in the theater, and as a memorial reconstruction by actors.

Traditionally, editors have conflated the Quarto and Folio texts and published a single text in which they chose what they considered the best readings from each edition. But after an influential paper by Michael Warren in 1978, several scholars adopted a "two-text hypothesis" in which the Quarto and Folio texts were treated as two distinct plays and were published separately. In 1987, Wells and Taylor's three-volume *The Oxford Shakespeare* included for the first time two separate texts of the play, based on the Quarto and Folio editions. But, as the most recent *Arden* editor remarked, "...none of the differences between Q and F radically affects the plot of the play, or its general structure, and there is every reason to think that we have two versions of the same play, not two different plays" (Foakes 118–9).[9]

It is accepted with little dissent among orthodox scholars that Shakespeare knew the earlier *King Leir* and based his own play on its plot and characters. Most scholars also agree that in dozens of places he used or modified words, phrases, ideas and dramatic devices from the old *Leir* play when composing *King Lear*.[10] In fact, several have described Shakespeare as "rewriting" the anonymous *Leir* (Bullough, *Narrative* 7:270; Duncan-Jones, *Ungentle* 185), and James Shapiro calls the canonical *King Lear* a "gut renovation" of the anonymous *Leir* (47). The subtitle of Sidney Lee's edition refers to it as "The Original of Shakespeare's 'King Lear'" (ix). There is some disagreement as to whether he had access to a text of *Leir*, merely saw a performance of it, or perhaps acted in it.[11] The uses that Shakespeare made of the *Leir* play, and the modifications he made in his revision are described below in "Relationships Between the Two *Lears*."

Of its more than 3300 lines, 2234 are in blank verse and 169 in rhyme. The 925 lines of prose are more than in any other Shakespearean tragedy, except *Hamlet*. There are a high number of split lines (243) and more short lines (191) than in any other Shakespeare play (Chambers, *William Shakespeare* 2:398–402).

## Sources of the Plays

The sources of *King Leir* and *King Lear* are difficult to pinpoint because of the multiple retellings of the legend during the previous four hundred years. Although virtually all of the more than fifty versions were based on Geoffrey of Monmouth's account, each author told the story differently, with numerous variations in the characters, events and details. The majority of these retellings were prose histories of some kind, many in French. The first of them to be printed, in 1480 by William Caxton, was *Chronicles of England*, an English translation of the *Brut*, a verse history of Britain composed in the Norman language about 1155 by the Anglo-Norman poet Wace. The *Brut* was based on Geoffrey's *Historia*, and was so popular that Caxton reprinted it ten times before 1528 (Perret 62–3).

In the 1490s, Robert Fabyan completed his *New Chronicles of England and France*, which also included the King Lear story. It was printed in 1516 and is considered "important as a basis for Holinshed" (Perret 76). Another popular chronicle of English history, by John Hardyng, that included the King Lear story was circulated in manuscript after 1463, and printed, with additions, by Richard Grafton in 1543. Geoffrey's *Historia*, of which more than two hundred manuscripts survive, was not translated into modern English until the seventeenth century. The interesting folk tale origins of the Lear story that were uncovered by the Italian scholar Giuseppe Cochiarra are described by F. D. Hoeniger (98–101).

Additional versions of the Lear story also appeared in three works of poetry published after 1550. These include *Albion's England*, a lengthy poem about English history by William Warner, the first four books of which were published in 1586; and the 1587 edition of *A Mirror for Magistrates*. In Canto X of Book II of Edmund Spenser's *The Fairie Queen*, published in 1590, six stanzas are devoted to the "King Leyre" story (300).

## The Anonymous Leir

The anonymous *Leir* is obviously based on the characters and events in Geoffrey's *Historia*, but the playwright added major and minor characters, a murder plot, two comic scenes involving watchmen and many details. He deleted other details and most of the events occurring after Leir's return from Gaul. The added characters include Skalliger, the evil counselor; Perillus, the faithful friend; the Messenger sent to kill Leir and Perillus; and Mumford, the King of Gaul's companion. Additions to Geoffrey's story are King Leir's sudden voluntary abdication, the thunderstorm that frightens the Messenger, the chance meeting and wooing of Cordella by the disguised King of Gaul, and the recognition scene between Leir and Cordella. Perhaps the most important modifications are the fate of Leir and Cordella, both of whom the playwright spares, and Leir's voluntary abdication in favor of the King of Gaul, thus inserting a happy ending that is absent from the previous versions.

Scholars have identified about a dozen details in the anonymous *Leir* that also appeared in the three poetical works mentioned above, and concluded that they were copied from those works by the author. These claims appear to be based on the belief that *Leir* was written about 1590. (For evidence that it was written many years earlier, see "Dates of the Two *Lears*," below.) Most of these details can be found in Geoffrey's *Historia* or in one or more of the other versions of the story that were available in manuscript or in print by 1550. Others might have been introduced independently by the author of *Leir*. Moreover, it has been shown that Warner, Spenser and the author of the relevant section of *A Mirror for Magistrates* all used the same older versions of the story as bases for their own accounts (Perrett 34, 85, 89, 90).

Rafael Holinshed's *Chronicles*, published in 1577, and in 1587, has also been mentioned as a source of *King Leir*, but according to the most extensive discussions of the question, there is little or no evidence that the playwright used either edition (Perrett 99).

## *The Canonical* Lear

It is widely agreed that Shakespeare used the anonymous *King Leir* as his main source for *King Lear*. Numerous scholars have identified similarities in structure, situation, thought and expression, as well as dozens of particular verbal parallels between the two plays (Greg, "Date" 386–97; Logan and Smith 222–4) These are treated in the next Section.

Another major source for *King Lear* is Philip Sidney's *The Countess of Pembroke's Arcadia*, the new version of which he completed in 1584, but was not published until 1590 (Duncan-Jones, *Courtier* 266, 276). The subplot involving Gloucester and his sons, Edmund and Edgar, appears to have been inspired by the story in Book 2, chapter 10 of *Arcadia* in which Plexirtus, the wicked, bastard son of the King of Paphlagonia, dethrones and then blinds his father after persuading him to denounce his elder, legitimate son. Several other details in *King Lear*, such as Gonerill's and Regan's lust for Edmund, Gonerill's suicide, and the storm in Act III, might also have been based on incidents in *Arcadia* (Halio 6).[12]

Another generally-accepted source of material in *King Lear*, especially in Act III, is Samuel Harsnett's *A Declaration of Egregious Popish Impostures, etc.,* published in 1603. Several dozen words, names, phrases and ideas that appear in *King Lear* are identical with those in Harsnett's book (Muir, "Harsnett"; Brownlow 107–132).

The notorious Annesley Case is frequently cited as a source, or inspiration, for *King Lear*, but, as noted above, this is unlikely. The additions made to *A Mirror for Magistrates* by John Higgins in 1574, the second book of the 1587 edition of Holinshed's *Chronicles*, and Canto X of Book II of Spenser's *The Fairie Queen* (1590) have also been cited by Geoffrey Bullough as sources for several details in *King Lear* (*Narrative* 7:323–34). He also cites Warner's *Albion's England* as a "possible source" (*Narrative* 7:335–6), but elsewhere states that "Nothing suggests that Shakespeare was influenced by this piece" (*Narrative* 7:276). Wilfrid Perrett, in the most exhaustive study of *Lear's* sources, sees only a few details from Holinshed in *Lear* (273); R. A. Law sees none ("Holinshed's Leir" 49–50). Both mention Holinshed's reliance on Fabyan's *Chronicles*. Perrett observes that Shakespeare used details from Layamon's *Brut*, an English translation of Wace's poem (44–5).

## Relationships Between the Two Lears

*King Leir* is similar to the four other apprenticeship plays described in this book in its anonymity, its plain and pedestrian style, and its competent and logical construction. It appears that the playwright did not return to *King Leir* until the last decade of his life, and the new play he created departed farther from the original than did any of his other four revisions. The characterization and verse in the canonical *Lear* are far superior to that in the anonymous *Leir*, and Shakespeare added a significant subplot and several new characters. In completely rewriting the verse, he elaborated or compressed the dialogue so as to create emotional intensity and darken the mood of the play. In doing so, he transformed a rather perfunctory and shallow romance, in which there is no violence and not a single death, into a tragedy riddled by humiliation, torture, suicide and murder. Charles Lamb remarked that *King Lear* "is essentially impossible to be represented on a stage" (Furness, ed. *King Lear* 421).

### Structure and Plot

From a close reading of the two *Lear* plays, it is obvious that Shakespeare used the old play as a template on which to construct a new play, and added a subplot that mirrors and complements the main story. But although his revision is longer by hundreds of lines, he compressed the original plot significantly, substituting a single scene, for instance, for the first seven in *King Leir*. In his revision, Shakespeare begins his play with the love test, which in *King Leir* doesn't occur until the third scene. In the source play, Leir has an altruistic reason for prescribing the love test for his daughters. Expecting each of them to profess that she loves him above all others, he plans to then reply to Cordella that she can please him by marrying a "king of Brittany."[13] His intent is to insure that she is provided with a well-fixed husband, her two sisters being already engaged to kings. There is no such intent in Shakespeare's revision, but a remnant of the old play remains in Lear's offer of the dowerless Cordelia to the Duke of Burgundy or the King of France, Burgundy refusing, France accepting, her. Nevertheless, once Cordella has responded coolly to the love test, Leir denounces and banishes her, just as he does in the canonical *Lear*.

The outcome of the love test and Leir/Lear's abdication are essentially the same in both plays, as are Cordella/Cordelia's departure to France and her marriage to the King. In both plays, Leir/Lear departs from the scene of his humiliation and rejection, in *Leir* to France with Perillus, in *Lear* to an unknown location with the disguised Kent and the Fool. Near the end of both plays, Cordella/Cordelia arrives at Dover with her new husband and his army. In *King Leir*, she is accompanied by her father after their having met in France and reconciled in an emotional scene. In *King Lear*, they have the same tearful reconciliation when he is brought to the French camp in a chair by servants. In both plays, Leir/Lear is ailing and confused and prepared to die when he and Cordella/Cordelia are reunited, and begs her forgiveness for his actions.

In the source play, the Gaulish army defeats the forces of Cornwall and Cambria, Leir and Cordella are triumphant, and Leir is restored to his throne. In his revision, Shakespeare, instead, has the British army defeat the French and capture Lear and Cordelia. In the final scene, Goneril and Regan quarrel over Edmund, and in short order all three are dead. Cordelia is hanged by mistake, and Lear himself dies, holding her in his arms.

Another significant revision that Shakespeare made was the insertion of a subplot in which another father, the Duke of Gloucester, and his two sons, one legitimate, one not, are drawn into the dispute between Lear and his daughters. Although Shakespeare dropped the evil counselor Skalliger, the addition of these three characters, and Goneril's servant Oswald, greatly thickens the plot. Oswald and Gloucester's son Edmund supply more than sufficient wickedness to make up for the loss of Skalliger. Shakespeare's Goneril and Regan are no less calculating and vicious than in *King Leir*, but he added a dimension to their immorality by assigning to each of them an adulterous lust for Edmund.

Shakespeare discarded the aborted murder-for-hire of Leir and Perillus initiated by Gonorill in his original play. In place of this single ineffectual threat, he added a vicious blinding (of Gloucester by Cornwall), four intended murders (of Lear and Cordelia by Edmund; of Gloucester by Oswald; of Albany by Edmund), five successful ones (of Cornwall by a servant; of the servant by Regan; of Oswald by Edgar; of Regan by Goneril; of Edmund by Edgar), an attempted suicide (Gloucester's), a successful one (Goneril's) and, finally, Cordelia's hanging before a tardy reprieve, and Lear's own death from grief.

Shakespeare replaced the overt but anomalous Christianity that pervades *King Leir* with a pagan world of anger, greed and treachery, where references to God are replaced by repeated entreaties to "gods" for support, pity or revenge. He dropped the farcical interludes involving the incompetent watchmen, and did not replace them with anything similar. The little humor there is in *King Lear* is the bitter humor of the Fool.

## CHARACTERS

In the same way that he retained the basic plot of *King Leir*, Shakespeare retained the seven main characters from the source play, using the same or similar names—and two others, whom he renamed, but kept in the same roles and relationships. The King, his three daughters and their husbands reappear in the same roles, but all have been transformed into articulate and fully-realized individuals. On the other hand, the repeated references to the action by the characters in *King Leir* sometimes makes their motivations clearer than in Shakespeare's revision.

Cordella/Cordelia plays the same role and behaves in the same way in both plays, but in the Folio *Lear* her role is less important, and she is given only half as many lines. The Cordella of *King Leir* is less complex and more religious than Cordelia, referring to her God and her church, where she intends to "pray unto my Savior" (IV.i.31).[14] In *Leir*, much is made of Cordella's beauty, but in *Lear* Shakespeare emphasizes her virtue.

The King Leir of the source play is irrational and stubborn, in the same way as the Lear of the Folio, as he conducts the love test, banishes Cordella, and then rejoices at his oldest daughters' imminent weddings. But in his next appearance, at Gonorill's castle, he has suddenly become sad and gloomy, and complains of his "troubled days" and the lack of "worldly joys"—"Then welcome sorrow, Leir's only friend." When Gonorill turns on him, calls him a "vild old wretch," and urges him to "seek some other place," he is quick to blame himself—"This punishment my heavy sins deserve." Weeping, he laments that he has lived too long and urges "gentle death" to end his sorrows "with thy fatal dart." He continues to bemoan his fate in the same way until well after his reconciliation with Cordella, only after which both of them denounce Gonorill and Ragan.

In the canonical *Lear*, however, when Goneril demands that he reduce his complement of knights, he reacts angrily, and directs a torrent of invective against her. Proceeding to Gloucester's castle, he is enraged to find Kent in the stocks, and when Regan invites him to return to Goneril, he denounces her in the same terms. At this point he begins to speak of madness, as distinguished from the simple eccentricity of the Leir of the source play. In this case, as with several other characters in the apprenticeship plays, Shakespeare has taken a simple, one-dimensional character and made of him one of the canon's most pitiable and tragic figures.

Two characters who were added to the story in the anonymous *King Leir* were carried over into Shakespeare's revision, but under different names. Gonorill's anonymous Messenger/Murderer is recast in *Lear* as Goneril's steward Oswald, who is dispatched by her with a letter to Regan, and who later contemplates murdering Gloucester. King Leir's faithful and truth-telling companion Perillus is recast as the Earl of Kent, a younger man who attempts to warn Lear of his folly in the same way as did Perillus. Both Perillus and Kent, at the same moment in each play, when the King has just banished Cordella/Cordelia, beg him to reconsider his rash act and restore her to his favor. Each is rebuked by the King in almost identical language:

| Leir. | Urge this no more, and if thou love thy life: | *King Leir* II.iii.99 |
|---|---|---|
| Lear. | Kent, on thy life, no more. | *King Lear* I.i.154 |

In the same conversation, both Perillus and Kent decry the King's decision and liken it to a type of moral blindness:

| Perillus. | Ah, who so blind, as they that will not see | |
| | The near approach of their own misery? | *King Leir* II.iii.106–7 |
| Kent. | See better, Lear; and let me still remain | |
| | The true blank of thine eye. | *King Lear* I.i.158–9 |

Both Perillus and Kent depart from the play shortly after their protests, Perillus on his own, but Kent by banishment. When Perillus returns several scenes later, Leir does not recognize him; when Kent reappears, he is disguised as Caius, a servant, and Lear does not recognize him until the final scene. Sidney Lee pointed out that "Hardly any of the speeches which Perillus and Leir address to one another failed to yield suggestion to Shakespeare" (ed. *King Leir* xxxix).

Another significant character added by Shakespeare is the Fool, who is alternately a loyal and loving supporter and a sympathetic taunter of the King. His role and function have been hinted at in the anonymous play by Perillus, Lear's loyal but tart companion. An example of this is the idea of the King as the shadow of himself that is raised in both plays in the dialogue between them:

| | | |
|---|---|---|
| *Leir.* | Cease, good Perillus, for to call me Lord, | |
| | And think me but the shadow of myself. | *King Leir* IV.ii.16–17 |
| *Lear.* | Who is it that can tell me who I am? | |
| *Fool.* | Lear's shadow. | *King Lear* I.iv.230–1[15] |

Leir's admonition of Perillus is one of the dramatist's earliest uses of the shadow/substance comparison, a motif that persists throughout the canon. His description of himself as a shadow, symbolizing his loss of legitimacy as a king, repeats an observation by King John in *Troublesome Reign* (*Pt. I*, 512–14),[16] and again in 3 *Henry VI*, when Warwick removes the captured King Edward's crown:

| | | |
|---|---|---|
| *War.* | But Henry now shall wear the English crown, | |
| | And be true king indeed, thou but the shadow. | |
| | | *3 Henry VI* IV.iii.49–50 |

Although Shakespeare dropped Skalliger, some traces of his language and behavior resurfaced in Edmund, one of the three major characters he added.

## VOCABULARY AND STYLE

Although Shakespeare retained the basic plot and the principal characters of *King Leir*, he rewrote the entire play, bringing to bear his immensely improved poetic skills and his heightened sense of the folly and wickedness of mankind. He replaced the loose, monotonous and jogging rhythm of the old play with a highly compressed language, often in split lines and broken-end speeches. Much of the dialogue is delivered with emotional intensity, with many exclamations, interjections and imprecations, etc. The frequency of feminine endings is among the highest in the canon. Rhyme occurs far less frequently than in *King Leir*, but more often than in any other tragedy (169 lines), except *Romeo and Juliet* (Campbell and Quinn 932). The use of imagery is greatly increased, and the images used, especially by King Lear himself, often simply express the speaker's feelings, rather than attempt to communicate.

There are more than forty citations from *King Lear* in Eric Partridge's *Shakespeare's Bawdy*, many more than in *King Leir*, but few of them are sexual puns. They are mostly what Partridge calls "non-sexual bawdy" or straightforward sexual imprecations, a great many of them by Lear himself, such as his extended diatribe on copulation in IV.vi.108–31. Sidney Lee observed that in *King Leir*, "There are farcical interludes ... which owe their ludicrous effect to their crudity, and occasionally to their childish obscenity" (ed. *King Leir* xvii–xviii). One example is the brief exchange about Cordella between Ragan and Gonorill:

*Ragan.*        She were right fit to make a parson's wife:

            For they, men say, do love fair women well,

            And many times do marry them with nothing.

*Gonorill.*     With nothing! Marry, God forbid! Why, are there any such?

*Ragan.*        I mean, no money.                                      *King Leir* 6.20–4

In this case, the word *nothing* denotes the absence of a penis. Shakespeare did not repeat the exchange or use the word in the same sense when rewriting the play, but he used it similarly in several other plays, most notably in III.ii of *Hamlet*, where the prince coarsely teases Ophelia by twisting her use of the word *nothing* to its vulgar meaning (112–121).[17]

In *King Leir*, there are more than fifty legal terms or ordinary words used in a legal sense. Examples are *abridge, assizes, confute, debar, enjoin, indictment, indubitate, letters of contract, prosecute, sequestered, upon condition,* etc. In contrast, the canonical *King Lear* contains about thirty legal terms and concepts, and none of the above words is used. Instead, the terms are more general in nature, such as *bastard, bond, dowry, murder, treason, usury, villein,* etc. It seems that the author, in his first version of the play, were intent on using legal terms to which he had just been exposed and, in his revision, perhaps thirty years later, no longer felt the need to display his specialized vocabulary.

As recounted in Chapter III, Shakespeare made frequent use of words about language—such as *speak, speech, language, name, voice, tongue, mouth, throat, ear, breath, pen, paper, ink,* and *parchment*—and they are abundant throughout the canon. In the early plays, these words are used at the rate of once in every twenty-four lines, and for the entire canon, once in twenty-six (Donawerth 141, 161). The frequency of these words in *King Leir* is higher still—110, once in every twenty-four lines.

Also noted in Chapter III, is a feature of Shakespeare's vocabulary that distinguishes him from all other Elizabethan playwrights—his repeated use of words with particular prefixes, most of them prefixes of inversion, especially *un.* In the accepted canon, he uses more than 600 words beginning with the *un* prefix, half of them only once (Brook 132). According to Alfred Hart, words beginning with *un* make up nearly 4 percent of his total vocabulary, and "about a quarter are 'new' to literature" (*Homilies* 253). In both the Quarto and Folio versions of *King Lear*, he uses the *un* prefix about sixty times. In *King Leir*, he uses more than thirty words beginning with *un* more than fifty times—figures consistent with Shakespeare's habit throughout his career (Thomson 85, n. 25; Hart. *Homilies* 253). Another distinctive characteristic of Shakespeare's verse is his frequent use of compound words, a practice shunned by other Elizabethan playwrights (*Homilies* 254). In *King Leir*, the playwright uses nearly fifty compound words, a dozen of which, according to the *OED*, were new to the language.

Both plays contain multiple allusions to the Bible and the Book of Common Prayer, but only a few from the anonymous *Leir* reappear in *King Lear*. In one case, the reference is to the same Biblical passage at the same psychological moment in the plot, suggesting that the same author is at work. The Kings in both plays allude to the same verses in the Sermon on the Mount—Matthew 5:33–7—in the last verse of which Jesus admonishes his disciples not to swear oaths, "But let your communication be, Yea: yea: Nay, nay. For whatsoever is more than these cometh of evil."[18]

In the anonymous play, Leir demands to know from the Messenger if it is true that he has been sent by Gonorill and Ragan to murder him. When the Messenger swears that it is true, Leir reacts angrily and warns him that swearing an oath will not save him from hell if he murders him (IV.vii.185–192). In *King Lear*, Shakespeare echoes the same verses from Matthew at a similar dramatic moment—IV.vi—when a mad Lear recalls the lies and flattery of Goneril and Regan, and exclaims:

> *Lear.*                                              To
>
> say "ay" and "no" to every thing that I said! "Ay,"
>
> and "no" too, was no good divinity.        *King Lear* IV.vi.98–100

That is, their seeming adherence to Jesus's admonition was not sufficient to save them from hell. A third use, in *Richard III*, of the same verses from Matthew is described below.

The following are three additional examples of the more than a dozen passages in the Folio *Lear* that strongly echo passages in the anonymous *Leir*.

In their first conversation after she has cut his allowance in half, Gonorill angrily taunts Leir and accuses him of fomenting strife between her and her husband Cornwall, who urges the King not to take offence. Leir replies weakly that she must be suffering the effects of her pregnancy:

> *Leir.*        Alas, not I: poor soul, she breeds young bones,
>
>                And that is it makes her so touchy, sure.    *King Leir* III.iii.27–8

In the Folio *Lear*, after Lear and Goneril have had an angry quarrel, he seeks refuge in Regan's household. There he excoriates Goneril at great length and calls on heaven to take vengeance on her unborn child:

*Lear.*          All the stor'd vengeances of heaven fall

On her ungrateful top! Strike her young bones,

You taking [infectious] airs, with lameness.

*King Lear* II.iv.162–4

In Act III of the anonymous *King Leir*, after Leir has banished Cordella and given his kingdom to Gonorill and Ragan, his friend Perillus appears alone on stage and decries Leir's actions. He anticipates that Leir will be mistreated by his older daughters, but will not complain:

*Perillus.*          But he, the mirror of mild patience,

Puts up all wrongs, and never gives reply:          *King Leir* III.i.12–13

This characterization of the King is echoed in the Folio text. With the Fool on the heath, Lear addresses the raging storm, urging it to do its worst, and at the same time complains that it acts in concert with his "pernicious daughters." Then, unaccountably, he resigns himself to silence, as he does in the source play:

*Lear.*          No, I will be the pattern of all patience;

I will say nothing.          *King Lear* III.ii.37–8

Words and actions in the last act of the anonymous *Leir* are repeated in two places in the Folio text. In the *dénouement* scene, with all the characters in the main plot on stage, Perillus rebukes Gonorill after she has threatened Cordella:

*Perillus.*          Nay, peace thou monster, shame unto thy sex:

Thou fiend in likeness of a human creature.          *King Leir* V.x.72–3

A moment later, Leir assails Ragan with similar language, brandishing the incriminating letters she has written:

*Leir.*          Out on thee, viper, scum, filthy parricide,

More odious to my sight than is a toad.

Knowest thou these letters?          [*She snatches them & tears them.*]

*King Leir* V.x.75–7

In the Folio text, after Albany and Goneril have turned against each other, he denounces her in similar language:

*Alb.*                                    See thyself, devil!

              Proper deformity [shows] not in the fiend

              So horrid as in woman.                    *King Lear* IV.ii.59–61

And in the last scene, he again rebukes her, and confronts her about her letters, forbidding her to tear them up, as Ragan did in *King Leir*:

*Alb.*                                    Shut your mouth, dame,

              Or with this paper shall I [stopple] it. Hold, sir—

              Thou worse than any name, read thine own evil.

              No tearing, lady, I perceive you know it.

*Gon.*        Say if I do, the laws are mine, not thine;

              Who can arraign me for't?

*Alb.*                                    Most monstrous! O!

              Know'st thou this paper?

*Gon.*        Ask me not what I know.          *Exit*          *King Lear* V.iii.155–61

As Kenneth Muir remarks,

> "Shame," "fiend," and "know'st thou" are common in both passages; "monster," "sex," and "these letters" are echoed in "monstrous," "woman," and "this paper," and the stage direction in the old play was remembered in Shakespeare's "no tearing."
>
> [ed. *King Lear* xxviii–xxix].

An example of Shakespeare's re-use of imagery from *King Leir* occurs in the first scene of his revision, where Lear wishes that Cordelia be no more "neighbour'd, pitied and relievéd" than the "barbarous Scythian" (I.i.116–119) who eats members of his own family. This allusion to cannibalism might well have been suggested by the passage in the anonymous *King Leir* where Leir and Perillus are faint from hunger, and Perillus offers his arm to Leir:

*Perillus.*     O, feed on this if this will do you good,

              I'll smile for joy, to see you suck my blood.    *King Leir* V.iv.36–7

Michael Schmidt points out, "In *King Lear*, the image is only once stated; but various allusions throughout the play refer back to the initial image. The imagery of tasting, digesting, dismembering and self-sacrifice (cf. the Pelican image) substantiate the original extended metaphor" (148). These examples, and many others, illustrate Shakespeare's familiarity with the older play, and the extent to which its words, phrases and images lingered in his mind as he rewrote it scene by scene.[19]

Another similarity between the two plays is their unusual length. At 2665 lines, *King Leir* is very close to Shakespeare's average, and hundreds of lines longer than the average play by Peele, Greene, Kyd or Marlowe (Hart, "Length" 149).

Two other small facts support the idea that Shakespeare was revising his own play. In the 1608 Quarto version of the extended dialogue in I.iv between Lear and the Fool, the latter refers to "That lord that counsell'd thee / To give away thy land" (140–1). But no one counseled Lear to do this in either version of the canonical *Lear*. While composing *King Lear*, the author failed to recall that he had deleted this crucial advice, which was given only by Skalliger, and only in *King Leir*. Moreover, as Eric Sams wrote, the 1608 Quarto "contains the *Leir* spelling Gonorill *passim* (not Goneril, as in the Folio text) and even the name 'Leir,' which twice (B4r, D2r) stayed in his mind and slipped from his pen" (*Real Shakespeare II* 274). In fact, Shakespeare called his king "Leir" four times in the 1608 Quarto of *King Lear*.

## Dramatic Devices

It has been noticed by more than one scholar that certain dramatic devices are used, and certain situations occur, in the anonymous *Leir* that are repeated in some variation or other in the canonical *Lear*. Aside from the obvious parallel of the love test, which is present in Geoffrey's *Historia*, these include the use of letters and disguises, the hiring or bribing of a murderer, the use of the weather as a factor in the action, and occasions when a character kneels before another. (Recurrences of these devices elsewhere in the canon are detailed in the next Section.)

Letters sent and letters intercepted are prominent in *King Leir*, at least eight being sent to or from the King. Several are intercepted and others substituted for them, and in the final confrontation Ragan snatches incriminating letters from Leir and tears them up. Similarly, in the canonical *King Lear*, at least eight letters written by half-a-dozen characters drive the action and mark crucial turning points in the plot. Edmund uses two forged letters to deceive his father and then incite Cornwall to blind him. The main characters repeatedly communicate with each other by letters, notes and "challenges," some of which are delivered, but others are intercepted, redirected, recalled, denied, concealed, misdelivered, undelivered or stolen.[20]

Deliberate disguises and failures of recognition are also significant features of both plays. After the departure of the King's loyal companion Perillus/Kent in both plays, Leir/Lear fails to recognize him when he reappears. In the anonymous *Leir*, the King and Perillus exchange clothes with mariners before they meet the disguised Cordella and her new husband, and in neither play do any of them recognize the others. In *King Lear*, both Edgar and the Earl of Kent successfully disguise themselves, Edgar as a mad beggar, Kent as a servant. The disguises and failures of recognition were introduced by the playwright of the anonymous *King Leir*. There are none in Geoffrey's *Historia*. It hardly need be noted that disguises, masks, deception and misrecognitions of all kinds are staples throughout the canon.

In the anonymous *Leir*, the King's second daughter Ragan hires a messenger to kill him and Perillus, a task from which he is eventually dissuaded in the so-called "begging scene" (IV.vii). In the canonical play, the same daughter bribes Oswald to murder Gloucester, at which he also fails; he is finally killed by Edgar, who is in disguise. In Act V, Edmund bribes the Captain to murder Lear and Cordelia, but he is also killed by Edgar, who with his last breath attempts to reverse the order, without success.

The Messenger whom Ragan has sent to murder Leir and Perillus is so frightened by sudden thunder and lightning and the "pains of hell" as he is about to do the deed that he reveals his mission and spares them. Similarly, a "storm and tempest" appears suddenly at the end of Act II in *King Lear*, and lingers into the next Act as the King shouts his defiance and rails over the injustices done him.

In V.iv of *King Leir*, the "recognition" or "kneeling" scene, Leir and his companion Perillus, both weary and faint from hunger, and wearing rough seamen's gowns that conceal their identity, come upon Cordella, her new husband, the King of Gaul, and his companion Mumford in the countryside. They are also not recognizable, being disguised as "country folk." Cordella and her husband take pity on the two strangers and offer them food and drink. Before long, Cordella recognizes her father's voice as he relates all that has happened to him. When he confesses that he has mistreated his youngest daughter and is now looking for her, she reveals herself to him with these words:

| | | |
|---|---|---|
| *Cordella.* | But look, dear father, look behold and see | |
| | Thy loving daughter speaketh unto thee. | [*She kneels.*] |
| *Leir.* | O, stand thou up, it is my part to kneel, | |
| | And ask forgiveness for my former faults. | [*He kneels.*] |

| | | |
|---|---|---|
| *Cordella.* | O, if you wish, I should enjoy my breath, | |
| | Dear father rise, or I receive my death. | [*He riseth.*] |
| *Leir.* | Then I will rise to satisfy your mind, | |
| | But kneel again, til pardon be resigned. | [*He kneels.*] |

*King Leir* V.iv.203–10

After several more words of reconciliation and forgiveness, he rises again, and Cordella kneels as she asks his forgiveness. Leir forgives and blesses her, and she rises and welcomes him and Perillus "to our court." At this point, the King of Gaul also kneels and vows to restore Leir's kingdom to him. As the King rises, Mumford himself kneels and rises, as if mocking the other kneelers, remarking that if he goes to Britain and returns without his wench, "Let me be gelded for my recompense " (V.iv.259).

Editors and critics have decried this episode as overdone and ludicrous, and so it is, ending with Mumford's customary off-color wisecrack. But Shakespeare chose to use the image, in a more restrained way, several times throughout his revision. The first occasion is when Lear kneels before Regan and begs for "raiment, bed, and food" (II.iv.154–6); the second when Gloucester kneels as he delivers his farewell to the world in the field near Dover (IV.vi.34–6). Again, in the recognition scene in *King Lear*, Shakespeare seemingly recalls the same scene in the anonymous *King Leir* when Cordelia says:

| | |
|---|---|
| *Cor.* | O, look upon me, sir, |
| | And hold your hands in benediction o'er me: |
| | [No, sir,] you must not kneel. |

*King Lear* IV.vii.57–9

Finally, when Lear and Cordelia are being led away to prison in the last scene, Lear exclaims:

| | |
|---|---|
| *Lear.* | No, no, no, no! Come, let's away to prison: |
| | We two alone will sing like birds i' the cage: |
| | When thou dost ask me blessing, I'll kneel down, |
| | And ask of thee forgiveness |

*King Lear* V.iii.8–11

As Sidney Lee remarked, "Lear's twice-repeated offer at the close to kneel for pardon at the feet of his injured daughter Cordelia is an inspiration of Shakespeare's predecessor" (ed. *Leir* xlii). Writing about the same time as Lee, Leo Tolstoy also decried "Shakespeare's long-drawn scene of Lear's interview with Cordelia and of Cordelia's unnecessary murder." But, virtually alone among critics, he praised the happy ending of *King Leir* and called the reconciliation scene "exquisite" and "unequaled by any in all Shakespeare's dramas" (44).

It seems clear that in rewriting the Lear story the dramatist was led to use several of the same dramatic devices—letters, disguises, kneeling characters, etc.—that he had used in his first version of the play. These same devices appear throughout the canon. Specific examples, especially of the kneeling episode, are described in the next Section.

## King Leir *and the Shakespeare Canon*

*King Leir* is probably the source of more words, phrases, images and ideas used in the canon than any other apprenticeship play. To quote one scholar of the play, "...enough evidence has been brought out, I believe, to convict Shakespeare of repeated borrowing from the anonymous play, especially in his earlier years (Law, "*King John*" 474). Another remarks, "Without [*King Leir*] we would not have *King Lear* or *As You Like It*, while *Richard III*, *The Merchant of Venice*, and *Hamlet* would be quite different plays" (Mueller 195).

Scholars have identified repetitions and echoes of phrases and thought, as well as dramatic devices, from *King Leir* in more than a dozen canonical plays, and in *Sir Thomas More* and *Venus and Adonis*. The echoes of language and thought are especially striking in *Much Ado About Nothing*, *Richard II*, *Richard III* and *Edward III*.

### MUCH ADO ABOUT NOTHING

Jacqueline Pearson has pointed out several instances of language and circumstance in *King Leir* that are echoed in *Much Ado About Nothing*.[21] In *King Leir*, for instance, the Messenger asserts his willingness to do Ragan's bidding, no matter the consequences:

*Messenger.*   Were it to meet the devil in his den,

          And try a bout with him for a scratchéd face,

          I'd undertake it, if you would but bid me.   *King Leir* IV.v.19–21

In *Much Ado*, Benedick facetiously hopes that Beatrice will stay in a peaceful mood:

*Bene.*       so that some gentleman or other shall scape a predes-

          tinate scratch'd face.       *Much Ado About Nothing* I.1.134–5

In the opening scene of *King Leir*, Ragan is concerned that Cordella will marry before her and Gonorill:

*Ragan.*      And we must be set by for working days.        *King Leir* I.ii.18

Ragan is suggesting that their marriages may be treated as ordinary and trivial.

In *Much Ado*, Beatrice refuses Don Pedro's humorous marriage proposal:

*Beat.*       No, my lord, unless I might have another

              for working-days.        *Much Ado About Nothing* II.i.327–8

Beatrice uses the same phrase to suggest that such a marriage would be socially inappropriate, and that she would need another for "every day."

The conversations between the watchmen in the two plays supply even more striking parallels, and illustrate how the playwright built upon two comical exchanges in *King Leir* to create Dogberry, the cowardly constable, and his assistant Verges, both masters of malapropism, in *Much Ado About Nothing*.

In two scenes near the end of *Leir*, two watchmen are instructed to watch "vigilantly" and to "fire the beacon" and "raise the town" if a fleet of enemy ships appears. The two proceed to garble their instructions with repeated malapropisms, and then begin drinking. Later, they are discovered, drunk, by two Captains and soundly berated. The first watchman protests that he is preparing "To fire the town, and call up the beacon" (V.ix.13), but the Gauls have already surprised the town and captured the inhabitants. In a similar episode in *Much Ado*, Dogberry and Verges deliver bungled and confusing instructions to two watchmen, who subsequently confront Borachio and Conrade and arrest them. Both episodes are peppered with comic misunderstandings and repeated malapropisms. In *King Leir*, the Captain instructs the watchmen to perform their tasks "vigilantly" (V.vii.3). In *Much Ado*, Dogberry urges the watchmen to "be vigitant" (III.iii.92). The second watchman in *King Leir* confuses "advice" and "vice" (V.vii.10) in the same way that Dogberry substitutes "comprehend" for "apprehend" (III.iii.25), "confidence" for "conference" (III.v.2), and "suspect" for "respect" (IV.ii.74–5), and so forth. As with the numerous other incidents in *King Leir* that recur in the Shakespeare canon, the editor of the play recognized that the watchmen are "close kin to Shakespeare's Dogberry and his Watch," but apparently cannot conceive of the possibility that the plays are by the same author (Michie 49).

Thomas McNeal has identified another passage in *King Leir* that appears to be the source of a speech by Beatrice in *Much Ado* ("Queens" 47). In her monologue that opens V.v of *King Leir*, Ragan frets about the Messenger she has sent to murder Leir and Perillus. She is afraid that he will be talked out of his mission:

Ragan.      A shame on these white-liver'd slaves, say I,

              That with fair words so soon are overcome.

              *O God, that I had been but made a man;*

              Or that my strength were equal with my will!

              These foolish *men are nothing but mere pity,*

              And *melt* as butter doth *against the sun.*     *King Leir* V.v.13–18

In the fourth Act of *Much Ado*, the high-spirited Beatrice echoes the same thought about men that Ragan expresses, and in similar language:

Beat.           *O that I were a man!* What, beat her in

              hand until they come to take hands, and then

              with public accusation, uncover'd slander, unmitigated

              rancor—*O God, that I were a man!* I would eat his

              heart in the market-place.   *Much Ado About Nothing* IV.i.303–7

Beat.           *O that I were a man for his sake!*

              or that I had any friend that would be a man for my sake!

              But *manhood is melted* in cour'sies, valor into compli-

              ment, and *men* are only turned into tongue, and

              trim ones too.     *Much Ado About Nothing* IV.i.317–21

                                  (McNeal's emphasis)

As McNeal notes, the same passage in *Leir* is echoed in Queen Margaret's remarks about her husband in *2 Henry VI*:

Queen.      Free lords, cold snow *melts with the sun's hot beams*:

              Henry my lord is cold in great affairs,

              Too full of *foolish pity;*      *2 Henry VI* III.i.223–25

Lastly, the sentiments of both Ragan and Beatrice are echoed in the memorable lines in *Macbeth*:

Lady M.                 Come, you spirits

              That tend on mortal thoughts, unsex me here,

              And fill me from the crown to the toe topful

              Of direst cruelty! Make thick my blood,

              Stop up th'access and passage to remorse,    *Macbeth* I.v.40–4

## RICHARD II

In her examination of the "mental climate in which Shakespeare's plays were written," Meredith Skura cites both the "begging scene" in *King Leir* (IV.vii) and the "recognition scene" (V.iv), described in the previous Section, as contributing to events in several canonical plays. In the "begging scene," King Leir and Perillus plead at length for mercy with the Messenger sent by Goneril to murder them. In *Richard II,* the entirety of V.iii, near the end of the play, consists of an extended episode in which "Aumerle," now the Earl of Rutland, and his mother, the Duchess of York, kneel before King Henry and beg his pardon for Aumerle's involvement in a conspiracy to kill him. At the same time, Aumerle's father, the Duke, kneels before the King, urging that his son be put to death for his treason. Skura also points out the influence of the begging scene on similar scenes in *King John, Cymbeline* and *Coriolanus* (285–6, n. 96).

There are further examples of words, phrases and images in *King Leir* that are repeated or paraphrased in *Richard II* (Pearson, "Influence"). Both King Leir and Richard use the same phrase in connection with their abdications:

| | | |
|---|---|---|
| *Leir.* | If they, for whom I have undone myself, | *King Leir* III.iii.85 |
| *K. Rich.* | Now mark me how I will undo myself: | *Richard II* IV.i.203 |

The King of Gaul in *King Leir* and Northumberland in *Richard II* both express pleasure with those in their presence, using identical phrases:

*King.* Thy pleasant company will make the way seem short

*King Leir* II.i.48

*North.* By this the weary lords

Shall make their way seem short, as mine hath done

By sight of what I have, your noble company.

*Richard II* II.iii.16–18

The King of Gaul counsels his new wife Cordella to put her painful banishment behind her:

*King.* Forget thy father and thy kindred now,

Since they forsake thee like inhuman beasts,

Think they are dead, since all their kindness dies,

And bury them, where black oblivion lies. *King Leir* IV.iv.19–22

In their last meeting before he enters the Tower, Queen Isabel urges Richard II not to "take correction lightly," and to react like the lion he is—"the king of beasts." In his reply, Richard also refers to beasts and counsels his wife with similar phrases:

K. Rich.     A king of beasts indeed—if aught but beasts,
             I had been still a happy king of men.
             Good sometimes queen, prepare thee hence for France.
             Think I am dead, and that even here thou takest,
             As from my death-bed, thy last living leave.   *Richard II* V.i.35–9

As King Leir prepares to divide his kingdom between his two older daughters and their new husbands, he compares himself to the pelican, which was thought to feed its young with its own blood:

Leir.     I am as kind as is the pelican,
          That kills itself, to save her young ones' lives:
                                                   *King Leir* II.iii.43–4

In *Richard II*, Shakespeare uses the same metaphor to illustrate an instance of filial ingratitude when John of Gaunt accuses Richard of feeding on the blood of his own family:

Gaunt.     That blood already, like the pelican,
           Hast thou tapp'd out and drunkenly carous'd.
                                                   *Richard II* II.i.126–7

In *Hamlet*, Laertes describes how he will distinguish between his dead father's enemies and his friends, as he seeks revenge for his murder by Hamlet:

Laer.     To his good friends thus wide I'll ope my arms,
          And like the kind life-rend'ring pelican,
          Repast them with my blood.          *Hamlet* IV.v.146–8

In the only other use of the pelican metaphor in the canon, Shakespeare, in *King Lear*, modifies it, so that Lear's reference is to the notion that pelican young were thought to attack their parents (Robin 68):

Lear.     Is it the fashion, that discarded fathers
          Should have thus little mercy on their flesh?
          Judicious punishment! 'twas this flesh begot
          Those pelican daughters          *King Lear* III.iv.72–75

In II.iv of *King Leir*, Cordella declares her love for the Palmer, not knowing that he is the King of Gaul in disguise:

Cordella.     I'll hold thy palmer's staff within my hand,

And think it is the sceptre of a queen,     *King Leir* II.iv.115–16

Richard II uses the same image in his list of the details of his offer of resignation:

K. Rich.     I'll give my jewels for a set of beads,

...

My sceptre for a palmer's walking-staff,     *Richard II* III.iii.147, 151

∞

In *King Leir*, when Mumford and the King of Gaul arrive in Britain, Mumford asks the King:

Mumford.     My Lord, how do you brook this British air?     *King Leir* II.iv.1

In *Richard II*, as Richard arrives in England from Ireland, his companion Aumerle asks him the same question, using the same phrase:

Aum.     How brooks your Grace the air?     *Richard II* III.ii.2

∞

The distinction between what is in the speaker's heart and what is expressed by the mouth is an idea that appears in the Shakespeare canon more than thirty times. The line is sometimes glossed as an allusion to Ecclesiastics 21.26—"The heart of fools is in the mouth; but the mouth of the wise men is in their heart." Perhaps the most notable instance occurs in I.i of *King Lear*, when Cordelia replies to her father:

Cor.     Unhappy that I am, I cannot heave

My heart into my mouth.     *King Lear* I.i.91–2

Among the half-a-dozen times that this idea is used in *King Leir* is one in which the disconnect between the heart and the tongue is specifically mentioned, as in this remark by Perillus:

Perillus.     My tongue doth fail, to say what heart doth think

*King Leir* V.iv.245

The same idea, using both *tongue* and *heart*, appears twice in *Richard II*:

*Ross.*      My heart is great, but it must break with silence,

Ere't be disburdened with a liberal tongue. *Richard II* II.i.228–9

*Groom.*    What my tongue dares not, that my heart shall say.

*Richard II* V.v.97

Similarly, Coriolanus, using the same words, asks if he must say to the people what he does not feel in his heart:

*Cor.*                                                                                          Must I

With my base tongue give to my noble heart

A lie that it must bear?                        *Coriolanus* III.ii.99–101

In *Edward III*, the King addresses Warwick, using the same image:

*K. Edw.*    O that a man might hold the heart's close book

And choke the lavish tongue when it doth utter

The breath of falsehood not charact'red there!

*Edward III* II.i.305–7

Clearly, the playwright was fond of this metaphor, and used it repeatedly.

## RICHARD III

The powerful scene in *Richard III*, in which two murderers conduct a lengthy conversation with Clarence in his prison cell and then murder him (I.iv), has no source in any chronicle account. According to one critic, "Shakespeare seems to have been indebted to his own imagination only for the scene of Clarence in prison, his beautiful narrative of his dream, and the less happy dialogue of the murderers" (Skottowe 1:194). But its remarkable similarity to the scene in *King Leir*, in which the Messenger confronts Leir and Perillus (IV.vii), has been detailed by Robert A. Law ("Richard"). The killings have been solicited previously in both plays, by Ragan in *King Leir*, by Richard, Duke of Gloucester, in *Richard III*. Among the following dozen features in *both* episodes, there are some forty-two separate points of resemblance[22]:

1. Men are hired to kill a man of noble birth by someone he does not suspect.
2. A document of some kind, a letter in *King Leir*, a warrant in *Richard III*, figures in the planning.
3. A reward is offered to the murderers.

4. The murderers are cautioned not to be talked out of their task by the victims.

5. The victims fall asleep and wake up frightened after dreaming that they have been murdered by those who have hired the murderers.

6. The murderers enter while the victims are asleep, and decide to speak with them before killing them.

7. The victims ask the murderers how they have offended them.

8. The victims ask the murderers who has sent them; when they are told, they are astonished. They believed that it was a sibling of the person named.

9. The victims ask for mercy, and predict divine punishment for the murderers.

10. After further pleas by the victims, the murderers reply that they are getting what they deserve.

11. The victims warn the murderers that they themselves may become victims of those who hired them.

12. The murderer in *King Leir* is frightened by thunder and lightning, and spares the victims. In *Richard III*, one murderer is frightened by the idea of judgment and damnation, and has second thoughts. But the other reassures him, and they complete the crime.

Although the outcome is different in each scene, the interactions among the characters have an eerie similarity, and many of the words and phrases are identical, or nearly so—the instructions to the murderers, for instance:

*Ragan.*      And then proceed to execution:

              But see thou faint not; for they will speak fair.

                                                    *King Leir* IV.v.51–2

*Glou.*       But, sirs, be sudden in the execution,

              Withal obdurate, do not hear him plead;

              For Clarence is well-spoken, and perhaps

              May move your hearts to pity if you mark him.

                                                    *Richard III* I.iii.345–8

Just before they fall asleep, all three of the intended victims express their weariness and need for sleep. The idea of one keeping another company enters the conversation:

| Leir. | 'Tis news indeed, I am so extreme heavy, |
| | That I can scarcely keep my eyelids open. |

… 

| Perillus. | I'll sit and pray with you for company; |
| | Yet was I ne're so heavy in my life.    *King Leir* IV.vii.3–4, 18–19 |
| Clar. | Keeper, I prithee sit by me a while. |
| | My soul is heavy, and I fain would sleep.    *Richard III* I.iv.73–4 |

The same thought occurs to the murderers as they stand over their sleeping targets:

| Messenger. | Now could I stab them bravely, while they sleep, |
| | *King Leir* IV.vii.31 |
| 2. Mur. | What, shall [I] stab him as he sleeps?    *Richard III* I.iv.100 |

The same fate is predicted in the same words for each of the villains:

| Perillus. | [to Ragan]      to send us both to heaven, |
| | Where, as I think, you never mean to come.    *King Leir* V.x.87–8 |
| Anne. | [to Richard] He is in heaven, where thou shalt never come. |
| | *Richard III* I.ii.106 |

The passage in which King Leir alludes to verses in Matthew as he admonishes the Messenger, described earlier, was echoed in *Richard III* long before the playwright re-used it in *King Lear*. When Leir demands to know if his daughters, Gonorill and Ragan, have hired the Messenger to kill him, the Messenger replies:

| Messenger. | That to be true, in sight of heaven I swear. |
| Leir. | Swear not by heaven, for fear of punishment |
| | The heavens are guiltless of such heinous acts. |
| Messenger. | I swear by earth, the mother of us all. |
| Leir. | Swear not by earth, for she abhors to bear |
| | Such bastards, as are murderers of her sons. |
| Messenger. | Why then, by hell, and all the devils I swear. |
| Leir. | Swear not by hell; for that stands gaping wide, |
| | To swallow thee, and if thou do this deed. |
| | *King Leir* IV.vii.184–92 |

A series of oaths is similarly rejected in *Richard III*, as John Dover Wilson points out (ed. *Richard III* xxxii; 236–7), in the exchange between Richard and the former Queen Elizabeth, in which he tries to persuade her of the sincerity of his proposal to her daughter Princess Elizabeth:

| | |
|---|---|
| *K. Rich.* | I swear— |
| *Q. Eliz.* | By nothing, for this is no oath: |

    …

| | |
|---|---|
| *K. Rich.* | Then, by my self— |
| *Q. Eliz.* | Thy self is self-misused. |
| *K. Rich.* | Now, by the world— |
| *Q. Eliz.* | 'Tis full of thou foul wrongs. |
| *K. Rich.* | My father's death— |
| *Q. Eliz.* | Thy life had it dishonor'd. |
| *K. Rich.* | When then, by [God]— |
| *Q. Eliz.* | [God's] wrong is most of all: |

*Richard III* IV.iv.368, 374–7

Several other such parallels of language and dramatic actions are scattered throughout each play. In the words of Robert A. Law, there exists "a remarkable analogy between the respective scenes—an analogy which can scarcely be explained as fortuitous, or as due to literary or dramatic conventions" ("Richard" 131). He further asserts that "the weight of the evidence points to Shakespeare as the borrower," but he cannot, as nearly all other scholars cannot, even entertain the idea that the plays were by the same man. Eric Sams, however, was confident that Shakespeare was rewriting his own play, not pilfering another's. Citing dozens of identical or nearly identical words and ideas, he concludes, "…that manuscript [*Leir*] anticipates *Lear* and *Richard III* in so many and such detailed respects that either Shakespeare plundered it wholesale for his own prestige and profit or else he wrote it" (*Real Shakespeare II* 274).

## EDWARD III

In *The Real Shakespeare II* (268–301), Sams makes a strong case for Shakespeare's authorship of *King Leir*, one aspect of which is the similarity of its language and imagery to that of *Edward III*, a play that Sams himself demonstrated belongs in the Shakespeare canon.[23] He cites more than a dozen words and phrases in *King Leir* that are echoed in *Edward III*, a play published in 1596, but probably written in the first half of the 1570s, a few years after *Leir*. In one example, Ragan uses a proverbial phrase to indicate that she will make a show of friendliness:

Ragan.          Yet will I make fair weather, to procure

                    Convenient means, and then I'll strike it sure.

                                                                    *King Leir* IV.ii.58–9

In Act I of *Edward III*, King David of Scotland, using the same phrase, assures the Duke of Lorraine that he will not halt his attack on the English without the agreement of King John of France:

K. Dav.          Touching your embassage, return and say

                    That we with England will not enter parley,

                    Nor never make fair weather, or take truce;

                                      … till your king

                    cry out "Enough! spare England now for pity."

                                                                    *Edward III* I.ii.21–34

Shakespeare uses this phrase a third time in an aside by Richard, Duke of York in Act V of *2 Henry VI*:

York.          But I must make fair weather yet awhile,

                    Till Henry be more weak and I more strong.

                                                                    *2 Henry VI* V.i.30–1

In IV.iii of *King Leir*, the Messenger brings a letter to Ragan from her sister Gonorill and describes her face as she reads it:

Messenger.     See how her color comes and goes again,

                    Now red as scarlet, now as pale as ash:     *King Leir* IV.iii.14–15

In Act II of *Edward III*, Lodowick, Edward's confidant, remarks how the King blushes at the Countess's reaction to him—using the same words as the Messenger:

Lod.          Anon, with reverent fear when she grew pale,

                    His cheeks put on their scarlet ornaments;

                    But no more like her oriental red,

                    Than brick to coral or live things to dead.     *Edward III* II.i.9–12

In V.xi of *King Leir*, the Gallian King and his army have defeated the forces of Cornwall and Cambria, and both armies exit the field. In the next scene, Gonorill's husband, the King of Cornwall, enters alone:

| | |
|---|---|
| *Cornwall.* | The day is lost, our friends do all revolt, |
| | And join against us with the adverse part:        *King Leir* V.xi.1–2 |

In Act IV of *Edward III*, the two French princes report that their troops have scattered, and urge their father, King John, to flee the field. But he exhorts them to renew the fight with the remaining men. He and Prince Charles use the same language as Cornwall:

| | |
|---|---|
| *K. John.* | Make up [fill up the gap] once more with me; the twentieth part |
| | Of those that live, are men enow [enough] to quail [defeat] |
| | The feeble handful on the adverse part. |
| *P. Cha.* | Then charge again: if heaven be not opposed, |
| | We cannot lose the day.                    *Edward III* IV.vii.31–4 |

## HAMLET

In 1940, W. W. Greg noticed a passage in *King Leir* that "seemed to be echoed in Hamlet."[24] In IV.vii, as the Messenger stands over the sleeping Leir and Perillus with two daggers in his hands, he says:

| | |
|---|---|
| *Messenger.* | Now could I stab them bravely, while they sleep, |
| | And in a manner put them to no pain; |
| | And doing so, I showed them mighty friendship: |
| | For fear of death is worse than death itself. *King Leir* IV.vii.31–4 |

In Act III of *Hamlet*, as Claudius kneels to pray, Hamlet says:

| | |
|---|---|
| *Ham.* | Now might I do it pat, now 'a is a-praying; |
| | And now I'll do't—and so 'a goes to heaven; |
| | And so am I reveng'd. That would be scann'd: |
| | ... |
| | O, this is hire and salary, not revenge    *Hamlet* III.iii.73–5, 79 |

## KING JOHN

In *King Leir*, Gonorill and Ragan each solicit the Messenger, in a round-about and guilty way, to kill their father. In both cases, the Messenger responds with pledges of obedience, and readily agrees to the task. Both daughters speak to him about money and "riches," and Gonorill gives him a purse, Ragan two purses (III.v.57–111; IV.v.7–59). In *King John*, these interactions are echoed as John solicits Hubert in the same roundabout way to kill his nephew Arthur and hints at a reward:

| | |
|---|---|
| *Hub.* | I am much bounden to your Majesty. |
| *K. John.* | Good friend, thou hast no cause to say so yet, |
| | But thou shalt have; and creep time ne'er so slow, |
| | Yet it shall come for me to do thee good. *King John* III.iii.30–32 |

## THE MERCHANT OF VENICE

In the opening passage in II.i of *King Leir*, the King of Gaul announces his plan to search for the three daughters of King Leir, and to see if they are as beautiful as they are said to be:

| | |
|---|---|
| *King.* | Dissuade me not, my Lords, I am resolved |
| | This next *fair wind* to sail for Brittany, |
| | In some disguise, to see if flying fame |
| | Be not too prodigal in the *wondrous* praise |
| | Of these three nymphs, the *daughters* of King Leir. |
| | If present view do answer present praise, |
| | And *eyes* allow of what our ears have heard, |
| | And Venus stand auspicious to my vows, |
| | And fortune favor what I take in hand; |
| | I will return seized of as rich a prize |
| | As *Jason*, when he won the *golden fleece.*   *King Leir* II.i.1–11 |

In the opening scene of *The Merchant of Venice*, Bassanio expresses a similar thought, using many of the same words, about the beauty of Portia. Both speakers allude to the same legend of Jason and the golden fleece from Book VII of Ovid's *Metamorphoses*:

| | |
|---|---|
| *Bass.* | In Belmont is a lady richly left: |
| | And she is *fair,* and *fairer,* than that word, |
| | Of *wondrous* virtues. Sometimes from her *eyes* |
| | I did receive *fair* speechless messages. |

Her name is Portia, nothing undervalu'd

To Cato's *daughter*, Brutus' Portia.

Nor is the wide world ignorant of her worth,

For the four *winds* blow in from every coast

Renownéd suitors: her sunny locks

Hang on her temples like a *golden fleece*,

Which makes her seat at Belmont Colchis' strond,

And any *Jasons* come in quest of her.

> *The Merchant of Venice* I.I.169–72 (my emphasis)

Among several other similarities in the two plays are further references to the same legend. In *King Leir*, Cordella finds her father thirsty and weak from hunger and urges him to drink:

*Cordella.*     And may that draught be unto him, as was

That which old Aeson drank, which did renew

His withered age, and made him young again.

> *King Leir* V.iv.95–7

In *The Merchant of Venice*, Jessica alludes to the same incident in the same story:

*Jes.*                              In such a night

Medea gathered the enchanted herbs

That did renew old Aeson.     *The Merchant of Venice* V.1.13–15

## AS YOU LIKE IT

The passage mentioned above, in which Perillus offers his arm as food for *King Leir*, appears to have been the source for a similar scene in *As You Like It*. In V.iv of *King Leir*, after being spared by their would-be assassin, Leir and Perillus have fled Britain and, exhausted and famished, find themselves lost "near the coast of Gallia." The starving pair comes upon a group of people about to enjoy a meal. It is Cordella, her husband, the King of Gaul, and his servant Mumford, all disguised as "country folk." Cordella offers food to Leir and Perillus, and Perillus urges Leir to sit and eat:

| | |
|---|---|
| *Perillus.* | Oh comfort, comfort! Yonder is a banquet, |
| | And men and women, my Lord; be of good cheer: |
| | For I see comfort coming very near. |
| | O my Lord, a banquet, and men and women! |

*King Leir* V.iv.75–9

In *As You Like It*, Orlando and the old servant Adam have fled Oliver's house into the Forest of Arden. Fatigued and hungry, Adam says that he cannot continue, but Orlando urges him to take heart:

| | |
|---|---|
| *Orl.* | Why how now Adam? No greater heart in |
| | thee? Live a little, comfort a little, cheer thy- |
| | self a little. If this uncouth forest yield any thing |
| | savage, I will either be food for it, or bring it for |
| | food to thee. |

*As You Like It* II.vi.5–8

In the next scene, Orlando comes upon Duke Senior and his lords, who are about to begin a feast. The Duke invites him to "sit down and feed, and welcome to our table" (II.vii.111). Orlando thanks him profusely and then adds that he will not eat until he brings his companion, "an old poor man" who is suffering from "two weak evils, age and hunger." When the Duke urges him to bring him, Orlando leaves and, when he returns with Adam on his back, invites him to "set down your venerable burden and let him feed" (II.vii.176–7). The scenes in the two plays are nearly identical in terms of situation, incident and language.

## JULIUS CAESAR AND MEASURE FOR MEASURE

An idea found in two places in *King Leir* reappears in two later plays in the canon.

In IV.vii of *King Leir*, as the Messenger/Murderer stands over the sleeping Leir and Perillus, he says "For fear of death is worse than death itself" (IV.vii.34). In a later scene in *King Leir*, mentioned above (V.iii), Perillus and the King have fled to Gaul to try to find Cordella. They have no money and no food, and. Leir is despondent and fearful that Cordella will not forgive him for his treatment of her. Perillus tries to comfort him:

| | |
|---|---|
| *Perillus.* | Why, say the worst. The worst can be but death, |
| | And death is better than for to despair: |
| | Then hazard death, which may convert to life; |
| | Banish despair, which brings a thousand deaths. |

*King Leir* V.iii.85–8

Donald Michie (229) has pointed out the similarity of the first passage to the lines in II.ii of *Julius Caesar*, where Calpurnia cautions Caesar against leaving the house, for fear he will be killed. Caesar replies:

Caes.          Cowards die many times before their deaths,

               The valiant never taste of death but once.

                                        *Julius Caesar* II.ii.32–3

In Act III of *Measure for Measure*, Isabel says to the condemned Claudio "The sense of death is most in apprehension" (III.i.77).

## TITUS ANDRONICUS

In his commentary on *King Leir*, Sidney Lee cites a line spoken by the King of Gaul:

King.          To utter grief, doth ease a heart o'ercharged.     *King Leir* II.iv.57

that is echoed by Marcus in *Titus Andronicus*:

Marc.          Sorrow concealed, like an oven stopp'd,

               Doth burn the heart to cinders where it is.

                                        *Titus Andronicus* II.iv.36–7

and again in *Venus and Adonis*:

               An oven that is stopp'd, or river stay'd,

               Burneth more hotly, swelleth with more rage;

               So of concealed sorrow may be said;

               Free vent of words love's fire doth assuage.

                                        *Venus and Adonis* 331–4

In another example from *Titus Andronicus*, noted by Meredith Skura, the kneeling scene in *King Leir* "…must have contributed to the kneelings that dominate *Titus Andronicus*, as victim after victim is surprised by his captor's cruel indifference" (285).

## CYMBELINE

Robert A. Law has found a "series of corresponding situations" in *King Leir* and *Cymbeline*, both romances set in early British history, that suggest a use by Shakespeare of a scene and language from the former as he composed the latter ("Unnoticed Analog" 133–5). In IV.vii of *Leir*, the King and Perillus are lured to "Cambria" under the pretext of meeting Cordella. A Messenger/ Murderer arrives and shows Leir a letter from Gonorill ordering him killed. Leir accedes to his own murder, declaring it "the will of God," but ultimately the Messenger refuses to kill him. Nevertheless, Leir is despondent and decides not to return to court or to stay in Britain. Perillus persuades him to sail to France in order to re-unite with Cordella.

The identical scenario takes place in III.iv of *Cymbeline*, when Imogen is lured to "Cambria" in the same way, by her husband's servant, Pisanio, on the pretext of meeting her husband Posthumus. Pisanio hands her a "paper" in which her husband instructs Pisanio to kill her because of her adultery. Imogen decries her husband's accusation, and protests her innocence, but orders Pisanio to do the deed, or she will do it herself. Pisanio relents and refuses to kill her, but she is despondent and refuses to return to court. Pisanio persuades her to disguise herself as a man, and then flee to Italy where Posthumus lives in exile.

## A MIDSUMMER NIGHT'S DREAM

Among several other repetitions of language and thought from *King Leir* in various Shakespeare plays, Thomas McNeal ("Margaret" 6–7) lists these three in *A Midsummer Night's Dream*:

| | |
|---|---|
| *Cornwall.* | The lady's love I long ago possessed |
| | But until now I never had the father's.   *King Leir* II.ii.39–40 |
| *Lys.* | You have her father's love, Demetrius, |
| | Let me have Hermia's; do you marry him. |

*A Midsummer Night's Dream* I.i.93–4

| | |
|---|---|
| *Cornwall.* | 'Twere pity such rare beauty should be hid |
| | Within the compass of a cloister's wall:   *King Leir* II.ii.59–60 |
| *The.* | Know of your youth, examine well your blood, |
| | Whether (if you yield not to your father's choice) |
| | You can endure the livery of a nun |
| | For aye to be in shady cloister mew'd. |

*A Midsummer Night's Dream* I.i.68–71

| | | |
|---|---|---|
| *Leir.* | Will soonest yield unto their father's hest | *King Leir* I.iii.36 |
| *The.* | To fit your fancies to your father's will | |

*A Midsummer Night's Dream* I.i.118

## 1 AND 2 HENRY VI

In the same article, McNeal cites a significant instance of language and thought in a speech by Cordella in *King Leir* that is "repeated first by Suffolk in *1 Henry VI*, and echoed again by York in *2 Henry VI*":

| | | |
|---|---|---|
| Cordella. | *I'll hold thy Palmer's staff within my hand,* | |
| | And think it is the *scepter of a queen.* | |
| | Sometime *I'll set* thy bonnet *upon my head,* | |
| | And think I wear *a rich imperial crown,* | *King Leir* II.iv.115–18 |
| Suf. | *I'll* undertake to make thee Henry's *queen,* | |
| | To put a golden *sceptre in thy hand,* | |
| | And *set a precious crown upon thy head,* | *1 Henry VI* V.iii.117–19 |
| York. | That *head of thine* doth not become a crown: | |
| | *Thy hand* is made to *grasp a palmer's staff* | |
| | And not to grace *an aweful princely sceptre.* | |

*2 Henry VI* V.i.96–8 (McNeal's emphasis)

He cites ten other linguistic parallels between *King Leir* and *1 Henry VI* that he calls sufficient "to refute a charge that we are here dealing with such common material and general Elizabethan style as to make findings worthless" ("Margaret" 4–5).

In another article, "Shakespeare's Cruel Queens," McNeal suggests that, in their characteristic strong wills, wickedness and contempt for their husbands, Leir's daughters, Gonorill and Ragan (they are queens in the anonymous *Leir*), are the originals of Queen Margaret in the *Henry VI* plays, as well as of Lady Macbeth. Besides the two examples given above, he compares Ragan's threat against her father in *King Leir*:

| | | |
|---|---|---|
| *Ragan.* | Well, it were best for him to take good heed, | |
| | Or I will make him hop without a head, | *King Leir* IV.iii.27–8 |

to Margaret's threat against Duke Humphrey:

| Queen. | Thy sale of offices and towns in France, |
|---|---|
| | If they were known, as the suspect is great, |
| | Would make thee quickly hop without thy head. |

*2 Henry VI* I.iii.135–7

As McNeal notes, this expression occurs in several Elizabethan plays, but only in these two plays is it used by "queens of identical nature" (46–7).

There is one additional striking parallel between *King Leir* and one of the *Henry VI* plays. In his description of himself as "kind as is the pelican," cited earlier, Leir adds:

| Leir. | And yet as jealous [watchful] as the princely eagle, |
|---|---|
| | That kills her young ones, if they do but dazzle |
| | Upon the radiant splendor of the sun.    *King Leir* II.iii.45–7 |

The reference is to the traditional notion that eagles test their young by forcing them to look steadily at the sun, and kill those who cannot do so without their eyes watering (Robin 162). The playwright uses it again in *3 Henry VI*, when Richard Plantagenet addresses his brother Edward:

| Rich. | Nay, if thou be that princely eagle's bird, |
|---|---|
| | Show thy descent by gazing 'gainst the sun;   *3 Henry VI* II.i.91–2. |

Further echoes of lines from *King Leir* in such other plays as *Two Gentlemen of Verona*, *Romeo and Juliet*, *Henry V* and *Othello* can be found in McNeal's "Margaret of Anjou" (6–7).

It should be noted here that not all scholars agree that these words, phrases and ideas in *King Leir* were the source or inspiration for their counterparts in Shakespeare's canonical plays. Richard Knowles, in particular, devotes ten pages to dismissing all of the above parallels, asserting instead that "the evidence for *Leir's* influence on Shakespeare's early plays is small at best and illusory at worst...." He writes that "no adequate explanation has been offered" for Shakespeare's familiarity with the play since it was not printed until 1605 (27). But neither he nor the great majority of Shakespeare scholars seem to realize that he knew it so well because he wrote it.

## King Leir *and Other Apprenticeship Plays*

The *King Leir* Quarto of 1605 was one of ten plays belonging to the Queen's Men that were registered for publication between 1591 and 1595. At the time, this company, which has been repeatedly linked to Shakespeare, was near the end of its London career (McMillin and MacLean 160–1). E. K. Chambers suggested that to sustain itself it sold publication rights to some of the plays it owned (*Elizabethan Stage* 2:114–115). Among them were three other apprenticeship plays— *Troublesome Reign, Famous Victories* and *The True Tragedy of Richard the Third,* all of which were rewritten and published under the Shakespeare pseudonym.

## THE TROUBLESOME REIGN OF JOHN, KING OF ENGLAND

The apprenticeship play most commonly associated with *King Leir* is the anonymous *Troublesome Reign,* published in 1591, but written perhaps twenty-five years earlier. Numerous parallels of language, thought and dramatic devices between *Leir* and *Troublesome Reign* have been detected by scholars attempting to ascertain the plays' authors. For instance, both contain similar interludes of farce in a style different from that of the rest of the play. This has led several to theorize that they had a common author. "A perusal of [*Troublesome Reign* and *Leir*] is very persuasive that the same author wrote them" (Furnivall and Munro, eds. *Troublesome Reign* xiii). In the words of Arthur Acheson, "The old *King Leir* was evidently written by the same author as *The Troublesome Reign of King John* [*sic*], which it strongly resembles, though the latter play is clearly the earlier composition" (165). Although Acheson was probably correct in dating *Troublesome Reign* earlier than *King Leir,* he thought Thomas Lodge was the author of both plays.

Several scholars have pointed to striking similarities between the Bastard Philip Falconbridge, King John's companion in *Troublesome Reign,* and Mumford, companion to the King of Gaul in *King Leir,* neither of whom is to be found in the historical sources of either play. Sidney Lee remarked that "Mumford ... is as brave a soldier as the Bastard in King John, and is cast in the same mould" (ed. *King Leir* xxxiii). Both have the same magnetic personality—bluff and outspoken, and the same function—companion to a King and commenter on the action of the play. Moreover, they have in common a personal quarrel with another character—the Bastard Falconbridge with Lymoges, a sometime enemy of his father, and Mumford with Ragan's husband, the King of Cambria. The outcome of these quarrels is nearly identical in both plays. In *Troublesome Reign,* Falconbridge conducts a running quarrel with Lymoges, calling him a "Base heardgroom, coward, peasant, worse than a threshing slave," before killing him (*1 TR* 565). The same confrontation, this time between Mumford and Cambria, takes place in *King Leir,* after the King of Gaul's army has defeated the army of Cornwall and Cambria. Mumford taunts Cambria as a "Welshman," and calls him a coward as he chases him off the stage:

*Mumford.*    Farewell (Welshman) give thee but thy due,

Thou hast a light and nimble pair of legs:

Thou art more in debt to them than to thy hands:

But if I meet thee once again today,

I'll cut them off, and set them to a better heart.

*King Leir* V.xi.9–13

Another similarity is the scene in each play in which an assailant is sent to harm or murder a specific victim(s), such as described above in *King Leir* and *Cymbeline*. In *Troublesome Reign*, King John sends Hubert to blind John's nephew Arthur to prevent him from competing with him for the throne. Hubert confronts Arthur in his prison cell and shows him the letter from the King with the instruction. Arthur warns Hubert of what will await him:

*Arthur.*    Hell, *Hubert*, trust me, all the plagues of hell

Hangs on performance of this damned deede.

This seale, the warrant of the bodies blisse,

Ensureth Satan chieftaine of thy soule:

…

Advise thee, *Hubert*, for the case is hard,

To lose salvation for a Kings reward

*1 TR* 1379–82, 1389–90

Hubert insists that he is bound to do what King John has commanded and, after many bitter words, Arthur finally gives in:

*Arthur.*    Then doo thy charge, and charged be thy soule

With wrongfull persecution done this day.        *1 TR* 1415–16

At this point, Hubert accedes to his conscience and spares Arthur any injury. In *King Leir*, the unnamed Messenger/Murderer sent by Leir's daughters, Ragan and Gonorill, confronts Leir and Perillus and tells them what he has been hired to do, showing them Gonerill's letter as evidence. Because of his guilt over the way he has treated Cordella, Leir assents to his own death. But Perillus warns the assassin about what his punishment will be:

*Perillus.*    Oh, then art thou for ever tied in chains

Of everlasting torments to endure,

Even in the hottest hole of grisly hell,

Such pains, as never mortal tongue can tell.

*King Leir* IV.vii.288–91

After an extended conversation, the Messenger/Murderer begins to worry about his own salvation, and decides to spare them, discarding his daggers.

In another example of similar language in the two plays, Arthur's mother Constance accuses Queen Eleanor in *Troublesome Reign* of blocking her son's claim to the throne. Exclaiming that the Queen is "the wretch that broacheth all this ill," she asks herself:

*Constance.*   Why flye I not upon the Beldames face,

And with my nayles pull foorth her hatefull eyes.   *1 TR* 812–13

In *King* Leir, Ragan uses almost exactly the same words to express her anger at Cordella. She thinks that Cordella was the "cause of this uncertain ill" and threatens to follow her to France:

*Ragan.*       And with these nails scratch out her hateful eyes:

*King Leir* V.ii.27

This particular literal image, of a woman attacking another's face with her nails, recurs in a dozen canonical plays—twice in *King Lear*—first, when an angry Lear castigates Goneril for demanding that he reduce his complement of knights in her castle:

*Lear.*        I have another daughter,

Who I am sure is kind and comfortable.

When she shall hear this of thee, with her nails

She'll flay thy wolvish visage.        *King Lear* I.iv.305–8

and again in Act III, as Gloucester tries to explain to Regan and Cornwall why he has sent Lear to Dover:

*Glou.*        Because I would not see thy cruel nails

Pluck out his poor old eyes,        *King Lear* III.vii.56–7

## EDMUND IRONSIDE

Eric Sams found dozens of parallels of words and phrases between *King Leir* and *Edmund Ironside*, leading him to assert that "...these two textual tapestries were woven by the same hand, from the same threads of discourse, at much the same time" ("King Leir" 270). Three examples:

1. In I.iii of *King Leir*, Perillus decries Leir's treatment of Cordella:

*Perillus.*    Reason to rage should not have given place,   *King Leir* I.iii.139

just as Edmund admonishes Canute in *Edmund Ironside*:

Edmund.                              ... govern thou
              thy surly terms with reason, not with rage.
                                        *Edmund Ironside* V.ii.1810–11[25]

2. In III.ii of *King Leir*, Gonorill complains to Skalliger about Leir's carp-
   ing at her spending:

Gonorill.     And saith, the [banquet's] cost would well suffice for twice.
                                        *King Leir* III.ii.16

Similarly, in *Edmund Ironside* Canute remarks on Southampton's largesse:

Canute.       half this [banquet's] expense would well have satisfied
                                        *Edmund Ironside* II.i.388

The identical thought is carried over to the canonical *King Lear* when Goneril
makes the same complaint about her father:

Gon.          His knights grow riotous, and himself upbraids us
              On every trifle.                    *King Lear* I.iii.6–7

3. In *King Leir*, Cornwall remarks on his messenger's delay:

Cornwall.     I'll teach him how to dally with his King,        *King Leir* IV.vi.5

In *Edmund Ironside*, Canute makes a similar comment about the English:

Canute.       I'll teach them what it is to play with kings
                                        *Edmund Ironside* II.iii.678

## THE FAMOUS VICTORIES OF HENRY THE FIFTH

Further evidence of a single mind at work is clear in short scenes in *Famous
Victories*, *King Leir*, *Edmund Ironside* and *Henry V*, in which a king falls instantly
in love with a girl he has just met. In all four instances, this whirlwind wooing
results in a prompt marriage. In the playwright's first dramatization of an
impetuous proposal of this kind, King Henry V, immediately after accepting
the surrender of the King of France in *Famous Victories*, decides that he is in
love with the King's daughter Katherine:

King of       Ay, but I love her, and must crave her—
England.      Nay, I love her, and will have her!    *Famous Victories* xviii.47–8

Katherine, aged nineteen at the time, responds by asking "How should I love him that hath dealt so hardly with my father?," but adds:

Katherine.    If I were of my own direction, I could give

you answer; but seeing I stand in my father's direction, I

must first know his will.

A moment later she agrees:

Katherine.    Whereas I can put your Grace in no assur-

ance, I would be loath to put you in any despair.

Famous Victories xviii.76–8; 81–2

In II.iv of *King Leir*, Cordella encounters the King of Gaul and Mumford, who are disguised as pilgrims. Both the King and Mumford are immediately attracted to her and, fewer than thirty lines later, the King declares:

King.         I am in such a labyrinth of love,

As that I know not which way to get out.    *King Leir* II.iv.46–7

He promptly proposes and she accepts. When they reappear several scenes later, they are married.

This scene is re-enacted in *Edmund Ironside*, when King Canute meets Egina, the underage daughter of the Earl of Southampton, offers her a cup of wine, and proposes to make her his Queen—all in the space of thirty lines. As did Katherine in *Famous Victories*, Egina defers to her father's judgment. When he readily assents, she promptly accepts Canute's proposal:

Egina.        What my dread sovereign and my father wills

I dare not, nay I will not, contradict. *Edmund Ironside* II.i.437–8

The scene is again recapitulated in the last act of *Henry V*, when Henry abruptly proposes to the French King's daughter Katherine. After a lengthy exchange, she replies that if it pleases her father, it will "content" her (V.ii.247–50).

## The Two Lears *and Edward de Vere*

There is little evidence to connect Edward de Vere with the anonymous *King Leir*. Although he eventually had three daughters, he first took up the story of King Lear during his teen years. What can be said is that since he is the actual Shakespeare and the author of the Folio *King Lear*, the play that is so obviously its original version must be his composition, as well. The same reasoning applies to the four other apprenticeship plays described in this book. Each of them has a strong connection to de Vere, and each is strikingly similar to *King Leir* in its relationship to a canonical play or plays.

It is also noteworthy that Oxford had access to multiple versions of the play's sources in the library of William Cecil in London (Jolly, "'Shakespeare' and Burghley's Library" 6). In addition to several copies of Geoffrey's *Historia* in manuscript (McKisack 51), Cecil's library contained an English-language manuscript of the *Brut* bearing Cecil's signature on its first page (Matheson 94), Caxton's printed versions of the *Brut,* and Polydore Vergil's *Anglica Historia,* which had been printed several times, in Latin, before 1560 (McKisack 99). Cecil also owned a manuscript of an English translation of Ranulf Higden's *Polycronicon,* a Latin adaptation of the *Brut* (J. Taylor 2–3), as well as a copy of Matthew Paris' *Chronica Majora,* which he loaned to Archbishop Parker, who printed it in 1567 and 1570 (Perrett 38–9). All these manuscripts and books contained a version of the King Lear story, each one slightly different in its details.

A couplet that Sir John Davies addressed to Susan Vere, Oxford's youngest daughter, in 1602 suggests that he was known as the author of *King Lear.* The lines allude to the conversation in the first scene in the play, and seem to identify her with Cordelia in *King Lear*:

> Nothing's your lott, that's more then can be told
> For nothing is more precious then gold.[26]

## *Dates of the Two* Lears

It is generally accepted that the *kinge leare* of which Philip Henslowe recorded two performances in April 1594 is the anonymous *King Leir* that John Wright published in 1605 (Greg, "Date" 378; Michie 4–5). Most editors date the composition of the play to c. 1590, apparently concluding that the similar elements in the three poetical works mentioned above were sources. It is true that these poems were published between 1586 and 1590, but it is more likely their authors borrowed names and phrases from a performance, or even a manuscript, of *King Leir,* or even from another source, possibly much older, that has not yet been identified. The evidence indicates that the play was written more than twenty years earlier, during or soon after Oxford's attendance at Gray's Inn in the late 1560s.

The excessive use of legal terms in *King Leir,* described above in "Vocabulary and Style," was a sharp departure from his practice in the four apprenticeship plays that he wrote before his exposure to legal language in 1567.

Moreover, the pedestrian language, clumsy dramaturgy, and dozens of monologues and speeches to the audience also suggest that the play was among the earliest he undertook.

The several elements carried over from Morality plays—the two counselors, one good, one evil; the simple one-sided characters that do not change; the happy ending in which goodness is rewarded—also suggest an early date. There is ample evidence of Oxford's poetic output at about that time, and of his entertaining the Queen with dramatic "devices" in the 1570s.[27] Besides the Gilbert Talbot letter mentioned in "The Author of the Canon," we have the testimony of Anthony Munday, who entered the service of the Earl of Oxford in 1578. In the epilogue to his novel *Zelauto*, published in 1580, Munday mentions the "devices" that are presented to entertain Elizabeth and her court by "her noble peers and lords that are about her." Munday adds that he is "much bound to one of them in especial…" (Stillinger 51–52). The word "device" has several meanings. In this context, it is a type of "dramatic representation" (*OED*, devise: 11). Lastly, Revels Office records indicate that there was a "vogue at Court of romances" such as *King Leir* during the twenty-five-year period beginning about 1570 (Michie 36; Harbage 62).

The composition of the canonical *King Lear* is traditionally dated to 1605/6 on the basis of two alleged sources—Harsnett's *A Declaration* and the English translation of Montaigne's *Essays*, both published in 1603—and it was certainly written at some time during the previous decade. There is a wealth of evidence that Oxford had access to Harsnett's source—a certain "book of Miracles" by the Jesuit priest William Weston, also known as "Edmunds," that was extant in the late 1580s.[28] Also, since Oxford was competent in French from his teen years, he could have read Montaigne when his *Essays* were published in French in 1580, 1588 and 1595.

Several references to eclipses, such as Gloucester's "these late eclipses of the sun and moon" (I.ii.103–4) have been alleged to refer to solar and lunar eclipses in 1605. But there were other pairs of eclipses in England that occurred, in 1590, 1598 and 1601 (Muir, ed. *King Lear* xix; Furness, ed. *King Lear* 379–80). Relevant to this is the discovery by German physicist Hanno Wember that only the March 7, 1598, solar eclipse was total in England; those of 1601 and 1605 were only partial, and much less likely to attract attention (35–8). Wember also reported that the 1598 solar eclipse passed diagonally across the western side of England, totally blacking out a wide swath of country from Cornwall to Edinburgh. The blackout was 93 percent in London. A related lunar eclipse, only slightly less than total, occurred two weeks earlier, on February 21st. The eclipse in 1605 passed across southern France, and would not have been noticed in England.

## Contrary Evidence

The anonymous *King Leir* has been ascribed to Marlowe (Robertson 400), Lodge (Acheson 164), Kyd (W. Wells, "Authorship" 434–8), Peele (Sykes, *Sidelights* 128), Greene (Law, *"King John* and *King Leir"*), Munday (Crundell 310–11), "Greene, Lodge, and Kyd" (Hopkinson vii) and "an imitator of Shakespeare" (P. Alexander, *Shakespeare* 171). In 2008, Brian Vickers used an anti-plagiarism software program to detect "identical threeword sequences" in a group of 75 plays written before 1596. He found "over 100 identical phrases" in *King Leir* that also appeared in two plays allegedly written by Kyd (*The Spanish Tragedy* and *Soliman and Perseda*) and one (*Cornelia*) that he translated from the French ("Thomas Kyd"). But "identical phrases" are only one part of the process of attribution, and the evidence adduced for each of the eight playwrights mentioned is far less convincing than that outlined above for the real Shakespeare.

In the opinion of Sidney Lee, the play's verse falls far below the level of Marlowe's, and if it were by Lodge, Kyd, Peele or Greene, "the publisher is not likely to have ... withheld all key to the dramatist's name from the title-page" (ed. *King Leir* xx). Lee introduced the name of William Rankins, the author of a play about one of King Lear's successors to the throne of Britain. But neither this play nor the three other historical plays by Rankins have survived, so the matter cannot be pursued. Lee also speculated that *King Leir's* author subsequently wrote *Locrine*, another play about an early British king, published in 1595, that appeared with the author's initials "W. S." on the title page.[29]

It is significant that all but a handful of modern critics and editors seem reluctant to assign an author to *King Leir*, choosing to refer to him as the "old playwright" or the "older journeyman dramatist" (H. B. Charlton 195). As noted in Chapter II, neither *King Leir*, nor any of the other apprenticeship plays described in this book, are included in collections of Shakespearean apocrypha.[30] The most recent editor of the play does not address the question at all, although he is confident that "we do know when it first appeared on stage," evidently assuming that the performance in April 1594 was the first (Michie 4).

It appears that the German critic Ludwig Tieck was the first scholar to assign *King Leir* to Shakespeare, in 1811 (C. F. T. Brooke ix–x), but it was not until the twentieth century that this opinion was again hazarded—by Ephraim Everitt in 1954 (173) and by Eric Sams in 1995 (*Real Shakespeare* 182–3).

## Conclusion

The evidence presented above demonstrates that the two *Lear* plays were written by the same person—the playwright who used the pseudonym William

Shakespeare. His first version of *King Leir* was a pleasant romance intended to instruct and entertain. It reflected his basic Protestant beliefs, his recent exposure to the law, and his substantial plotting ability—but also his undeveloped poetic skills.

Three decades later, the author had a different view of life and the Creator, and a different message to convey. He transformed this simple tale, infused with Christian piety, into a powerful and violent tragedy in which pagan Gods are repeatedly invoked, and the very idea of justice is questioned. The depth and meaning he added to the story cannot be calculated. One critic remarked upon "…the distance which Shakespeare has traveled into complexity, ambiguity and dubiety in his new creation" (Elton 71).

To argue that *Leir* cannot be by Shakespeare because of its elementary plot, wooden characters and pedestrian verse is to say that there was no period of experimentation and practice, no apprenticeship before he wrote *The Comedy of Errors* or *Titus Andronicus*, or whatever was the earliest canonical play. As Eric Sams wrote, "The dismissive reflex that Leir cannot possibly be by Shakespeare, because it is 'inferior' (as if he alone, among all the world's great creative artists, never developed from youth to maturity but always had only the one style) is just as worthless in this context as in all others" (*Real Shakespeare II* 273). Denying him the authorship of the anonymous *King Leir* presupposes an imaginary "older journeyman dramatist" of whom no trace can be found in the Elizabethan theatrical world.

# A Summing Up

The evidence presented in the preceding pages demonstrates that five anonymous plays performed or published during the reign of Elizabeth, for which no credible attribution to any other author has been made, actually belong in the Shakespeare canon. The evidence for this is both internal and external, and supports, in terms of his personal life and activities, the claim that the actual author of the Shakespeare canon was Edward de Vere, seventeenth Earl of Oxford. Although no single element of the argument is conclusive, the accumulation of historical, theatrical and literary evidence is substantial and compelling.

Each anonymous play has a corresponding counterpart in the accepted canon that includes in its cast the same or similar historical and fictional characters, many with the same name or with a different name, but in the same role as in the earlier play.

Each anonymous play has a structure and plot that are identical or similar to those in its counterpart in the canon, with many identical plot elements arranged in the same order. In the corresponding canonical plays, Shakespeare reduced the cast, added a subplot or plot elements, and completely rewrote and expanded the dialogue.

Moreover, in each of the seven canonical plays emanating from these plays, Shakespeare carried over dramatic devices, ideas, metaphors, and other linguistic markers from its anonymous counterpart. But in each of them, he has rendered his characters more complex and more believable. A pantheon of memorable Shakespearean characters—Falstaff, Poins, Mistress Quickly, the Bastard Falconbridge, Oswald, Petruchio, Kate—all originated in one or the other of these five anonymous plays. Equally memorable, but minor, characters, such as the stubborn porter in *Macbeth*, the reluctant murderer in *Richard III* and the farcical Dogberry in *Much Ado about Nothing* all had the same origin.

Despite claims to the contrary by some scholars, there is clear documentary evidence that each anonymous play was printed or performed long before its canonical counterpart, two of which, *King John* and *The Taming of the Shrew*, were unpublished until their appearance in the First Folio. These five anonymous plays form a distinct group of initial versions of later plays that is unique in Elizabethan drama. A similar body of first efforts has not survived for any other playwright of the time.

The titles of four of the anonymous plays differ from those in the canon only in spelling or in modifying adjectives. The fifth, *The Famous Victories of Henry the Fifth*, was expanded into three plays, each bearing the name of a king appearing in the earlier play. *The Troublesome Reign of John* was twice attributed to Shakespeare on its title page and, along with *The Taming of a Shrew*, was considered by printers and publishers of the time to be merely an earlier version of its counterpart in the canon.

Four of the five anonymous plays have concrete links to the Earl of Oxford, and can be dated, on the basis of those links, to the six or seven years of his teen age. The paucity of legal issues and legal language in each of them is convincing evidence, but not the only evidence, that he wrote them before his exposure to the law and the language of the law during his tenure at Gray's Inn, which began in 1567. The fifth play, *King Leir*, is replete with legal language, but is so similar to the other four in terms of its simple characters and prosaic plot that it clearly belongs in the same period, but near the end of it. In two of the plays, the role of the Earl of Oxford has been unhistorically expanded and glorified—a sign of the youthful hubris and pride of the author, a practice that he abandoned thereafter.

The dating of these five Shakespeare plays prior to 1570 virtually eliminates the authorship theory based upon William Shakspere of Stratford-upon-Avon, who was not yet ten years old when they were written. Such dating also provides a road map to the composition dates of the plays of the first half of the Shakespeare canon. For example, in the forty-year writing career of the Earl of Oxford, the creation of *Henry V* in 1583 occurs naturally at about the mid-point, just as it is claimed to occur at the mid-point, 1599, of the career of the author alleged in the Stratfordian theory. The sixteen-year difference between the two dating schemes—Stratfordian and Oxfordian—reflects the nearly fifteen-year difference in their birth dates, 1550 and 1564. In the orthodox sequence of the composition of the thirty-nine-play canon, *Henry V* is the eighteenth or nineteenth play, and the last history play, that Shakespeare wrote, except for *Henry VIII* (Chambers, *William Shakespeare* 1:246–50; Wentersdorf, "Chronology" 164).

It is therefore reasonable to conclude that the body of plays dated prior to *Henry V* by scholars of all persuasions belongs in the decade before 1583. Within this group, *The Comedy of Errors, Titus Andronicus* and the first tetralogy were probably written before Oxford's trip to France and Italy in 1575–6. Following this line of reasoning, it seems clear that he wrote most of his Italian and French plays during the half-a-dozen years after his arrival in Italy in 1575.

This radical redating of the first half of the Shakespeare canon coincides roughly with the orthodox dating sequence, but only in terms of sequence. The messy and incomplete record of performance and publication dates of the apocryphal and canonical plays is an unreliable and misleading guide to their composition dates. It is clear that most of Oxford's plays did not appear in print or reach the public stage until many years after he wrote them. Half of them were not published until years after his death, and for several there is no record of their existence until they appeared in the First Folio in 1623. This is consistent with the finding that he wrote for "royalty, the nobility, educated aristocrats, their retainers and court officialdom" (Whalen, "Shakespeare's Audience" 9), and made no effort to profit from the publication of his plays or from their performance in public theaters.

In view of this compendium of evidence, it is astonishing that virtually all scholars, critics and editors of Shakespeare have overlooked, disputed or disparaged the idea the he had anything to do with any of them. Nor have they provided any credible evidence that they are the work of any other dramatist. As previously mentioned, the plays are not even included in collections of Shakespearean "apocrypha."

It appears that this attitude is based on two premises—that Shakespeare could not have written a bad play, and that the author of the canon, the most brilliant dramatic achievement in the history of the theater, was a businessman and actor from a provincial town for whom there is no credible evidence that he was even literate. The first premise is questionable on the face of it, and should not be the basis for any kind of literary judgment. The second premise is the crux of the problem, and deserves the most searching scrutiny, something that has been entirely absent from orthodox Shakespearean scholarship.

Such scrutiny has not only been absent, it has been actively discouraged to such an extent that conference appearances and publications in scholarly journals by those who question the Stratfordian theory have been routinely rejected by the academic establishment. With only occasional exceptions, universities do not offer courses, sponsor research, or grant advanced degrees that may imply that there is a question about the author of the Shakespeare canon. Columbia University English professor, James Shapiro, acknowledges this fact in *Contested Will* (5).

If there is a conspiracy associated with the Shakespeare authorship question, as orthodox spokesmen claim, it is a conspiracy of Stratfordian scholars to conceal the truth, and to suppress efforts to reveal it.

The addition of these five plays to the canon makes available more than ten thousand new lines of Shakespeare's verse and prose for study and analysis. Many of them clarify and explain phrases and passages in the canon that have puzzled scholars. Comparison of the apprenticeship plays with their canonical counterparts reveals Shakespeare's thought processes, especially his second thoughts, and his increasing skill as a dramatist, as he built new plays on the plot structures of his earliest efforts.

Although *Shakespeare's Apprenticeship* is focused on demonstrating that Shakespeare is the author of five anonymous plays heretofore excluded from the canon, it supplies further evidence, found in the plays themselves, that "William Shakespeare" is a pseudonym—the most successful pseudonym in literary history.

The revelation of the person behind the pseudonym allows those of us who read, watch or act in Shakespeare plays to not only appreciate and understand them more fully, but also to connect their characters and situations to the personality and circumstances of a known author. The repeated rewriting of the scanty biography of the alleged Stratfordian author attests to the immense and persistent interest in the life of the person behind the world's most distinguished canon of dramatic work. *Shakespeare's Apprenticeship* reveals the early work of that person, and adds to the evidence that he was Edward de Vere, seventeenth Earl of Oxford.

# Chapter Notes

## The Author of the Canon

1. "Shakespeare" Identified in Edward de Vere, Seventeenth Earl of Oxford.

2. Although Boas claims that Shakespeare was more familiar with Oxford than anywhere else in England, except Stratford and London, he is able to cite only two references to it in the canon, in Henry VIII and The Taming of the Shrew, both general in nature (Shakespeare and the Universities 46–7). Furthermore, the Welsh-hating Dr. Caius, who is a significant character in The Merry Wives of Windsor, was obviously based on Dr. John Caius, a scholar and physician who had co-founded Gonville and Caius College, Cambridge (Nutton). See also Gilvary, "Queens' College Cambridge."

3. Oleum magistrale (1574) by George Baker; Divers and Sundry Waies of Two Parts in One, to the Number of Fortie, uppon One Playn Song (1591) and English Madrigals (1599) by John Farmer; and Defence of the Militarie Profession (1579) by Geoffrey Gates. See Chiljan, Dedications, pp. 41, 94, 98. John Harrison, the publisher of the Gates volume, also published Venus and Adonis and Lucrece.

4. The most comprehensive treatment of the subject is Fowler.

5. Among the earliest to write on the subject were C. Brown in 1838 (100) and Karl Elze in 1874 (Chap. V).

6. The concept is explained more fully in Price, "Stigma." See also Sheavyn at 162–3, 168.

7. For the association of Athena with spear-shaking and dramatic poetry, see Anderson at xxviii.

8. See also Farina at 82–7.

9. These are explained more fully in Altschuler, "Searching."

10. Anderson cites several at 397–8 and 572.

11. The matter is treated more fully by Ogburn Jr. at 204–206. The entire preface is printed in Chambers, William Shakespeare 2:216–17.

## Chapter I

1. The wording of the title pages of the acknowledged Shakespeare plays is most accessible in Bartlett (25–9) or in Chambers, William Shakespeare 1:375–78, 388–89, and that of Famous Victories in Pitcher (167).

2. Quotations from Famous Victories are from Pitcher's ed. Division of scenes 4–6, and line numbers throughout are slightly different among the various editions of the play.

3. The title page of Locrine (1595) bore the words "Newly set foorth, overseen and corrected, By W. S." (Chambers, Elizabethan Stage 4:28.) Although it appeared in the Third and Fourth Folios, modern scholars do not consider it a Shakespeare play. Both Locrine and The London Prodigal have been edited by William Kozlenko, and appear in his collection of "disputed" plays.

4. Four leaves have survived from an even earlier Quarto, apparently printed in the same year (Humphries lxvi).

5. The circumstances of this entry are

explained by Gurr in his edition of *Henry V* at 224–8.

6. The episode of the Jaggard/Pavier quartos is explained by E. K. Chambers in *William Shakespeare* 1:133–37.

7. Although the actual title of Edward Hall's work is *The union of the two noble and illustre famelies of Lancastre and Yorke*, it is routinely referred to as Hall's *Chronicle*.

8. The text and sources of the *Vita Henrici Quinti* by Titus Livius are in Kingsford's *The First English Life*.

9. The French Dauphin was routinely mocked by the English as the "Dolphin."

10. Kingsford, *English Historical Literature in the Fifteenth Century*; Corbin and Sedge, 177.

11. Stow's *Summarie* was published under slightly different titles between 1565 and 1604. Its sources are listed in B. L. Beer's edition.

12. *Narrative* v. 4: ix–xi. Bullough prints excerpts from Stow's *Chronicles of England* (1580) at 4:215–219.

13. The collection was expanded and reissued half-a-dozen times before 1600.

14. J. D. Wilson, ed. *Henry IV, Part 1*, 191–6; Kastan, ed. *King Henry IV, Part 1*, 343–4; in Humphries, ed. *King Henry IV, Part 1*, they are included in footnotes throughout the text.

15. The confrontation in *Famous Victories*, in which Prince Hal strikes the Chief Justice and is then ordered to jail by him, is absent from *2 Henry IV*, but both actions are referred to on two occasions, suggesting that the author had his original version in mind as he composed the play.

16. The three other identical plot elements—Prince Hal's accession to the throne, the English invasion of France, and the English victory are uncontroversial historical facts.

17. Additional specific details are listed in Greer's article and in Dutton ("Famous Victories" 137–8.)

18. Nor are there any comics in the two anonymous history plays, *The Troublesome Reign of John* and *The True Tragedy of Richard the Third*, that Shakespeare wrote during this same period.

19. Geoffrey Bullough summarizes many of the similarities described in this Section (*Narrative* 4:347–9.)

20. Humphries, ed. *King Henry IV, Part II*, xl–xli, with additional details.

21. This close relationship was first suggested by James Monaghan in "Falstaff and His Forebears."

22. This concept is developed more fully in D. B. Landt's article in *Shakespeare Quarterly* and by Pitcher at 104–108.

23. "Dame Partlet" is really an inside literary joke and poetic reference to Chaunticleer the rooster's wife/sister in *The Nun's Priest's Tale* (Delahoyde 155).

24. There is an extended discussion of the matter in Corbin and Sedge at 2–30.

25. In the Folio and many modern editions of *1 Henry VI*, the name is spelled "Falstaffe." But there is no connection between Fastolf and the fat knight of the *Henry IV* plays. See Burns 111–112, 289 and Hattaway 64.

26. Additional instances of Derick's and Falstaff's similar language and behavior are detailed in Champion's article.

27. Additional examples can be found in Monaghan, Greer, Pitcher (120–62) and in Eric Sams' *The Real Shakespeare II*.

28. Quartos 1, 2, 3, 5, 6 only.

29. Quotations from *True Tragedy* are from the Malone Society reprint, edited by W. W. Greg. Slight changes in certain spellings have been made.

30. Quotations from *The Taming of a Shrew* are from Miller's edition. In his annotation of this passage, Miller writes, "This idea that a play might be mistaken for reality, brilliantly exploited in *Span. Trag.*, is much evident in Shakespeare," and cites *MND* and *Hamlet* (114).

31. Gad's, or Vagabond's, Hill is located about 2½ miles northwest of Rochester on the road to Gravesend and London.

32. In *The Tragedy of Richard II, Part One* (*Thomas of Woodstock*), a Shakespeare play that has not yet been added to the canon, the Duchess of Ireland briefly mentions her former husband, Robert de Vere, ninth Earl of Oxford (III.iii.10–12). See M. Egan, ed. *Tragedy* 1:575.

33. Keen and Lubbock 7, 211. According to John Rollett, who examined the book several times, the Italic "Edward" is located opposite a line in the text that includes the word "Oxford," referring to the city ("Elizaforum" Bulletin Board, 23 March 2005).

34. This is also the opinion of A. P. Rossiter, whose article constitutes Appendix IV in Keen and Lubbock (184–5).

35. The evidence consists of a passage from the 1611 edition of *Tarlton's Jests* (24–5), describing his roles as the Lord Chief Justice and the Clown. Quoted by Pitcher at 180–1.

36. http://ericsams.org/index.php/shakespeare-archive/the-real-shakespeare-ii/283-17b-the-famous-victories-of-henry-v. Para. 15.

37. Both are quoted in Jamison at 115 and 121.

38. On the title page of *Romeus and Juliet*, published in 1562, are the words "by Ar. Br.," ostensibly Arther Brooke (c. 1545–1563).

39. De Ayala and Guéno 38, 72; Tennyson i.

40. The conversation is slightly different in the Quartos.

41. Exception: the "Notes on Henry V" in Miller's edition of Clark's *Hidden Allusions* (782–5). Ogburn Jr. also equates *Harry of Cornwall* with *Henry V* (692n.3).

42. Elizabeth's letters to Essex on this occasion are printed in G. B. Harrison's collection at 263–76.

43. Bacon 3:150.

44. Guy 447–8. Annabel Patterson suggests that this may have been the reason that the Choruses were omitted from all three Quartos (86–7).

45. The documents attesting to the affair are cited in Hammer at 320–1. See also Anderson at 297 and 538.

46. Lee, "Butler, Thomas" 80; D. Edwards, *Ormond Lordship* 98–103.

47. D. Edwards, "Butler, Thomas."

48. *Calendar of State Papers relating to Ireland, etc.* 1867. v. 105, pp. 478, 480.

49. Camden, *Annales.* 2001 ed. (1583, item 22); Holinshed 6:454.

50. The *OED* cites the use of the verb "broach" (v.1) in this specific passage to support the definition "To stick (something) on a spit or pointed weapon." But Oxford had used "broach" in a similar sense in *3 Henry VI* (II.iii.16) and *Titus Andronicus* (IV.ii.86).

51. The letter can be seen at http://www.oxford-shakespeare.com/StatePapersOther/SP_63-51-3_%20ff_92-3.pdf

52. Carte 1: cv–cvi. According to Carte, Robert Dudley, Earl of Leicester, and his supporters "took care to misrepresent his conduct...."

53. In the words of another scholar, "the Folio version is a text intended for a special performance before a selected audience" (Albright 753).

54. J. D. Wilson. ed. *King Henry V* 122. Creizenach describes the customary garb of the Prologue/Chorus, and comments further that the *Henry V* Chorus "occupies a place apart. Its services ... could well have been spared; it seems rather as if the author's object had been to give direct expression to his patriotic enthusiasm for the glorious deeds of his favorite hero by breaking through the dramatic form" (275–6).

55. "Dig at theater where Shakespeare worked uncovers a surprise." Associated Press. May 21, 2016.

56. Astington, "Inigo Jones" 46–56. See illustrations on pp. 86 and 88.

57. According to theater historian John H. Astington, "The Cockpit at Whitehall had a longer career as a temporary performance space than it did as permanent playhouse" ("Whitehall Cockpit" 301). "The enclosed Cockpit, when used for plays before 1629, would resemble a smaller version of the Swan ("Whitehall Cockpit" 310).

58. With respect to the orthodox dating of the play to the spring or summer of 1599, it is significant that the Court Calendar indicates that the Queen resided at Richmond, Greenwich and Nonsuch between February and October of that year. Although there was a cockpit at the Greenwich Palace, I have found no evidence that it was ever used for the performance of plays. Furthermore, the Court Calendar records no performances of plays before the Queen between February and December of 1599 (Chambers, *Elizabethan Stage* 4:111–12).

59. In another record, Treasurer of the Chamber's Accounts, the payee listed for the performances on March 3 was John Lyly (Colthorpe, "The Elizabethan Court Day by Day." March 3, 1584). At the time, Lyly was employed by the Earl of Oxford.

60. According to Chambers, the Children of the Chapel were under the patronage of Oxford in 1583–4 (*Elizabethan Stage* 2:37, 101, 497).

61. Duncan-Jones. *Courtier Poet* 164–5,

322. The most complete account of the affair is in B. M. Ward (*Seventeenth Earl* 165–74).

62. Sidney, *Miscellaneous Prose* 59–60. *Sidney, A Critical Edition* xxii. Duncan-Jones, *Courtier Poet* 230.

63. Clough, "Broken English" Table 1. Clough also lists *Hymenaeus* (1579), a play attributed to Abraham Fraunce, but its text is in Latin, and Fredericus, the "foreigner" employs a medley of Latin, Dutch, and German.

64. Chambers, *Elizabethan Stage* 4:28. Both plays have been edited by W. W. Greg.

65. Fluellen has been identified by most orthodox editors as a portrait of Sir Roger Williams, a Welshman in the service of the Earl of Oxford, c. 1580. See C. W. Barrell "Shakespeare's "Fluellen." On the other hand, in *I, William Shakespeare*, Leslie Hotson suggests that Fluellen is based on the astronomer and military theorist Thomas Digges (111–124). Hotson's evidence is the more convincing, but in either case the connection to Oxford is a strong one.

66. In the First Folio there is no Chorus preceding Act IV, which is actually marked "Actus Tertius." The second half of the original Chorus to Act III (marked "Actus Secundus" in the Folio) was transferred to its current place preceding Act IV by later editors.

67. Alwin Thaler makes the same observation on pp. 19–20 of *Shakespeare and Sir Philip Sidney*. Another commentator on *Henry V*, Robert Ornstein, writes that "the apology is as sly as it is gratuitous" in *A Kingdom for a Stage*, p. 176.

68. *Courtier Poet*, 237; some background on this issue is supplied by Heninger in his introduction to Watson's *Hekatompathia* at xiv–xvi.

69. In her comment on this sonnet, Duncan-Jones makes the same observations about Sidney and horses that I make in this Section (*Critical Edition* 363).

70. The choruses are also absent from the Quartos, but Gurr didn't omit them from his *Henry V*. The connection between III.vii in *Henry V* and Sidney's fondness for horses was first noticed by Gerit Quealy.

71. They are fully explained by Partridge at 40–1. Four prominent editors of the play (Gurr), *The Oxford Shakespeare* (G. Taylor) and *The Riverside Shakespeare* (Evans and

Tobin), appear to have been unaware of them.

72. The idea is more fully developed by Desper (25). In the same paper, Desper suggests that the "stars or suns" phrase later in the passage (not quoted) is an allusion to the thirteenth Earl of Oxford's role in the Battle of Barnet in 1471.

73. Looney, "The Earl of Oxford as Shakespeare, New Evidence." Reprinted in Looney, *"Shakespeare" Identified.* 2:168–76. See also Ogburn, *Mysterious* 486–7, and Brazil, "Unpacking The Merry Wives."

74. Slender refers to Shallow as both "uncle" and "cousin."

75. III.iii.43. The "Second Song" in *Astrophil and Stella* begins with "Have I caught my heavenly jewel." The editors of the Arden, Cambridge, Oxford and Riverside editions of the play all note the use of Sidney's line, but none of them recognizes the satire. A more perceptive scholar writes, "…in the witty and corpulent Falstaff, we can see Shakespeare metamorphosing Sidney's brilliant persona Astrophil into an almost wholly comic figure" (Duncan-Jones, "Liquid Prisoners" 12).

76. *"Shakespeare" Identified* 1:248–50. Looney also associated the name "Boyet" and its "old equivalent" "knave" with "Knyvet," Sir Thomas Knyvet being Oxford's "most profound foe" (1:251).

77. Further caricatures of Sidney in Act V can be seen in Miller's ed. of Clark's *Hidden Allusions* at 247–8.

78. A resemblance between Slender and Aguecheek was recognized in 1911 by Shakespearean scholar Edward Dowden, who suggested that "when he has grown some years older," Slender "may walk arm-in-arm in our fancy with Sir Andrew Aguecheek" (139). See also Bloom at 237.

79. *Cymbeline* IV.ii.184. See Evans, ed. *The Riverside Shakespeare* at p. 1595.

80. Some scholars see the characters in *Cymbeline* as representing Oxford's portrayal of the courtship of Elizabeth by the Duke of Alençon—Cloten representing Alençon, and his mother the Queen representing Catherine De Medici, Alençon's mother (Ogburn and Ogburn 151; Clark 85–95; Berney 18–19). But Oxford favored the French marriage, and is not likely to have caricatured Alençon as Cloten.

81. The best known manuscript of the music is "the keyboard version by William Byrd, in the so-called Fitzwilliam Virginal Book" (Sternfeld 152–3). Byrd's relationship with de Vere is well-known. He wrote three pieces of music for him; the first, "The Earl of Oxford's March," was published in the same Fitzwilliam Virginal Book (Mosher 18, 23).

82. The painting appears in D. Edwards' biography of Thomas Butler in the *ODNB*. Unfortunately, it was not made available for inclusion in this book. The "General's cut" phrase may have been retained in the Quarto of 1600 as an actual reference to Essex.

83. This suggestion will be elaborated in the following chapters.

## Chapter II

1. For instance, in the collections edited by C. Brooke, Baldwin Maxwell, Kozlenko, Bate and Rasmussen, and recently, in Gary Taylor, et al., eds. *The New Oxford Shakespeare*.

2. F. G. Fleay asserted that *True Tragedy* was "played at court" (*Biographical Chronicle* 2:315).

3. For their narratives of the period covered by the plays, both Grafton and Hall used, in addition to More, material from Polydore Vergil's *Anglica Historia* (Basle 1534), which each translated independently (Hanham 202–3).

4. J. D. Wilson, ed. *Richard III* xxiii–xxviii. *The Mirror for Magistrates* has been edited by Lily B. Campbell.

5. A useful summary of all the alleged sources of *Richard III* is provided in Siemon's edition at 51–79.

6. Quotations from *True Tragedy* are from W. W. Greg's edition. Slight changes in certain spellings have been made.

7. Moorman 90ff. The anonymous *Locrine* has been edited by Jane L. Gooch, and *The Spanish Tragedy* by David Bevington. *The Misfortunes of Arthur* and *The Scottish History of James the Fourth* were written by Thomas Hughes and Robert Greene, respectively.

8. Both plays are included in the Bate and Rasmussen, Kozlenko, and C. F. T. Brooke collections.

9. By Arthur Golding and others. See "The Date of Famous Victories" in Chapter I.

10. Further evidence of an interest in the events of 1485 by those in the neighborhood of Hedingham Castle might be suggested by a stone bas-relief depicting the moment of downfall of Richard III at Bosworth that was discovered in 1736 at Halstead, less than fifteen miles from the Castle (McLatchie 4).

11. As noted earlier, there are myriad differences between the Quarto texts of *Richard III* and the Folio. In this particular scene, the names of the three lords accompanying Richmond—Oxford, Blount and Herbert, are named in the Folio, but not in the Quartos.

12. *Chronique* 2:406. Cited in Ross at 82.

13. In stage directions, speech prefixes and dialogue in both the Quarto and the Folio, the Stanley/Derby character is variously designated as Stanley or Derby, but before October 1485, there was no Earl of Derby. See Smidt 70; Hammond 13. In 2000, John Jowett published an extended discussion of these variations, and their bearing on the question of memorial reconstruction ("'Derby,' 'Stanley'").

14. Greg, *Editorial Problem* 80–1; J. D. Wilson, "Shakespeare's *Richard III*" xxix–xxx; Bullough, *Narrative* 3:222; Jowett 24; Bevington, ed. *Richard III* 148; Lull 3.

15. *Elizabethan Stage* 4:43–4. In his later *William Shakespeare*, however, he writes that, along with *The Famous Victories of Henry the Fifth*, *True Tragedy* "may belong" to the mid–1580s (1:32).

16. *Calendar of State Papers, Foreign Series*. v. 1:32–3, 51, 53, 72, 90–1, 103, 109, 167–8.

17. This identification was regularly made in publications of the time. Another example occurs in the "Oration of John Hales to the Queen's Majesty," included by John Foxe in his *Acts and Monuments* in 1563 (8:673–79). See also Neale 62, 91, 178, 403.

18. "Turk Gregory never did such deeds in arms as I have done this day" (V.iii.44).

19. *New Cambridge Modern History* 2:587. This should not be confused with the Treaty of Prague, signed in 1635.

20. The sixteenth Earl of Oxford also accompanied Henry VIII on this expedition (J. Hughes).

21. The most popular of all Elizabethan miscellanies, *Paradyse*, though not published until 1576, was compiled, according to its publisher Henry Disle, by Edwards, who died in 1566 (Rollins and Baker 212–14).

# Chapter III

1. Chambers, *William Shakespeare* 1:338–40. The printers and publishers associated with these three editions were John Danter (1597), Thomas Creede (1599), Cuthbert Burby (1599) and John Smethwick (1609). Burby published Shakespeare's *Edward III* anonymously in 1596 and 1599, and *Love's Labor's Lost* in 1598 as "Newly corrected and augmented by W. Shakespeare." He was also one of the publishers of Meres' *Palladis Tamia* in 1598.
2. They are *Richard II* (1597), *Richard III* (1597) and *Henry IV Part 1*(1598).
3. See Chap. II, note 1.
4. Edward Capell, 1: pt.1:115 (quoted in Furness, ed. *King John* 448).
5. Symonds, 299 (quoted in Furness, ed. *King John* 465).
6. E. B. Everitt, "Young Shakespeare"; Eric Sams, "Troublesome Wrangle" and *The Real Shakespeare* 146–55.
7. Cairncross, *Hamlet* 136–43; P. Alexander, *Shakespeare's Life and Art* 85.
8. An extended discussion of the issue of priority can be found in Sider's edition at xx–xliii.
9. Sider at xliv–xlv. For Grafton as a source, see Forker's introduction to his edition of the play at 101, n. 64.
10. J. D. Wilson, ed. *King John* xxxiv; A. and J. Nicoll 1; R. A. Law, "On the Date of *King John*" 125; Mincoff 52.
11. References to and quotations from the two parts of *Troublesome Reign* (abbreviated *1 TR* and *2 TR*), including stage directions and emphases, are from Bullough's original-spelling text (*Narrative* v. 4.)
12. Quotations from Shakespeare are from *The Riverside Shakespeare*, ed. G. Blakemore Evans. 2nd ed. 1997.
13. Several other historical bastards who may have contributed to Philip's character and circumstances are listed by J. D. Wilson in his edition of *King John* at xxxviii–xli.

14. For more on Oxford's distaste for Essex, see "The Prince Hal Plays and Edward de Vere" in Chapter I.
15. John Dover Wilson lists nearly a dozen "points" in *King John* that are "quite unintelligible" without reference to *Troublesome Reign* (ed. *King John* xxi–xxvi).
16. In this connection, it is noteworthy that all the versions of *King John* brought to the stage up to the retirement of John Kemble in 1817 included passages from *Troublesome Reign* as a way of clarifying the action (Sprague 25). Also, Harold Child, in J. D. Wilson, ed. *King John* lxviii.
17. Unfortunately, Forker was convinced that the author of *Troublesome Reign* was George Peele. See "A Mistaken Ascription to George Peele."
18. The amount of the dowry was actually "20,000 silver marks" (Gies 98) and the marriage "took place at the castle and the church of St Martin in the district of Château-Neuf in Pontmort" (http://www.portmort.com/blanchedecastille.htm#).
19. McMillin and MacLean xv, 160–1. The three others are *King Leir*, *The Famous Victories of Henry the Fifth*, and *The True Tragedy of Richard the Third*.
20. Wells 218–19. *Edward III* was included in the 2nd edition of *The Riverside Shakespeare* in 1997 and in the New Cambridge series in 1998.
21. According to the Chadwyck-Healey database, *English Drama*, this parallel is "unique in plays written before 1642" (Forker, "Intertextuality" 135).
22. This is another parallel that is "unique in plays written before 1642" (Forker, "Intertextuality" 135).
23. Forker cites two more uses of the rare verb *unsay*, of just four in the canon ("Intertextuality" 130).
24. Spurgeon 13; "indoor life" 43; 112ff.
25. Spurgeon 90–1; The twelve additional dramatists Spurgeon studied were Marlowe, Kyd, Lyly, Greene, Peele, Dekker, Jonson, Heywood, Chapman, Beaumont, Fletcher and Massinger (362–3).
26. Donawerth, 141, 161. Also, Eric Sams, *Shakespeare's Edmund Ironside*, 334.
27. Hart, "Vocabularies of Shakespeare's Plays" and "The Growth of Shakespeare's Vocabulary."
28. Hart, "Growth" 249. Hart also counted

2976 different words in *Edward III* (*Shakespeare and the Homilies* 220.)

29. Honigmann, "Self-Repetitions" 183. The emphasis is Honigmann's.

30. Findlay, App. 253–5. Findlay excluded from her analysis plays dealing with "bastard baby situations."

31. The titles were extracted from Chambers, *The Elizabethan Stage*, v. 4 by S. Schoenbaum, and are listed in his *Internal Evidence, etc.*, at xvii–xviii. *Clyomon and Clamydes* was edited by Betty L. Littleton in 1968. *Alphonsus, Emperor of Germany* was edited by Herbert F. Schwarz in 1913 and attributed to George Chapman, an attribution that has found little acceptance.

32. Quotations from *David and Bethsabe* are from Horne's ed. of v. 1 of Peele's *Dramatic Works*.

33. Quotations from *The Arraignment of Paris* are from Benbow's edition of v. 3 of Peele's *Dramatic Works*.

34. Vickers added that the phrase "Their wither'd flower" is from the second edition (1604) of *The Tale of Troy* (81).

35. Quotations from *Edward I* are from Hook's edition of v. 2 of Peele's *Dramatic Works*.

36. These figures obtained from Timberlake at 121.

37. Chambers, *William Shakespeare* 2:400. Timberlake records a percentage of 5.5 percent in *Edward III* (77).

38. In an official expurgation of the Second Folio made in Spain c. 1650, so it could be used in the English College at Valladolid, twenty-two lines or parts of lines were cut from King John's tirade against the Catholic establishment. Excisions, mostly of anti-Catholic material, were made in at least ten other plays; also deleted was the entire text of *Measure for Measure* (Frye 275–93).

39. Egan must be credited, however, with proving Shakespeare's authorship of another anonymous Elizabethan history play—*Thomas of Woodstock*, which he calls *1 Richard II*. His exceptional work, *The Tragedy of Richard II, Part One: A Newly Authenticated Play by Shakespeare*, presents a totally convincing case.

40. G. E. Bentley discusses methods of collaboration in *The Profession of Dramatist* at pp. 227–34.

41. Anderson 24, 437. The only surviving document, a response to the claim by Edward's uncle Arthur Golding, can be seen at http://www.oxford-shakespeare.com/ StatePapers12/SP_12-29-8_ff_11-12.pdf. An extended description of the episode appears in Golding at pp. 37–46.

42. The complete poem is printed in Looney, *'Shakespeare' Identified* 1:580–1 and in Chiljan, *Letters and Poems* 162. See also Hyder E. Rollins, ed. *Paradyse*.

## Chapter IV

1. Harington owned a copy of *A Shrew*, and fifteen other quartos of Shakespeare plays. See Furnivall, "Sir John Harington's Shakespeare Quartos."

2. The rhyme with "bestow" accords with the pronunciation called for in both the anonymous *Shrew* (3.154; 15.16) and the canonical *Shrew* (V.ii.28–9; V.ii.188–9).

3. In *The Real Shakespeare*, Eric Sams makes the most compelling case on record for Shakespeare's authorship of *A Shrew* (136–45). But he assigns it to William Shakspeare of Stratford, and dates it to 1588.

4. Stage directions are similarly varied and elaborate in *A Shrew*.

5. Aside from Brunvand's own book, and his earlier article in *Shakespeare Quarterly*, useful discussions of his findings are in Hodgdon's edition of *The Shrew* (44–5) and in Miller's edition of *A Shrew* (12–16).

6. Gascoigne's mask for the two children of Anthony Browne, first Viscount Montague, was published in *A Hundreth Sundrie Flowres* in 1573 (Prior 444–49).

7. Quotations from *A Shrew* are from Miller's edition.

8. B. M. Ward claims that Gascoigne and Oxford were well-acquainted by 1566, but his evidence is flimsy (*Hundreth* 36–9). In 1561, Gascoigne married Elizabeth, daughter of John Bacon (1521?–1559), cousin of Sir Nicholas Bacon (1509–1579). In 1553, Sir Nicholas had married Anne Cooke, sister of Mildred, William Cecil's second wife (Palmer 8). It appears that in 1576 Gascoigne performed diplomatic services for Cecil (Ward, *Hundreth* 25, 55).

9. Looney was also the first to connect the names of the two Italian men with the

name of Katherina's father ('*Shakespeare' Identified* 1:226-7).

10. Further details of Burby's acquaintance with Munday are included in Julia C. Wright's article.

11. The subject is treated more completely in Pointon at 146-8.

12. Barrell's article, "'Shake-speare's,' Unknown Home," contains the details of Oxford's connections to the area, and a map showing Bilton and Bourton.

## Chapter V

1. In succeeding entries on the same page of his Diary, Henslowe mentions the production in the following June of three other plays whose titles also suggest Shakespeare plays, viz. *andronicous, hamlet* and *the tamynge of A shrowe* (21-2).

2. Wright was subsequently one of the booksellers of *Shake-speare's Sonnets* in 1609.

3. The Quartos are *Richard III,* Q2, Q4-Q8; *Richard II,* Q2-Q5; *1 Henry IV,* Q2-Q9; *Hamlet,* Q1; *King Lear,* Q1, Q2 and Q3 (1655). Most of the title page wording can be found in Chambers, *William Shakespeare,* v.1; all of it in Bartlett. See also Steinburg at 395.

4. Cordell and the middle sister Grace were Maids of Honor to the Queen.

5. A more recent proponent of this theory was A. L. Rowse in *Shakespeare's Southampton* (199-200).

6. The Lear story appears in Book II of the *Historia,* pp. 36-44 in Reeves' edition.

7. *Narrative* 7:277. The anonymous *A Knack to Know a Knave* has been edited by G. R. Proudfoot.

8. The pun on the surname Blount is repeated in Thomas Thorpe's dedication of Marlowe's translation of the first book of Lucan (1600) to his friend Edward Blount: "Blount, I purpose to be blunt with you."

9. The edition of *King Lear* cited is *The Riverside Shakespeare,* 2nd ed., a conflated text based on the Folio. Material appearing only in the Quarto is included, within brackets. Small variations among the texts are described in the Textual Notes (1345-1354).

10. A. S. Cairncross, in *The Problem of Hamlet* (136) and Peter Alexander, in *Shakespeare* (171), are the only prominent scholars

who place the composition of *King Lear* before that of the anonymous *King Leir.*

11. Muir (ed. *King Lear* xxix) and Weis (68) suggest that Shakespeare had performed in the play, most likely the part of Perillus.

12. An expanded list of verbal similarities between *Lear* and *Arcadia* can be found in the Muir and Danby article, and in Hardin Craig, "Motivation" (32-3). Both versions of *Arcadia* are included in Kimbrough's and Duncan-Jones's editions of Sidney's works.

13. In this instance, Brittany is a variant form of Britain.

14. Quotations from *King Leir* are based on Sidney Lee's edition.

15. In the Quarto, Lear answers his own question, at I.iv.218-19.

16. Quotations from *Troublesome Reign* are based on Bullough's text in *Narrative and Dramatic Sources,* vol. 4.

17. Some scholars find "hidden sexual significance" in Cordelia's "nothings." See David Willbern's "Shakespeare's Nothing."

18. The verse is identical in the Geneva Bible of 1560 and in the King James Version.

19. Michie (26-34) and Greg ("Date" 386-97) list several dozen between them. A summary of Shakespeare's "reshaping" of *King Leir* can be seen in Peter Pauls' article.

20. "At a conservative estimate, 111 letters appear on stage in the course of Shakespeare's plays..." (Stewart 4). There are more in *King Lear* than in any other.

21. "*Much Ado About Nothing* and *King Leir.*"

22. These are listed by Law ("Richard" 130-1) and expanded by Sams in *The Real Shakespeare II* (279-80).

23. *Shakespeare's Edward III, An early play restored to the canon* (1996).

24. "Shakespeare and *King Leir.*"

25. Quotations from *Edmund Ironside* are based on Eric Sams' edition of the play.

26. John Manningham recorded the couplet in his *Diary* (182). The background and reasoning behind the allusion is explained in the Warren Hope article.

27. Jiménez, "Oxford's Fifty-Play Canon" 12.

28. Much of the evidence is covered in Part 1 of Brownlow (21-164). See also G. Bowen and pp. 235-43 in v. 2 of Looney's

"'*Shakespeare' Identified*," in which part of Bowen's essay is reprinted.

29. The texts of *Arden of Faversham* and *Locrine* are in included in the collections of apocrypha edited by Kozlenko and C. F. T. Brooke.

30. The titles are listed in the first note in Chapter II. Moreover, in the collection of apocryphal plays edited by Jonathan Bate, et al., these five plays are not only excluded, they are not even mentioned in the section titled "Plays Excluded from This Edition" (724–9).

# Bibliography

The Oxfordian, The Shakespeare Oxford Newsletter, Brief Chronicles and Shakespeare Matters can be accessed at https://shakespeareoxfordfellowship.org/ The Oxford English Dictionary (OED) and The Oxford Dictionary of National Biography (ODNB) are available online through subscribing libraries. Articles by Charles Wisner Barrell and Gwynneth Bowen can be accessed at http://www.sourcetext.com/sourcebook/index.htm

Acheson, Arthur. Shakespeare, Chapman and Sir Thomas More. London: Bernard Quaritch, 1931.

Adams, Barry B., ed. John Bale's King Johan. San Marino, California: The Huntington Library, 1969.

Adams, Joseph Quincy. Shakespearean Playhouses: A History of English Theatres from the Beginnings to the Restoration. London: Houghton Mifflin, 1917.

Akrigg, George P.V. Shakespeare and the Earl of Southampton. London: Hamish Hamilton, 1968.

Albright, Evelyn M. "The Folio Version of Henry V in Relation to Shakespeare's Times." PMLA. v. 43, no. 3 (1928) pp. 722–56.

Alexander, Mark Andre. "Shakespeare's Knowledge of Law: A Journey through the History of the Argument." The Oxfordian. v. 4 (2001) pp. 51–120.

Alexander, Peter. Shakespeare. London. Oxford University Press, 1964.

_____. Shakespeare's Life and Art. London: James Nisbet, 1939.

_____. "The Taming of a Shrew." TLS. (16 September 1926) p. 614.

Allen, Percy. The Life Story of Edward de Vere as "William Shakespeare. London: C.

Palmer, 1932. Allen, Don Cameron. The Star-crossed Renaissance: The Quarrel About Astrology. Durham, NC: Duke University Press, 1941.

Altschuler, Eric. "Searching for Shakespeare in the Stars." 23 October 1998. https://archive.org/details/arxiv-physics9810 042 [accessed 10 September 2017].

Anderson, Mark K. "Shakespeare." by another Name, The Life of Edward de Vere, Earl of Oxford, the Man Who Was Shakespeare. New York: Gotham Books, 2005.

Arber, Edward, ed. An English Garner. 8 v. London: Arber, 1877–96.

_____, ed. A Transcript of the Registers of the Company of Stationers of London: 1554–1640, A.D. 5 v. Birmingham: Privately printed, 1875–77.

Armstrong, Edward A. Shakespeare's Imagination. (1946) Lincoln: University of Nebraska Press, 1963 ed.

Ascham, Roger. The Schoolmaster. (1570) Lawrence V. Ryan, ed. Ithaca, NY: Cornell University Press, 1967.

Astington, John H. "Inigo Jones and the Whitehall Cockpit." The Elizabethan Theatre. VII G.R. Hibbard, ed. 1980. pp. 46–64.

_____. "The Whitehall Cockpit: The Building and the Theatre." *English Literary Renaissance.* v. 12:3 (Sept. 1982) pp. 301–18.

Auden, W.H., ed. *19th Century British Minor Poets.* New York: Delacorte, 1966.

Ayala, Roselyne de, and Jean-Pierre Guéno. *Brilliant Beginnings: The Youthful Works of Great Artists, Writers, and Composers.* John Goodman, tr. New York: Harry N. Abrams, 2000.

Bacon, Francis. *The Letters and the Life of Francis Bacon: Including All His Occasional Works.* James Spedding, ed. London: Longmans, Green, Reader, and Dyer, 1868.

Bagwell, Richard. *Ireland Under the Tudors.* 3 v. London: Longmans, Green & Co., 1909–16.

Baker, George. *Oleum magistrale.* (1574) Amsterdam: Theatrum Orbis Terrarum, Da Capo Press, 1969.

Baldwin, T.W. *On the Literary Genetics of Shakespeare's Plays 1592–94.* Urbana: University of Illinois Press, 1959.

Bale, John. *Select Works of John Bale.* (1849) Henry Christmas, ed. New York: Johnson reprint, 1968.

Barrell, Charles W. "Shakespeare's 'Fluellen' Identified As a Retainer of the Earl of Oxford." *The Shakespeare Fellowship News-Letter (American).* v. 2:5 (August 1941) pp. 59–63.

_____. "Shakespeare's *Henry V* Can Be Identified as Harry of Cornwall in Henslowe's Diary." *Shakespeare Fellowship Quarterly (American).* v. VII, no. 4 (October 1946) pp. 49–54.

_____. "'Shake-speare's' Unknown Home on the River Avon Discovered." *Newsletter of the Shakespeare Fellowship.* v. 4:1 (Dec. 1942) pp. 1–8. Reprinted in Looney, "*Shakespeare*" *Identified* 2:355–69.

Bartlett, Henrietta C. *Mr. William Shakespeare, Original and Early Editions of his Quartos and Folios.* New Haven: Yale University Press, 1922.

Bate, Jonathan. *Soul of the Age: The Life, Mind and World of William Shakespeare.* New York: Viking, 2008.

_____, and Eric Rasmussen, with Jan Sewell and Will Sharpe, eds. *William Shakespeare & Others, Collaborative Plays.* Basingstoke, Hampshire: Palgrave Macmillan, 2013.

Beaurline, L.A., ed. *King John.* Cambridge: Cambridge University Press, 1990.

Beckerman, Bernard. *Shakespeare at the Globe.* New York: Macmillan, 1962.

Benbow, R. Mark, ed. *The Dramatic Works of George Peele.* v. 3. *The Arraignment of Paris.* New Haven: Yale University Press, 1961.

Bennett, Josephine Waters. "Oxford and Endimion." *PMLA.* v. 57 (June 1942) pp. 354–69.

Bentley, Gerald E. *The Profession of Dramatist in Shakespeare's Time, 1590–1642.* Princeton: Princeton University Press, 1971.

Berek, Peter. "Tamburlaine's Weak Sons: Imitation as Interpretation Before 1593." *Renaissance Drama.* v. 13 (1982) pp. 55–82.

Berney, Charles V. "*Cymbeline*: the Hidden History Play." *The Shakespeare Oxford Newsletter.* v. 51:4 (Fall 2015) pp. 18–21.

Bevington, David. *Tudor Drama and Politics.* Cambridge: Harvard University Press, 1968.

_____, ed. *Henry IV, Part 1.* (1987) Oxford: Oxford University Press, 1994 ed.

_____, ed. *Richard III.* New York: Bantam, 1988.

_____, ed. *The Spanish Tragedy.* Manchester: Manchester University Press, 1996.

_____, and Jay L. Halio, eds. *Shakespeare: Pattern of Excelling Nature.* Newark: University of Delaware Press, 1978.

Bloom Harold. *Shakespeare, The Invention of the Human.* London: Fourth Estate, 1999.

Boas, Frederick A. "The Play within the Play." *A Series of Papers on Shakespeare and the Theatre.* London: Oxford University Press, 1927. pp. 134–56.

_____. *Shakespeare and the Universities.* Oxford: Basil Blackwell, 1923.

_____, ed. *The Taming of a Shrew.* London: Chatto and Windus, 1908.

Bond, R.W., ed. *Complete Works of John Lyly.* 3 v. Oxford: The Clarendon Press, 1902.

_____, ed. *The Taming of the Shrew.* (1904) London: Methuen, 2nd ed. 1929.

Boswell-Stone, W.G. *Shakespeare's Holinshed.* 2nd ed. 1907. New York: Dover Publications, 1968.

Bourne, Henry R.F. *Sir Philip Sidney: Type of English Chivalry in the Elizabethan Age.* New York: G.P. Putnam's Sons, 1891.

Bowen, Gwynneth M. "Hackney, Harsnett and the Devils in King Lear." *Shake-*

spearean Authorship Review. #14 (Autumn 1965) pp. 2–7. Reprinted in Looney, 'Shakespeare' Identified. 1975 ed. 2:237–43.

Bowsher, Julian. Shakespeare's London Theatreland, Archaeology, History and Drama. London: Museum of London Archaeology, 2012.

Boyd, Brian, ed. Words that Count. Newark: University of Delaware Press, 2004.

Brandes, Georg. William Shakespeare. (1898) New York: Macmillan, 1935 ed.

Braunmuller, A.R., ed. The Life and Death of King John. Oxford: Oxford University Press, 1989.

Brazil, Robert. "Unpacking The Merry Wives." The Oxfordian. v. 2 (1999) pp. 117–37.

Brockbank, Philip. "Shakespeare: His Histories, English and Roman." English Drama to 1710. Christopher Ricks, ed. pp. 148–81.

Bronson, Bertrand H., ed. with Jean M. O'Meara. Selections from Johnson on Shakespeare. New Haven: Yale University Press, 1986.

Brook, G.L. The Language of Shakespeare. London: Andre Deutsch, 1976.

Brooke, Arthur. Brooke's Romeus and Juliet. J.J. Munro, ed. London: Chatto & Windus, 1908.

Brooke, C.F. Tucker. The Shakespeare Apocrypha. Oxford: Clarendon Press, 1908.

Brown, Barbara. "Sir Thomas More and Thomas Churchyard's Shore's Wife." Yearbook of English Studies. v. 2 (1972) pp. 41–8.

Brown, C. Armitage. Shakespeare's Autobiographical Poems. London: James Bohn, 1838.

Brownlow, Frank W. Shakespeare, Harsnett, and the Devils of Denham. Newark, DE: University of Delaware Press, 1993.

Brunvand, Jan Harold. "The Folktale Origin of The Taming of the Shrew." Shakespeare Quarterly. v. 17 (1966) pp. 345–59.

_____. The Taming of the Shrew, A Comparative Study of Oral and Literary Versions. New York: Garland, 1991.

Bruster, Douglas. "Shakespeare the Stationer." Shakespeare's Stationers: Studies in Cultural Bibliography. Marta Straznicky, ed. Philadelphia: University of Pennsylvania Press, 2013. pp. 112–31.

Bullough, Geoffrey. "King Lear and the An-

nesley Case: A Reconsideration." Festschrift Rudolf Stamm. Eduard Kolb and Jorg Hasler, eds. München: Francke, 1969. pp. 43–9.

_____. Narrative and Dramatic Sources of Shakespeare. 6 v. New York: Columbia University Press, 1957–75.

Bulman, James C., ed. King Henry IV, Part 2. Arden 3rd ser. London: Bloomsbury, 2016.

Burns, Edward, ed. King Henry VI, Part 1. Arden 3rd ser. London: Thomson Learning, 2000.

Cairncross, Andrew S. The Problem of Hamlet: A Solution. London: Macmillan, 1936.

_____. ed. King Henry VI, Part I. Arden 2nd ser. London: Methuen, 1962.

Camden, William. Annales. (1615) Dana F. Sutton, trans. 2001. http://www.philological.bham.ac.uk/camden/ [accessed 15 December 2015].

Campbell, Lily B. Shakespeare's Tragic Heroes, Slaves of Passion. Cambridge: Cambridge University Press, 1952.

_____, ed. The Mirror for Magistrates. (1559) Cambridge: Cambridge University Press, 1938.

Campbell, O.J., and Edward G. Quinn, eds. The Reader's Encyclopedia of Shakespeare. New York: MJF Books, 1966.

Capell, Edward. Mr. William Shakespeare's Comedies, Histories and Tragedies. London: J. and R. Tonson, 1767–68.

Capp, Bernard. "Harvey, Richard (bap. 1560, d. 1630)." ODNB. Oxford University Press, 2004.

Cardano, Girolamo. Cardanus Comforte. (1576) Facsimile. New York: Da Capo Press, 1969.

Carte, Thomas. The Life of James, Duke of Ormond. 6 v. Oxford: Oxford University Press, new ed. 1851.

Castiglione, Baldasar. The Book of the Courtier. (1528) Leonard E. Opdyke, ed. Wordsworth Editions: Ware, Hants., 2000.

Chambers, Edmund K. The Elizabethan Stage. 4 v. Oxford: Clarendon Press, 1923.

_____. The Mediaeval Stage. 2 v. London: Oxford University Press, 1903.

_____. William Shakespeare. A Study of Facts and Problems. 2 v. Oxford: Clarendon Press, 1930.

Champion, Larry S. "Shakespeare's Source for 2 Henry IV, II, i." American Notes and Queries. v. 5, no. 5 (Jan. 1967) pp. 69–70.

Charlton, Derran. "*Doctor Faustus, Tamburlaine* and *The Taming of the Shrew.*" *The Oxfordian.* v. 12 (2010) pp. 108–118.

Charlton, H.B. *Shakespearian Tragedy.* Cambridge: Cambridge University Press, 1948.

Cheyney, E.P. *Readings in English History Drawn from the Original Sources.* (1908) Boston: Ginn & Co., 1922.

Chiljan, Katherine. "Oxford and *Palamon and Arcite.*" *The Shakespeare Oxford Newsletter.* v. 35:1 (Spring 1999) pp.10–13.

_____, ed. *Book Dedications to the Earl of Oxford.* San Francisco, 1994.

_____, ed. *Letters and Poems of Edward, Earl of Oxford.* San Francisco, 1998.

Churchill, George B. *Richard the Third Up to Shakespeare.* Berlin: Mayer and Muller, 1900.

Churchyard, Thomas. *A Critical Edition of Churchyard's Challenge* (1593) Charles A. Rahter, ed. Diss. Philadelphia: University of Pennsylvania, 1958.

_____. *The First Part of Churchyard's Chips.* (1575) Facsimile. Menston, Yorkshire: Scolar Press, 1973.

_____. *A Scourge for Rebels.* London: Thomas Cadman, 1584.

Cicero, Marcus Tullius. *Cicero's Letters to Atticus.* Harmondsworth: Penguin Books, 1978.

Cioni, Fernando. "*A Shrew* and *The Shrew*: Shakespeare, Plautus and the 'Bad Quarto.'" *Textus.* v. 11 (1998) pp. 235–60.

Clare, Janet. "Medley History: *The Famous Victories of Henry the Fifth* to *Henry V.*" *Shakespeare Survey.* v. 63 (2010) pp. 102–113.

Clark, Eva Turner. *Hidden Allusions in Shakespeare's Plays.* (1931) Ruth L. Miller, ed. Port Washington, NY: Kennikat Press, 3rd ed. 1974.

Clemen, Wolfgang. *English Tragedy Before Shakespeare.* T.S. Dorsch, tr. London: Methuen, 1961.

Clough, Wilson O. "The Broken English of Foreign Characters of the Elizabethan Stage." *Philological Quarterly.* v. 12 (1933) pp. 255–68.

Cochiarra, Giuseppe. *La Leggenda di re Lear. Studi di etnologia e folklore.* v. 1. Torino: Fratelli Bocca, 1932.

Coggeshall, Ralph of. *Radulphi de Coggeshall Chronicon anglicanum.* (1875) Joseph

Stevenson, ed. Wiesbaden: Kraus reprint, 1965.

Colie, Rosalie L. and F.T. Flahiff, eds. *Some Facets of 'King Lear': Essays in Prismatic Criticism.* Toronto: University of Toronto Press, 1974.

Collier, John, ed. *The Complete Works of William Shakespeare.* New York: Cooledge, c. 1855.

Collins, Arthur, ed. *Letters and Memorials of State in the Reigns of Queen Mary, Queen Elizabeth, King James,* etc. (1746) 2 v. New York: AMS reprint, 1973.

Colthorpe, Marion E. "The Elizabethan Court Day by Day." Folgerpedia. Folger Shakespeare Library. https://folgerpedia. folger.edu/The_Elizabethan_Court_ Day_by_Day (accessed September 26, 2017).

Corbin, Peter, and Douglas Sedge, eds. *The Oldcastle Controversy.* Manchester: Manchester University Press, 1991.

Courthope, W.J. *A History of English Poetry.* 6 v. New York: Macmillan, 1904–11.

Craig, Hardin. "Hamlet's Book." *Huntington Library Bulletin.* v. 6 (November 1934) pp. 17–37.

_____. "Motivation in Shakespeare's Choice of Materials." *Shakespeare Survey.* v. 4 (1951) pp. 32–3.

Craig, Hugh. Review of *Words that Count,* Brian Boyd, ed. *Shakespeare Quarterly.* v. 56:4 (2005) pp. 496–498.

Craig, W.J. *The Comedies of Shakespeare.* London: Oxford University Press, 1911.

Craik, T.W., ed. *King Henry V.* Arden 3rd ser. London: Routledge, 1995.

Creizenach, Wilhelm. *The English Drama in the Age of Shakespeare.* New York: Russell & Russell, 1916.

Crundell, H.W. "Anthony Munday and 'King Leir.'" *Notes and Queries.* v. 166 (May 5, 1934) pp. 310–11.

Crystal, David, and Ben Crystal. *Shakespeare's Words.* London: Penguin, 2002.

Curren-Aquino, Deborah. "Self-Naming in Shakespeare's Early Plays." *Names.* v. 35 (September–December 1987) pp. 147–63.

Daniel, P.A. "Introduction" to *The Famous Victories of Henry the Fifth.* Charles Praetorius, ed. London, 1887. http://babel. hathitrust.org/cgi/pt?id=hvd.32044 014365993;view=1up;seq=1 (accessed September 10, 2017).

Daniel, Samuel. *The Civil Wars.* (1595;1609) Laurence Michel, ed. New Haven: Yale University Press, 1958.

Davies, John. *The Complete Works of John Davies of Hereford.* 2 v. A.B. Grosart, ed. Edinburgh: T. and A. Constable, 1878.

Davis, Frank M. "Shakespeare's Medical Knowledge: How Did He Acquire It?" *The Oxfordian.* v. 3 (2000) pp. 45–58.

Davis, Herbert, and Helen Gardner, eds. *Elizabethan and Jacobean Studies Presented to Frank Percy Wilson.* Oxford: Oxford University Press, 1959.

Davison, Peter, ed. *The First Quarto of King Richard III.* New York: Cambridge University Press, 1996.

Deese, Helen R. "Two Unpublished Emerson Letters: To George P. Putnam on Delia Bacon and to George B. Loring." *Essex Institute Historical Collections.* v. 122:2 (April 1986) pp. 101–125.

Delahoyde, Michael. "Subliminal Chaucer in Shakespeare's History Plays." *The Oxfordian.* v. 17 (2015) pp. 153–62.

Desper, Richard. "'Stars or Suns': The Portraits of the Earls of Oxford in Elizabethan Drama." *Shakespeare Matters.* v. 5:4 (Summer 2006) pp. 1, 25–30.

*Dictionary of National Biography.* 63 v. Leslie Stephen, ed. London: Smith, Elder, and Co., 1885–1900.

"Dig at Theater Where Shakespeare Worked Uncovers a Surprise." Associated Press. May 21, 2016. http://www.sfgate.com/entertainment/article/Dig-at-theater-where-Shakespeare-worked-uncovers-7929431.php [accessed 12 September 2017].

Donawerth, Jane. *Shakespeare and The Sixteenth-Century Study of Language.* Urbana: University of Illinois Press, 1984.

Doran, Madeline. "Elements in the Composition of *King Lear.*" *Studies in Philology.* v. 30 (1933) pp. 34–58.

Dorsten, Jan van. "Literary Patronage in Elizabethan England: The Early Phase." *Patronage in the Renaissance.* Guy F. Lytle and Stephen Orgel, eds. 1981. pp. 191–206.

Dowden, Edward. Introduction to *The Merry Wives of Windsor. The Comedies of Shakespeare.* W.J. Craig, ed.

Draper, John W. "Shakespeare and Florence and the Florentines." *Italica.* v. 23:4 (1946) pp. 287–93.

Drayton, Michael, Anthony Munday, Richard Hathaway and Robert Wilson. *The Life of Sir John Oldcastle.* (1600) Percy Simpson, ed. Oxford: Malone Society reprint, 1908.

du Bartas, Guillaume de Salluste, Sieur. *The Works of Guillaume de Salluste Sieur du Bartas. A critical edition.* Urban Tigner Holmes, Jr., John Coriden Lyons and Robert White Linker, eds. 3 v. Chapel Hill: University of North Carolina Press, 1935–1940.

Duncan-Jones, Katherine. "Liquid Prisoners: Shakespeare's Re-writings of Sidney." *Sidney Journal.* v. 15:2 (Fall 1997) pp. 3–21.

_____. *Sir Philip Sidney, Courtier Poet.* New Haven: Yale University Press, 1991.

_____. *Ungentle Shakespeare.* London: Thomson Learning, 2001.

Duthie, G.I. "*The Taming of a Shrew* and *The Taming of the Shrew.*" *The Review of English Studies.* v. 19 (October 1943) pp. 337–56.

Dutton, Richard. "*The Famous Victories* and the 1600 Quarto of *Henry V.*" *Locating the Queen's Men, 1583–1603.* H. Ostovich, H.S. Syme, and A. Griffin, eds. 2009. pp. 135–44.

_____. "'Methinks the Truth Should Live from Age to Age': The Dating and Contexts of Henry V." *Huntington Library Quarterly.* v. 68 (2005) pp. 173–204.

Eccles, Mark. "Elizabethan Actors IV: S to End." *Notes and Queries.* v. 40:2 (June 1993) pp. 165–76.

Edelman, Charles. *Brawl Ridiculous, Swordfighting in Shakespeare's Plays.* Manchester: Manchester University Press, 1992.

_____. *Shakespeare's Military Language: A Dictionary.* London: Athlone Press, 2000.

Edwards, David. "Butler, Thomas, tenth earl of Ormond and third earl of Ossory (1531–1614)." *ODNB.* Oxford University Press, 2004.

_____. *The Ormond Lordship in County Kilkenny 1515–1642: The Rise and Fall of Butler Feudal Power.* Dublin: Four Courts Press, 2003.

Edwards, Richard, ed. *The Paradyse of Dainty Devices.* (1576) Hyder Rollins, ed. Cambridge: Harvard University Press, 1927.

_____. *Richard Edwards' Damon and Pithias: a critical old-spelling edition.* D. Jerry White. ed. New York: Garland, 1980.

Edwards, Thomas. *Cephalus and Procris.*

*Narcissus.* (1595) W.E. Buckley, ed. London: Nichols and Sons, 1882.

Egan, Gabriel. "The 1599 Globe and its modern replica: Virtual Reality modelling of the archaeological and pictorial evidence." *Early Modern Literary Studies.* Special Issue. v. 13:5 (2004) pp. 1–22. http://purl.oclc.org/emls/si-13/egan [accessed September 11, 2017].

Egan, Michael. "King John." *The Greenwood Companion to Shakespeare.* v. 1 *Overviews and the history plays.* Joseph Rosenblum, ed. pp. 156–89.

_____, ed. *The Tragedy of Richard II, Part One: A Newly Authenticated Play by Shakespeare.* 3 v. Lewiston, ME: Edwin Mellen Press, 2005.

Elson, John. "Studies in the King John Plays." *Joseph Quincy Adams Memorial Studies.* James G. McManaway, et al., eds. pp. 183–97.

Elton, William R. *King Lear and the Gods.* San Marino, CA: Huntington Library, 1966.

Elyot, Sir Thomas. *The Book Named the Governor.* (1531). New York: Dutton, 1962.

Elze, Karl. *Essays on Shakespeare.* London: Macmillan & Co., 1874.

Emerson, R.W. *Emerson's Poetry and Prose.* Joel Porte and Saundra Morris, eds. New York: W.W. Norton, 2001.

Erasmus, Desiderius. *Collected Works of Erasmus.* Craig R. Thompson, tr. v. 39 "Colloquies." Toronto: University of Toronto Press, 1997.

Erne, Lukas. *Shakespeare as Literary Dramatist.* (2003) Cambridge: Cambridge University Press, 2nd ed. 2013.

Evans, G. Blakemore, et al., eds. *The Riverside Shakespeare.* Boston: Houghton Mifflin, 2nd ed. 1997.

Everitt, Ephraim B. "Six Early Plays Related to the Shakespeare Canon." *Anglistica.* XIV, 1965.

_____. "The Young Shakespeare: Studies in Documentary Evidence." *Anglistica.* II, 1954.

Fabyan, Robert. *The New Chronicles of England and France, in two parts.* (1513) London: F.C. & J. Rivington, 1811.

Falconer, A.F. *A Glossary of Shakespeare's Sea and Naval Terms Including Gunnery.* London: Constable, 1965.

Falls, Cyril B. *Elizabeth's Irish Wars.* London: Methuen, 1950.

Farina, William. *De Vere as Shakespeare: An Oxfordian Reading of the Canon.* Jefferson, NC: McFarland, 2006.

Farmer, John. *Divers and Sundry Waies of Two Parts in One, to the Number of Fortie, uppon One Playn Song.* London: Este, 1591.

_____. *The First Set of English Madrigals to Four Voices.* (1599) Cambridge: Chadwyck-Healey, 1992.

Farmer, John Stephen. *The True Chronicle History of King Leir.* (1605) London: Tudor Facsimile Texts, 1910. AMS Press reprint, 1970.

Fay, Edwin C. "Further Notes on the Mostellaria of Plautus." *American Journal of Philology.* v. 24:3 (1903) pp. 245–77.

Feldman, A. Bronson. "Othello in Reality." *American Imago.* v. 11:1 (Spring 1954) pp. 147–79.

Feuillerat, Albert. *The Composition of Shakespeare's Plays.* New Haven: Yale University Press, 1953.

Fiehler, Rudolph. "How Oldcastle Became Falstaff." *MLQ.* v. 16 (1955) pp. 16–28.

Field, Barron, ed. *The True Tragedy of Richard the Third; to which is appended the Latin play of Richardus Tertius.* London: The Shakespeare Society, 1844.

Findlay, Alison. *Illegitimate power: bastards in Renaissance drama.* Manchester: Manchester University Press, 1994.

Fleay, F.G. *A Biographical Chronicle of the English Drama, 1559–1642.* 2 v. (1891) New York: B. Franklin, 1969 ed.

_____. *Shakespeare Manual.* London: Macmillan & Co., 1876.

Foakes, R.A., ed. *King Lear.* Arden 3rd Ser. London: Thomson Learning, 1997.

Forker, Charles R. "*The Troublesome Reign, Richard II,* and the Date of *King John*: A Study in Intertextuality." *Shakespeare Survey.* v. 63 (2010) pp. 127–48.

_____, ed. *The Troublesome Raigne of John, King of England.* Manchester: Manchester University Press, 2011.

Fowler, William Plumer. *Shakespeare Revealed in Oxford's Letters.* Portsmouth, NH: W.P. Fowler, 1986.

Foxe, John. *The Acts and Monuments of John Foxe.* (1563) 8 v. George Townsend, ed. New York: AMS Press reprint, 1965.

Fraunce, Abraham. *Hymenæus: A comedy acted at St. John's College, Cambridge.* G.C.

Moore Smith, ed. Cambridge: Cambridge University Press, 1908.

Freeman, Thomas S. "Foxe, John (1516/17–1587)." *ODNB*. Oxford University Press, 2004.

Frey, Albert R., ed. *The Taming of the Shrew: The Players Text of "The Taming of a Shrew of 1594."* The Bankside Shakespeare. v. 2. New York: The Shakespeare Society of New York, 1888.

Frye, Roland M. *Shakespeare and Christian Doctrine.* Princeton: Princeton University Press, 1963.

Furness, Horace H., ed. *King John.* Philadelphia: J.B. Lippincott, 1919.

_____, ed. *King Lear.* (1880) New York: Dover, 1963 ed.

_____, ed. *The Merchant of Venice.* Philadelphia: J.B. Lippincott, 1888.

_____, ed. *The Tragedy of Richard the Third: with the Landing of Earle Richmond, and the Battell at Bosworth.* Philadelphia: J.B. Lippincott, 1909.

Furnivall, F.J. "Sir John Harington's Shakespeare Quartos." *Notes and Queries.* ser.7 v. ix (May 17, 1890) pp. 382–3.

_____, and John Munro, eds. *The Troublesome Reign of King John, being the original of Shakespeare's "Life and death of King John."* London: Chatto and Windus, 1913.

Garber, Marjorie. *Shakespeare After All.* New York: Anchor Books, 2004.

Gates, Geoffrey. *The Defence of the Militarie Profession.* (1579) New York: Da Capo Press, 1973.

Gayley, Charles M. *Representative English Comedies.* 4 v. (1903) New York: AMS Press reprint, 1969.

Geoffrey of Monmouth. *History of the Kings of Britain.* Michael Reeve, ed. Neil Wright, tr. Woodbridge, UK: Boydell Press, 2007.

George, David. "Shakespeare and Pembroke's Men." *Shakespeare Quarterly.* v. 32 (1981) pp. 305–33.

Gibson, James M. "Shakespeare and the Cobham Controversy: The Oldcastle/Falstaff and Brooke/Broome Revisions." *Medieval and Renaissance Drama in England.* v. 25 (2012) pp. 94–132.

Gies, Frances. *Women in the Middle Ages.* New York: Crowell, 1978.

Gillespie, Stuart. *Shakespeare's Books: a dictionary of Shakespeare's Sources.* London: Athlone Press, 2001.

Gilvary, Kevin. "Queens' College Cambridge and the Henry VI Plays." *The De Vere Society Newsletter.* v. 15, no. 2 (June 2008) pp. 5–6.

_____, ed. *Dating Shakespeare's Plays.* Tunbridge Wells: Parapress, 2010.

Gooch, Jane L., ed. *The Lamentable Tragedy of Locrine: A Critical Edition.* (1595) New York: Garland: 1981.

Great Britain. Public Record Office. *Calendar of State Papers, Foreign Series, of the Reign of Elizabeth, 1558–1568.* London: Longman, Roberts, & Green, 1863–1950.

_____. *Calendar of State Papers Relating to Ireland, of the Reign of Elizabeth, 1574–1585.* London: Public Record Office, 1867.

Green, V.H.H. *Renaissance and Reformation.* London: Arnold, 1952.

Greene, Robert. *Menaphon.* Edward Arber, ed. London: Edward Arber, 1880.

_____. *The Scottish history of James the Fourth.* Norman Sanders, ed. London: Methuen, 1970.

Greer, Clayton A. "Shakespeare's Use of 'The Famous Victories of Henry V.'" *Notes and Queries.* v. 199 (June 1954) pp. 238–41.

Greg, W.W. *A Bibliography of English Printed Drama to the Restoration.* Oxford: Oxford University Press, 1939–59.

_____. "The Date of *King Lear* and Shakespeare's use of earlier versions of the Story." *The Library.* v. 20 (1940) pp. 377–400.

_____. *The Editorial Problem in Shakespeare.* Oxford: Clarendon Press, 1954.

_____. "Shakespeare and *King Leir.*" *TLS.* v. 39 (9 March 1940) p. 124.

_____, ed. *The Interlude of Wealth and Health.* London: The Malone Society, 1907.

_____, ed. *The Rare Triumphs of Love and Fortune.* London: The Malone Society, 1931.

_____, ed. *The True Tragedy of Richard the Third 1594.* Oxford: The Malone Society, 1929.

Gregory's Chronicle. *The Historical Collections of a Citizen of London.* (1876) James Gairdner, ed. New York: Johnson Reprint Corp., 1965.

Grehan, Ida. *Irish Family Histories.* Toronto: Key Porter Books, 1993.

Griffin, Benjamin. *Playing the past: Approaches*

to *English Historical Drama, 1385–1600.* Woodbridge, Suffolk; D.S. Brewer, 2001.

Grillo, Ernesto. *Shakespeare and Italy.* Glasgow: Robert Maclehose, 1949.

Gurr, Andrew. "Richard III and the Democratic Process." *Essays in Criticism.* v. 24 (1974) pp. 39–47.

_____. *The Shakespearean Stage, 1574–1642.* Cambridge: Cambridge University Press, 3rd ed., 1994.

_____, ed. *The First Quarto of King Henry V.* Cambridge: Cambridge University Press, 2000.

_____, ed. *King Henry V.* "Updated Edition." Cambridge: Cambridge University Press, 2005.

Guy, John. *Tudor England.* Oxford: Oxford University Press, 1988.

Habicht, Werner, D.J. Palmer and Roger Pringle, eds. *Images of Shakespeare: proceedings of the Third Congress of the International Shakespeare Association. 1986.* Newark, DE: University of Delaware Press, 1988.

Hakluyt, Richard. *The Principal Navigations, Voyages, Traffiques and Discoveries.* (1589) Reprint 10 v. London: J.M. Dent, 1927.

Halio, Jay L., ed. *Critical Essays on Shakespeare's King Lear.* New York: G.K. Hall, 1996.

_____, ed. *The Tragedy of King Lear.* Cambridge: Cambridge University Press, 1992.

Hall, Edward. *The union of the two noble and illustre famelies of Lancastre and Yorke.* (1548; 1550) H. Ellis, ed. New York: AMS Press reprint, 1965.

Hamill, John. "Shakespeare's Sexuality and how it affects the Authorship Issue." *The Oxfordian.* v. 8 (2005) pp. 25–59.

_____. "The Ten Restless Ghosts of Mantua: Shakespeare's Specter Lingers Over the Italian City." *"Report My Cause Aright." The Shakespeare Oxford Society Fiftieth Anniversary Anthology.* The Shakespeare Oxford Society, 2007. pp. 86–102.

Hamilton, Charles. *In Search of Shakespeare.* Harcourt Brace Jovanovich: San Diego, 1985.

Hammer, Paul E.J. *The Polarisation of Elizabethan Politics: The Political Career of Robert Devereux, 2nd Earl of Essex, 1585–1597.* Cambridge: Cambridge University Press, 1999.

Hammond, Anthony, ed. *King Richard III.* (1981) Arden 2nd series. London: Thomson Learning reprint, 2002.

Hanham, Alison. *Richard III and His Early Historians 1483–1535.* Oxford: Clarendon Press, 1975.

Harbage, Alfred. *Shakespeare and the Rival Traditions.* New York: Macmillan, 1952.

Hardyng, John. *The Chronicle of John Hardyng.* (1543) Henry Ellis, ed. London: F.C. and J. Rivington, 1812.

Harington, Sir John. *A New Discourse of a Stale Subject, called the Metamorphosis of Ajax.* (1596) Elizabeth S. Donno, ed. London: Routledge and Kegan Paul, 1962.

Harner, James L. "Jane Shore in Literature: A Checklist." *Notes and Queries.* v. 28 (December 1981) pp. 496–507.

Harris, Jesse W. *John Bale: A Study in the Minor Literature of the Reformation.* Urbana: Illinois University Press, 1940.

Harrison, G.B. *Shakespeare: The Complete Works.* New York: Harcourt, Brace, 1948.

_____, ed. *The Letters of Queen Elizabeth.* Westport, CT: Greenwood Press, 1938.

Harrold, William E. "Shakespeare's Use of *Mostellaria* in *The Taming of the Shrew.*" *Shakespeare Jahrbuch* (West). v. 106 (1970) pp. 188–94.

Harsnett, Samuel. *A Declaration of Egregious Popish Impostures, etc.* (1603) Frank W. Brownlow, ed. *Shakespeare, Harsnett, and the Devils of Denham.* 1993. pp. 184–335.

Hart, Alfred. "The Growth of Shakespeare's Vocabulary." *The Review of English Studies.* v. 19 (1943) pp. 242–54.

_____. "The Length of Elizabethan and Jacobean Plays." *The Review of English Studies.* v. 8 (1932) pp. 139–54.

_____. *Shakespeare and the Homilies.* Melbourne: Melbourne University Press, 1934.

_____. *Stolne and Surreptitious Copies, A Comparative Study of Shakespeare's Bad Quartos.* Melbourne: Melbourne University Press, 1942.

_____. "Vocabularies of Shakespeare's Plays." *The Review of English Studies.* v. 19 (1943) pp. 128–40.

Hattaway, Michael, ed. *The First Part of King Henry VI.* Cambridge: Cambridge University Press, 1990.

Hayward, Sir John. *The First and Second Parts of John Hayward's The Life and Raigne of*

*King Henrie IIII.* (1599) John J. Manning, ed. Camden 4th series. v. 42. London: Royal Historical Society, 1991.

Hazlitt, William C. *Shakespeare's Library.* (1875) 6 v. New York: AMS Press reprint, 1965.

Henslowe, Philip. *Henslowe's Diary.* R.A. Foakes, ed. Cambridge: Cambridge University Press, 2nd ed. 2002.

Hess, W. Ron. *The Dark Side of Shakespeare.* 3 v. New York: iUniverse, 2003.

Hibbard, G.R., ed. *The Elizabethan Theatre VII.* Port Credit, Ontario: P.D. Meany, 1980.

_____, ed. *The Taming of the Shrew.* London: Penguin Group, 1968.

Higden, Ranulf. *The Description of Britain [Polycronicon].* (1480) John Trevisa, tr. New York: Da Capo Press, 1971.

Hodgdon, Barbara, ed. *The Taming of the Shrew.* Arden 3rd series. London: Methuen, 2010.

Hoeniger, F.D. "The Artist Exploring the Primitive: King Lear." *Some Facets of 'King Lear.'* Rosalie L. Colie and F.T. Flahiff, eds. 1974. pp. 89–102. Reprinted in *Critical Essays on Shakespeare's King Lear.* Jay Halio, ed. 1996. pp. 75–87.

Holinshed, Raphael. *Holinshed's Chronicles of England, Scotland, and Ireland.* (1577; 1587) Henry Ellis, ed. 6 v. London: J. Johnson, 1807–08.

Honigmann, E.A.J. "King John, The Troublesome Reigne, and 'documentary links': A Rejoinder." *Shakespeare Quarterly.* v. 38:1 (Spring 1987) pp. 124–126.

_____. *Shakespeare: The Lost Years.* Manchester: Manchester University Press, 2nd ed. 1998.

_____. *Shakespeare's Impact on his Contemporaries.* London: Macmillan, 1982.

_____. "Shakespeare's 'Lost Source Plays.'" *Modern Language Review.* v. 49 (1954) pp. 293–307.

_____. "Shakespeare's Self-Repetition and *King John.*" *Shakespeare Survey.* v. 53 (2000) pp. 175–83.

_____, ed. *King John.* Arden 2nd series. London: Methuen, 1954.

Hook, Frank S., ed. *The Dramatic Works of George Peele.* v. 2. *Edward I.* New Haven: Yale University Press, 1961.

Hope, Jonathan. *The authorship of Shakespeare's plays: a socio-linguistic study.* Cambridge: Cambridge University Press, 1994.

Hope, Warren. "Lear's Cordelia, Oxford's Susan, and Manningham's Diary." *The Elizabethan Review.* v. 5:2 (Autumn 1997) pp. 123–6.

Hopkinson, A.F., ed. *The True Chronicle History of King Leir.* London: M.E. Sims, 1895.

Horne, David, ed. *The Dramatic Works of George Peele.* v. 1. *The Life and Minor Works.* New Haven: Yale University Press, 1961.

Hosley, Richard. "Sources and Analogues of *The Taming of the Shrew.*" *Huntington Library Quarterly.* v. 27 (1963–64) pp. 289–308.

Hotson, Leslie. *I, William Shakespeare.* London: Jonathan Cape, 1937.

Hughes, Jonathan. "Vere, John de, sixteenth earl of Oxford (1516–1562)." *ODNB.* Oxford University Press, 2004.

Hughes, Stephanie Hopkins. "Oxford's Childhood Part II: The first four years with Smith." *The Shakespeare Oxford Newsletter.* v. 42:3 (Fall 2006) pp. 1, 5–15.

Hughes, Thomas. *The misfortunes of Arthur: a critical, old-spelling edition.* Brian Jay Corrigan, ed. New York: Garland, 1992.

Humphries, A.R., ed. *King Henry IV, Part I.* (1960) Arden 2nd series. London: Routledge, 1989.

_____, ed. *King Henry IV, Part II.* Arden 2nd series. London: Methuen, 1966.

Hunter, G.K. *John Lyly, The Humanist as Courtier.* London: Routledge and Kegan Paul, 1962.

_____. Review of T.W. Baldwin's *On the Literary Genetics of Shakspere's Plays 1592–94. The Review of English Studies.* n.s. v. 12, no. 46 (May 1961) pp. 189–195.

Ioppolo, Grace. *Revising Shakespeare.* Cambridge, MA: Harvard University Press, 1991.

Jackson, MacD. P. *Studies in Attribution: Middleton and Shakespeare.* Salzburg: University of Salzburg, 1979.

Jamison, Kay Redfield. *Touched with Fire: Manic-Depressive Illness and the Artistic Temperament.* New York: Free Press, 1993.

Jenkins, Harold, ed. *Hamlet.* Arden 2nd series. London: Methuen, 1982.

Jiménez, Ramon. "Oxford's Fifty-Play Canon and When It Was Written (Part II)." *The Shakespeare Oxford Newsletter.* v. 50:1 (Winter 2014) pp. 1, 12–17.

_____. "Shakespeare in Stratford and London: Ten Eyewitnesses Who Saw Nothing." *"Report My Cause Aright." The Shakespeare Oxford Society Fiftieth Anniversary Anthology.* The Shakespeare Oxford Society, 2007. pp. 74–85.

Johnson, Samuel, ed. *The Plays of William Shakespeare.* 8 v. London: J. and R. Tonson, 1765.

Jolly, Eddi. "'Shakespeare' and Burghley's Library: *Biblioteca Illustris: Sive Catalogus Variorum Librorum.*" *The Oxfordian.* v. 3 (2000) pp. 3–18.

_____, and Patrick O'Brien. "Shakespeare's Sources and Sir Thomas Smith's Library." *The De Vere Society Newsletter.* (July 2001) pp. 19–21. Reprinted in Richard Malim, ed. *Great Oxford.* 2004. pp. 22–5.

Jolly, Margrethe. *The First Two Quartos of Hamlet, A New View of the Origin and Relationship of the Texts.* Jefferson, NC: McFarland, 2014.

Jones, G.P. "'Henry V': The Chorus and the Audience." *Shakespeare Survey.* v. 31 (1978) pp. 93–104.

Jonson, Ben. *The Cambridge Edition of the Works of Ben Jonson.* 7 v. David Bevington, Martin Butler and Ian Donaldson, eds. Cambridge: Cambridge University Press, 2012.

Jowett, John. "'Derby,' 'Stanley,' and Memorial Reconstruction in Quarto *Richard III.*" *Notes and Queries.* v. 245 (March 2000) pp. 75–9.

_____, ed. *The Tragedy of Richard III.* Oxford: Oxford University Press, 2000.

Kabel, Paul. *Die Sage von Heinrich V. bis zu Shakespeare.* Berlin: Mayer & Müller, 1908.

Kastan, David Scott, ed. *King Henry IV, Part 1.* Arden 3rd series. London: Thomson Learning, 2002.

Keen, Alan and Roger Lubbock. *The Annotator.* New York: Macmillan, 1954.

Kennedy, Richard. "The Woolpack Man: John Shakespeare's Monument in Holy Trinity Church, Stratford-on-Avon." http://webpages.charter.net/stairway/WOOLPACKMAN.htm [accessed 12 September 2017].

Kernan, Alvin B. *Shakespeare, The King's Playwright: Theater in the Stuart Court, 1603–1613.* New Haven: Yale University Press, 1995.

Kesson, Andy, and Emma Smith, eds. *The Elizabethan Top Ten: Defining Print Popularity in Early Modern England.* Ashgate: Farnham, Surrey, 2013.

King, John N. "Bale, John." *ODNB.* Oxford University Press, 2004.

Kingsford, C.L. "The Early Biographies of Henry V." *The English Historical Review.* v. 25 (1910) pp. 58–92.

_____. *English Historical Literature in the Fifteenth Century, with an appendix of chronicles.* Oxford: The Clarendon Press, 1913.

_____. Review of *Die Sage von Heinrich V. bis zu Shakespeare* by Paul Kabel. 1908. *The English Historical Review.* v. 24, no. 96 (Oct. 1909) pp. 785–787.

_____, ed. *Chronicles of London.* (1905) Dursley, Gloucestershire: A. Sutton, 1977.

_____, ed. *The First English Life of King Henry the Fifth.* Oxford: The Clarendon Press. 1911.

Kirschbaum, Leo. "The Copyright of Elizabethan Plays." *The Library.* ser. 5, v. 14:4 (December 1959) pp. 231–50.

Knight, Charles, ed. *The comedies, histories, tragedies, and poems of William Shakspere.* 12 v. 2nd ed. London: Charles Knight & Co., 1842–1844.

Knolles, Richard. *The generall historie of the Turkes.* London: A. Islip, 1603.

Knowles, Richard. "How Shakespeare Knew *King Leir.*" *Shakespeare Survey.* v. 55 (2002) pp. 12–34.

Kolb, Eduard, and Jorg Hasler, eds. *Festschrift Rudolf Stamm.* Munich: Francke, 1969.

Kozlenko, William. *Disputed Plays of William Shakespeare.* New York: Hawthorne Books, 1974.

Kuhl, Ernest P. "The Authorship of *The Taming of the Shrew.*" *PMLA.* v. 40, no.3 (September 1925) pp. 551–618.

Landt, D.B. "The Ancestry of Sir John Falstaff." *Shakespeare Quarterly.* v. 17:1 (1966) pp. 69–76.

Lake, David. *The Canon of Thomas Middleton's Plays.* Cambridge: Cambridge University Press, 1975.

Lancashire, Ian. *Dramatic Texts and Records of Britain: A Chronological Topography to 1558.* Toronto: University of Toronto Press, 1984.

Law, Robert A. "The Choruses in Henry the Fifth." *University of Texas Studies in English.* v. 35 (1956) pp. 11–21.

_____. "Holinshed's Leir Story and Shakespeare's." *Studies in Philology*. v. 47 (1950) pp. 42–50.

_____. "*King John* and *King Leir*." *Texas Studies in Literature and Language*. v. 1 (1960) pp. 473–6.

_____. "On the Date of *King John*." *Studies in Philology*. v. 54 (1957) pp. 119–57.

_____. "*Richard the Third*: A Study in Shakespeare's Composition." *PMLA*. v. 60, no. 3 (Sept. 1945) pp. 689–96.

_____. "Richard the Third, Act I, Scene 4." *PMLA*. v. 27, no. 2 (June 1912) pp. 117–41.

_____. "An Unnoticed Analog to the Imogen Story." *Texas Studies in English*. v. 7 (1927) pp. 133–5.

Layamon. *Layamon's Brut: A History of the Britons*. Donald G. Bzdyl, tr. Binghamton, N.Y.: Medieval & Renaissance Texts & Studies, 1989.

Lee, Sidney. "Butler, Thomas, tenth Earl of Ormond." *Dictionary of National Biography*. v. 8. 1886. pp. 79–81.

_____. *A Life of William Shakespeare*. (1898) 14th ed. New York: Dover reprint, 1931.

_____. "Vere, Edward de, seventeenth Earl of Oxford." *Dictionary of National Biography*. v. 58. 1899. pp. 225–29.

_____, ed. *The chronicle history of King Leir: the original of Shakespeare's 'King Lear.'* London: Chatto and Windus, 1909. https://archive.org/stream/chroniclehistory00leesuoft/chroniclehistory00leesuoft_djvu.txt [accessed 12 September 2017].

Lefranc, Abel. *Under the Mask of William Shakespeare*. (1919) Cecil Cragg, tr. Braunton, Devon: Merlin, 1988.

Legge, Thomas. *Richardus Tertius*. Robert J. Lordi, ed. New York: Garland, 1979.

Lennon, Colm. *Sixteenth Century Ireland: The Incomplete Conquest*. New York: St. Martin's Press, 1995.

Littleton, Betty L., ed. *Clyomon and Clamydes, A critical edition*. Paris: Mouton, 1968.

Lock, Julian. "Brooke, William, tenth Baron Cobham (1527–1597)." *ODNB*. Oxford University Press, 2004.

Logan, T.P., and D.S. Smith, eds. *The Predecessors of Shakespeare*. Lincoln, NB: University of Nebraska Press, 1973.

Looney, John Thomas. "The Earl of Oxford as Shakespeare, New Evidence." *The Golden Hind*. v. 1:1 (October 1922).

_____. "*Shakespeare*." *Identified in Edward de Vere, Seventeenth Earl of Oxford*. (1920) 3rd ed. Ruth L. Miller, ed. 2 v. Port Washington, NY: Kennikat Press, 1979.

Lordi, Robert J. "The Relationship of Richardus Tertius to the Main Richard III Plays." *Boston University Studies in English*. v. 5 (1961) pp. 139–53.

Lull, Janice, ed. *King Richard III*. Cambridge: Cambridge University Press, 1999.

Lyly, John. *Euphues: The Anatomy of Wit* and *Euphues and His England*. (1578; 1580) Leah Scragg, ed. Manchester: Manchester University Press, 2009.

Lyne, Raphael. "Churchyard, Thomas (1523?–1604)." *ODNB*. Oxford: Oxford University Press, 2004.

Lytle, Guy F., and Stephen Orgel, eds. *Patronage in the Renaissance*. Princeton, NJ: Princeton University Press, 1981.

Magri, Noemi. "No Errors in Shakespeare: Historical Truth and *The Two Gentlemen of Verona*." *The De Vere Society Newsletter*. v. 2:12 (May 1998) pp. 9–22. Reprinted in *Great Oxford*. Richard Malim, ed. 2004, pp. 66–78.

_____. "Places in Shakespeare: Belmont and Thereabouts." *The De Vere Society Newsletter*. v. 10 (June 2003) pp. 6–14. Reprinted in *Great Oxford*. Richard Malim, ed. 2004, pp. 91–106.

_____. "Shakespeare and Italian Renaissance Painting, The three wanton pictures in *The Taming of the Shrew*." *The De Vere Society Newsletter*. v. 12 (May 2005) pp. 4–12.

Maguire, Laurie E. *Shakespearean Suspect Texts: The "Bad" Quartos and Their Contexts*. New York: Cambridge University Press, 1996.

Mahood, Molly M. *Bit Parts in Shakespeare's Plays*. Cambridge: Cambridge University Press, 1992.

Malim, Richard C. "They Haven't the Necessary Will." Letter. *The Spectator*. No. 280 (9 January 1999) p. 24.

_____, ed. *Great Oxford*. Tunbridge Wells: Parapress, 2004.

Malone, Edmund. *The Plays and Poems of William Shakespeare*. 21 v. James Boswell, ed. London: F.C. and J. Rivington, et al. 1821.

Manningham, John. *The Diary of John Man-ningham of the Middle Temple 1602–1603.* (1868) Robert Parker Sorlien, ed. Hanover, NH: The University Press of New England, 1976.

Marcus, Leah S. "The Shakespearean Editor as Shrew-Tamer." *English Literary Renaissance.* v. 22 (1992) pp. 177–200.

Marlowe, Christopher. *Doctor Faustus and Other Plays.* David Bevington and Eric Rasmussen, eds. Oxford: Oxford University Press, 1998.

_____. *The Works of Christopher Marlowe.* 3 v. A.H. Bullen, ed. London: John C. Nimmo, 1885.

Marston, John. *The Scourge of Villanie.* (1599) G.B. Harrison, ed. London: John Lane, 1925.

Martyr, Peter. *The Decades of the Newe Worlde or West India.* (1511–32) Richard Eden, tr. London: Guilhelmi Powell, 1555. Reprinted in *The first Three English books on America.* Edward Arber, ed. 1885.

Matheson, Lister M. *The Prose Brut: The Development of a Middle English Chronicle.* Tempe, AZ: Medieval and Renaissance Texts & Studies, 1998.

Maxwell, Baldwin. *Studies in the Shakespeare Apocrypha.* New York: Greenwood Press, 1956.

Maxwell, J.C. "'The Shrew' and 'A Shrew': The Suitors and the Sisters." *Notes and Queries.* Arden 2nd series. v. 213 (April 1968) pp. 130–1.

_____, ed. *Titus Andronicus.* London: Methuen, 1961.

May, Steven W. *The Elizabethan Courtier Poets, the Poems and their Contexts.* Columbia, MO: Missouri University Press, 1991.

_____. "The Poems of Edward de Vere and Robert Devereux." *Studies in Philology.* v. 22:5 (1980).

McDiarmid, Matthew P. "Concerning 'The Troublesome Reign of King John.'" *Notes and Queries.* v. 202 (October 1957) pp. 435–38.

McKisack, May. *Medieval History in the Tudor Age.* Oxford: The Clarendon Press, 1971.

McLatchie, Linda B. "De Vere and the Battle of Bosworth." *The Shakespeare Oxford Society Newsletter.* v. 29:4 (Fall 1993) pp. 4–6.

McManaway, James G., Giles E. Dawson and

Edwin E. Willoughby, eds. *Joseph Quincy Adams Memorial Studies.* Washington: The Folger Shakespeare Library, 1948.

McMillin, Scott and Sally-Beth Maclean. *The Queen's Men and their Plays.* Cambridge: Cambridge University Press, 1998.

McNeal, Thomas H. "Margaret of Anjou: Romantic Princess and Troubled Queen." *Shakespeare Quarterly.* v. 9 (1958) pp. 1–10.

_____. "Shakespeare's Cruel Queens." *Huntington Library Quarterly.* v. 22 (1958–9) pp. 41–50.

Melchiori, Giorgio, ed. *The Second Part of King Henry IV.* Cambridge: Cambridge University Press, 1989.

Meres, Francis. *Palladis Tamia.* London. Cuthbert Burbie, 1598.

Meyers, Carole, ed. *Women in Scripture.* Boston: Houghton Mifflin, 2000.

Michie, Donald M. *A Critical Edition of The True Chronicle History of King Leir And His Three Daughters, Gonorill, Ragan and Cordella.* New York: Garland, 1991.

Miller, Stephen Roy, ed. *The Taming of a Shrew, The 1594 Quarto.* Cambridge: Cambridge University Press, 1988.

Mincoff, Marco. "The Dating of *The Taming of the Shrew.*" *English Studies.* v. 54 (1973) pp. 554–65.

Mish, Charles G. "The Waking Man's Dream." *TLS.* v. 50 (28 December 1951) p. 837.

Moffett, Thomas. *Nobilis; or, A view of the life and death of a Sidney, and Lessus lugubris.* (1594) Virgil B. Heltzel and Hoyt H. Hudson, eds. and trs. San Marino, Calif.: The Huntington Library, 1940.

Molinet, Jean. *Chronique de Jean Molinet.* J.-A.C. Buchon, ed. 5 v. Paris: Verdiére, 1827–1828.

Monaghan, James. "Falstaff and His Forebears." *Studies in Philology.* v. 18 (1921) pp. 353–61.

Montaigne, Michel de. *The Essayes of Montaigne.* (1603) John Florio, tr. New York: The Modern Library, 1933.

Moore, Peter R. *The Lame Storyteller, Poor and Despised: Studies in Shakespeare.* Buchholz, Germany: Uwe Laugwitz, 2009.

Moorman, F.W. "The Pre-Shakespearean Ghost." *Modern Language Review.* v. 1:2 (January 1906) pp. 85–95.

More, Sir Thomas. *The History of King Richard III.* (1548) George Logan, ed.

Bloomington, IN: Indiana University Press, 2005.

Morris, Brian, ed. *The Taming of the Shrew*. Arden 2nd series. London: Methuen, 1981.

Mosher, Sally. "Music Named for Edward de Vere." *The Shakespeare Oxford Newsletter*. v. 32:3 (Summer 1996) pp. 18, 23.

Mott, Lewis. "Foreign Politics in an Old Play." *Modern Philology*. v. 19 (1921) pp. 65–71.

Mueller, Martin. "From *Leir* to *Lear*." *Philological Quarterly*. v. 73 (1994) pp. 195–218.

Muir, Kenneth. "A Reconsideration of *Edward III*." *Shakespeare Survey*. v. 6 (1953) pp. 39–48.

_____. "Samuel Harsnett and *King Lear*." *The Review of English Studies*. n.s. v. 2 (1951) pp. 11–21.

_____. "Source Problems in the Histories." *Shakespeare-Jahrbuch*. v. 96 (1960) pp. 47–63.

_____, ed. *King Lear*. Arden 2nd series London: Methuen, 1972.

_____, and J.F. Danby. "*Arcadia* and *King Lear*." *Notes and Queries*. v. 195 (4 February 1950) pp. 49–51.

Nashe, Thomas. *The Works of Thomas Nashe*. (1904–10) 5 v. R.B. McKerrow, ed. Rev. ed. by F.P. Wilson. London: Basil Blackwell, 1958.

Neale, J.E. *Queen Elizabeth*. (1934) Garden City, NY: Doubleday, 1957.

*New Cambridge Modern History*. v. 2. Cambridge: Cambridge University Press, 1990.

Nichols, John B. *Progresses and Public Processions of Queen Elizabeth*. 3 v. (1823) New York: AMS reprint, 1968.

Nichols, Louise. "'My Name was known before I came': The Heroic Identity of the Prince in *The Famous Victories of Henry V*." *Other Voices, Other Views*. H. Ostovich, Mary V. Silcox and Graham Roebuck, eds. pp. 154–75.

Nicoll, Allardyce. *A History of Restoration Drama*. Cambridge: Cambridge University Press, 1923.

_____, and Josephine Nicoll. *Holinshed's Chronicle as Used in Shakespeare's Plays*. London: J.M. Dent, 1927.

Norwich, J.J. *Shakespeare's English Kings*. New York: Simon and Shuster, 1999.

Nutton, Vivian. "Caius, John (1510–1573)." *ODNB*. Oxford: Oxford University Press, 2004.

Ogburn, Charlton, and Dorothy Ogburn. *This Star of England*. New York: Coward-McCann, 1952.

Ogburn, Charlton, Jr. *The Mysterious William Shakespeare*. McLean, VA: EPM Publications, 2nd ed. 1992.

Oliver, H.J., ed. *The Taming of the Shrew*. Oxford: Oxford University Press, 1982.

Onions, C.T. *A Shakespeare Glossary*. (1911) Oxford: Clarendon Press, 2nd ed. rev., 1958.

Ordish, T.F. *Shakespeare's London, a commentary on Shakespeare's life and work in London*. (1897) London: J.M. Dent, 1904 ed.

Orgel, Stephen. "A Bumper Year." Review of *1599 A Year in the Life of William Shakespeare* by James Shapiro. *TLS* (19 August 2005) p.11.

Ornstein, Robert. *A Kingdom for a Stage*. Cambridge, MA: Harvard University Press, 1972.

Ostovich, Helen, Holger Schott Syme, and Andrew Griffin, eds. *Locating the Queen's Men, 1583–1603: material practices and conditions of playing*. Farnham, Surrey: Ashgate, 2009.

Ostovich, Helen, Mary V. Silcox and Graham Roebuck, eds. *Other Voices, Other Views: Expanding the Canon in English Renaissance Studies*. Newark, DE: University of Delaware Press, 1999.

Ovid (Publius Ovidius Naso). *Ovid's Metamorphoses*. (1567) Arthur Golding, tr. John Frederick Nims, ed. New York: Macmillan, 1965.

*Oxford Dictionary of National Biography*. Oxford: Oxford University Press, 2004; online ed. May 2012.

*Oxford English Dictionary*. Oxford: Oxford University Press, 2nd ed. 1989.

Pafford, J.H.P., ed. *King Johan by John Bale*. Oxford: The Malone Society, 1931.

Palmer, Alan, and Victoria. *Who's Who in Shakespeare's England*. New York: St. Martins Press, 1981.

Palmer, William. *The Problem of Ireland in Tudor Foreign Policy, 1485–1603*. Woodbridge, Suffolk: The Boydell Press, 1994.

Paris, Matthew. *Chronica Majora*. 7 v. (1872–83) H.R. Luard, ed. v. 1, *The Creation to 1066*. v. 2, *A.D. 1067 to A.D. 1216*. New York: Cambridge University Press, 2012.

Parrott, Thomas Marc. *Shakespeare: Twenty-Three Plays and the Sonnets*. (1938) New

York: Charles Scribner's Sons reprint, 1953.

Partridge, Eric. *Shakespeare's Bawdy.* (1948) New York: E.P. Dutton, rev. ed. 1969.

Patterson, Annabel. *Shakespeare and the Popular Voice.* Oxford: Basil Blackwell, 1989.

Pauls, Peter. "The True Chronicle History of *King Leir* and Shakespeare's *King Lear.*" *The Upstart Crow.* v. 5 (1984) pp. 93–107.

Peacham, Henry. *Minerva Britanna* (1612) New York: Da Capo Press, 1971.

Pearson, Jacqueline. "The Influence of *King Leir* on Shakespeare's *Richard II.*" *Notes and Queries.* v. 227 (April 1982) pp. 113–15.

_____. "*Much Ado About Nothing* and *King Leir.*" *Notes and Queries.* v. 226 (April 1981) pp. 128–9.

Pendleton, Thomas A. "'this is not the man': On Calling Falstaff Falstaff." *AEB, Analytical & Enumerative Bibliography.* n.s. v. 4 (1990) pp. 59–71.

Perrett, Wilfrid. *The Story of King Lear from Geoffrey of Monmouth to Shakespeare.* Berlin: Mayer & Müller, 1904.

Pinciss, G.M. "Thomas Creede and the Repertory of the Queen's Men 1583–1592." *Modern Philology.* v. 67 (1970) pp. 321–30.

Pitcher, Seymour M. *The Case for Shakespeare's Authorship of "The Famous Victories."* New York: State University of New York, 1961.

Plato. *The Axiochus of Plato.* (1592) Edmund Spenser, tr. F. M, Padelford, ed. Baltimore: Johns Hopkins Press, 1934.

Plautus, Titus Maccius. *Miles Gloriosus.* Mason Hammond, Arthur M. Mack and Walter Moskalew, eds. Cambridge, MA: Harvard University Press, 2nd ed. 1970.

_____. *Mostellaria.* Frank O. Copley, ed. and tr. New York: Liberal Arts Press, 1955.

Pointon, A.J. *The Man who was Never Shakespeare.* Tunbridge Wells, Kent: Parapress, 2011.

Pope, Alexander. *The Works of Shakespeare.* 6 v. London: Jacob Tonson, 1723–5.

Praetorius, Charles, ed. *The Famous Victories of Henry the Fifth, The Earliest Known Quarto 1598.* Facsimile "from the unique copy in the Bodleian Library." London: Charles Praetorius, 1887.

Preston, Thomas. *A Critical Edition of Thomas Preston's Cambises.* Robert Carl Johnson, ed. Salzburg: Institut fur Englis-che Sprache und Literatur, Universitat Salzburg, 1975.

Price, Diana. "The Mythical 'Myth' of the Stigma of Print." http://www.shakespeareauthorship.com/resources/stigma.asp. [accessed 17 March 2017].

_____. *Shakespeare's Unorthodox Biography: New Evidence of an Authorship Problem.* Westport, CT: Greenwood Press, 2000.

Prior, Roger. "Gascoigne's Posies as a Shakespearean Source." *Notes and Queries.* v. 47 (Dec. 2000) pp. 445–49.

Proudfoot, G.R., ed. *A Knack to Know a Knave.* (1594) Oxford: The Malone Society, 1964.

Quealy, Gerit. "Who Really Won the Tennis Court Quarrel?." *The De Vere Society Newsletter.* v. 21:3 (October 2014) pp. 7–11.

Quiller-Couch, Arthur, and John Dover Wilson, eds. *The Taming of the Shrew.* Cambridge: Cambridge University Press, 1928.

Quintilian. *The Institutio Oratoria of Quintilian.* 4 v. H.E. Butler, tr. New York: William Heinemann, 1922.

Radford, John. *Child Prodigies and Exceptional Early Achievers.* New York: The Free Press, 1990.

Raleigh, Sir Walter A. *Shakespeare.* New York: Macmillan, 1907.

_____, Sidney Lee and C.T. Onions, eds. *Shakespeare's England.* 2 v. Oxford: Clarendon Press, 1916.

Read, Conyers. *Mr. Secretary Cecil and Queen Elizabeth.* New York: Knopf, 1955.

Rhodes, Neil. "Shakespeare's Popularity and the Origins of the Canon." *The Elizabethan Top Ten: Defining Print Popularity in Early Modern England.* A. Kesson and E. Smith, eds., pp. 101–22.

Ribner, Irving. *The English History Play in the Age of Shakespeare.* (1957) New York: Octagon Books, rev. ed., 1965.

Richmond, Hugh M. *Shakespeare's Theatre: a Dictionary of His Stage Context.* London: Continuum, 2002.

Ricks, C., ed. *English Drama to 1710.* (1971) New York: Penguin Books, 1993.

Riggs, David. *Ben Jonson, A Life.* Cambridge: Harvard University Press, 1989.

Robertson, John M. *An Introduction to the Study of the Shakespeare Canon.* London: G. Routledge, 1924.

Robin, P. Ansell. *Animal Lore in English Lit-*

*erature.* (1932) Folcroft, PA: Folcroft Press reprint, 1970.

Roe, Richard P. *Shakespeare's Guide to Italy Then and Now.* Rosalie Books. no. loc., 2010.

Rollins, Hyder E., ed. *A Handful of Pleasant Delights.* (1584) Cambridge: Harvard University Press, 1924.

_____, and Herschel Baker, eds. *The Renaissance in England.* Boston: D.C. Heath, 1954.

Root, Robert K. *Classical Mythology in Shakespeare.* (1903) New York: Gordian Press reprint, 1965.

Rosenblum, Joseph, ed. *The Greenwood Companion to Shakespeare.* 4 v. v. 1. *Overviews and the history plays.* Westport CT: Greenwood Press, 2005.

Ross, James A. *The Foremost Man of the Kingdom, John de Vere, Thirteenth Earl of Oxford (1442–1513).* Woodbridge, Suffolk: The Boydell Press, 2015.

Rossiter, A.P. "Prognosis on a Shakespeare Problem." *Durham University Journal.* v. 33, no. 2 (Mar. 1941) Reprinted in Keen and Lubbock, *The Annotator.* pp. 164–85.

Rowan, Arthur B. "Desmond Papers." *Kerry Magazine.* v. 1, no. 7. (July 1, 1854) pp. 97–100.

Rowe, Nicholas, ed. *The Works of Mr. William Shakespear.* 6 v. (1709) New York: AMS Press reprint, 1967.

Rowlands, Samuel. *The Complete Works of Samuel Rowlands 1598–1628.* Edmund W. Gosse, ed. Glasgow: The Hunterian Club, 1880.

Rowley. Samuel. *When you see me, you know me.* (1605) F.P. Wilson, ed. London: The Malone Society, 1952.

Rowse, A.L. *Shakespeare's Southampton.* New York: Harper, 1965.

Salingar, Leo. *Shakespeare and the Traditions of Comedy.* Cambridge: Cambridge University Press, 1974.

Sams, Eric. "King Leir and Edmond Ironside." *Notes and Queries.* v. 48 (September 2001) pp. 266–70.

_____. "Oldcastle and the Oxford Shakespeare." *Notes and Queries.* v. 240 (June 1993) pp. 180–5.

_____. "The Troublesome Wrangle Over King John." *Notes and Queries.* v. 233 (March 1988) pp. 41–4.

_____. *The Real Shakespeare, Retrieving the Early Years, 1564–1594.* New Haven: Yale University Press, 1995.

_____. *The Real Shakespeare II, Retrieving the Later Years, 1594–1616.* http://ericsams.org/index.php/shakespeare-archive/the-real-shakespeare-ii [accessed June 17, 2017].

_____, ed. *Shakespeare's Edward III, An early play restored to the canon.* New Haven, CT: Yale University Press, 1996.

_____, ed. *Shakespeare's Lost Play, Edmund Ironside.* Aldershot, Hants: Wildwood House, 1986.

Satin, Joseph. *Shakespeare and his Sources.* Boston: Houghton Mifflin, 1966.

Schäfer, Jürgen. *Documentation in the OED: Shakespeare and Nashe as Test Cases.* Oxford: Clarendon Press, 1980.

Schmidt, Michael. "Cannibalism in *King Lear.*" *Notes and Queries.* v. 18 (April 1971) pp. 148–49.

Schoenbaum, Samuel. *Internal Evidence and Elizabethan Dramatic Authorship.* Evanston: Northwestern University Press, 1966.

Schwartz, Herbert F., ed. *Alphonsus Emperor of Germany.* (1654) New York: G.P. Putnam's Sons, 1913.

Schwartz, Murray M. and Coppélia Kahn, eds. *Representing Shakespeare.* Baltimore: Johns Hopkins University Press, 1980.

Scoufos, Alice-Lyle. *Shakespeare's Typological Satire.* Athens, OH: Ohio University Press, 1979.

Seward, Desmond. *Henry V, The Scourge of God.* New York: Viking, 1988.

_____. *The Wars of the Roses.* New York: Penguin, 1996.

Shaheen, Naseeb. "Shakespeare and *The True Tragedy of Richard the Third.*" *Notes and Queries.* v. 32 (March 1985) pp. 32–3.

Shapiro, James. *Contested Will, Who Wrote Shakespeare?* New York: Simon & Schuster, 2010.

_____. *The Year of Lear.* New York: Simon & Schuster, 2015.

Sharpe, Will. "Authorship and Attribution." *William Shakespeare & Others, Collaborative Plays.* Jonathan Bate, et al., eds. 2013. pp. 641–745.

Sheavyn, Phoebe A.B. *The Literary Profession in the Elizabethan Age.* Manchester: Manchester University Press, 1987.

Sheehan, Anthony J. "The Killing of the Earl of Desmond." *Cork Archaeological and His-*

torical Society Journal. ser. 2, v. 88 (1983) pp. 106–110.

Sherbo, Arthur. "Shakespeare's Legal Language." *Notes and Queries.* v. 57 (March 2010) pp. 112–118.

Sider, J.W., ed. *The Troublesome Raigne of John, King of England.* New York: Garland, 1979.

Sidney, Philip. *An Apology for Poetry.* F.G. Robinson, ed. Indianapolis: Bobbs Merrill, 1970.

_____. *An Apology for Poetry.* Geoffrey Shepherd, ed. (1965) Manchester: Manchester University Press, 1973.

_____. *Miscellaneous Prose.* Katherine Duncan-Jones & J. v. Dorsten, eds. London: Oxford University Press, 1973.

_____. *Sir Philip Sidney, A Critical Edition of the Major Works.* Katherine Duncan-Jones, ed. Oxford: Oxford University Press, 1989.

_____. *Sir Philip Sidney, Selected Prose and Poetry.* Robert Kimbrough, ed. San Francisco: Rinehart Press, 1969.

Siemon, James R. *King Richard III.* Arden 3rd series. London: Methuen, 2009.

Simmons, J.L. "Shakespeare's *King John* and its Source." *Tulane Studies in English.* v. 17 (1969) pp. 53–72.

Skottowe, Augustine. *The Life of Shakespeare, etc.* 2 v. London: Longman, 1824.

Skura, Meredith. *Shakespeare the Actor and the Purposes of Playing.* Chicago: University of Chicago Press, 1993.

Smallwood, R.A., ed. *King John.* London: Penguin Books, 1974.

Smidt, Kristian. *Unconformities in Shakespeare's History Plays.* London: Macmillan, 1982.

Smith, George C. Moore. *College Plays Performed in the University of Cambridge.* Cambridge: The University Press, 1923.

Smith, G. Gregory, ed. *Elizabethan Critical Essays.* 2 v. Oxford: Oxford University Press, 1904.

Smith, W.D. "The Henry V Choruses in the First Folio." *Journal of English and Germanic Philology.* v. 53 (1954) pp. 38–57.

Sobran, Joseph. *Alias Shakespeare, Solving the Greatest Literary Mystery of All Time.* New York: Free Press, 1997.

Sokol, B.J. and Mary Sokol. *Shakespeare's Legal Language: A Dictionary.* London: Athlone Press, 2000.

Somerset, Anne. *Elizabeth I.* New York: St. Martins Press, 1991.

Spencer, Hazelton, ed. *The Tragedy of King Richard the Third.* Boston: Heath, 1933.

Spenser, Edmund. *The Complete Poetical Works of Spenser.* (1908) R.E. Neil Dodge, ed. Cambridge, MA: Houghton, Mifflin, 1932 ed.

Spevack, Marvin. "Shakespeare's English: The Core Vocabulary." *Review of National Literature.* v. 3 (1972) pp. 106–22.

Sprague, Arthur C. *Shakespeare's Histories: Plays for the Stage.* London: Society for Theatre Research, 1964.

Spurgeon, Caroline. *Shakespeare's Imagery and What It Tells Us.* (1935) Boston: Beacon Press, 1958.

Squire, W. Barclay. "Music." *Shakespeare's England.* W.A. Raleigh, S. Lee and C.T. Onions, eds. 2:15–49.

Steevens, George. *Twenty of the Plays of Shakespeare.* (1760) New York: AMS Press reprint, 1968.

Steinburg, Steven. *I Come to Bury Shakespeare.* (2011) no loc. Café Padre, rev. ed. 2013.

Sternfeld, Frederick W. "Shakespeare's Use of Popular Song." *Elizabethan and Jacobean Studies.* Herbert Davis and Helen Gardner, eds. 1959. pp. 150–66.

Stewart, Alan. *Shakespeare's Letters.* Oxford: Oxford University Press, 2008.

Stillinger, Jack, ed. *Anthony Munday's Zelauto: The Fountaine of Fame.* (1580) Carbondale, IL: University of Southern Illinois, 1963.

Stokes, Francis G. *A Dictionary of the Characters and Proper Names in the Works of Shakespeare.* (1924) New York: Dover Publications, 1970 ed.

Stopes, Charlotte C. *The Life of Henry, Third Earl of Southampton, Shakespeare's Patron.* Cambridge: Cambridge University Press, 1922.

Stow, John. *The chronicles of England: from Brute vnto this present yeare of Christ.* London: H. Bynneman, 1580.

_____. *Summarie of the Chronicles of England.* (1565) Barrett L. Beer, ed. Lewiston: Edwin Mellen Press, 2008.

_____. *A Survey of London.* (1603) C.L. Kingsford, ed. 1908. 2 v. Oxford: Oxford University Press, 1971.

Strachey, Lytton. *Elizabeth and Essex.* (1928)

Harmondsworth, Middlesex: Penguin Books reprint, 1971.

Strecche, John. "The Chronicle of John Strecche for the Reign of Henry V (1414–1422)." Frank Taylor, ed. *Bulletin of the John Rylands Library*. v. 16 (1932) pp. 137–87.

Streitberger, W.R., ed. *Jacobean and Caroline Revels Accounts 1603–1642*. Oxford: Malone Society, 1986.

Stritmatter, Roger. "The Not-Too-Hidden Key to *Minerva Britanna*." *The Shakespeare Oxford Newsletter*. v. 36:2 (Summer 2000) pp. 1, 9–15, 17.

———. "'Tilting Under Frieries': *Narcissus* (1595) and the Affair at Blackfriars." *Cahiers Élisabéthains*. No. 70 (Autumn 2006) pp. 39–42; also *Shakespeare Matters*. v. 6:2 (Winter 2007) pp. 1, 18–20.

———, and Lynne Kositsky. "Shakespeare and the Voyagers Revisited." *The Review of English Studies*. v. 58 (2007) pp. 447–72.

Strype, John. *The Life of the Learned Sir Thomas Smith Kt., Doctor of Civil Law*. (1698) New York: Franklin reprint, 1974.

Swan, Marshall W.H. "The Sweet Speech and Spenser's (?) Axiochus." *English Literary History*. v. 11 (1944) pp. 161–81.

Sykes, H. Dugdale. *The Authorship of "The Taming of a Shrew," "The Famous Victories of Henry V" and the Additions to Marlowe's "Faustus."* London: Chatto and Windus, 1920.

———. *Sidelights on Shakespeare*. Stratford-upon-Avon: Shakespeare Head Press, 1919.

Symonds, J.A. *Shakespeare's Predecessors in the English Drama*. (1884) London: Smith, Elder, 1967.

Tacitus, Cornelius. *The annales of Cornelivs Tacitvs. The description of Germanie*. Richard Greneway, tr. London: Bonham and John Norton, 1598.

Tarlton, Richard. *Tarlton's jests, and News out of purgatory*. (1611) James O. Halliwell, ed. London: The Shakespeare Society, 1884.

Tait, James. "Stanley, Thomas, first Earl of Derby." *Dictionary of National Biography*. Leslie Stephen, ed. v 54. London: Smith, Elder & Co., 1898. pp. 25–8.

Taylor, Alva Park. *Thomas Churchyard, his life and works*. Diss. University of California, Berkeley, 1929.

Taylor, Gary. "William Shakespeare, Richard James, and the House of Cobham." *The Review of English Studies*. v. 38 (1987) pp. 334–54.

———, ed. *Henry V*. Oxford: Oxford University Press, 1982.

———, John Jowett, Terri Bourus and Gabriel Egan, eds. *The New Oxford Shakespeare: The Complete Works*. Oxford: Oxford University Press, 2016.

Taylor, John. *The 'Universal Chronicle' of Ranulf Higden*. Oxford: The Clarendon Press, 1966.

Taylor, Rupert. "A Tentative Chronology of Marlowe's and other Elizabethan Plays." *PMLA*. v. 51, no. 3 (1936) pp. 642–88.

Tennyson, Charles, ed. *The Devil and the Lady, and Unpublished Early Poems by Alfred Tennyson*. (1930/1) Bloomington: Indiana University Press, 1964.

Terence (Publius Terentius Afer). *Eunuchus*. A.J. Brothers, ed. and tr. Warminster, UK: Aris & Phillips, c. 2000.

Thaler, Alwin. *Shakespeare and Sir Philip Sidney*. Cambridge, MA: Harvard University Press, 1947.

Theobald, Lewis, ed. *The Works of Shakespeare*. 7 v. (1733) New York: AMS Press reprint, 1968.

Theobald, William. *The Classic Element in the Shakespeare Plays*. London: Robert Banks, 1909.

Thomas, Sidney. "'Enter a sheriffe': Shakespeare's *King John* and *The Troublesome Raigne*." *Shakespeare Quarterly*. v. 37:1 (Spring 1986) pp. 98–100.

Thompson, Ann, ed. *The Taming of the Shrew*. Cambridge: Cambridge University Press, 1984.

Thomson, Leslie. "'Pray you, undo this button': Implications of 'Un' in *King Lear*." *Shakespeare Survey*. v. 45 (1993) pp. 79–88.

Thurley, Simon. *Whitehall Palace, The Official Illustrated History*. London: Merrell, 2008.

Tillyard, E.M.W. *Shakespeare's History Plays*. (1944) Collier Books: New York, 1962 ed.

Timberlake, Philip W. *The Feminine Ending in English Blank Verse*. Menasha, WI: George Banta, 1931.

Tolman, Albert H. "Shakespeare's Part in the 'Taming of the Shrew.'" *PMLA*. v. 5, no. 4 (1890) pp. 201–278.

Tolstoy, Leo. *Tolstoy on Shakespeare.* V.G. Tchertkoff, ed. and tr. Christchurch, Hants: Free Age Press, 1907.

Tottel, Richard. *Tottel's Miscellany.* (1557–1587) Hyder Rollins, ed. Cambridge: Harvard University Press, 1965.

Trevor-Roper, Hugh. "What's in a name?." *Réalités.* No. 144 (November 1962) pp. 41–3.

Trim, D.J.B. "Norris, Sir John (c. 1547x50–1597)." *ODNB.* Oxford University Press, 2004.

Tyler, Sharon. "Minding true things: the Chorus, the audience, and Henry V." *The Theatrical Space, Themes in Drama.* v. 9. James Redmond, ed. 1987. pp. 69–80.

van Dam, B.A.P. "The Taming of a Shrew." *English Studies.* v. 10 (1929) pp. 97–106.

Vergil, Polydore. *Three books of Polydore Vergil's English history: comprising the reigns of Henry VI, Edward IV, and Richard III.* (1555) H. Ellis, ed. London: Camden Society, v. 29, 1844.

Vickers, Brian. *Shakespeare, Co-Author.* Oxford: Oxford University Press, 2002

_____. "Thomas Kyd, the secret sharer—A new software program should restore Kyd to the eminence he deserves." *TLS.* (19 April 2008) pp. 13–15.

_____. "*The Troublesome Reign,* George Peele, and the Date of *King John.*" *Words that Count.* Brian Boyd, ed. 2004. pp. 78–116.

Wace (Robert). *The Brut; or, The Chronicles of England.* Friedrich W.D. Brie, tr. London: Oxford University Press, 1960.

Waldo, T.R., and T.W. Herbert. "Musical Terms in *The Taming of the Shrew:* Evidence of Single Authorship." *Shakespeare Quarterly.* v. 10 (1959) pp. 185–99.

Warburton, William, ed. *The Works of Shakespeare.* 8 v. (1747) New York: AMS Press reprint, 1968.

Ward, Bernard M. "The Famous Victories of Henry the Fifth: Its Place in Elizabethan Dramatic Literature." *The Review of English Studies.* v. 4 (July 1928) pp. 270–94.

_____.*The Seventeenth Earl of Oxford 1550–1604.* London: John Murray, 1928.

_____, ed. *A Hundreth Sundrie Flowres.* (1573) Port Washington, NY: Kennikat Press, 1975.

Warner, William. *Albion's England.* (1586). New York: G. Olms, 1971.

Warren, Michael. "Quarto and Folio King Lear and the Interpretation of Albany and Edgar." *Shakespeare: Pattern of Excelling Nature.* David Bevington and Jay L. Halio, eds. 1978. pp. 95–107.

Warren, W.L. *King John.* Berkeley: University of California Press, 1961.

Watson, Thomas. *Hekatompathia.* (1582) S.K. Heninger, Jr., ed. Gainesville, FL: Scolars' Facsimiles & Reprints, 1964.

Weever, John. *Mirror of Martyrs. or The life and death of that thrice valiant Capitaine, and most godly Martyre Sir Iohn Old-castle knight, Lord Cobham.* (1601) https://babel.hathitrust.org/cgi/pt?id=ien.35556006752661;view=1up;seq=91;size=150 [Accessed June 17, 2017].

Weil, Herbert, and Judith Weil, eds. *The First Part of King Henry IV.* "Updated Edition." Cambridge: Cambridge University Press, 2007.

Weimann, Robert. *Shakespeare and the Popular Tradition in the Theater.* (1967) Robert Schwartz, ed. Baltimore: Johns Hopkins University Press, rev. ed. 1978.

Weis, Rene, ed. *King Lear: A Parallel Text Edition.* (1993) London: Pearson Education, 2nd ed. 2010.

Wells, Stanley. "The Unstable Image of Shakespeare's Text." *Images of Shakespeare.* W. Habicht, D.J. Palmer and Roger Pringle, eds. 1988. pp. 305–13.

Wells, Stanley, and Gary Taylor, eds. *Modernizing Shakespeare's Spelling: With Three Studies in the Text of Henry V.* Oxford: Clarendon Press, 1979.

_____, and _____. *William Shakespeare, A Textual Companion.* (1987) New York: W.W. Norton, 1997 ed.

_____ and _____, eds. *The Oxford Shakespeare.* 3 v. Oxford: Oxford University Press, 1987.

Wells, William Smith. "The Authorship of 'King Leir.'" *Notes and Queries.* v. 177 (December 1939) pp. 434–8.

_____. "Thomas Kyd and the Chronicle-History." *Notes and Queries.* v. 178 (March 1940) pp. 218–34.

Wember, Hanno. "Illuminating Eclipses: Astronomy and Chronology in *King Lear.*" *Brief Chronicles.* v. 2 (2010) pp. 33–43.

Wentersdorf, Karl P. "The Authenticity of The Taming of the Shrew." *Shakespeare Quarterly.* v. 5 (1954) pp. 11–32.

_____. "Shakespearean Chronology and the Metrical Tests." *Shakespeare-Studien: Festschrift fur Heinrich Mutschmann.* Walther Fischer and Karl Wentersdorf, eds. Marburg: Elwert, 1951. pp. 161–93.

West, F.J. "Burgh, Hubert de, earl of Kent (c. 1170–1243)." *ODNB.* Oxford University Press, 2004; online ed. Jan 2008.

Whalen, Richard F. "A Dozen Shakespeare Plays Written after Oxford Died? Not Proven!" *The Oxfordian.* v. 10 (2007) pp. 75–84.

_____. *Shakespeare, Who Was He?* Westport, CT: Praeger, 1994.

_____. "Shakespeare's Audience: A Reassessment of the Stratfordian View." *The Shakespeare Oxford Newsletter.* v. 40:4 (Fall 2004) pp. 1, 7–9.

_____. "The Stratford Bust: A monumental fraud." *The Oxfordian.* v. 8 (2005) pp. 7–24.

White, R. Grant, ed. *Mr. William Shakespeare's Comedies, Histories, Tragedies and Poems.* Boston: Houghton, Mifflin, 1883.

Whitman, Walt. *The Complete Poetry and Prose of Walt Whitman.* 2 v. New York: Pellegrini and Cudahy, 1948.

Whittemore, Hank. "Abstract and Brief Chronicles." *The Shakespeare Oxford Newsletter.* v. 35:2 (Summer 1999) pp.1, 10–14, 22.

_____. "Oxford's Metamorphoses." *The Shakespeare Oxford Newsletter.* v. 32:4 (Fall 1996) pp. 1, 11–15.

Whitworth, Charles. Review of *The Troublesome Raigne of John.* Charles Forker, ed. *Cahiers Élisabéthains.* v. 82 (2012) pp. 93–4.

Wickham, Glynne. *Early English Stages: 1300–1660, Volume Two 1576 to 1600, Part II.* New York: Columbia University Press, 1972.

Willbern, David. "Shakespeare's Nothing." Murray M. Schwartz and Coppélia Kahn, eds. *Representing Shakespeare.* 1980. pp. 241–63.

Wilson, John Dover. "The Origins and Development of Shakespeare's Henry IV." *The Library.* 4th series v. 26:1 (June 1945) pp. 2–16.

_____. "Shakespeare's *Richard III* and *The True Tragedy of Richard the Third* 1594." *Shakespeare Quarterly.* v. 3 (1952) pp. 299–306.

_____, ed. *Henry IV, Part 1.* Cambridge: Cambridge University Press, 1946.

_____, ed. *Henry IV, Part 2.* Cambridge: Cambridge University Press, 1953.

_____, ed. *Henry V.* Cambridge: Cambridge University Press, 1947.

_____, ed. *King John.* (1936) Cambridge: Cambridge University Press, 1969 ed.

_____, ed. *King Richard II.* Cambridge: Cambridge University Press, 1939.

_____, ed. *Richard III.* (1954) Cambridge: Cambridge University Press, rev. ed. 1961.

_____, ed. *Titus Andronicus.* (1948) Cambridge: Cambridge University Press, rev. ed. 1968.

Woudhuysen, H.R., ed. *Samuel Johnson on Shakespeare.* London: Penguin Books, 1989.

_____. *Sir Philip Sidney and the Circulation of Manuscripts 1558–1640.* New York: Oxford University Press, 1996.

Wright, Daniel L. "'Ver-y Interesting,' Shakespeare's treatment of the earls of Oxford in the history plays." *The Shakespeare Oxford Newsletter.* v. 36:1 (Spring 2000). pp. 1, 14–21.

Wright (Turner) Julia C. "Anthony Mundy, 'Edward' Spenser, and E.K." *PMLA.* v. 76, no. 1 (1961) pp. 34–9.

# Index

Numbers in **bold italics** indicate pages with illustrations

Milton Keynes UK
Ingram Content Group UK Ltd.
UKHW031148121124
451045UK00015B/291

9 781476 672649